IDAHO'S PLACE

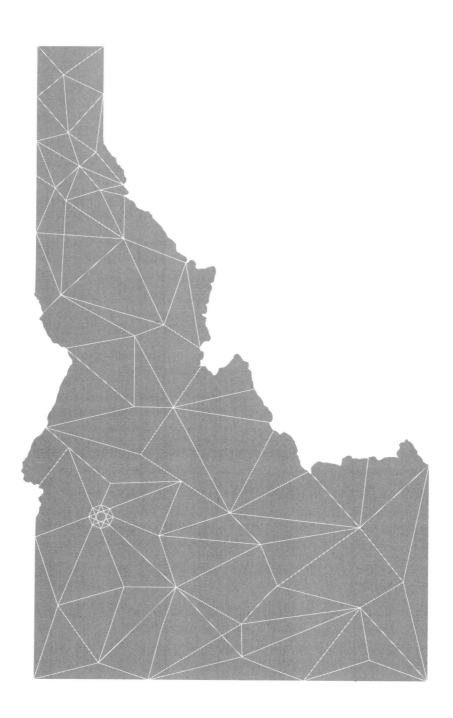

Idaho's Place

A NEW HISTORY OF THE GEM STATE

EDITED BY

Adam M. Sowards

UNIVERSITY OF WASHINGTON PRESS
SEATTLE AND LONDON

PROGRAM IN PACIFIC NORTHWEST STUDIES
UNIVERSITY OF IDAHO

© 2014 by the University of Washington Press
Printed and bound in the United States of America
Design by Dustin Kilgore
Composed in Chaparral, a typeface designed by Carol Twombly
17 16 15 14   5 4 3 2 1

University of Washington Press
PO Box 50096, Seattle, WA 98145, USA
www.washington.edu/uwpress

Program in Pacific Northwest Studies
Department of History
University of Idaho
875 Perimeter Drive MS 3175
Moscow, ID 83844-3175

"Rabbit and Jack Rabbit" reprinted by permission from Rodney Frey, *Landscape Traveled by Coyote and Crane: The World of the Schitsu'umsh (Coeur d'Alene Indians)* (Seattle: University of Washington Press, 2001), 112.

Library of Congress Cataloging-in-Publication Data
Idaho's place : a new history of the Gem State / edited by Adam M. Sowards. — 1st edition.
     pages   cm
   Includes bibliographical references and index.
   ISBN 978-0-295-99367-6 (cloth : alk. paper)
1. Idaho—History. 2. Idaho—Civilization. 3. Ethnology—Idaho. 4. Idaho—Ethnic relations.   I. Sowards, Adam M., editor of compilation.   II. University of Idaho. Program in Pacific Northwest Studies.
   F746.I24 2014
   979.6—dc23
2013041645

To all my teachers and students
in western and northwestern history

Contents

Acknowledgments   ix

1. Idaho's Place: Reckoning with History   3
    ADAM M. SOWARDS

2. The Confluence of Rivers: The Indigenous Tribes of Idaho   13
    RODNEY FREY AND ROBERT McCARL

IDAHO VOICES: *Native American History*   42

3. Crossing Divides: An Environmental History of Idaho   44
    KEVIN R. MARSH

IDAHO VOICES: *Environmental History*   73

4. Idiosyncrasy and Enigma: Idaho Politics   76
    KATHERINE G. AIKEN

IDAHO VOICES: *Political History*   105

5. The Power and the Glory: Idaho's Religious History   108
    JILL K. GILL

IDAHO VOICES: *Religious History*   136

6. Defying Boundaries: Women in Idaho History   138
    LAURA WOODWORTH-NEY AND TARA A. ROWE

IDAHO VOICES: *Women's History*   165

7. Confronting Race and Creating Community: Idaho's Ethnic History 167
    LAURIE MERCIER

IDAHO VOICES: *Ethnic History*   198

8. Latinos in Idaho: Making Their Way in the Gem State 201
   ERROL D. JONES

IDAHO VOICES: *Latino History* 235

9. Shifting Currents: Cultural Expressions in Idaho 238
   RICHARD W. ETULAIN

IDAHO VOICES: *Cultural History* 260

10. Telling Stories: Idaho's Historians 263
   JUDITH AUSTIN

IDAHO VOICES: *Historians* 289

Contributors 291

Index 295

Acknowledgments

Among the many who have helped create this book, those who work at the Idaho State Historical Society deserve prominent thanks. Oral historians, past and present, preserved important materials that I drew on. Kathy Hodges made a research trip to Boise pleasant and productive. On that same trip, I drew on Judy Austin's generosity and detailed knowledge of the society's photographic holdings, making my task far easier. I also am exceedingly grateful to the Idaho Humanities Council for a grant to help offset the funding for this book; Rick Ardinger graciously helped facilitate that process. Further funding and support came through the University of Idaho's Program in Pacific Northwest Studies. Katherine G. Aiken, the former dean of the College of Letters, Arts, and Social Sciences and current provost for the university, ensured funding for the program, even in times of financial challenges, and has been a supporter of this project from its inception. Elizabeth Carney, Mark Fiege, Troy Reeves, Jeff Sanders, and Kelley Sowards gave the introduction helpful critiques that have helped me improve my ideas and expression. Aaron Schab and Shane Garner provided editorial assistance. Marianne Keddington-Lang of the University of Washington Press gave this project early support and excellent suggestions. Ranjit Arab inherited the project when Marianne semiretired; he has been the perfect combination in an editor, prodding and persistent, encouraging and helpful. The rest of the press staff have been models of professionalism. Most of all, I thank the authors of these essays for their fine work, their infinite patience, and their (usually) good cheer in the face of what has seemed to us all to be endless delays. I can only hope that the book meets their expectations. Lastly, as with all projects, I thank my family—near and far, old and new—for their forbearance and support. The book is dedicated to all my teachers and students in western and northwestern history; from them, I have learned and continue to learn so much.

IDAHO'S PLACE

1

Idaho's Place

Reckoning with History

ADAM M. SOWARDS

SNOW AND RAIN FALL FROM THE IDAHO SKIES. AS WATER, IT
rolls or seeps down hillsides and into creeks. It collects into larger
streams and then into rivers. Then rivers converge into larger rivers. It is
an impressively complex system in which several parts exist individually,
but as they move through space and time, those independent pieces gather together and collect into something larger and then larger still. At the
headwaters, the water system seems simple. By the time we see the river
downstream, it is the accumulation of countless tributaries and all that
flows into each of them.

History is like that, too.[1] It begins with small things—an individual, a
family, a village, a year. They interact and accumulate and converge, adding
and changing into something altogether new—a town, a region, an economy, an era. Later, "downstream," as it were, those constituent parts are
so intermingled, so entangled, that it is impossible to discern one strand
from another, and we find each piece wrapped up with all the others. So it
is with Idaho and its rich past. The waterways of history are abundant. This
book helps us chart them. It shows us how the streams and rivers have created—and continue to create—this vibrant place, Idaho.

What is Idaho's place? It is a deceptively simple question. The answer, of
course, is, it depends. It depends partially on how we frame the question. If
we consider it geographically, Idaho is a meeting ground of the Great Basin,
Rocky Mountains, and Columbia Plateau and is characterized by stunning
sagebrush, majestic mountains, and roiling rivers. If we examine it politically, Idaho is as conservatively Republican as any state today, but beginning
in 1971, two Democratic governors served six consecutive terms, and the

3

state has long been represented by fiercely independent Republicans *and* Democrats unafraid of bucking their party establishments and serving the state more than a party's ideology. If we conceive of it ethnically, Idaho is one of the most homogeneous states in the nation, yet once nearly one-third of its population was Chinese, a long and proud Basque tradition strongly influences cultural events and identities, and its many tribal members represent a continuing vital presence.

This list of paradoxes could go on. The contradictions could be described by the common quip that Idaho is the only state with three capitals—Salt Lake City, Boise, and Spokane—which shows the cultural, political, and economic scattering of the state. They could highlight how the state possesses some of the largest and longest-protected wilderness areas amid a population that exhibits some of the nation's most hostile attitudes toward environmental protection. They could feature the simultaneous opportunities and obstacles, discrimination and tolerance faced by diverse Idahoans while they were trying to make a successful life in the state. In other words, the state is a diverse and in-between place where there is far more than first meets the eye or than is revealed by the popular stereotypes of famous potatoes, Aryan Nations, and open spaces. To place Idaho, to define this state, we must reckon first and last with its history. This book takes on this task.

A leading historian of the region once remarked that the Pacific Northwest was far away from and behind the times of mainstream America. And it is easy to conclude from existing regional writing that Idaho is the most distant and most delayed of the states with which it is usually linked.[2] But such a characterization conceals more than it reveals and depends largely on comparisons with New York or North Carolina, Massachusetts or Missouri. Yet even historians of the American West marginalize Idaho, paying more attention to its neighbors, perhaps because its complex history defies easy incorporation into larger narratives.[3] The casual reader, resident, or visitor to the state could be forgiven for thinking that not much happened there or that events in Idaho's history reveal little of importance more broadly. This simply is not true.

Even the more flattering portraits do not adequately represent Idaho. Consider Leonard J. Arrington's description from his thorough, two-volume *History of Idaho*: "[T]he peoples of Idaho have adjusted to these divers tugs and pulls, and a resolute citizen loyalty to the state has emerged. Idahoans enjoy their historical uniqueness. . . . Indeed, Idahoans take pride in their singularity—their unique blend of conservatism and progressivism, their free-wheeling democracy, and their deep commitment to traditional values."[4] As astute an observer as any, Arrington sketches the state as singular when in fact most western states, perhaps all states, would be equally well characterized by the generalities he employs.

I noticed this tendency to displace or misplace Idaho, despite good reasons not to, when I moved from teaching Northwest history at an urban college in Seattle to doing so at a rural university in Moscow, Idaho. It was easy to find history—excellent history, in fact—about Idaho. Sensitive portrayals of Idaho tribal culture, surprising insights about the social and environmental history of irrigation, and a best-selling account of industrial violence and political retribution had all been published in the few years before my move.[5] Despite this work and much more that continues to appear year after year, Idaho's history has remained disconnected and disjointed, much the same as the state's sprawling landscape.[6]

Understanding Idaho's place and putting it in context requires a guidebook. This book attempts to remedy the current scattershot understanding of the state's past. To date, those interested in religious history might know of Idaho's Church of Jesus Christ of Latter-day Saints or Christian Identity sects; immigration historians might know of its working-class miners or agricultural workers; cultural historians might know of its writers or artists. But those topics have tended to remain diffused. What the fine authors in this volume have done is collect and synthesize the best of Idaho history. Consider, then, this book a report on the state of the state's history. Readers who pick up this volume—whether they are longtime residents or newcomers, onetime tourists or seasonal dwellers, policy makers or historians—will be treated to a rich past, one in which the many streams of Idaho's history intermingle to produce this beautiful, interesting, and sometimes confounding state.

What does this work reveal about Idaho? It would be redundant to summarize each chapter here, but it may be useful to point out to readers some ways various elements of Idaho history intersect, both thematically and chronologically, as reflected by these gathered texts. As already suggested,

6   ADAM M. SOWARDS

paradox is a prime characteristic of this state; puzzles about Idaho's past are plain in almost all the essays that follow. More self-consciously than any other available source, this book traces how Idaho's political or cultural paradoxes evolved so that the state becomes comprehensible, not just a collection of inexplicable oddities. Political patterns, environmental divisions, racial challenges, and cultural trends all emerge from these pages in ways that make clear what at first might seem confusing or contradictory. The reason for the clarity, for the unraveling of these paradoxes, is that the authors root their analyses in historical developments. What might seem enigmatic in the twenty-first century looking backward makes sense when seen on the past's own terms. Or, to return to the river metaphor, we can find our way best through Idaho's watersheds by tracing them from the headwaters of the past through their confluences with the present.

Another leitmotif in the following chapters is how Idahoans built their communities, sometimes in the face of strong counterpressures. Whether emphasizing the roles of women and churches, economic and political roots, or ethnic and cultural traditions, the authors show commonalities that bound Idahoans to one another as they made their way in the world. In the face of sometimes harsh physical and social environments, Idahoans banded together to create places in their towns, their state, and their social institutions where they felt at home and that promoted a sense of well-being, community, and identity. Such havens—powwows, churches, political parties, women's clubs, labor unions, and more—offered mutual aid in trying times, a sense of identity and belonging, and connections to other communities within and beyond Idaho's borders.

Integral to this community building and togetherness, though, were the hostility and discrimination many communities faced while making their way. Latter-day Saints and Chinese miners, women and American Indians, Latino migrants and Japanese farmers, and more faced unequal conditions. Such inequality took many forms, from officially sanctioned legal discrimination to interpersonal violence. Idaho individuals and communities persisted, survived, and flourished despite pressures to assimilate, disappear, or remain in the shadows. This thriving—so apparent in the following pages and as one travels the state—illuminates Idahoans' power of persistence, individuality, and community.

Diversity is another prevalent theme. Whether it is the diversity of environments, cultural practices, political sensibilities, economic structures, or community beliefs and traditions, Idahoans have made and encountered differences and have necessarily defined themselves as part of such mosaics. Idaho resists easy characterization. Consequently, these writers have provided a signal service in their careful and sensitive reconstruction of the state's peoples and the broader forces with which they interacted to create history.

Within this multiplicity of themes, the authors help us identify some trends; they help us, in other words, in distinguishing some of those streams of history from others. One important duty for historians is to periodize the past, recognizing that major turning points for one group or region may be almost irrelevant to another;[7] that is, by examining broad scales of time, historians can identify periods when important shifts and emerging trends marked a new age. Across these essays, some common shifts coalesce at important, if imprecise, transition points.

Following the emergence of Native peoples in the region, the first transition came when Euro-Americans arrived with their animals, plants, and diseases, after which all Idahoans would reckon with the consequences of contact until the 1880s. Beginning around the turn of the eighteenth century, trade networks brought the biological armada (e.g., horses, pathogens) that irrevocably altered Idaho's ecological and cultural relationships. In effect, this meant incorporating new economic patterns and fashioning new cultural interdependencies for all. Gold and silver traded hands alongside salmon and mountain goats, Christianity added to indigenous spirituality, and the Coeur d'Alene became successful farmers while Italian and Welsh immigrants forged unions of hard-rock miners. Puzzling out those initial changes initiated by colonialism remained the primary task of all Idahoans, Native and newcomer alike. Until the next transition.

By the time Idaho gained statehood in 1890, Euro-Americans asserted power through political, economic, and religious institutions, entities that sometimes quite harmfully entwined with or overpowered indigenous institutions and landscapes. Political leaders established Idaho's boundaries and governing bodies, and capitalists constructed an industrial system that transformed economic and ecological structures. The extension and consequences of those developments occupied much of the succeeding century. New technologies and migrations moved Idaho toward and into the twentieth century with much the same impact as in other western places. Ethnic groups arrived and worked in the fields, forests, and mines; modern industrial techniques accelerated economic growth and increased the pace at which Idahoans transformed nature into commodities to be traded in national and global markets. Policies—federal and state, formal and informal—facilitated these changes, generally pursuing what most Americans thought to be the common good while expressing little concern for negative consequences for Native peoples, the working classes, or ecosystems. Conservation policies funded dams for irrigation and hydropower, while foresters managed land for timber and game production; immigration policies encouraged and then discouraged and finally selected who could immigrate to Idaho (and the United States generally) to labor in the state's economy and build its communities. Meanwhile, women, workers, Latter-day Saints, and others not in the male, WASP (white Anglo-Saxon Protestant) elite achieved greater recognition, rights, and power, although discrimination and power imbalances endured.

By the 1930s and 1940s, Idahoans felt federal involvement in their lives and livelihoods to a greater degree as the government attempted to check capitalism's excesses and abuses. Moreover, changes in governance on Indian reservations (e.g., the Indian Reorganization Act of 1934) and in labor and immigration practices (e.g., the bracero program) similarly modified social patterns. Close examination in the following pages will reveal that cultural practices, political desires, and economic dynamics had shifted noticeably by then, but in many respects it was only the emphases that changed—a shift in degree, not kind; that is, rather than a full-scale departure from an earlier period, the Depression, World War II, and postwar years found Idahoans adjusting to modern life and the institutions that had grown up with the state, consolidating and expanding power in familiar state structures.

By the 1980s, however, Idahoans were forging a new historical era. The nature of this transition was complex and not uniform, and its implications are still unfolding in ways that historians are puzzling through. Nevertheless, in the past three decades, Idahoans have asserted themselves in unprecedented ways. Idaho's indigenous nations have pursued, along with some changes in federal policy, self-determination and sovereignty with great success; Latinos, Basques, and other ethnic communities have publicly celebrated their traditions, and the Aryan Nations and Christian Identity movements found transitory refuges in which to express their own violent versions of racial pride and hate. Meanwhile, politicians and the public have become more combative, with the state's conservative base strengthening, and new issues—from religious expression to women's rights to endangered species—animating the state's public debates and leading to well-publicized and hotly contested campaigns. This assertiveness, then, includes mixed signs—vigorous public participation and rising cultural pride, ubiquitous political conflict, and tiresome xenophobia. These elements have roots stretching back throughout Idaho's history, although as the writers that follow make clear, sometimes subtly and sometimes explicitly, something shifted around 1980 to heighten and make more strident these divisions. When Idahoans produce the next transition is impossible to predict, for historians can only forecast the past, not the future.

It is time to place Idaho securely within its historical context, and *Idaho's Place* does that. By recognizing that historical developments in this state are neither as distant nor as inconsequential as some may think, this volume suggests that Idaho's place is properly understood to be a product of its spaces, cultures, and times. Part and parcel of the North American West, Idaho reveals a rich past of struggle and achievement, of diversity and common interests, of continuities and changes, of creativity and imitation. As a dynamic place and meeting ground, the state has struggled at times with finding a common identity. But Oregon and Washington routinely experience chafing between their eastern and western halves; sprawling Texas includes both high-tech Houston and empty western plains; and distant upstate New York does battle with its downstate metropolis. In other words, lack of coherence is not uniquely Idaho's burden, and reckoning with that seeming incoherence is best done through history. The here and now of the state, after all, is the product of its past. Writing Idaho history is an ongoing and necessarily incomplete process. Nevertheless, in this volume, students and teachers, residents and visitors have a historical guidebook that can help them begin piecing together the story of this place. Within these pages, readers will find enough details to challenge their stereotypes, deepen their understanding, and answer the question, *What is Idaho's place?*

As much of Idaho's water leaves the state via the Snake River at Lewiston, Idaho's lowest point, it carries with it sediments of the state's past, the fragments of its history, the thorough commingling of people and place and time. If it could speak, it could tell of Shoshones hunting deer and gathering pine nuts; of explorers, traders, missionaries, and emigrants exchanging ideas and goods with indigenous groups; of prospectors and town builders, boosters, and ministers, Natives and newcomers making homes and communities amid constantly shifting circumstances. The waters would have witnessed confrontation and cooperation in forests and fields, in courtrooms and the legislature, among farmers and ranchers, unionists and executives. They would carry with them runoff from irrigation and pollution from mining, be slowed by dams and turbines, and swirl around invasive carp and declining salmon. Such water would have provided good health for families, relief during a hot day's work, and inspiration for writers and artists. Each stream, each witnessing, each confluence adds to the weight of history in those waters.

A NOTE ON ORAL HISTORIES

In addition to the excellent scholarship reflected in the following pages, this book includes excerpts from oral histories. The Idaho State Historical Society has been collecting oral histories since 1978, and its Oral History Center is a treasured repository of the state's history. The voices of Idahoans remain central to writing and understanding the state's many pasts. I hope that the short excerpts included here will make the history come alive, seem more real, personified in ways that oral histories especially can achieve. I also hope that you will participate in and support the state's oral history program, so that these valuable resources will continue to be available to our future historians and citizens.[8]

Notes

1   I am indebted to Rodney Frey and Robert McCarl, the authors of chapter 2 in this book, whose metaphor of rivers and confluence prompted this discussion.

2   Carlos Arnaldo Schwantes, *The Pacific Northwest: An Interpretive History*, rev. ed.

(Lincoln: University of Nebraska Press, 1996), 16. Schwantes extracted the Idaho portions of the first edition of *The Pacific Northwest*, reshaped and added to them, and published the result as *In Mountain Shadows: A History of Idaho* (Lincoln: University of Nebraska Press, 1991). Still, Idaho remains the clear minority partner in the region's published history. As another example, *Terra Pacifica*, a fine collection of essays on Northwest history, includes only a single essay on Idaho. See Paul W. Hirt, ed., *Terra Pacifica: People and Place in the Northwest States and Western Canada* (Pullman: Washington State University Press, 1998). William G. Robbins and Katrine Barber's new text on the greater Northwest improves the representation, but even so, Idaho remains outside the heart of their treatment. See *Nature's Northwest: The North Pacific Slope in the Twentieth Century* (Tucson: University of Arizona Press, 2011).

3 Gary Clayton Anderson and Kathleen P. Chamberlain, *Power and Promise: The Changing American West* (New York: Pearson Longman, 2008); Anne M. Butler and Michael J. Lansing, *The American West: A Concise History* (Malden, MA: Blackwell, 2008); Richard W. Etulain, *Beyond the Missouri: The Story of the American West* (Albuquerque: University of New Mexico Press, 2006); Carol L. Higham and William H. Katerberg, *Conquests and Consequences: The American West from Frontier to Region* (Wheeling, IL, and Cody, WY: Harlan Davidson and the Buffalo Bill Historical Center, 2009); Robert V. Hine and John Mack Faragher, *The American West: A New Interpretive History* (New Haven, CT: Yale University Press, 2000); Patricia Nelson Limerick, *The Legacy of Conquest: The Unbroken Past of the American West* (New York: Norton, 1987); Richard White, *"It's Your Misfortune and None of My Own": A New History of the American West* (Norman: University of Oklahoma Press, 1991). In none of these texts does Idaho figure prominently.

4 Leonard J. Arrington, *History of Idaho* (Moscow and Boise: University of Idaho Press and Idaho State Historical Society, 1994), 1:xvii.

5 I am thinking in particular of Rodney Frey, in collaboration with the Sch_itsu'umsh, *Landscape Traveled by Coyote and Crane: The World of the Sch_itsu'umsh (Coeur d'Alene Indians)* (Seattle: University of Washington Press, 2001); Mark Fiege, *Irrigated Eden: The Making of an Agricultural Landscape in the American West* (Seattle: University of Washington Press, 1999); J. Anthony Lukas, *Big Trouble: A Murder in a Small Western Town Sets Off a Struggle for the Soul of America* (New York: Simon and Schuster, 1997).

6 *Idaho Yesterdays* is the state's peer-reviewed history journal of record and the best starting point for staying abreast of historical developments. See http://www .idahoyesterdays.com (accessed March 15, 2011). Since I arrived at the University of Idaho, several important scholarly and popular books on Idaho history have appeared, demonstrating this vibrancy: Katherine G. Aiken, *Idaho's Bunker Hill: The Rise and Fall of a Great Mining Company, 1885–1981* (Norman: University of Oklahoma Press, 2005); Karl Boyd Brooks, *Public Power, Private Dams: The Hells Canyon High Dam Controversy* (Seattle: University of Washington Press, 2006); Timothy Egan, *The Big Burn: Teddy Roosevelt and the Fire That Saved America* (Boston: Houghton Mifflin Harcourt, 2009); Robert Terry Hayashi, *Haunted by Waters: A Journey through Race and Place in the American West* (Iowa City: University of Iowa Press, 2007); John W. Heaton, *The Shoshone-Bannocks: Culture and Commerce at Fort Hall, 1870–1940* (Lawrence: University Press of Kansas, 2005); Gregory E. Smoak, *Ghost Dances and Identity: Prophetic Religion and American Indian Ethnogenesis in the*

Nineteenth Century (Berkeley: University of California Press, 2006); Elliott West, *The Last Indian War: The Nez Perce Story* (New York: Oxford University Press, 2009); Laura Woodworth-Ney, *Mapping Identity: The Creation of the Coeur d'Alene Indian Reservation, 1805–1902* (Boulder: University Press of Colorado, 2004).

7   This is a significant lesson brought to the fore by women's historians. Laura Woodworth-Ney and Tara A. Rowe make much the same argument in chapter 5 in this volume.

8   The Oral History Collection webpage offers information about its holdings, including a list of narrators. See http://idahohistory.cdmhost.com/cdm/search/collection/p15073coll1 (accessed August 7, 2013).

2

The Confluence of Rivers

The Indigenous Tribes of Idaho

RODNEY FREY AND ROBERT McCARL

L IKE THE CONFLUENCE OF GREAT RIVERS, THE HISTORIES OF the indigenous tribes of Idaho represent the intermingling of the waters of distinct rivers. Among the many rivers, there are two pivotal rivers that are essential to understanding these rich histories. One carries the waters of each tribe's particular oral traditions, its indigenous culture. These waters are rich with languages, songs, and aesthetics, with family, kinship, and ecological orientations, and with stories of creation, such as those of Coyote, Grizzly Bear, and other Animal Peoples. This is a river expressive of the unique heritage and dreams of sovereign peoples. Flowing between the banks of another, altogether different river are the waters of Euro-American contact history.[1] These are waters expressive of the effects of the horse and smallpox, and of encounters with the Lewis and Clark Expedition, fur traders, missionaries, military generals, and treaty commissioners. This is the river of federal acts creating reservations and allotments, of federal acts of reorganization, self-determination, and gaming, of Euro-American influences continuing into the present. Found here are the waters that have fortuitously, or more often by intent, sought to redefine, modify, destroy, or deny the sovereignty of the tribes.

An appreciation of the specific intermingling of both rivers, at the point of confluence, is essential to understanding the history of any given tribe. That confluence differs in specific character and content from locale to locale, contributing to the unique histories of each tribe. Nevertheless, common to the confluences of all the tribes are certain shared experiences related to the quest to maintain tribal sovereignty in the face of assimilation by Euro-American influences. As the histories of the Idaho tribes are far too

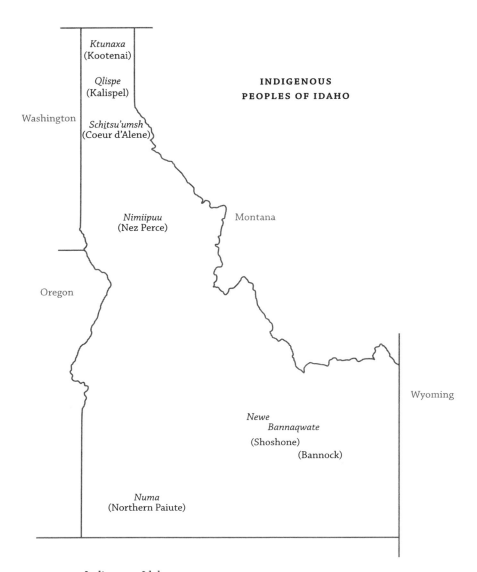

Washington

Ktunaxa
(Kootenai)

Qlispe
(Kalispel)

Schi̱tsu'umsh
(Coeur d'Alene)

INDIGENOUS
PEOPLES OF IDAHO

Nimiipuu
(Nez Perce)

Montana

Oregon

Wyoming

Newe
Bannaqwate

(Shoshone)

(Bannock)

Numa
(Northern Paiute)

FIGURE 2.1. Indigenous Idaho

extensive to be adequately conveyed here, the intent in this chapter is to highlight but a few representative currents from both rivers and provide a historical overview of Idaho's indigenous peoples. In so doing, we are sensitive to Indian perspectives on their own histories and seek to integrate their viewpoints into this essay.[2]

There are seven indigenous peoples of Idaho, each with its own distinctive ancestry linking it to the aboriginal landscape. Reflecting the influences of both the Animal Peoples and Euro-American rivers, each of these peoples is known by two sets of names—the name asserted by the people themselves and the name given to them by newcomers. In their aboriginal homeland and extending far beyond the boundaries of what would become Idaho, from north to south, are the Ktunaxa (Kootenai), the Qlispé (Kalispel), the Schitsu'umsh (Coeur d'Alene), the Nimíipuu (Nez Perce), the Newe (Shoshone), the Bannaqwate (Bannock), and the Numa (Northern Paiute). Today, these tribal groups reside on six reservation communities in Idaho, as well as in reservation communities in neighboring British Columbia, Alberta, Montana, Wyoming, Utah, Nevada, Oregon, and Washington.[3]

The Ktunaxa (a term of self-designation, applied to all Kootenai bands, the meaning of which is unclear) or Kootenai (derivative of *Ktunaxa*) have traditionally resided in a large region that would become southern British Columbia and Alberta and the northwest, northern, and northeastern areas of what would become Montana, Idaho, and Washington respectively. This is the region of the Kootenay/Kootenai and Columbia Rivers and the banks of the Arrow Lakes. Their language is an isolate, linguistically unrelated to any other tribal language in the region. In Idaho, one band of the Ktunaxa, the ?aq'anqmi ("People of the island" [pronounced with an initial glottal stop], in reference to the band's location on the Kootenai River near Bonners Ferry), reside on the 19-acre Kootenai Indian Reservation near Bonners Ferry, with an enrolled tribal membership of more than two hundred individuals. Other Ktunaxa bands reside on the 1.3-million-acre Flathead Indian Reservation of Montana or on various reserves throughout southeastern British Columbia and southwestern Alberta, Canada.[4]

The Qlispé (meaning unknown, though it may refer to a place-name location) or Kalispel (from the Salishian term *qlispé*) were a river-oriented people, traditionally living along the Clark Fork River in Montana, the shores of Lake Pend Oreille, and along the Pend Oreille River into Canada, who inhabited more than 3 million acres of aboriginal territory. Linguistically affiliated with their neighbors, the Coeur d'Alene, Spokane, and Flathead, the Qlispé speak a Salishian language. Today, the descendants of the Qlispé live primarily on either the Flathead reservation of Montana, numbering an estimated 500 descendants, or on the 4,600-acre Kalispel Indian Reservation in Washington, which has an enrollment of more than 250 members.[5]

The Schitsu'umsh ("The ones who were found here," referring to Lake Coeur d'Alene), or Coeur d'Alene (from the French *coeur d'alêne*, or "heart of the awl," referring to the tribe's skills in trading), have traditionally resided in what would become northern Idaho and eastern Washington, along the banks of the Coeur d'Alene, St. Joe, and Spokane Rivers and the shores of Lake Coeur d'Alene. The Schitsu'umsh speak a Salishian language. Their homeland of 5 million acres was reduced to a reservation of some 345,000 acres with an enrolled membership of about two thousand individuals.[6]

The Nimíipuu (the People), or Nez Perce (from the French *nez percé*, or "pierced noses"), have resided in the country of the Clearwater and Snake River drainages of what would become north-central Idaho, southeastern Washington, and northeastern Oregon, including Wallowa Lake—in all, more than 13 million acres. Closely related linguistically to such tribes as the Umatilla, Yakama, and Warm Springs, who live along the Columbia River, the Nimíipuu are part of the Sahaptian language family. Most Nimíipuu reside on the 750,000-acre Nez Perce Reservation located in north-central Idaho, with an enrolled membership of more than 3,300. The Nimíipuu descendants of the Nez Perce War of 1877 live on the Colville Reservation in north-central Washington.[7]

The aboriginal lands of southern Idaho were home to numerous bands of Shoshone and Paiute people. Today, the descendants of these bands reside on three federally recognized communities, the Fort Hall and Duck Valley Reservation and the Northwestern Band of Shoshone Nation.[8]

The people of the Fort Hall Reservation, just north of Pocatello, are made up of the Newe ("the People" [with stress on the first syllable]) or Northern Shoshone (the term *shoshone* is derived from the Shoshoni word *sosoni*, the plural of *sonipe*, likely meaning "grass people," in reference to their grass lodges) and the Bannaqwate ("From across the water," in reference to the Hells Canyon and Snake River area where they were from) or Bannock (the Scots-English term *bannock* refers to a "flat cake made of oatmeal," and this name may have been used by whites because it sounds like Bannaqwate, the name the tribe used for itself).[9]

The Fort Hall Indian Reservation is also the home of the descendants of Newe who once lived on the 64,000-acre Lemhi Indian Reservation. They called themselves the Agai-deka' (Salmon eaters), also spelled Akaitteka', or Lemhi Shoshone (derived from the Mormon name given to the area of the Agai-deka'), and the Duku-deka' (Sheep eaters), also spelled Tukkutte-ka'. But in 1907, after their reservation had been terminated, they resettled at Fort Hall. Today, while these terms are still in use, the people are also collectively called the Yahan-deka' (Groundhog eaters) as well as Newe.[10]

Many of the Great Basin cultures of southern Idaho and adjacent west-ern Wyoming, northern Utah, Nevada, and Oregon were gatherer-hunters of the larger linguistic groups of Shoshone and Paiute, with each band re-ferred to by its seasonal resource or location. The name Agai-deka' means "Salmon eaters" and was used to describe Shoshones when they fished for salmon on the Snake River. The name Kamme-deka', or "Jackrabbit eaters," was given to those Shoshones who were gathering and hunting from the Snake River farther south. The Yahan-deka', "Groundhog eaters," were the Shoshones of the lower Boise and Weiser basin. The Duku-deka', "Sheep eaters," referred to the Shoshones residing in the Sawtooth Range during part of the year. The fluidity of the names matched the seasonal move-ments of these band societies and has led to some confusion among out-siders who tend to apply the seasonal resource name in use at the time of Euro-American contact. Collectively, all these Shoshone bands also refer to themselves as Newe.[11]

The aboriginal territory of the Newe and Bannaqwate included all of the Snake as well as upper Salmon River drainages, encompassing much of the central and all of the eastern area of what would become the state of Idaho south of the Salmon River, more than 30 million acres in all. While the Newe were originally made up of distinct Shoshone bands and the Ban-naqwate were a distinct Paiute band, all groups speak a variation of the Numic branch of the Uto-Aztecan language family. Today, the vast majority of these descendants, numbering more than 5,800 people, reside on or near the 544,000-acre Fort Hall Reservation.[12]

The people of the Duck Valley Reservation, which straddles the Idaho-Nevada border south of Mountain Home, are made up of bands of Newe or Northern Shoshone, along with bands of the Numa (the People) or Northern Paiute (the derivation of *Paiute* is uncertain). They had inhabited the aboriginal lands associated with the Boise, Bruneau, Owyhee, Payette, and Weiser Rivers, as well as lower regions of the Snake and Salmon Rivers. This area would become southeastern Oregon, northern Nevada, and western Idaho and encompasses more than 20 million acres. Both the Newe and the Numa speak variations of the Numic branch of the Uto-Aztecan language family and reside in the Duck Valley Indian Reservation. Today, the reservation covers some 293,000 acres and is home to approximately 1,500 people.[13]

The people of the Northwestern Band of the Shoshone Nation are descendants of the Newe, residing on scattered locations over southeastern Idaho and northern Utah, including one tract of 187 acres, with tribal offices in Pocatello, Idaho, and Brigham City, Utah. Today, this band numbers more than 600 enrolled members.[14]

THE RIVER OF THE ANIMAL PEOPLES

To begin our appreciation of the confluences, we must briefly travel the landscape ahead of the confluence, before the Euro-American riverbed was channeled into the landscape. Running through this aboriginal landscape is the river of tribal oral traditions, itself the culmination of its own tributaries. These are the waters of stories told and songs sung, of family and community practices and rituals, of dance and the regalia worn, and of languages spoken. These are the waters of the Animal Peoples and their creation. These are the waters of independent, sovereign peoples. Although certainly defined in distinct ways by each tribe, sovereignty was and continues to be understood as the ability of a people to make decisions for themselves, in all realms of life, unimpeded by outside influences. Sovereignty is established and asserted by the will of a people. It is not ultimately contingent on some other nation granting it to them, as, for example, the United States. The tribes were sovereign nations long before Meriwether Lewis and William Clark gave peace medals to many of them—long before Christopher Columbus set foot on the shores of his new world. The indigenous peoples of Idaho shared a landscape that offered many different resources: food, water, shelter, and spiritual renewal. Occasionally the desire for a particular resource might bring the members of different tribes or bands into conflict. More typically, however, traditional areas of use and stewardship, rather than ownership, precluded any protracted warfare or conflict over resources in a region that demanded regular seasonal movement. These are waters that would continue to flow, intermingling with the waters of another river newly forged through the landscape.

To appreciate the waters of the Animal Peoples, let us travel downriver with Rabbit and Jack Rabbit. Their story is but one small example from one tribe, the Schitsu'umsh, of a vast body of oral traditions held by the Idaho tribes.

RABBIT AND JACK RABBIT

Rabbit and Jack Rabbit are cousins and friends. Rabbit lives in the mountains around DeSmet, near Moses Mountain here. Jack Rabbit lives on the prairie of the Big Bend country, from Rosalia out toward the Davenport area there. The winter is hard.

When it clears after a big snow, Jack Rabbit looks toward the mountains here. The trees are heavy with snow; the branches interlock. Jack Rabbit says, "I wonder what he eats? I think Rabbit must be dead." Then Jack Rabbit says, "I think I'll take my cousin some bitterroot, camas, dried salmon eggs." He puts them in a bundle and packs it on his back. Then he starts off to Rabbit's home.

Rabbit looks toward the prairie there. Then he says, "Poor Jack Rabbit! I wonder if he has a fire in this cold weather. I'll go see." He gathers pitch shavings, makes as large a pack as he can carry. Then he starts off with it toward Jack Rabbit's home.

Rabbit comes up the north side of Tekoa Mountain. Then he sets down at the edge of the woods. He says, "I wonder where Jack Rabbit lives? I don't know exactly."

Jack Rabbit comes over the prairie, up the south side of the mountain. Then he sees Rabbit sitting. He says, "Why, here he is!" Rabbit stands up. He sees Jack Rabbit. Then they walk toward each other, shake hands.

"You're still alive, my cousin!" says Rabbit. "And you're still alive, my cousin," says Jack Rabbit. "I was just coming to look for you. I was worried about you" says Rabbit. "Why, I was coming to look for you too. I was worried about you. I thought you might be hungry," says Jack Rabbit.

"No, I'm not hungry. I found green grass under that tree. I ate it. It's you I worry about. I thought you might get cold so I brought these pitch shavings for you to start a fire," says Rabbit. "No, I'm not cold. You worry for no reason. When it snows and drifts, I find a dry spot under this sage brush. That's where I stay. I thought you might need some food so I brought you some camas and bitterroot," says Jack Rabbit. Then they both laughed.

"I'll throw away the pitch." Then Rabbit unties his pack, dumps it out. "I'll dump what I brought to feed you." Then Jack Rabbit unties his pack, dumps it out. Then Rabbit and Jack Rabbit go their separate ways.

The next spring the pitch grows into pitchy trees and the bitterroot and camas into rock roses. When you go to Tekoa Mountain, you will find pitch pine trees. You will find patches of bitterroot and camas.[15]

Through the actions of the Animal Peoples, the world is "prepared for the coming of Human Peoples," as commonly expressed and understood by elders. Coyote and Wolf, Grizzly Bear and Salmon, and Rabbit and Jack Rabbit are among the Animal Peoples, along with a host of others. While the physical characteristics of these beings typically are not described, the Animal Peoples travel a primordial landscape, talking and relating to one another like humans, with motivations and personalities, and with the power to transform that landscape. Often understood as having been sent by the Creator, Animal Peoples encounter and slay dangerous monsters.[16] The terrain of the landscape is given its characteristics and made habitable, placing within it certain quintessential "gifts" that the Human Peoples will need. Such gifts include the creation of navigable rivers and mountains and prairies endowed with an abundance of roots, animals, and fish. Still another gift is spiritual power, as well as the rituals of healing and nurturing that access and direct these powers for the benefit of humans. And there are the gifts of "teachings," pragmatic as well as moral and ethical in nature, which the Human Peoples will need as they interact with one another and their world. These teachings are etched into the landscape by the Animal Peoples as rock outcroppings, river bends, and hilltops, as "textbooks" held sacred and to be "read." In the story, Rabbit and Jack Rabbit leave pitch, camas, and bitterroot on a hillside for those who would be coming, as well as a certain teaching, an ethic of sharing. Finally, it is through the actions of Coyote or Wolf that the Human Peoples are brought forth and given their particular characteristics and homelands. For the Nimíipuu, Coyote was able to trick the Swallowing Monster, kill it, free all the Animal Peoples it had gobbled up, and throw its cut-up body parts in many directions, creating the Human Peoples. The monster's heart is still visible as a hill along the Clearwater River near Kamiah.[17]

It is also important to understand how these more mythological stories provide a reorientation away from a preoccupation with measurement and time and toward a timeless focus on relationships between sentient beings and the land. "Rabbit and Jack Rabbit" transcends the historical to define the feelings that these people have for each other. The term "relative-friend," their mutual concern for the other's welfare over the long winter (undercut by the mildly insulting notion that the other might not know how to take care of himself), and the intended exchange of goods provide a glimpse into the timeless way in which the Schitsu'umsh themselves relate to one another. Walking the land, harvesting food, demonstrating concern for friends and kin, and finding joy in the antics of Coyote and other trickster figures reinforce the beliefs that continually invigorate this worldview.[18]

Among the Newe and the Numa, Coyote also plays an important role as he offers valuable knowledge about the variable seasonal and regional groupings of animals and plants found throughout the traditional homelands of these peoples. As he travels in the more arid southern regions, Coyote competes with Antelope, Deer, and Beaver for pine nuts, and when he travels in northern areas in search of salmon, he often competes with Mountain Sheep, Bear, and Wolf for sustenance and protection. These regional varieties of flora and fauna reflect the ever-so-subtle shades of seasonal and environmental change, the knowledge of which, conveyed in Coyote's stories, was so crucial to the survival of these people. Similarly, the extensive narratives involving Water Babies, mysterious yet dangerous spirit beings who lived around pools or springs in the arid regions, reiterate the care and respect the people must maintain if they are to continue accessing and using this precious resource.[19]

Among some of the essential teachings, shared by all the tribes of Idaho, are certain quintessential values. These include the understanding that the landscape is spiritually endowed and that its gifts of plants, animals, and even rocks are equally so endowed. Among the various Peoples—be they human, animal, plant, or a mountain or river—all share in a kinship with one another; all are "Peoples." The dynamic relationships between kinsmen are governed by mutual respect and an ethic of sharing, giving unselfishly to those in need, as Rabbit and Jack Rabbit so aptly demonstrate. The actions of the First Peoples not only reinforce the linkage of all living things to a timeless and evolving history; they also establish territorial boundaries between tribal people with regard to specific ecologies and food sources. This does not mean that northern Paiutes living in Idaho, for example, cannot travel south to California and Nevada in order to harvest pine nuts. It simply means that acknowledging tribal areas and seeking permission to harvest in certain places ensure the values of good stewardship and reciprocity.[20]

It is among these values that a people bases its sense of identity, heritage, and aspirations. These are the teachings that help define the nature of family and tribe, as well as relationships with plants and animals and between friend and foe. These are values that continue to influence how tribes address issues of health care, economic development, governance, and education. These are the values that reaffirm a will to be sovereign. In addition, the values of people in the tribes are reflected and passed on via material traditions. Baskets, dance regalia, drums, and even the harvesting of traditional foods like salmon, camas root, antelope, and rock chuck conform to millennia of stewardship and interaction with specific areas of Idaho. Nez Perce elder Horace Axtell creates traditional deer-hide drums by hunting, dressing, and processing the hide and consuming the venison in a prescribed, sacred manner. The songs that he sings using the drum are thereby enriched by the beliefs constructed in the drum itself.[21]

The particular and vital significance of the oral traditions is to be found not only in *what* they convey—the teachings, as critical as they are—but in *how* they are conveyed, in the telling, singing, and doing of these oral traditions. It is in these acts of giving voice to the Animal Peoples that the teachings are brought forth, vitalized, and perpetuated in the world. Some of this vitalizing power can be glimpsed by considering the act of storytelling.

FIGURE 2.2. Indigenous people often adapted traditional values to new contexts. Mrs. Lawyer winnows near Kamiah, Idaho. Photo courtesy of Idaho State Historical Society, 63–221.4a.

When an elder tells of one of the Animal People, his or her techniques include adept use of body language, hand gestures, and voice intonation, all intended to draw listeners into the story as participants. There is extensive use of phrase and sequence repetition, with Coyote's particular action highlighted by repetition of key phrases. The participation of listeners is actually monitored. In a traditional setting, as the story unfolds, listeners acknowledge their participation by periodically responding with the linguistic equivalent of "yes." As long as there are responses, the story continues, but should there be only silence, the story would cease, regardless of whether or not the teller had reached the end of the story, for there would no longer be any participants.

The animation of the story is fully realized when the power of language is itself brought to bear. Words spoken in the Native languages are understood to do more than simply describe the world; they have a "transformative power" to affect it.[22] This notion is expressed, for example, when one receives one's "Indian name." The ritually bestowed name, often descriptive of the actions of some animal, helps the child grow to become the words of that name—Running Deer or Soaring Eagle, for example. Similarly, saying "good-bye" is "too final," as one may never see the other person again. Instead, one says, "I'll see you later." One does not speak of a particular sickness out of fear of manifesting that affliction. When storytellers weave the fibers of the words into the tapestry of an oral tradition, the spoken words bring forth that which they portray. Phenomena are spoken into existence; the world is vitalized and perpetuated. When a Schitsu'umsh elder tells of Coyote tricking the Rock Monster, causing it to roll through a berry patch into the lake, the "blue" of Lake Coeur d'Alene is revitalized.[23] The storytelling techniques of the elder and the power of words coalesce, allowing listeners to run with Grizzly Bear or Coyote. They re-witness the transformation of the landscape of the creation time, as well as the revitalization of the landscape of the current time, they being one in the same landscapes. They return to the creation time, running with Grizzly Bear or Coyote, as the events of time are themselves perennially reengaged. In the waters of this river, we witness the actions of the many Animal Peoples.

So why have the elders continued to give voice to the Animal Peoples? The oral traditions of story, song, dance, and ritual at once reveal that which was established by the Animal Peoples, allowing discovery of what is most meaningful in the landscape, the teachings, providing an emotional tone to life and guidance in traveling the difficult trails encountered by Idaho's tribes. And in the very acts of telling, singing, and dancing the stories of the Animal Peoples, their journeys are continued, bringing forth, forming, and manifesting the creation time in the experiential world. The world is made and rendered meaningful in the act of revealing Coyote's story of it.

THE EURO-AMERICAN RIVER

The arrival of Euro-Americans forged a new riverbed through the indigenous landscape. And with it came altogether new sorts of waters, intermingling with, and at times threatening, the confluence with the waters of the Animal Peoples.

As we begin our journey down this river, we witness the first of many newcomers to the landscape: the horse. Through trade and the northern migration of wild herds, the Spanish-derived horse was first encountered

by the Numa and later the Nimíipuu as early as the late seventeenth century and was fully adopted into their cultures by the 1730s. The ability to
communicate with the Comanche and Mexican tribes such as the Tarahu-
mara via the Numic language aided the Shoshone and Paiute peoples in
acquiring horses, which had been taken from the Spanish by Indian people
conscripted into the ranchero workforce. The horse increased mobility
and enhanced intertribal trade, as people could travel greater distances
and transport larger cargos. In addition, the Comanche-Shoshone rapidly
transformed their culture by developing extremely mobile, mounted "light
infantry" that outmaneuvered their Indian and Anglo foes for more than
one hundred years after the horse's introduction. The horse made the buffalo country of Montana and Wyoming and the salmon and trading country
at Celilo Falls on the Columbia River much more accessible. The Nimíipuu,
in fact, bred the horse to be more agile and responsive to have tremendous
endurance. For all the tribes, the horse became a source of pride and wealth,
of pleasure and artistic expression, and of spiritual power. Some families
had herds numbering more than a thousand. This newcomer certainly contributed to the sovereignty of the people.[24]

As we continue our journey downriver, we see a second newcomer to
the indigenous landscape. But unlike the horse, it would threaten tribal
sovereignty. A series of deadly smallpox, diphtheria, and other epidemics swept the landscape as early as the mid-eighteenth century, as Kevin
Marsh explains in chapter 3 in this volume. For instance, a series of smallpox and other epidemics hit the Schitsu'umsh between 1770 and 1850.
The Schitsu'umsh, who had no previous exposure or acquired immunity,
were devastated by the epidemics, which reduced their numbers from an
estimated 5,000 to 500 in just eighty years. The Nimíipuu, numbering some
6,000 at the time Lewis and Clark passed through their lands, experienced
similar ravages, with only an estimated 1,600 left by the end of the nineteenth century. The impact of smallpox was particularly devastating for the
tribes, as their most susceptible members were the youth, who embodied
the future hopes of the tribes, and the elderly, who were the caretakers
of their collective wisdom. With the pre-contact population in Idaho estimated to be around 20,000, by the mid-nineteenth century there were only
about 4,000 indigenous people in the state.[25]

FIGURE 2.3. Natives incorporated horses into their cultures. Coeur d'Alene Indians identified as Andrew SiJohn, Susan Frank, Louie Pierre, and Lucy SiJohn at Tekoa, Washington, near the Idaho border. Photo courtesy of Idaho State Historical Society, 76–2.52d.

Following Lewis and Clark's Corps of Discovery contacts with the Nimíipuu, Schitsu'umsh, and Newe between 1805 and 1806, fur trappers and traders arrived. They had only a marginal effect on some tribes, like the Nimíipuu, but for others, like the Qlispé, Schitsu'umsh and Newe, the fur trade greatly added to their technology that made life easier, as least while the trade continued. By the early 1820s, the Hudson's Bay Company was actively involved with the Qlispé, Schitsu'umsh, and Ktunaxa at Kully-spell House (at Lake Pend Oreille), Saleesh House (near Thompson Falls), and Spokane House (along the Spokane River). Among the Newe, the 1828 expedition of Peter Ogden presaged the scorched-earth policy of white expansionism, as Ogden and his trappers found many beavers along the Humboldt River and other tributaries, which they proceeded to trap out. Metal axes, knives, and pots, woven blankets and clothes, and firearms were among the items incorporated into the technology of the tribes. The traders also introduced alcohol, which had deleterious effects on the native population. After the world demand for fur hats dried up in the 1840s, so, too, did the trade in beaver and, along with it, the sources of these newly incorporated technologies. As metal tools wore out or broke and supplies of musket lead and gunpowder diminished, many tribes struggled to compensate for these loses.[26]

As we continue downriver, we witness yet another threat to tribal sovereignty in the form of military confrontations with the U.S. government. For the Schitsu'umsh, war came in May 1858 with an unprovoked invasion by about 150 federal soldiers and fifty of their Nez Perce allies. Lieutenant Colonel Edward Steptoe and his troops met heavy resistance from the combined forces of Schitsu'umsh, Spokane, Palouse, Kalispel, and Yakama near Rosalia, Washington. Surrounded and facing certain defeat, Steptoe negotiated with the Schitsu'umsh to surrender, having his troops leave their weapons behind and promising not to return. But in August 1858, Colonel George Wright brought a much larger, better-armed force, to "avenge this humiliation," and defeated the area tribes in two decisive battles near Spokane, Washington. In the ensuing days, he pursued a scorched-earth policy, all the way up to the Cataldo Mission itself. Wright ordered the destruction of food stores intended for the coming winter, the killing of hundreds of Indian horses, and, without trial, the hanging of many of the leaders. Both the families who had supported the resistance and those who had stayed out of the fighting faced punishment.[27]

On January 29, 1863, a group of some five hundred Newe, under the leadership of a local chief named Bear Hunter, was wintering in the Cache Valley near Franklin, just south of the Utah-Idaho border. Tensions were high between white settlers, who were arriving in increasing numbers, and the Newe, who wanted to protect their land and water. Colonel Patrick Connor and his California Volunteers initiated battle against Newe warriors. The Newe repelled the first attack, but, after that, outgunned and out of ammunition, Connor's troops overran the Newe camp. The soldiers proceeded to indiscriminately kill men, women, and children, committing all sorts of atrocities against the remaining Newe. As the Bear River Massacre occurred during the height of the Civil War and western expansionism, it has received little historical attention.[28]

For the Nimíipuu, war with the U.S. military came in 1877. While not party to the Treaty of 1863, the Wallowa bands of Nimíipuu in northeastern Oregon found that their homelands were no longer within the boundaries of the much reduced reservation. Their chiefs—among them, Looking Glass, Joseph, and White Bird—began the move to their new home. On their way, tensions erupted when some Nimíipuu warriors killed several settlers in retribution for Nimíipuu murders. To prevent a possible Indian uprising, General Oliver Howard sent his troops against the Wallowa bands. A three-month and 1,600-mile struggle to reach Canada ensued. The Nimíipuu numbered about 750, less than half of whom were warriors, yet they managed to elude a far superior military force, even defeating or repelling the troops in several encounters at White Bird, along the Clearwater River, at Big Hole, and through the newly established Yellowstone National Park. But the toll on lives was heavy, as government soldiers targeted children, women, and the elderly as well as warriors. Exhausted and running short on supplies, some 400 Nimíipuu, under Joseph's leadership surrendered to Colonel Nelson Miles, just forty miles from Canada and safety. Sent to Oklahoma, many Nimíipuu died along the way. Eventually, Joseph and about 150 other non-Christian Nimíipuu were exiled to the Colville Indian Reservation in Washington, where their descendants continue to reside today, far from their homeland.[29]

In 1878, having lost access to some of their traditional lands around the Camas Prairie area near Fairfield, a group of Niwi and Newe from the Fort Hall Reservation, joined by some Umatillas from Oregon, directed their frustration at nearby settlers. The fighting continued as the leader, Buffalo Horn, was joined by allies among Weiser Shoshones and Northern Paiutes under the leadership of Paddy Cap. However, defeat was imminent. When they were eventually captured by the U.S. Army, Paddy Cap and his followers were sent to the Yakama Indian Reservation in Washington. Eventually, he and many of his followers were provided with land on the northern part of the Duck Valley Indian Reservation, where they settled in 1885.[30]

The enactment of a series of treaties and executive orders further eroded tribal sovereignty during the mid- to late nineteenth century. These "agreements" established reservations, diminishing the tribes' land base. Although the U.S. Congress ceased negotiating formal treaties with Indian nations after 1871, the federal government continued to establish nation-to-nation relations and negotiate exchanges of resources for land in the form of executive orders. Executive orders have the same legal authority as treaties.

Ironically, while seeking to inhibit tribal sovereignty, treaties and executive orders helped establish a legal basis on which federal interactions with the tribes acknowledge a limited form of tribal sovereignty. The U.S. Supreme Court, based on the rulings known as the Marshall Trilogy, handed down during the tenure of Chief Justice John Marshall, had long recognized that Indian nations were "distinct political communities, having territorial boundaries, within which their authority is exclusive, and having a right to all the lands within those boundaries" (*Worcester v. Georgia*, 1832). Though the Indian tribes were not to be considered foreign nations, they did constitute "distinct political" communities within the United States, known as "domestic, dependent nations" (*Cherokee Nation v. Georgia*, 1831). This notion helped establish the guardian-to-ward relationship between the federal government and the tribes, giving birth to federal trusteeship of Indian affairs.[31]

Nevertheless, as described in Article VI, Section 2, of the U.S. Constitution, treaties are bilaterally constructed, nation-to-nation agreements, the "supreme law of the land," intended to be legally binding for all time. Treaties acknowledged that tribal property should not be taken without consent of the Indian tribe in question and, further, that the ownership of land is to be held by the tribe unless explicitly relinquished in the language of a treaty. For example, ownership of a lake, if not explicitly granted to the United States, would remain with the tribe. As such, the agreements entered into were not grants of rights to Indians but rather grants of rights from tribes to the United States; this principle is known as the reserved rights doctrine. Courts also affirmed that treaties are to be interpreted as their original signers had intended, a system known as the canons of construction. And finally, in exchange for ceding vast tracts of land and resources, the tribe would receive educational and health benefits as well as other services. Such services and allocations are legally understood as akin to "purchased" and "contracted" services, not "social entitlements" or "special rights."[32]

The ultimate effect of the treaties and executive orders was to contribute to the assimilation of Indians and infringement on tribal sovereignty. Implicit in the treaty process was the assertion of federal congressional plenary power—the ability of Congress to unilaterally abrogate any provision of a treaty. This power would be exemplified in the imposition of the Dawes Severalty Act of 1887, as well as in the termination policy of the 1950s.

Between 1873 and 1889, a series of rather heavy-handed executive orders were negotiated with the Schitsu'umsh, reducing the tribe's original 5-million-acre homeland to a reservation of 345,000 acres. Interestingly, their beloved Sacred Heart Mission at Cataldo was not included within the reservation boundaries. This dislocation from their traditional lands was further compounded after the implementation of the Dawes Act in 1909. Each tribal member was limited to owning 160 acres of land. So-called surplus lands, totaling more than 300,000 acres, were opened up to non-Indian homesteading. Today, within a reservation boundary encompassing 345,000 acres, only 70,000 acres are actually owned by tribal members. Before allotment, the Schitsu'umsh were some of the most successful farmers on the Palouse of north-central Idaho. Families typically owned two homes, one on their farm of 1,000–2,000 acres and the other in DeSmet, where they assembled on weekends to celebrate Mass and socialize. During this period, the Schitsu'umsh utilized state-of-the-art farm implements, hired non-Indians as laborers, and produced impressive harvests, for example, in 1894, more than 100,000 bushels of wheat. After allotment, with their land base so diminished, the Schitsu'umsh lost their economic independence, as did so many other tribes.[33]

The Newe and Numa received federal recognition in the Treaty of Ruby Valley of 1863. The boundaries of their Duck Valley Indian Reservation, which straddles the states of Idaho and Nevada, were established by executive order on April 16, 1877. Their aboriginal lands of some 20 million acres were reduced to a 289,667-acre reservation, increased in 1886 by an additional 4,000 acres when Paddy Cap's band of Northern Paiutes settled on the northern parts of the reservation. As the federal government never designated Duck Valley Indian Reservation for the Allotment Act, all of its lands are still owned by the tribes.

The 1868 Fort Bridger Treaty established the Fort Hall reservation for the Newe and Bannaqwate. The reservation initially covered some 1.6 million acres but has been reduced by allotment, homesteading, and other agreement concessions to 544,000 acres today. The Fort Hall reservation has also become home to the Agai-dika and Duku-deka', who had their own Lemhi Indian Reservation in north-central Idaho of some 64,000 acres established in 1875. However, the agreement creating the Lemhi reservation was unilaterally dissolved by the U.S. government in 1880 over the objections of the Agai-deka' and Duku-deka'. These tribes were eventually moved to Fort Hall in 1907, but their descendants continue to seek the reestablishment of the reservation.[34]

The Idaho Qlispé were party to two federal negotiations, both of which led to resettlement out of state. In the Hellgate Treaty of 1855, several families of Qlispé agreed to join the much larger populations of Bitterroot Salish, Kootenai, and other Qlispé in resettling on the Flathead Reservation of some 1.3 million acres. The federal government pressured the remaining Qlispé families to relocate from their Idaho homes onto the Colville, Coeur d'Alene, or Flathead reservations, but the families staunchly resisted. Finally, a 1914 executive order established the 6,400-acre Kalispel Indian Reservation near Usk, Washington, where the remaining families settled. Allotment had devastating effects on both reservations, with the Flathead Indian Reservation reduced by more than half. Allotment was imposed on the Kalispel reservation in 1924, but unlike other reservation allotments of 160 acres, the parcels assigned to the Qlispé were limited to 40 acres each, typically on lands that were not suitable for farming.[35]

The indigenous peoples of Idaho witnessed their aboriginal lands of more than 60 million acres eventually reduced to five Idaho reservations of some 3.2 million acres and then experienced the further loss of those lands through allotment and other concessions. While the tribes retain jurisdiction over all the lands within their original reservation boundaries, the actual land owned today by the membership of individual tribes or collectively by the tribes is a little more than a million acres of their once expansive homeland.

As we continue downriver, we see another threat, an assault on the cultural practices of the Idaho Indians through the activities of Christian missionaries and the establishment of boarding schools. For example, Jesuit missionaries first came to the Schitsu'umsh in 1842, wearing black robes.

The Mission of the Sacred Heart, or Old Mission, at Cataldo was completed in 1850. In an attempt to further control a nomadic people, the Jesuits implemented a "reduction system," moving and settling Schitsu'umsh families at DeSmet, between 1876 and 1877. The trauma administered by the hands of Jesuit missionaries was most pronounced from the late 1890s through the early 1930s. One elder, voicing a Schitsu'umsh sentiment, said that "everything we do is considered a sin."[36] Sacred objects were confiscated and publicly burned. All forms of spiritual and social dancing were prohibited. Christian names replaced Indian names, both personal and geographic. Animal spirits gave way to Christian saints and notions of heaven, hell, and salvation. Children were rounded up, removed from their families, and forced to attend the Sisters of Charity Boarding School at DeSmet. Upon arrival, and to begin the "civilizing" process, students' hair was cut short, they were given uniforms to wear, and they were forbidden to speak their native language. Ironically, the Schitsu'umsh cut their hair at the time of the passing of a relative, as a sign of respect and mourning. The new Catholic education undermined traditional Indian values and teachings, as new industrial skills were taught and new ways of viewing the world instilled. The focus was now on building a self-reliant individual, no longer on supporting the extended family; traveling a secular landscape, no longer accompanied by spirit Animal Peoples; moving along a chronological path in which time is measured linearly, no longer able to return with the Animal Peoples to the creation time when the events of time are perennially reoccurring. And with the new Jesuit administration, virtually all forms of decision making, within the family, community, and tribe, were taken away from the hereditary headmen and family elders and placed in the hands of the priests and their most devout Indian adherents, the Soldiers of the Sacred Heart.[37]

During this period of land and habitat loss, cultural destruction, and violence toward Indian people, a religious revival occurred in southern Idaho and northern Nevada. A young Paiute ranch hand who had taken the name Jack Wilson had a vision that Indian people could revitalize Indian life and culture by dancing the "ghost dance," living a clean life without alcohol, and returning to their native beliefs and rituals. Wilson's vision became known as the Ghost Dance religion, and the songs, stories, and rituals associated with it spread throughout the West. Delegations from the Sioux and Kiowa met with Wilson, who took the Indian name Wovoka. The U.S. military, in response to what it considered a threat from Sioux who might become violent toward the army, saw the Ghost Dance as a call to arms among the relatively peaceful Sioux. This fear and the inability of Sitting Bull and other Sioux leaders to negotiate a relationship of trust between his people and the soldiers during the winter of 1890 resulted in the slaughter of Sioux men, women, and children at Wounded Knee. Tragically, eighty-five years later, this violent episode was followed by another violent clash between federal law enforcement officials and members of the American Indian Movement at Wounded Knee, which also resulted in bloodshed and a life sentence for Leonard Peltier.[38]

By the middle of the nineteenth and well into the first half of the twentieth century, the tribes of Idaho were thus anything but sovereign peoples. Healers and warriors could no longer offer protection against their enemies, and headmen could no longer negotiate with their enemies from a position of strength. Euro-American governmental and missionary institutions controlled virtually all educational, spiritual, economic, social, and political decision making for the tribes. It was a period of dependency as well as spiritual, economic, and psychological challenge, despair, and trauma for the indigenous peoples of Idaho. Elders recall this period as the "dark age." Even into the early 1950s, there was the federal initiative known as the Termination Policy, which abrogated federal relations with and obligations to the tribes, eliminating not only reservations but also the health care, educational, economic, and administrative infrastructures supporting those communities. Idaho tribes aggressively and successfully fought this policy.

During this dark age, many tribal families sought to maintain their heritage and identity by going underground. While they were not always able to challenge the authority of missionaries or government agents, they continued practicing their traditional activities, such as powwow dancing and singing, the stick game, sweat bathing, and ceremonial dancing, but out of the gaze of authorities. Such continued practices sowed the seeds of the cultural revival and renewed sovereignty seen today.

As we continue downriver toward a confluence, we notice the waters slowing and warming. Under the guidance of John Collier, commissioner of the Bureau of Indian Affairs (1933–45), federal assimilation policies were

redirected. In these initiatives, prime among them the Indian Reorganization Act of 1934, Collier sought self-determination for the tribes, establishing their own governance and constitutions, educational opportunities,
economic development endeavors, and religious freedoms and terminat-
ing the Dawes Act. The Schitsu'umsh established their first tribal council in 1936 and tribal constitution in 1947. Coinciding with federal policy
changes, by the 1930s, many missionary activities had shifted from repress-
ing indigenous religious expression to encouraging a rebirth in Native arts
and cultural expression. In 1975, the federal government enacted the Self-
Determination Act, followed in 1995 by the Self-Governance Act. Through
these measures, tribes could assume control of their education, health care,
natural resource management, and law enforcement. Tribes also sought out
regional and national alliances through such organizations as the National
Congress of American Indians (founded in 1944) and the Affiliated Tribes of
Northwest Indians (founded in 1953), both dedicated to protecting Indian
rights. Idaho tribes were beginning to assert a rejuvenated sovereignty.[39]

Gaming, as expressed in stick games or horse-racing competitions and
betting, has always been an important social activity among the tribes of
Idaho. During the 1980s, some Idaho tribes began envisioning economic development and employment opportunities through casino-style entertainment projects. Seeking to establish a regulatory framework that would gov-
ern these gaming endeavors while still encouraging economic development,
the United States established the Indian Gaming Regulatory Act of 1988.
The act specifies that each tribe must establish a gaming compact with the
appropriate state government and grants the tribe the authority to pursue
gaming only at the level permitted by that state. In Idaho, Class III games
commonly played at Las Vegas–style casinos, such as blackjack and roulette,
are not allowed. Nevertheless, gaming and entertainment operations on
the Coeur d'Alene, Fort Hall, Kootenai, and Nez Perce reservations, as well
as the Kalispel operation west of Spokane, Washington, have proved to be
very successful. The Coeur d'Alene Casino Resort Hotel, for example, had approximately five hundred employees and generated more than $20 million
in profits in 2008. It has shared its success by donating millions of dollars
to local school districts, both on and off the reservation. In conjunction
with other tribal initiatives, it has reduced unemployment on the Coeur

d'Alene Reservation from 70 percent in the 1970s to single digits today.[40]

While most thought the last Indian war ended in the nineteenth century, the Ktunaxa of northern Idaho had different plans. In September 1975, a small band of Ktunaxa near Bonners Ferry declared war on the United States. As it had not been part of the treaty process and thus was not federally recognized, the band did not have an assigned reservation and basic services for its population. The Ktunaxa instituted tolls and placed armed guards on roads running through traditional tribal lands. The funds collected went to support housing and health care for tribal elders. In a concession, the federal government granted this Ktunaxa band, the ʔaq'anqmi, tribal recognition and a small reservation of 12.5 acres, which was subsequently enlarged to almost 20 acres.[41]

Another group of Newe families resisted federal government attempts at relocation to the Fort Hall and Duck Valley Reservations and remained in scattered locations across southeastern Idaho and northeastern Utah. These individual families were federally recognized as the Northwestern Band of the Shoshone Nation on April 29, 1987. With elected tribal officials and an enrollment of about five hundred, the tribe staffs offices in Pocatello, Idaho, and Brigham City, Utah. In 1989, the Church of Jesus Christ of Latter-day Saints gave the tribe 184 acres of land, which today constitutes its reservation. Additional privately owned Indian lands are held in trust by the Bureau of Indian Affairs in northern Utah and southern Idaho. The 26-acre Bear River Massacre site (near Preston, Idaho) was donated to the tribe on March 24, 2003.[42]

THE CONFLUENCE

In the intermingling of the waters of two distinct rivers are the histories of the indigenous peoples of Idaho. In one river are the experiences of Euro-American contact, a chronology of struggle, loss, and trauma but also of opportunity. In the other river, Coyote and the Animal Peoples ran in a world perennially re-created, brought forth each time the stories were told, the dances danced, the songs sung, the languages spoken, and the landscapes traveled. One river sought to impose its will on Indians, to modify, if not undermine, their sovereignty, while the other river sought to assert the will of Indians, seeking sovereignty.

With the ebb and flow of the two rivers beginning in the late seventeenth century, we see an oscillation between rivers, but in the confluence of these waters during the past thirty years, one river is emerging as dominant. We witness the Ktunaxa, Qlispé, Schitsu'umsh, Nimíipuu, Bannaqwate, Newe, and Numa applying the teachings of the Animal Peoples as they mediate and render the lingering effects of contact history meaningful within the context of their cultural heritage. As they had done with the horse, the tribes are consciously embracing and adapting elements of Euro-American society, to enhance the quality of life of their peoples.

Each time a high school gym is converted into a powwow dance floor, the Ktunaxa, Qlispé, Schitsu'umsh, Nimíipuu, Bannaqwate, Newe, and Numa are reasserting their tribal identities and reclaiming their landscapes in the face of Euro-American assimilation. At the powwow, beginning with the grand entry, we see an unfolding transformation. The eagle feather staff, "the Indian flag," leads the way, with the Stars and Stripes a step behind, both held high by military veterans, followed by elders and youth, men and women, all in regalia of animal skins, bird feathers, and bright-colored clothing.[43] With the drumbeat, the honor song, and the dance step, the procession cleanses the ground, as if making its way to the ancestral mountain valley, prairie, or lakeshore. Handshakes and smiles are frequently exchanged, renewing bonds of family and friendship. As the dances continue into the evening, with the traditional men's, owl, or women's fancy shawl dance, the dancers themselves become Butterfly, Wolf, or Soaring Eagle. And the Animal Peoples are seen once again.

On the Duck Valley Indian Reservation, federal government and church officials opposed the annual fandangos and traditional dances that marked the early summer season for the Newe and Numa. Round dances, stick games, courting rituals, and family giveaways had characterized these meeting of the bands for millennia. Rather than simply give up these traditions, however, tribal leaders at Duck Valley, as well as at the Fort Hall Reservation, organized Fourth of July celebrations that allowed all of these events to continue within the acceptable context of a national holiday. The flag song sung in Paiute, the rodeo featuring Indian events like bronc roping and relay racing, the night-long stick games and songs, and the combination of traditional round dances with more pan-Indian powwow dances all provide tribal members with traditional resources within a national holiday. The role of the veteran at these holiday events has been an interesting development. Indian veterans are highly honored in all reservation communities, and the dancing, singing, and recognizing of individual sacrifices on behalf of tribal and national goals is a central part of the event.[44]

The trauma felt, sacrifices made, and courage shown during the Nez Perce War of 1877 are relived in the annual pilgrimages made by the Nimíipuu. The battle sites of White Bird, Big Hole, and Bear Paw are as significant to the cultural landscape of the Nimíipuu as is the Heart of the Monster, the birthplace of the people near Kamiah. Each year, youth and adults retrace the steps of their ancestors, not only participating in the victories and defeats, but also experiencing the despair, sacrifice, and freedom that are part of being Nimíipuu. In this way, a historical event is transformed into a perennially reengaged Nimíipuu oral tradition.

For the Schitsu'umsh, the voices of the Animal Peoples are clearly heard in their casino, tribal school, and medical center. The very successful Coeur d'Alene Casino and Circling Raven Golf Course function as a family, with their "hunters bringing home jobs and hope." A significant portion of the annual profit is routinely distributed, with no strings attached, to area schools in need, many off the reservation. The state-of-the-art Coeur d'Alene Tribal School and Benewah Medical and Wellness Center, funded through tribal initiatives and resources, maintain an open-door policy. The educational and health care opportunities these facilities provide are offered to all in the community who are in need, Indian and non-Indian alike. As in the distribution of gaming revenues, the example of Rabbit and Jack Rabbit and their ethic of sharing orients how the Schitsu'umsh are constructing much of their contemporary landscape.

In these and many other examples too numerous to detail here, we witness the voices of the army generals, Christian missionaries, and treaty commissioners being either silenced altogether or rendered benign and culturally redefined by the voices of the Animal Peoples. We witness lineal time and the chronology of cultural assimilation being replaced by perennial time and the cultural rejuvenation of tribe and landscape. We witness the tribes successfully addressing issues related to educational and employment opportunities, health care and social services, economic development, law enforcement and jurisdictional claims, and tribal administration. We witness the the Ktunaxa, Qlispé, Schi̱tsu'umsh, Nimíipuu, Bannaqwate, Newe, and Numa reasserting their sovereignty.

Notes

1   The term *contact history* refers to the varied interactions between indigenous and Euro-American societies, from the moment of initial contact and continuing into the present.

2   The content of this chapter is informed not only by the sources cited in the notes but by the cumulative knowledge derived from interviews and participant-observations with elders and consultants from Idaho's tribes over many years of ethnographic research.

3   Additional details about the lands, languages, and populations described in this chapter can be found on official tribal websites: the Coeur d'Alene Tribe, http://www.cdatribe.com (accessed March 17, 2011); Kootenai Tribe of Idaho, http://www.kootenai.org (accessed March 17, 2011); the Nez Perce Tribal Web Site, http://www.nezperce.org (accessed March 17, 2011); Shoshone-Bannock Tribes, http://shoshonebannocktribes.com (accessed March 17, 2011); Shoshone Paiute Tribes of the Duck Valley Indian Reservation, http://shopaitribes.org/spt-15/ (accessed March 17, 2011); and Robert McCarl, "Shoshone-Paiute 'Pakkiata' in the Great Basin," *Idaho Issues Online* (Fall 2004), http://www.boisestate.edu/research/history/issuesonline/fall2004_issues/2f_numa.html (accessed July 11, 2011). See also Warren D'Azevedo, ed., *Handbook of North American Indians,* vol. 11, *Great Basin* (Washington, DC: Smithsonian Institution Press, 1986); Robert Ruby and John Brown, *A Guide to the Indian Tribes of the Pacific Northwest* (Norman: University of Oklahoma Press, 1986); Deward Walker, ed., *Handbook of North American Indians,* vol. 12, *Plateau* (Washington, DC: Smithsonian Institution Press, 1998); and Deward Walker, *Indians of Idaho* (Moscow: University of Idaho Press, 1982).

4   References to pronunciation acknowledge the importance of the spoken word. The tribes of Idaho are anchored in their oral traditions and the spoken word and, as part of their renewed tribal sovereignty, are seeking to rejuvenate their tribal identities and spoken languages. Bill B. Brunton, "Kootenai," in Walker, *Handbook*, vol. 12, *Plateau*, 223–37. A complicating factor with regard to the Shoshone and other tribes in the Great Basin is the varying names used by Indian people in the region based on their primary subsistence area or source. Those people living in the northern part of the Great Basin (northern Nevada and southern Idaho) relied heavily on pine nuts and they were referred to as *tipatikka* (pine nut eaters), while those from the Ruby Valley area in Nevada who settled in Duck Valley and Fort Hall Reservations, were called *watatikka* (eaters of ryegrass seed); David Hurst Thomas, Lorann S. A. Pendleton, and Stephen C. Cappanari, "Western Shoshone," in D'Azevedo, *Handbook*, vol. 11, *Great Basin*, 281–83.

5   Sylvester L. Lahren, Jr., "Kalispel," in Walker, *Handbook*, vol. 12, *Plateau*, 283–96.

6   Rodney Frey, in collaboration with the Schi̱tsu'umsh, *Landscape Traveled by Coyote and Crane: The World of the Schi̱tsu'umsh (Coeur d'Alene Indians)* (Seattle: University of Washington Press, 2001), 3; Gary B. Palmer, "Coeur d'Alene," in Walker, *Handbook*, vol. 12, *Plateau*, 313–26.

7   Deward E. Walker, Jr., "Nez Perce," in Walker, *Handbook*, vol. 12, *Plateau*, 420–38.

8   We are indebted to Chris Loether, professor of anthropology, Idaho State University, to Josie Shottanana, director of cultural resources for the Kootenai Tribe, and to Francis Cullooyah, director of cultural resources for the Kalispel Tribe, for helping clarify the terms used by the Shoshone and Bannock, the Kootenai, and the Kalispel peoples respectively.

9   Robert F. Murphy and Yolanda Murphy, "Northern Shoshone and Bannock," in D'Azevedo, *Handbook*, vol. 11, *Great Basin*, 284–307.

10   Ibid. In the history written by the tribe, the authors use the symbol + to indicate the vowel sound between *i* and *u*, as in "Tag+d+ka." See *Newe: A Western Shoshone History* (Reno: Intertribal Native Council of Nevada and University of Utah Printing Service, 1976), 4.

11   Murphy and Murphy, "Northern Shoshone and Bannock."

12   Ibid. The historical depth and geographic breadth of the Uto-Aztecan language and cosmology are discussed in Daniel J. Gelo, "Recalling the Past in Creating the Present: Topographic References in Comanche Narrative," in L. Daniel Myers, ed., *Numic Mythologies: Anthropological Perspectives in the Great Basin and Beyond* (Boise: Boise State University, 2006), 81–93. As Gelo illustrates, the relationships between humans and the landscape are mediated by animal spirits that respond to various physical features (mountains, streams, valleys) in positive or negative ways. Based on these beliefs, Numic societies, from the Aztec to the Shoshone and Paiute, inhabit a landscape that reinforces vigilance and awareness of, as well as respect for, these positive and negative forces.

13   Murphy and Murphy, "Northern Shoshone and Bannock"; David H. Thomas, Lorann S. A. Pendleton, and Stephen C. Cappannari, "Western Shoshone," in D'Azevedo, *Handbook*, vol. 11, *Great Basin*, 262–83.

14   Murphy and Murphy, "Northern Shoshone and Bannock"; Thomas, Pendleton, and Cappannari, "Western Shoshone"; Patty Timbimboo-Madsen, director, Cultural and Natural Resources for the Northwestern Band of the Shoshone Nation, personal communications, February 2, 2009, and June 29, 2011.

15   "Rabbit and Jack Rabbit" is reprinted by permission from Rodney Frey, *Landscape Traveled by Coyote and Crane: The World of the Schitsu'umsh (Coeur d'Alene Indians)* (Seattle: University of Washington Press, 2001), 112. This text was modified based on the telling by Schitsu'umsh elder Dorothy Nicodemus (undated manuscript) and also recorded in Gladys Amanda Reichard, *An Analysis of Coeur d'Alene Indian Myths* (Philadelphia: Memoirs of the American Folklore Society, 1947), 192–93.

16   Frey, *Landscape*, 109–51; also Allen Slickpoo Sr., Leroy Seth, and Deward Walker, Jr., *Nu Mee Poom Tit Wah Tit (Nez Perce Legends)* (Lapwai, ID: Tribal Publications, 1972). In addition to the sources cited in the notes, for further information on the oral traditions of Idaho's indigenous peoples, see Haruo Aoki, *Nez Perce Texts*, University of California Publications in Linguistics 90 (Berkeley: University of California Press, 1979); Haruo Aoki and Deward Walker, *Nez Perce Oral Narratives*, University of California Publications in Linguistics 104 (Berkeley: University of California Press, 1989); Beverly Crum and Jon P. Dayley, *Shoshoni Texts*, Occasional Papers and Monographs in Cultural Anthropology and Linguistics, vol. 2 (Boise: Boise State University, 1997); Isabel T. Kelly, "Northern Paiute Tales," *Journal of American Folklore* 52 (October–December 1938): 363–438; Wick Miller, *Newe Natekwinappeh: Shoshoni*

Stories and Dictionary, Anthropological Papers no. 94 (Salt Lake City: University of Utah, 1972); Myers, *Numic Mythologies*; Archie Phinney, *Nez Perce Texts*, Columbia University Contributions to Anthropology 23 (New York: Columbia University Press, 1934); Anne Smith, *Shoshone Tales* (Salt Lake City: University of Utah Press, 1993); Deward Walker, *Myths of Idaho Indians* (Moscow: University of Idaho Press, 1980); Walker, *Blood of the Monster: The Nez Perce Coyote Cycle* (Worland, WY: High Plains Publishing Company, 1994).

17   Rodney Frey, ed., *Stories That Make the World: Oral Literature of the Indian Peoples of the Inland Northwest, As Told by Lawrence Aripa, Tom Yellowtail, and other Elders* (Norman: University of Oklahoma Press, 1995); and Frey, *Landscape*, 3–13, 152–256; Slickpoo, Seth, and Walker, *Nu Mee Poom Tit Wah Tit*.

18   Robert McCarl, "A Spatial Analysis of Coeur d'Alene Traditional Literature: Aquatic Culture and Cultural Survival through Narrative" (Seattle: Institute of the North American West, 1993), 2–5. Expert testimony submitted to the United States Department of Justice, *United States v. Idaho*, July 15, 1996.

19   Water babies and malevolent spirits and their association with particularly lonely or threatening places are discussed in Gelo, "Recalling the Past," 81–93; Judith Vander, *Shoshone Ghost Dance Religion: Poetry Songs and Great Basin Context* (Urbana: University of Illinois Press, 1997), 45; also see Earl Dean Harney with Beverly Crum and Earl Crum, "Western Shoshone Place Names," in Beverly Crum and Jon P. Dayley, eds., *Shoshoni Texts* (Boise: Boise State University, Department of Anthropology, 1997), 192–93.

20   Unless otherwise noted, the analysis of oral tradition in this chapter is elaborated on in Frey, *Stories*, esp. 10–14, 39–44, 52–61, 63–70, 141–58, 169–77, and 214–16.

21   Horace Axtell and Margo Aragon, *A Little Bit of Wisdom: Conversations with a Nez Perce Elder* (Lewiston, ID: Confluence Press, 1997), 209–11.

22   Frey, *Landscape*, 197–98.

23   Frey, *Stories*, 71–75.

24   Walker, *Handbook*, vol. 12: *Plateau*; Demitri B. Shimkin, "Introduction of the Horse," in D'Azevedo, *Handbook*, vol. 11: *Great Basin*, 517–24. Also see Walker, *Indians of Idaho*, 89–90.

25   Frey, *Landscape*; demography estimates derived from various sources in the *Handbook of North American Indians* series, especially Joy Leland, "Population," in D'Azevedo, *Handbook*, vol. 11: *Great Basin*, 608–19; Robert T. Boyd, "Demographic History until 1990," in Walker, *Handbook* , vol. 12: *Plateau*, 467–83.

26   Murphy and Murphy, "Northern Shoshone," 295, 302; Carling I. Malouf and John Findlay, "Euro-American Impact before 1870," in D'Azevedo, *Handbook*, vol. 11, *Great Basin*, 503–6; Deward E. Walker, Jr., and Roderick Sprague, "History until 1846," in Walker, *Handbook*, vol. 12, *Plateau*, 140–44; Brunton, "Kootenai," 232–33; Lahren, "Kalispel," 293–94; Walker, "Nez Perce," 429; Theodore Stern, "Columbia River Trade Network," in Walker, *Handbook*, vol. 12, *Plateau*, 650–52.

27   Frey, *Landscape*, 83–84; Laura Woodworth-Ney, *Mapping Identity: The Creation of the Coeur d'Alene Indian Reservation, 1805–1902* (Boulder: University Press of Colorado, 2004), 57–69.

28   Brigham Madsen, *The Bannock of Idaho* (Caldwell, ID: Caxton, 1958), 111–38.

29   Nez Perce Tribal Web Site, http://www.nezperce.org; Alvin M. Josephy, *The Nez Perce Indians and the Opening of the Northwest* (New Haven, CT: Yale University Press,

1965), is the best-known account, see esp. 443–644. See also Robert R. McCoy, *Chief Joseph, Yellow Wolf, and the Creation of Nez Perce History in the Pacific Northwest* (New York: Routledge, 2004), esp. 99–184.

30 Whitney McKinney, *A History of the Shoshone-Paiutes of the Duck Valley Indian Reservation* (Salt Lake City: Institute of the North American West and Howe Brothers, 1983), 57–61; Richard O. Clemmer and Omer C. Stewart, "Treaties, Reservations and Claims," in D'Azevedo, *Handbook*, vol. 11: Great *Basin*, 525–57.

31 The third in the trilogy is *Johnson v. M'Intosh* (1832).

32 For a definitive guide to the legal framework within which Indian people live in the United States, see Stephen L. Pevar, *The Rights of Indians and Tribes: The Authoritative ACLU Guide to Indian and Tribal Rights*, 4th ed. (New York: Oxford University Press, 2010).

33 These trends are found throughout Frey, *Landscape*, and Woodworth-Ney, *Mapping Identity*.

34 Richard O. Clemmer and Omer C. Stewart, "Treaties, Reservations, and Claims," in D'Azevedo, *Handbook*, vol. 11, *Great Basin*, 525–57; Brigham D. Madsen, *The Lemhi: Sacajawea's People* (Caldwell, ID: Caxton, 1979).

35 Lahren, "Kalispel," 294; Sylvester L. Lahren, Jr., "Reservations and Reserves," in Walker, *Handbook* , vol. 12, *Plateau*, 490–94.

36 Frey, *Landscape*, 72.

37 Frey, *Landscape*, 62–78; Jacqueline Petersen, *Sacred Encounters: Father DeSmet and the Indians of the Rocky Mountains* (Norman: University of Oklahoma Press, 1993); Father Nicolas Point, *The Wilderness Kingdom: Indian Life in the Rocky Mountains, 1840–1847* (New York: Holt, Rinehart and Winston, 1967); Woodworth-Ney, *Mapping Identity*, 23–41.

38 James Mooney, "The Ghost Dance Religion and the Sioux Outbreak of 1890," *14th Annual Report of the Bureau of American Ethnology for the Years 1892–1893, Part 2*, (Washington, DC: Smithsonian Institution, 1896), 641–1136; Peter Matthiessen, *In the Spirit of Crazy Horse* (New York: Penguin, 1992).

39 John Fahey, *Saving the Reservation: Joe Garry and the Battle to Be Indian* (Seattle: University of Washington Press, 2001); Frey, *Landscape*, 100–103.

40 CDA Casino, http://www.cdacasino.com (accessed March 17, 2011).

41 Kootenai Tribe of Idaho website; Brunton, "Kootenai," 235; Lahren, "Reservations," 494.

42 Timbimboo-Madsen, personal communications.

43 Horace Axtell is an exemplar. See Axtell and Aragon, *Little Bit of Wisdom*. A more general description of the techniques and meaning of powwow dancing and singing can be found in George P. Horse Capture, *Pow Wow* (Cody, WY: Buffalo Bill Historical Center, 1989).

44 Steven J. Crum, *Po'I Pentum Tammen Kimmappeh: The Road on Which We Came; A History of the Western Shoshone* (Salt Lake City: University of Utah Press, 1994), 59–63.

Nez Perce Allen Slickpoo recalls the trauma that missionaries and other officials inflicted on Native peoples.

Okay, first of all, when the missionaries came, the Buckskin and the Eagle Feather became the work of the white man's devil. In other words, we were told that it was evil to wear a buckskin, it was evil to wear feathers on your hairdo, and that people should cut their hair and not have braids. From some of the experiences that we had historically with missionaries, for instance, I recall elderly people talking about Reverend Spalding. When Reverend Spalding put the people to work on his garden or whatever—hard, laborious tasks—he would tell them that they were doing it for the Great Spirit, or for God; they're doing for the church. In other words, to me, that would be indirectly next to what I would call slavery. And these people believed him; they believed what they were being told. At one time or another, the religion was so strong, the white man's religion was so strong, that even our own people—mind you, full-blooded Nez Perces—denied their culture, denied their heritage. Anything that would be going on that related to cultural activities was strictly prohibited among the congregation of that particular church. So you can, perhaps, understand that from the teachings that were given by the missionaries was to totally forget your culture. In other words, genocidal aims, the role of genocidal aims was very important on the part of the missionaries, on the part of the Indian agent, on the [part of the] federal government in general.

* * *

Amy Trice, former chair of the Kootenai Tribe, explains the conditions in Kootenai country.

TRICE: Well, I have a particular picture that I'd like to show you, share with you, that shows the kind of condition it was in, because at that time, if I describe it, it wouldn't, you wouldn't really know. And that was one of the reasons I had the Bureau of Indian Affairs get a hold of the people in Washington to come down here to see for themselves that we knew what we were talking about, that we wanted, you know, help for our people. Because at that time, they were—it was so pathetic. I had one of the people from Washington say that the houses that the people, the old people were living in here, wasn't fit for their dog. That's how bad it was, and I have a picture. And it's, you know, it's sad, but it did happen. And I must say it's much better now than it was then, the homes anyhow. We still have problems today, and that's drugs and alcohol, but we hope to accomplish that in the near future.

INTERVIEWER: Were people, what were they living in?

TRICE: Just anything, any place. It was sad. We had a man that died just down, right down here, he was—at that time we didn't know he had Alzheimer's disease, and he was living there. His water was frozen— . . . there's holes in the roof, it was snowing and he died of exposure. That's how sad it was. Nobody seemed to care. Because they didn't know what to do anyway, they just went amok, and there was nobody that—we tried to get help from the local people here. Well, they figure—well, let, "a good Indian is a dead Indian" is their motto. I think they changed their ways, though. I mean, they believe differently now. But that's the kind of feeling everybody—well, not everybody, some of the people—I know that we were ridiculed when we first started, and then they realized we meant business, you know, that we weren't going to be—here is the picture of one of the houses, and that's the way it looked inside.

Note

Allen Slickpoo spoke with an unknown interviewer, September 19, 1988, near Lapwai, ID, Idaho Educational Public Broadcasting System/Idaho Public Television, transcript (OH0949) Oral History Center/Idaho State Historical Society, 13–14. Used with permission of Idaho Public Television.

Amy Trice spoke with an unknown interviewer, Kootenai Reservation, January 11, 1988, Idaho Educational Public Broadcasting System/Idaho Public Television, transcript (OH0957) Oral History Center/Idaho State Historical Society, 4–5. Used with permission of Idaho Public Television.

3

Crossing Divides

An Environmental History of Idaho

KEVIN R. MARSH

WHEN MERIWETHER LEWIS REACHED THE SUMMIT OF LEMHI
Pass with an advance party of the Corps of Discovery on August
12, 1805, he looked out for the first time over the land that would become
Idaho. His dream—one shared by European explorers for centuries—of
finding an easy navigation route to the Pacific Ocean was dashed by the
"immence ranges of high mountains still to the West of us with their tops
partially covered with snow."[1] With help from the Lemhi Shoshone people
and their horses, William Clark and the remainder of the Corps of Discovery joined with Lewis to enter present-day Idaho fourteen days later. Over
the next several weeks, they traveled circuitously through the mountains
and river valleys of central Idaho, seeking a route to the Columbia River.
In that stretch, the expedition experienced the highest and lowest points
along the entire seven-thousand-mile journey, from the fortuitous reunion
of Sacajawea with her brother Cahmeawait, chief of the local Lemhi band,
to the near starvation of the entire exploratory party when they stumbled
out of the Bitterroot Mountains onto the Weippe Prairie on September 20.[2]

Lewis and Clark's crew traversed an enormous range of environments
and cultures; the land of Idaho was a crossroads for the Corps of Discovery,
a geographic link—however disjointed—between the Missouri River and
the Columbia, the Atlantic Ocean and the Pacific. Although the dream of a
simple Northwest Passage died there in the Beaverhead Range, mocked by
the mountains and canyons of central Idaho, the explorers' experience highlighted many themes that would rise to prominence in the region's history
over the following two centuries. In Idaho, they crossed not only the divide
between rivers but divides between distinct environmental regions and be-

tween different culture groups who had developed dissimilar traditions of land use. They also introduced a new set of cultural attitudes toward the environment that would instigate further divisions over the following two centuries. Distinct and contrasting environments within Idaho's borders and competing visions of how to best use those environments have since been consistent themes in the state's history.

Historians in recent years have emphasized the role of Idaho as a crossroads of the northern West, a place where multiple factors and divergent groups of people have crossed paths in ways that left lasting legacies for this region and beyond, as indicated in chapter 1 of this book.[3] This approach has helped to expand our understanding of the overland trails of the mid-nineteenth century, irrigation projects of the early twentieth century, and political debates over damming Hells Canyon in the 1950s. The environmental history of the state, those compiled interactions between humans and nonhuman elements that lie at the core of the human experience, reinforces the theme of Idaho as crossroads.

The field of environmental history works with the assumption that we cannot fully understand human experiences without considering the broader context of landscape and other environmental factors that shape events and how humans change those elements in ways that affect people in later periods. History is shaped by the constant interaction between humans and the nonhuman factors of plants, animals, climate, and disease organisms.

Environment is key to how people define Idaho, whether they be outsiders or Natives. The most prominent elements of Lewis and Clark's reports of Idaho were the abundant beaver and the rugged terrain. Tourist brochures—from railroad promotions of the late nineteenth century to contemporary websites—focus on mountains, rivers, and open spaces, and residents have long prized easy access to outdoor recreation. No symbol is more ubiquitous than the potato, a distinctly nonhuman immigrant that mid-twentieth-century marketing campaigns succeeded in making synonymous with Idaho. The potato was first planted in Idaho soil at the Lapwai mission farms in 1837 and commercially developed in southern Idaho by the early twentieth century.[4] Like other immigrants, its arrival in Idaho after a circuitous global journey was a crossroads for both the state and itself.

Before 1800, Idaho was a junction for two of the most powerful environmental factors to reshape the history of the region: horses and disease. Both followed well-established trade routes to reach the area yet had opposite impacts on indigenous Idahoans. The horse initiated a revolution in transportation and provided an impressive increase in military power and material wealth for most communities, as Rodney Frey and Robert McCarl detail in chapter 2 in this volume. Although people in the region retained aspects of their basic lifeways and traditions, the adoption of this new animal greatly expanded their range, and they rapidly used the horse to aid their established seasonal migrations. For people in eastern Idaho, horses "facilitated mobility and increased subsistence options." Shoshone and Bannock people obtained horses from Comanches and Utes to the south around 1700. Early in the eighteenth century, the Shoshone came to be the foremost society of the Rockies and northwestern Plains, reflecting the success of the Comanches, who were even more dominant in the southern Plains. "The titans of their realm," historian John Heaton called the Shoshone, due to their successful integration of horses ahead of rival tribes farther north, such as the Blackfeet.[5] French fur traders on the Great Plains in the 1740s recorded a pervasive fear in the region of raids from the mounted "Gens de Serpents," or Snake Indians, as the Shoshone were often called. By the mid-eighteenth century, the Cayuse from the northwest and the Blackfeet from the north had gathered the courage to steal Shoshone horses, thus spreading the new animal farther and leveling the strategic balance of power in the region. Shortly thereafter, according to tribal lore, the Nez Perce bought a pregnant white mare from the Shoshones and, through selective breeding, eventually developed the Appaloosa and some of the most impressive horse herds on the continent.[6]

When indigenous Idahoans met with the horse, their lives changed significantly. The Nez Perce began to travel much greater distances for food, especially the upper bands living along the Clearwater River who arranged annual bison-hunting trips on the Great Plains. This brought them greater material wealth through trade and allowed them to adopt a number of cultural traditions from the Plains, such as the teepee. Historian Elliott West argues that because the "lower bands were less likely to join the journeys," this helped to create a long-standing cultural split within the tribe. In addition, the Coeur d'Alene tribe developed a more centralized social structure, partially to help organize and coordinate the buffalo hunts but also to help defend themselves from the increased number of mounted raiding parties that terrorized the region.[7]

The spread of disease has been a dominant factor in human history throughout the world, and Idaho is no exception. Smallpox was the greatest killer. It developed as an endemic "crowd disease" within the Old World after the Agricultural Revolution, five thousand to ten thousand years ago. Native peoples of the Americas had no genetic or acquired immunity to this disease. The lack of immunity usually combined with social and environmental stress, and the disease tore through Indian communities with horrifying consequences. Around 1780, the Shoshone received smallpox just as they had acquired horses, through their close ties with the Comanches. This was part of the pandemic that spread across North America, from Boston to Mexico to Puget Sound, beginning around 1775. From southern Idaho, it continued northward into the Columbia Basin and the northern Great Plains, killing most of the people it encountered. Historians suggest that the cultural integration of Northern Paiute, or Bannocks, into Shoshone society occurred partially in response to disease and the changing balance of power in the eighteenth century.[8]

Beginning at Lemhi Pass, the Corps of Discovery met Native Idahoans whose lives and environments had been deeply transformed by the powerful convergence of horses, guns, and disease in the previous century, brought to them along the indigenous trading routes that crossed paths in their territory. The explorers also faced a crossroads of multiple culture groups that retained diverse land-use patterns. This did not surprise them; they understood the varied cultures of Native Americans from firsthand experience. These voyagers met first with the Lemhi band of the Shoshone and later with the Flathead and Nez Perce tribes. From these visits, they learned what every contemporary Idahoan realizes: northern and southern Idaho are distinctly different, both in culture and in environment.[9]

Indigenous peoples of southern Idaho had developed means and methods of using natural resources that were different from those used in the north. The arid deserts of the south are distinct from the relatively well-watered forests and grasslands of the north, a factor that has long shaped the region's history. Ethnologists group Idaho's tribes into two broad cul-

ture groups, mainly to reflect adaptations to regional environments: tribes
in southern Idaho are categorized as part of the Great Basin culture, and
those in the north are listed within the Columbia Plateau cultural region.[10]

In the sagebrush of the Snake River Plain, Shoshone-Bannock and
Northern Paiute people adapted to the scarce food resources by living in
small communities and moving frequently in established patterns throughout the year. They harvested nuts, seeds, roots, insects, birds, and small and
large game animals for food. Shoshone and Bannock peoples accommodated their lives to seasonal cycles of scarcity and abundance.[11] Success in
this region required extensive knowledge of plants and animals. Following
seasonal cycles, Shoshone-Bannocks traveled to the mountains for hunting,
gathered grass seed and camas bulbs in the valleys, took fish from the Snake
and Salmon Rivers, and migrated south to collect pine nuts. Before the introduction of cattle grazing in the region in the late nineteenth century,
the Snake River Plain had more grass and less sagebrush than it does today.
Shoshone-Bannocks gathered seeds from the grass, wove it in baskets, and
built conical huts with it for shelter.[12]

The tribes of northern Idaho, including the Nez Perce, Coeur d'Alene,
Kalispel, and Kootenai, relied more heavily on the river systems for food
and transportation, with salmon and other fish making up much of the
typical diet. They also cultivated and harvested camas bulbs. The relative
abundance of food allowed Plateau people to live in larger communities
and establish permanent winter villages.[13] Just as trade to the south with
Comanches shaped the life and history of Shoshone-Bannocks, the Plateau
tribes were greatly influenced by frequent trading connections with the
Northwest Coast and the Great Plains. The Nez Perce, especially, were integral to what historian James P. Ronda labeled the "Pacific-Plateau economic
and cultural network." They took bison hides and meat along with horses
down the Columbia River to trade for dried salmon and European-man-
ufactured goods, available from coastal traders since the late eighteenth
century. Despite differences in land use, tribes in both the Great Basin and
Plateau regions physically shaped their environments in order to maximize
their resources, such as by using fire in cultivating camas, which prepared
habitat and improved yield.[14]

Lewis and Clark came from the east as leaders of a U.S. government expedition, but the first significant commercial influence to arrive in the region came from the north. David Thompson, a fur trader for the Montreal-based Northwest Company, founded Kullyspell House on the shores of Lake Pend Oreille in September 1809, the first in a string of fur trading posts that stretched across much of Idaho by the 1830s.[15] Eventually monopolized by the Hudson's Bay Company, this system of fur trading with local tribes dominated the first era of large-scale natural resource extraction in Idaho. The fur trade introduced global market forces into the region, changing land use and the environment through extensive exploitation of beaver and accelerating the spread of European diseases. Beginning in 1823, the Hudson's Bay Company embarked on an effort to slow the influx of American traders by creating a "fur desert" in the Snake River Plain. Over the course of the next twenty years, company trappers killed thirty-five thousand beaver, severely degrading riparian habitats, but Americans continued to arrive anyway.[16]

The fur trade had a massive impact on the beaver population in the region; however, fur traders and trappers did not fundamentally alter the land-use patterns practiced by Native communities. This began to change in the 1830s, as missionaries and settlers arrived, seeking to create a sedentary agricultural society, as noted in chapter 2 in this volume. Missionaries sought to change the seminomadic traditions of Indians and convert them to both farming and Christianity. Although most tribes resisted the missionaries, the cultural elements of agrarian life eventually revolutionized land use in Idaho, as it did around the world.

Henry and Eliza Spalding traveled west through the Snake River Plain in 1836, guided by fur trappers and inspired by a religious fervor to convert the Nez Perce. After resting with the regional director of the Hudson's Bay Company in Fort Vancouver, the Spaldings established Lapwai Mission in 1836. There they offered training in Christianity, English, and agriculture. An early Idaho photograph shows Reverend Henry Spalding with the tools of his trade: a Bible in one hand and a hoe in the other. Farming and Scripture were the two pillars of life for many mid-nineteenth-century Protestant Americans, and the Spaldings sought to share that vision with the Nez Perce. In doing so, they fostered deep divides between their imported cultural values and indigenous attitudes toward the use of land and resources.[17]

The mid-nineteenth-century agricultural expansion westward in the United States was a revolutionary force. As historian Steven Stoll explains, "Farmers have served as the shock troops of the earth's environmental transformation." Marcus Whitman, who, along with his wife, Narcissa accompanied the Spaldings westward and established the Waiilatpu Mission in the Walla Walla Valley, referred to the agricultural settlement of the Northwest as "one of the onward movements of the world." The Spaldings and Whitmans were one vanguard in that movement, what Elliott West calls "an enveloping force," and they sought nothing less than the massive transformation that altered the American landscape and the lifeways of its inhabitants.[18]

The power to implement agrarian ideals and to cultivate order on the landscape came with the growing number of overland migrants to the Northwest and with improved transportation ties to expanding commercial markets. However stern and committed the Spaldings and other missionaries may have been, they never could compete with commerce as a driving force of change. The lure of gold in the hills of Idaho brought a flood of immigrants in the 1860s. Idaho City became the largest town in the Northwest, surpassing Portland, Oregon, in 1865. Commercial farming and ranching began in Idaho in order to supply mining camps. In the Treasure Valley, along the Boise River, farmers sold produce to miners in the Boise Basin or the Owyhee Mountains. "By the summer of 1864," claims historian Leonard Arrington, "all the river bottom land in Boise Valley was under irrigation."[19]

The earliest agricultural development of the Palouse Hills north of Lewiston was sparked by opportunities to supply the mining camps of the Clearwater and Salmon River country. Most of these settlers initially raised cattle. By the 1870s, production shifted toward annual grain crops, especially after overgrazing had reduced forage for livestock. Mining camps provided a financial incentive for northern Idaho and eastern Washington farmers, though transportation of food remained difficult and the camps themselves, given their boom-and-bust character, were unreliable sources of customers. Agriculture in Idaho remained small-scale and regional until improved transportation networks ensured more dependable access to distant markets.[20]

One question Idahoans ask repeatedly is, for whom should resources be extracted? Should it be done to supply the needs of a defined community? Or should these valuable commodities be made available to individual entrepreneurs, who can profit from selling those resources to customers near and far? Such questions faced farmers in Idaho as industrial capitalism reshaped land use across the world, and the state was, for a time, caught between competing ideas on who should benefit from its agricultural resources.[21]

Franklin was the earliest-incorporated town in the future territory and state of Idaho. Beginning in 1860, members of the Church of Jesus Christ of Latter-day Saints moved northward from the Salt Lake basin, bringing with them a deep desire for order in society as well as in nature. They had transformed the harsh deserts around the Great Salt Lake by channelizing water, and by the 1860s they had brought this technique northward into the tributary valleys of the Snake River and then farther north, to Henry's Fork and the South Fork of the Snake, beginning in 1879. Unlike most new arrivals in Idaho's mining regions and elsewhere in the West, Mormon settlers tried to avoid involvement in the expanding global economy. These agrarian communities sought to be more communal, not commercial. Leadership of the church, especially in the last decade of Brigham Young's life, promoted economic independence, and church members in newly established towns were expected to place the interests of the community above individual profit.[22]

Some observers outside the church admired this cooperative form of social organization and land use. John Wesley Powell, the famed explorer and surveyor who had a deep influence on the development of the American West, "found among the Mormons an inspiring model of adaptation and innovation." Powell's biographer, historian Donald Worster, explained that Mormon cooperative efforts in land and water distribution defied the individualistic ethos of capitalism and "profoundly influenced his thinking and the message he took to Washington." In the wake of the financial panic of 1873, which destabilized much of the mining industry in Idaho, Powell was not the only person to admire the relative stability of Mormon land use. One Idaho writer noted in 1884, "Probably nowhere in the civilized world is cooperation carried on so successfully as it is among this peculiar people."[23]

Eventually, however, cooperatives failed and market forces brought an end to the sought-after isolation. Railroads, which came first to Franklin in 1874, opened Mormon communities to the outside world, bringing in cheaper manufactured goods and a large influx of non-Mormons to southeastern Idaho. Church leaders gave up their campaign for self-contained settlements and communal use of environmental resources, just as they accommodated political and social pressures to end polygamy. Contemporary historians of the church explain that, after 1890, "the Mormons, once isolated, now became capitalistic, conservative, pro-American individualists." As Idaho gained statehood at the end of the nineteenth century, agricultural development came under "the all-embracing influence of capital as an agent of change."[24]

The arrival of the railroads, with four transcontinental lines crossing the state between 1883 and 1909, did not initiate mining, lumbering, ranching, and farming, but it transformed them into the dominant economies of Idaho. Resource extraction was fundamental to Idaho land use as early as the fur trade and continued with the gold rushes and Mormon cooperatives of the 1860s, but the scale of raw materials hauled out of Idaho's mountains, forests, rangelands, and farms rose rapidly to unprecedented heights after the arrival of the railroads and extensive investment of outside capital. In the first half of the twentieth century, Idaho established an economy of industrial resource extraction, though that economy maintained regional distinctions.[25]

Mining remained most significant in the central and northern parts of the state. Although the industry had lagged through the depression of the 1870s, strikes in the Coeur d'Alene region of northern Idaho spurred a new gold rush. More importantly, in 1885, galena ore, containing silver and lead, was discovered in the hills above the Coeur d'Alene River. The legendary discovery by prospector Noah Kellogg and his cantankerous mule marks a notable crossroads for the region's history. In the following century, miners working for large corporations such as the Bunker Hill and Sullivan Mining and Concentrating Company (renamed Bunker Hill Company in the 1950s) would extract more silver there than in any other mining district in the world. Prospectors like Kellogg were left behind, quaint relics of a preindustrial era, while investors from around the world supplied capital to fund the mines, wageworkers, and machinery needed to extract the resources of

FIGURE 3.1. Mining served as one of the principal economies of Idaho. This shows the scale of the enterprise at Black Jack Mine in the Owyhee District, Silver City, Idaho, around the turn of the twentieth century. Photo courtesy of Idaho State Historical Society, 60–120.11.

the Silver Valley. As railroads arrived in the new town of Kellogg in the late 1880s, so did outside capital. Simeon Reed of Oregon bought the Bunker Hill mine and mill for $750,000 in 1887.[26]

As mining towns became firmly established in the landscape of northern Idaho, conflict over resources and the implications of industrial resource extraction also became familiar historical landmarks. Growing mineral operations throughout the Silver Valley led to conflicts over environmental pollution, from both mining debris and smelter smoke. As early as 1899, farmers downstream on the Coeur d'Alene River complained that effluent from the mines was harming their crops and livestock. Within ten years, sixty-five farmers had joined to file suit against the various companies operating upstream. The Mine Owners' Association, originally formed to combat union organizing among workers, marshaled tremendous resources to fight the claims against its members. It successfully fought proposed injunctions

that would have shut down the company's operations. Although the farmers' claims exceeded $1 million, a federal court awarded them only $1 each.[27]

The pollution from the mines grew, especially as smelter operations expanded in the second decade of the twentieth century. Bunker Hill managers understood the health damage caused by lead sent up the smokestack in
Kellogg. They secured promises from the federal government that it would
not pursue legal claims for the damage they expected smelter smoke would
inflict on the surrounding national forests. Farmers and loggers, however,
continued to file lawsuits against the company for increasing amounts of
damage. With its extensive political clout and effective counsel, the company avoided liability for any of these cases through the mid-twentieth century.[28] Mining pollution remained, however, as a stark example of Idahoans' conflicting attitudes toward environmental resource use, and the issue
plagued the Bunker Hill mine, not to mention its workers and neighbors,
up to and beyond its closure in 1981 and its designation as a Superfund
clean-up site in 1983.

Forests represented the other main leg of the extractive economy of
northern Idaho, and the rise of the lumber industry also stemmed from
the arrival of railroads and capital investment from outside the region. The
earliest commercial harvest of timber occurred along the upper reaches of
the Palouse River. Felled trees were floated downstream on the spring flood
to mills in the towns of Palouse and Colfax, Washington, and from there
sold to farmers in the Palouse Hills. Just as limited transportation access
minimized the growth of farms in the Palouse into the 1880s, the same
isolation also hindered expansion of the lumber industry, which remained
local and small-scale.[29]

Industrialization had already revolutionized the American lumber industry by the time its leaders took notice of the rich stands of northern
Idaho. By the late nineteenth century, midwestern companies had depleted
much of the stands of white pine in the Great Lakes region. The industry had
always been migratory, and many of those same companies, having already
harvested in Maine, moved on from the Midwest. Boosters and speculators
in Idaho and elsewhere in the Northwest eagerly awaited their arrival.[30]

Charles Brown, a veteran of the lumber industry in northern Michigan,
traveled to Idaho by train in 1893, planning to get a jump on the shift of

timber operations out of the Midwest. He homesteaded in Latah County among, as he described it, "the largest cedar I have ever seen." He spent the next several years trying to convince major lumber manufacturers to set up operations in Idaho. Echoing the plea thirty years earlier of Caleb Lyon, the second territorial governor of Idaho, who encouraged residents to recruit outside capital investment "as the bedrock of Idaho's prosperity," Brown said to a Boise audience, "To these people we must appeal."[31] At the top of that list of names was Frederick Weyerhaeuser of Saint Paul, Minnesota, the most influential lumberman in the country, who oversaw management of the Weyerhaeuser syndicate, dozens of timber and financial firms. In 1900, Weyerhaeuser secretly sent two representatives, John Glover and James Johnson, to meet with Brown and tour potential timber holdings in Latah County. In January of that year, he purchased nearly one million acres of timberland in Washington State. By year's end, he led a group that purchased two hundred thousand acres in Idaho and soon established multiple lumber firms, including the Potlatch Lumber Company in 1903.[32]

The investments of the Weyerhaeuser syndicate spurred a rush of buying and speculating in parts of Idaho that had not yet seen extensive settlement and development. At the turn of the twentieth century, however, those rich forest resources became the subject of a broader national debate over who should have ownership and control of the trees. Fear of a "timber famine" and monopoly control of the forests, along with the desire to protect the watersheds of navigable rivers, spurred the nascent conservation movement, which called for government management of selected forest resources. Sparked by growing public concern and angered by several prominent scandals involving corrupt sales of public lands in other states, Congress passed a law in 1891 allowing the president to set aside forest reserves and in 1905 transferred the land to a new agency, the U.S. Forest Service. By 1907, more than twenty million acres in Idaho were protected within seventeen national forests.[33]

The creation of forest reserves represented a major shift in land management, because it established public lands as a permanent part of the western landscape. As a result, more than two-thirds of the land in Idaho is publicly owned and managed, mainly by agencies of the federal government. Land laws passed before 1891 assumed that the federal government would distribute all lands to private owners, but this was clearly unrealistic by the end of the nineteenth century, as much of the West was too dry, rugged, or both, to be desirable to private owners. Many who had homesteaded or otherwise claimed land had failed, and their property was returned to public custody. Most of Idaho, with its extensive mountains and deserts, remained unclaimed by private owners. Idaho history in the succeeding century often has focused on questions of how to manage those public lands and for whose benefit.

The national forests and the prominent chief forester, Gifford Pinchot, sparked heated debate at the beginning of the twentieth century. Pinchot famously defined the mission of the Forest Service as to pursue "the greatest good for the greatest number," but there was often disagreement over what would be the greatest good and for whom. In the lumber and mining country of northern Idaho, opinion ran strongly against "Czar Pinchot," condemning his agency as a tool of the elite, to be used to prevent settlement and economic development. U.S. Senator Weldon Heyburn of Wallace led the opposition. In southern Idaho, there was a broader current of support for federal protection of timberland and the rangelands that made up much of the national forests. Farmers there relied almost exclusively on irrigation from surface water streams and rivers running down from the various mountain ranges. For them, protecting the watersheds from overcutting and overgrazing was a practical measure that ensured their livelihoods. Cities in the south also supported federal conservation of forests as a way of securing their municipal water supply; Pocatello petitioned for the creation of the Pocatello Forest Reserve in 1903, and Senator Fred Dubois supported federal forest conservation efforts. Other prominent political leaders, such as Governor James Brady, of Pocatello, were able to compromise with the Forest Service yet expressed concern about excessive federal control of state land.[34]

Pinchot visited Idaho on a public relations campaign almost annually until 1910. His visits helped to sway the attitude of prominent journalists such as *Idaho Statesman* publisher Calvin Cobb and may have assuaged some of the public's concerns: in 1909, one survey found that 80 percent of Idahoans supported Forest Service projects.[35] Given that the majority of the population lived in the southern part of the state, this may not have indicated the end of the regional divide over how to use public forestlands in Idaho, most of which were in the north. To this day, the Forest Service divides its management of the state into two distinct regions, one headquartered in Ogden, Utah, the other in Missoula, Montana.

For the first half of the twentieth century, the national forests were used mostly for grazing cattle and sheep; little timber was sold until the 1940s. Despite demands to eliminate grazing on public lands, Pinchot ensured continued use of public rangelands by ranchers under government scrutiny. Thus, grazing became a fundamental use of the national forests, and government rangers helped to exterminate predators such as wolves. Ranchers secured grazing rights for summer range and agreed, often reluctantly, to specific restrictions on the numbers of livestock.[36] This was a major shift from the open range beginnings of the cattle industry in Idaho.

From the 1860s to the 1880s, cattlemen grazed their stock on the open range with little regulation, selling meat and hides to regional mining camps. Overgrazing led to loss of native grasses and an infestation of invasive Russian thistle, or tumbleweed. Devastating drought in 1889 followed by a brutal winter initiated the collapse of the cattle business across the Great Basin. In the wake of this tragedy, sheep ranchers used the lands that could no longer support cattle. They hired immigrants from the Basque country and elsewhere to trail their herds to high-elevation pastures and back each year. Conflicts arose between cattlemen and sheep ranchers over access to the range, each arguing that the other's animals were more environmentally destructive. For both cattle and sheep, the era of the open range had ended by the 1890s, and ranchers turned to growing hay for winter feed and accepted government oversight of public rangelands. Historian Richard White observed, "Ranchers replaced reliance on the natural production of the land with reliance on a managed and transformed environment." Oversight of grazing on public lands outside the national forests became more intensive after passage of the Taylor Grazing Act of 1934. With most of Idaho's livestock grazing on the public domain, tensions between ranchers and federal managers, exacerbated by changing public attitudes, remained a consistent theme through the twentieth century.[37]

The rapidly growing population of southern Idaho farmers relied directly on another central plank in the national conservation strategy of the

Progressive era: reclamation. How to irrigate the dry lands of the Snake River Plain had been a crucial question for several decades. Some had even wondered whether it would ever be possible to raise crops there, a region that Reverend Henry Spalding recalled as "that 'great and terrible wilderness' of death."[38]

The earliest irrigation efforts came at mission stations in Lapwai and Lemhi, though both were temporary. By the 1880s, Mormon settlers had created a series of small, cooperative irrigation systems along tributaries of the upper Snake River, and other farmers had established themselves tight alongside riverbanks, such as in the Boise Valley. Privately financed efforts arose to bring water to the broad plains away from, and often high above, the rivers. Arthur Foote's dream of diverting the Boise River out onto the sagebrush-covered benchlands brought him and his wife, Mary Hallock Foote, to Boise in 1884, the same year the Oregon Short Line introduced transcontinental train service through southern Idaho. They toiled for six years, overseeing labor, engineering designs, and cultivating outside investment. In 1890, they left their unfinished project for the last time. Mary recalled, "We did not lose our bones on that battlefield, but we left pretty much everything else we had." Their greatest frustration lay in the vagaries of distant investors. "Whenever a squall struck big business in the East," Mary wrote, "the ground swell rocked our boat," a phrase that could have described the misfortune of any effort at large-scale resource extraction in Idaho.[39] Despite decades of effort, farming in southern Idaho remained very limited at the beginning of the twentieth century.

During a lull in financing in 1889, Arthur Foote took a job with the U.S. government working on irrigation surveys higher up the Snake River. Looking to the federal government when private financing failed would become the standard procedure for Idaho agriculture. Successful expansion of farming along the Snake River came as a result of federal initiatives. The Carey Act of 1894 subsidized private irrigation development by providing federal land grants to states. Although the plan failed in most western states, its impact in Idaho was impressive. Milner Dam, miles of irrigation canals in Magic Valley, and the city of Twin Falls were all facilitated by the Carey Act. These landmarks made Idaho an exception to a policy that failed in most states, yet Congress passed the Reclamation Act of 1902 (also known as the

FIGURE 3.2. Agriculture awaited irrigation to fully develop in southern Idaho. Here, celery is growing near Twin Falls, Idaho. Photo courtesy of Idaho State Historical Society, 73–221.264.

Newlands Act), which established direct federal involvement in construction, maintenance, and regulation of large-scale irrigation systems and created the U.S. Reclamation Service. This left a powerful legacy of agricultural development, including dams at Arrowrock on the Boise River and American Falls on the Snake, the Minidoka and Boise projects of irrigated farming communities, and cities such as Rupert. In its creation of the Boise Project, the U.S. Reclamation Service stepped in to finish the work of Arthur Foote by completing Diversion Dam and the New York Canal.[40]

The development of federal reclamation projects was accompanied by lofty dreams and idealistic visions of the ability of modern technology and society to transform nature. Historian Laura Woodworth-Ney describes the faith maintained by settlers on the Minidoka Project near Rupert in 1904, who believed that "government aid could do what individual investors could not—turn Idaho's windswept lava-rock-strewn desert into an agrarian oasis." Community boosters, railroad advertising agents, and government planners all promoted a mythic story of transformation, in which the deserts of southern Idaho would become a lush and productive Eden. People celebrated the new infrastructure, from large dams to canal headgates, that harnessed the Snake River and beat back the desert. In lyrics he composed in 1905 for Boise Valley settlers, the Reverend H. N. Ruddock proclaimed:

> For genial showers you need not wait,
> You only have to hoist the gate,
> And let the waters overflow,
> Our valleys rich in Idaho.

The landscape of Idaho came to represent Progressive-era ideals of engineering, efficiency, and democracy, with oversight from federal agencies.[41]

Despite the success of federal irrigation in southern Idaho, the development of the soil and water of the Snake River Plain was not without conflict. Fundamental questions remained about who should benefit the most from the water. The 1890 Idaho constitution codified prior appropriation, a legal doctrine that recognized water rights based on use and gave seniority to those with the earliest established use of that water. Idahoans followed the pattern of other western states in declaring that "all water belongs to the public, or the state," and that individual rights to water would be based on use. "First in time is first in right" became the determining factor in any dispute over who should benefit from a limited supply of water, and there would be no shortage of disputes. In July 1919, William Grover, Jr., killed his neighbor with a shovel in an argument over access to water from the canal they shared near Blackfoot. Historian Mark Fiege explains that their duel "was not an isolated incident; rather, it represented but one small fight in a broader, ongoing struggle over Idaho's water." Arguments also arose between those who owned water rights and the federal and state agencies responsible for facilitating the legal and physical structures of irrigation. The Boise Project failed to meet many of its objectives, and federal officials and local farmers blamed each other.[42]

The conflict between hydroelectricity and irrigation has frequently drawn attention to disputed claims over how to use the state's water. One use requires maintaining stream flow; the other demands removing water from the stream. In the years immediately following World War II, Hells Canyon on the Snake River was the place where that conflict came to a head in a way that dramatically highlighted the continuing differences between resource use in the northern and southern sections of the state. The U.S. government, buoyed by expansive growth during the war, sought to complete a regional network for managing the environmental resources of the Northwest on behalf of economic development. High Hells Canyon Dam would have been the keystone of that system and the largest dam on earth. Proponents of the dam touted the production of electricity for the region, which could also provide the power needed for an elaborate scheme to take water from the Payette and Boise Rivers to irrigate new farms in Mountain Home Desert. In the tradition of public power advocates since the Progressive era, they felt that public agencies, not encumbered by the profit motive, could best harness a resource like the Snake River and distribute its wealth to the broadest number of people.

Similar idealism inspired the founders of the national forests and public irrigation projects, and, in Idaho, this push for a public dam was met by familiar criticisms of an expanding federal government infringing upon the rights of states and private companies. This time, however, farmers in southern Idaho strongly opposed the federal initiative, because the high dam proposal was effectively presented by critics such as Governor Len Jordan as a threat to individual water rights. Supported also by a national conservative backlash against the centralized policies of the New Deal era, these critics of federal management of environmental resources helped to block approval of the proposed high dam. Meanwhile, the Idaho Power Company gained federal approval to construct three smaller dams in Hells Canyon, upstream from the proposed federal dam.

Historian Karl Brooks has observed a regional divide in this debate, with Hells Canyon as the geographic and political fault line. Northern Idaho, with its historic ties to the Columbia River Basin, benefited from the dramatic development of a manufacturing economy in the years immediately preceding and during World War II. Federal planners had hoped to expand this new infrastructure, based on cheap electricity, to southern Idaho, but the linchpin of their plans, High Hells Canyon Dam, was seen as a distinct threat to the agricultural economy of the Snake River Plain. For Brooks, the division was not simply between southern and northern Idaho; it was between two broad regions in the Pacific Northwest, one focused on the Snake River and the other on Puget Sound and the Columbia: "People in both basins relied on distinctive forms of controlling water to sustain their characteristic modes of adapting to nature." In the early 1950s, the debate over Hells Canyon was seen as a test of priorities, a new Northwest of factories humming on cheap hydropower versus an old Northwest of irrigated farms.[43]

Both visions for Hells Canyon in the 1950s centered on extracting resources from the river; they differed on the question of who should benefit most directly. Both entailed a form of production—one of power, the other of potatoes. There had long been a background voice in Idaho and across the nation suggesting an alternative to consumption that called for preserving nature for its aesthetic or recreational values. In 1967, Supreme Court justice William O. Douglas, a Pacific Northwesterner, spoke out loudly in favor of preserving a free-flowing river. In a case over whether federal agencies or private companies should build a new large dam farther downstream from the earlier proposal, the court insisted that the parties involved consider the question of whether a dam should be built at all and, in doing so, expanded the assessment of public interest to include wild, free-flowing rivers and native fisheries. At the same time, Congress, led by Senator Frank Church of Idaho, was finalizing legislation for the Wild and Scenic Rivers Act, which would grant federal protection to specific stretches of intact river systems. At the top of Church's list of threatened rivers was the Salmon River, which gained protection from any dams upon passage of the new law in 1968. Senator Church, along with Len Jordan, led the effort to create the Hells Canyon National Recreation Area and Wilderness Area in 1974, preventing construction of dams along that stretch of the Snake River. The question of whether or not to extract environmental resources for production often replaced the questions of how and for whom these resources should be extracted and became a dominant issue in Idaho in the last several decades of the twentieth century.[44]

Recreation and aesthetic beauty had long been valued by Idahoans when

assessing the state's environment, though they usually were given secondary status when making political and economic decisions on how to use resources. A short-lived campaign to create a national park at Shoshone Falls
on the Snake River ended around 1900, when Governor Frank Steunenberg
and others noted that doing so might infringe on irrigation projects then
under construction. With the closure of Milner Dam in 1905, the flow of
water over the falls, once billed as the "Niagara of the West," was often inter-
rupted. If no clear conflict emerged with resource extraction, however, then
preservation efforts often moved forward. Heyburn State Park, Idaho's first
state park, was established in 1908 and provided for both recreation and
logging during its first few decades.[45] The Sawtooth Mountains became a
central site for recreation in the early twentieth century. A movement arose
in 1911, led by Boise clubwoman Jean Conly Smith, in support of creating
a national park there out of lands managed by the Forest Service. In an
interagency rivalry with the National Park Service, the Forest Service effectively undermined the park proposal by creating its own recreational
infrastructure, much of which remains today.[46] Opponents of the park did
not object to preservation and recreational use; instead, they succeeded by
accommodating those demands in the case of the Sawtooths.

Economic and political shifts toward a more urban, manufacturing society in the post–World War II years and growing awareness of the scarcity of
lands and resources raised environmental concerns. Many historians point
to a national shift in favor of environmental protection following the war,
and Idaho both participated in that rise of consciousness and was deeply
affected by it, particularly regarding use of public lands and waterways. Idahoans had long loved recreational fishing, but a 1954 ballot measure demonstrated its growing political clout. The Idaho Wildlife Federation, a voice
for conservation throughout most of the twentieth century, sponsored an
initiative to tighten state regulation of dredge mining activities. Mining
companies fiercely opposed the bill, but it passed with overwhelming support statewide.[47]

Wilderness debates became a flashpoint for these competing visions of
the land, and Idaho played a major role in the national history of wilderness
legislation. Even before the Forest Service devised a system to preserve "wilderness areas" in 1929, Idahoans clearly valued the solitude and primitive

recreation offered in such places. In the fall of 1927, Harry Shellworth, an executive with the Boise Payette Lumber Company, invited some friends into a remote area of the national forest along the Middle Fork of the Salmon River to discuss how to preserve the backcountry from development. With him was an influential group, including Governor H. Clarence Baldridge, mining executive Stanley Easton, and District Forester Richard H. Rutledge. All active in the state Republican Party, they worked to achieve their shared dream of protecting the area. In 1931, the Forest Service designated it as part of the Idaho Primitive Area, and in 1980, Congress included it in the River of No Return Wilderness Area.[48]

That executives from major mining and timber companies along with a leading Republican politician would spearhead creation of one of the nation's largest wilderness areas demonstrates the complexity of environmental politics, and the fact that this lineup seems surprising to many suggests the strength of the caricatures often used in portraying wilderness debates. Yes, Idahoans were deeply divided over whether and where to protect wilderness areas, but the disputes could not be attributed to cultural, economic, or political identities. Wilderness was not a simple north-south issue, nor were positions always consistent with the urban-rural divide. The roots of both supporters and detractors had always been prevalent in the cultural attitudes of the region: the desire to attain wealth and prosperity by manipulating and extracting the state's abundant resources coincided with reverence for the aesthetic power of the landscapes. By drawing firm boundaries between these two traditional values, wilderness protection distilled inherent contradictions.

Throughout much of the history of wilderness after World War II, one constant seems to stand out: the presence of Senator Frank Church. Church was elected to the U.S. Senate in 1956 and served for twenty-four years. Although he initially backed efforts to extract resources for economic development, he increasingly began to champion efforts to protect wilderness and wild rivers. He pursued a political strategy intended to "achieve what he believed was a practicable balance between development and preservation." Some have argued that no one was more important to passage of the Wilderness Act of 1964 than Church. Although prominent Idahoans thought his support for wilderness preservation was political suicide, he was reelected time and again as chronicled by Katherine G. Aiken in chapter 4 of this volume, perhaps demonstrating his success at achieving the balance he sought.[49]

Church supported environmental protection out of both his passion for the outdoors in Idaho and his growing frustration with the federal agencies that managed most of the land. The Forest Service in particular angered him with what he perceived to be an arrogance of administrative authority. The main implications of the Wilderness Act of 1964 included the protection of particular areas on the ground (nearly five million acres in Idaho as of 2009) and, perhaps most important, democratization of land-use decisions. Church repeatedly emphasized that one of the main points of the law was to take those decisions out of the secluded realm of the Forest Service and into the open arena of public debate. As a result, wilderness became one of the most heated and publicly accessible issues in American history.[50] In Idaho, these questions remained among the most visible and contentious policy debates of the past forty years, a stark reminder of the competing visions of Idahoans on how to use their state's environment.

A prime example of Church's efforts to allow more public input and also to reach pragmatic compromises came in the effort to create the Gospel Hump Wilderness Area in north-central Idaho. Seeking to focus on "their mutual interest in the land and its resources," Church gathered local residents from Grangeville along with representatives of both the timber industry and environmental organizations so that they could develop a compromise on land-use boundaries for several thousand acres of national forest. Out of the meetings came proposals for setting aside 220,000 acres of new wilderness area and opening 123,000 acres to logging. Although he did not campaign as a supporter of an expanded federal government, Congressman Steve Symms, who eventually defeated Church in 1980, complained about the "federal government's loss of control over the national forest system." The agreement, passed mostly intact into law in 1978, angered many on both sides of the issue, though some were very impressed by the collaborative process. One journalist wrote at the time, "They've wrested government from the big guy and returned it to Grangeville."[51]

By the early twenty-first century, wilderness was still a heated topic of debate statewide. Conflicting values had created a stalemate, leading some to adopt a collaborative model for land-use planning proposals in the Owyhee Canyonlands and for the White Clouds and Boulder Mountains. Competing groups formed the Owyhee Initiative in 2001 and sat together for many years, developing new guidelines designed to address the concerns of ranchers, conservationists, off-road vehicle riders, the Paiute tribe, and federal land managers. With support from Senator Mike Crapo and the entire state delegation, Congress passed this agreement for the Owyhees into law in 2009, designating 517,000 acres of new wilderness while releasing 200,000 acres from wilderness study status, supporting ranching in the area, protecting the cultural resources of the Paiute, and securing access for off-road vehicles.[52]

The White Cloud Mountains had been the focus of controversy in the 1960s, when ASARCO, the American Smelting and Refining Company, sought to develop an open-pit molybdenum mine near Castle Peak. The conflict between development and preservation became the focus of the 1970 gubernatorial campaign between incumbent Don Samuelson and Orofino legislator Cecil Andrus. Andrus campaigned to prevent the mine and won the election. "The battle over the White Clouds," he later recalled, "would help make me the first Western governor elected on an environmental platform."[53] Although as governor Andrus had little influence over management of the Challis National Forest, the proposed site for the mine, Idaho's congressional delegation set out to deal with the issue. Church had revived the idea of a national park in the Sawtooth Mountains in 1960, and he eventually collaborated with Republican senator Len Jordan to establish the Sawtooth National Recreation Area in 1972.[54] Though the law created the Sawtooth Wilderness Area and blocked mining in the neighboring White Cloud Mountains, it left broader land use for the White Cloud range undecided, setting the stage for the collaborative discussions spearheaded by Congressman Mike Simpson. While it is too early to tell whether these efforts signal a major shift in the environmental history of Idaho, they stem from a long-running series of conflicts that grew more heated in the decades after World War II.

Conflicts over environmental resources in Idaho seized front page headlines throughout the late twentieth and early twenty-first centuries, but the passion with which Idahoans faced the issues of access to natural resources has a long legacy. No place in history is devoid of environmental interactions, but in Idaho these often seem to take center stage. The state contains a dramatic and diverse set of landscapes that serves as more than a backdrop to history. People from around the world have crossed paths in this land, seeking profit from the various environments and competing against others with conflicting interests in those same resources. As a crossroads of nature, culture, and capital, Idaho presents a diverse and dynamic history.

Retracing the route of Lewis and Clark today, one encounters a place where land use is very different from what it was in their time, but the issue remains central to the lives of local people. The natural environment of the state has lost none of its importance over the course of two centuries, though people's interactions with the land have shifted. The Lemhi Shoshone and the Nez Perce who assisted the Corps of Discovery had undertaken dynamic adaptation to new environmental factors before 1805 and have continued to do so to this day. Scattered ranches and logging operations tell of the extraction economy that matured a century after Lewis and Clark's visit but has waned in recent decades. Recreational visitors—from whitewater rafters putting in on the Salmon River, to RV motorists cresting Lost Trail Pass, to backpackers and backcountry horse travelers embarking at Wilderness Gateway along the Lochsa River into the Selway Bitterroot Wilderness—are now the most common users.

Taken as a whole, Idaho's environmental history has also undergone consistent change, although contention over access to resources and ways of using the land has not disappeared. As Idaho has spanned such a broad range of environments and served as a crossroads for an array of cultural and economic values, its history reflects the complicated implications of these factors. While Idahoans' passion for defending their values and the land may not (and should not) subside, it is valuable to understand the dynamic nature of the history of how people have interacted with the remarkable landscape of Idaho.

NOTES

1   Meriwether Lewis, August 12, 1805, entry, in *The Journals of the Lewis and Clark Expedition*, ed. Gary Moulton (Lincoln: University of Nebraska Press, University of Nebraska–Lincoln Libraries–Electronic Text Center, 2005), http://lewisandclarkjournals.unl.edu.

2   James P. Ronda, *Lewis and Clark among the Indians* (Lincoln: University of Nebraska Press, 1984), 139–62; Alvin M. Josephy, Jr., *The Nez Perce Indians and the Opening of the Northwest* (Boston: Houghton Mifflin Co., 1997), 5.

3   See Peter Boag, "Mountain, Plain, Desert, River: The Snake River Region as a Western Crossroads," in *Many Wests: Place, Culture, and Regional Identity*, ed. David M. Wrobel and Michael C. Steiner (Lawrence: University Press of Kansas, 1997), 177–97; Katherine Aiken, Kevin R. Marsh, and Laura Woodworth-Ney, *Idaho: The Heroic Journey* (Encino, CA: Cherbo Publishing Group, 2006), 26.

4   James W. Davis, *Aristocrat in Burlap: A History of the Potato in Idaho* (Boise: Idaho Potato Commission, 1992), 1–7; Mark Fiege, *Irrigated Eden: The Making of an Agricultural Landscape in the American West* (Seattle: University of Washington Press, 1999), 155–70. Also see Michael Pollan, "Desire: Control/Plant: The Potato," in *Botany of Desire: A Plant's-Eye View of the World* (New York: Random House, 2001), 181–238; Redcliffe N. Salaman, *The History and Social Influence of the Potato* (1949; repr., New York: Cambridge University Press, 1985); Larry Zuckerman, *The Potato: How the Humble Spud Rescued the Western World* (New York: North Point Press, 1998).

5   John W. Heaton, *The Shoshone-Bannocks: Culture and Commerce at Fort Hall, 1870–1940* (Lawrence: University Press of Kansas, 2005), 29; Pekka Hämäläinen, *The Comanche Empire* (New Haven: Yale University Press, 2008); Elizabeth Fenn, *Pox Americana: The Great Smallpox Epidemic of 1775–82* (New York: Hill and Wang, 2001), 207.

6   Colin G. Calloway, *One Vast Winter Count: The Native American West Before Lewis and Clark* (Lincoln: University of Nebraska Press, 2003), 293–301; Fenn, *Pox Americana*, 203–8; Josephy, *Nez Perce Indians*, 28–29.

7   Calloway, *Winter Count*, 300–301; Elliott West, *The Last Indian War: The Nez Perce Story* (New York: Oxford University Press, 2009), 15–18; Laura Woodworth-Ney, *Mapping Identity: The Creation of the Coeur d'Alene Indian Reservation, 1805–1902* (Boulder: University Press of Colorado, 2004), 13–14.

8   Alfred W. Crosby, *Ecological Imperialism: The Biological Expansion of Europe, 900–1900* (Cambridge: Cambridge University Press, 1986), 30; Calloway, *Winter Count*, 418–26; Fenn, *Pox Americana*, 203–23. For a discussion of the complex interaction of disease with other factors, see David S. Jones, "Virgin Soils Revisited," *William and Mary Quarterly* 60, no. 4 (October 2003): 703–42. Heaton, *Shoshone-Bannocks*, 31–32.

9   The literature on the north-south divide of Idaho is extensive. For an overall discussion, see Carlos A. Schwantes, *In Mountain Shadows: A History of Idaho* (Lincoln: University of Nebraska Press, 1991), 1–12. Specific interpretations include Judith Austin, "Desert, Sagebrush, and the Pacific Northwest," in *Regionalism and the Pacific Northwest*, ed. William G. Robbins, Robert J. Frank, and Richard E. Ross (Corvallis: Oregon State University Press, 1983), 129–47; Karl Boyd Brooks, *Public Power, Private Dams: The Hells Canyon High Dam Controversy* (Seattle: University of Washington Press, 2006), 23–26; Donald W. Meinig, *The Great Columbia Plain: A Historical Geography, 1805–1910* (Seattle: University of Washington Press, 1968), 359–64; David H. Stratton, "Hells Canyon: The Missing Link in Pacific Northwest Regionalism," *Idaho Yesterdays* 28, no. 3 (Fall 1984): 3–9.

10   Deward E. Walker, Jr., *Indians of Idaho* (Moscow: University Press of Idaho, 1978), 25–27; Schwantes, *Mountain Shadows*, 14. For thorough coverage of the two culture regions that overlap in Idaho, see Warren D'Azevedo, ed., *Great Basin*, vol. 11 of *Handbook of North American Indians*, ed. William C. Sturtevant (Washington, DC: Smithsonian Institution Press, 1986); , and Deward E. Walker, Jr., ed., *Plateau*, vol.

12 of *Handbook of North American Indians*, ed. William C. Sturtevant (Washington, DC: Smithsonian Institution, 1998). For a development of tribal cultures since 1805, see Sven S. Liljeblad, *The Idaho Indians in Transition, 1805–1960* (Pocatello: Idaho State University Museum, 1972).

11   Ethnologist Deward Walker, Jr., wrote in the 1970s, "The margin of survival was thin, resulting in occasional starvation and frequent movement in search of food"; however, more recent research has documented that Shoshone and Bannocks were more successful than marginal. Walker, *Indians of Idaho*, 26.

12   Robert F. Murphy and Yolanda Murphy, "Northern Shoshone and Bannock," in D'Azevedo, *Great Basin*, 285–89; Heaton, *Shoshone-Bannocks*, 28–32; Walker, *Indians of Idaho*, 27; Liljeblad, *Idaho Indians in Transition*, 12–13. John W. W. Mann, in *Sacajawea's People: The Lemhi Shoshones and the Salmon River Country* (Lincoln: University of Nebraska Press, 2004), 143–78, notes that the Lemhi tradition of fishing later helped Shoshone-Bannocks of the Fort Hall Reservation to assert tribal fishing rights through much of southern Idaho.

13   Deward E. Walker, Jr., "Introduction," in Walker, *Plateau*, 3–6; Walker, *Indians of Idaho*, 25–26.

14   Ronda, *Lewis and Clark*, 169–70; Walker, "Introduction," 1–7; William E. Tydeman, "No Passive Relationship: Native Americans in the Environment," *Idaho Yesterdays* 39, no. 2 (Summer 1995): 23–28; and Alan G. Marshall, "The Nez Perce and Wild Horticulture on the Eastern Columbia Plateau," in *Northwest Lands, Northwest Peoples: Readings in Environmental History*, ed. Dale D. Goble and Paul W. Hirt (Seattle: University of Washington Press, 1999), 173–87.

15   David Thompson's extraordinary impact on the region is well described in Jack Nisbet, *Sources of the River: Tracking David Thompson through North America* (Seattle: Sasquatch Books, 1994), and by the explorer himself in David Thompson, *Columbia Journals*, ed. Barbara Belyea (Montreal: McGill-Queens University Press, 1994).

16   Jennifer Ott, "'Ruining' the Rivers in the Snake Country: The Hudson's Bay Company's Fur Desert Policy," *Oregon Historical Quarterly* 104, no. 2 (Summer 2003): 166–95; Meinig, *Great Columbia Plain*, 74, 82–87.

17   On the Spaldings, see West, *Last Indian War*, 39–51; and Clifford Merrill Drury, *Henry Harmon Spalding* (Caldwell, ID: Caxton Printers, 1936).

18   Steven Stoll, "Farm against Forest," in *American Wilderness: A New History*, ed. Michael Lewis (New York: Oxford University Press, 2007), 56; Whitman, quoted in Meinig, *Great Columbia Plain*, 140; West, *Last Indian War*, 46.

19   Schwantes, *In Mountain Shadows*, 52; Leonard Arrington, *History of Idaho* (Moscow: University of Idaho Press; Boise: Idaho State Historical Society, 1994), 1:473.

20   Andrew Duffin, *Plowed Under: Agriculture and Environment in the Palouse* (Seattle: University of Washington Press, 2007), 38–41.

21   The broader prevalence of these questions is noted in Richard White, *"It's Your Misfortune and None of My Own": A History of the American West* (Norman: University of Oklahoma Press, 1991), 236–68.

22   Lawrence G. Coates, Peter G. Boag, Ronald L. Hatzenbuehler, and Merwin R. Swanson, "The Mormon Settlement of Southeastern Idaho, 1845–1900," *Journal of Mormon History* 20, no. 2 (Fall 1994): 49–53, 62; Dean May, "Mormon Cooperatives in Paris, Idaho, 1869–1896," *Idaho Yesterdays* 19, no. 2 (Summer 1975): 20–30; White, *"It's Your Misfortune,"* 241–42.

23   Donald Worster, *A River Running West: The Life of John Wesley Powell* (New York: Ox-

ford University Press, 2001), 351–54; *History of Idaho Territory* (1884; repr., Fairfield, WA: Ye Galleon Press, 1973), 134–35.

24 Coates et al., "Mormon Settlement," 56–58; Claudia Lauper Bushman and Richard Lyman Bushman, *Building the Kingdom: A History of Mormons in America* (New York: Oxford University Press, 2001), 75–76; William G. Robbins, *Colony & Empire: The Capitalist Transformation of the American West* (Lawrence: University Press of Kansas, 1994), ix.

25 A general overview of the shift to industrial-scale extraction in the West is found in White, *"It's Your Misfortune,"* 236–68; for an explanation of the resulting boom in agriculture, see Duffin, *Plowed Under*, 38–45.

26 The most thorough coverage of the Silver Valley comes from a study of its largest company, Katherine G. Aiken, *Idaho's Bunker Hill: The Rise and Fall of a Great Mining Company, 1885–1981* (Norman: University of Oklahoma Press, 2005); for the discovery of the ore lode and investment of outside capital, see 3–9.

27 Ibid., 63–65.

28 Ibid., 92–94.

29 Keith C. Petersen, *Company Town: Potlatch, Idaho, and the Potlatch Lumber Company* (Pullman: Washington State University Press; Moscow: Latah County Historical Society, 1987), 6–12.

30 The migratory character and industrialization of the lumber frontier is documented in Michael Williams, *Americans and Their Forests: A Historical Geography* (Cambridge: Cambridge University Press, 1989), 193–330.

31 Brown, quoted in Petersen, *Company Town*, 18–19; Lyon, quoted in John Mullan, *Miners and Travelers' Guide to Oregon, Washington, Idaho, Montana, Wyoming, and Colorado* (New York: Wm. M. Franklin, 1865), 130.

32 Petersen, *Company Town*, 18–34; Williams, *Americans and Their Forests*, 310.

33 Harold K. Steen, *The U.S. Forest Service: A History*, centennial ed. (Durham, NC: Forest History Society, 2004), 22–46; J. Anthony Lukas, *Big Trouble: A Murder in a Small Western Town Sets Off a Struggle for the Soul of America* (New York: Simon & Schuster, 1997), 615–24.

34 J. M. Neil, *To the White Clouds: Idaho's Conservation Saga, 1900–1970* (Pullman: Washington State University Press, 2005), 1–12; James G. Lewis, *The Forest Service and the Greatest Good: A Centennial History* (Durham, NC: The Forest History Society, 2005), 59–64; Glen Barrett, "James H. Brady," in *Idaho's Governors: Historical Essays on Their Administrations*, ed. Robert C. Sims and Hope A. Benedict (Boise: Boise State University, 1992), 60–61.

35 Lukas, *Big Trouble*, 615–31; Steen, *U.S. Forest Service*, 86.

36 Steen, *U.S. Forest Service*, 65–67, 87–89.

37 White, *"It's Your Misfortune,"* 225–27; John Bieter and Mark Bieter, *An Enduring Legacy: The Story of Basques in Idaho* (Reno: University of Nevada Press, 2000), 37–38, 82–83.

38 Eliza Spalding Warren, comp., *Memoirs of the West: The Spaldings* (Portland, OR: Press of the Marsh Printing Company, 1916), 102.

39 Mary Hallock Foote, *A Victorian Gentlewoman in the Far West: The Reminiscences of Mary Hallock Foote*, ed. Rodman W. Paul (San Marino, CA: The Huntington Library, 1972), 274–330 (quotations from 329, 286).

40 For a survey of reclamation history, see Leonard J. Arrington, "Irrigation in the

Snake River Valley: An Historical Overview," *Idaho Yesterdays* 30, nos. 1–2 (Spring–Summer 1986): 3–11.

41 Laura Woodworth-Ney, "Water, Culture, and Boosterism: Albin and Elizabeth De-Mary and the Minidoka Reclamation Project, 1905–1920," in *The Bureau of Reclamation: History Essays from the Centennial Symposium* (Denver: U.S. Department of the Interior, Bureau of Reclamation, 2008), 385; Ruddock, quoted in Fiege, *Irrigated Eden*, 184.

42 H. E. Thomas, *Ground Water and the Law*, Geological Survey Circular 446 (Washington, DC: U.S. Geological Survey, 1961), 2; Dennis C. Colson, *Idaho's Constitution: The Tie That Binds* (Moscow: University of Idaho Press, 1991), 161–76; Fiege, *Irrigated Eden*, 81–84; Jane Morgan, "'Have Faith in God and U.S. Reclamation': Failure on the Boise Project, 1905–1924," *Idaho Yesterdays* 50, no. 1 (Spring 2009), available at http://134.50.3.223/idahoyesterdays/index.php/IY/article/view/11/11.

43 Karl Boyd Brooks, *Public Power, Private Dams: The Hells Canyon High Dam Controversy* (Seattle: University of Washington Press, 2006), 3–26 (quotation from 25).

44 Adam M. Sowards, *The Environmental Justice: William O. Douglas and American Conservation* (Corvallis: Oregon State University Press, 2009), 120–22; Sara Dant, "Making Wilderness Work: Frank Church and the American Wilderness Movement," *Pacific Historical Review* 77, no. 2 (2008): 252–53.

45 Neil, *White Clouds*, 25–30; Thomas R. Cox, *The Park Builders: A History of State Parks in the Pacific Northwest* (Seattle: University of Washington Press, 1988), 19–23.

46 Douglas Dodd, "A National Park for the Gem State?: The Forest Service, the National Park Service, and the Sawtooth National Park Campaign in Idaho, 1911–1926," *Idaho Yesterdays* 50, no. 1 (Spring 2009), http://134.50.3.223/idahoyesterdays/index.php/IY/article/view/10/10.

47 The leading interpretation of national trends in environmental politics after the war remains Samuel P. Hays, *Beauty, Health, and Permanence: Environmental Politics in the United States, 1955–1985* (New York: Cambridge University Press, 1987). J. M. Neil suggests through anecdotal evidence that the shift occurred in Idaho in the 1930s; see *White Clouds*, 70. For an explanation of the growing recreation boom after the war, see Peter Boag, "Outward Bound: Family, Gender, Environmentalism and the Postwar Camping Craze, 1945–1970," *Idaho Yesterdays* 50, no. 1 (Spring 2009), http://134.50.3.223/idahoyesterdays/index.php/IY/article/view/9/9. On the dredging initiative, see Neil, *White Clouds*, 106–13.

48 Dennis Baird and Lynn Baird, "A Campfire Vision: Establishing the Idaho Primitive Area," *Journal of the West* 26, no. 3 (July 1987): 50–58.

49 Dant, "Making Wilderness Work," 241, 243–47. On Church's political evolution, see Sara E. Dant Ewert, "Evolution of an Environmentalist: Senator Frank Church and the Hells Canyon Controversy," *Montana: The Magazine of Western History* 51, no. 1 (Spring 2001): 36–51.

50 Kevin R. Marsh, *Drawing Lines in the Forest: Creating Wilderness Areas in the Pacific Northwest* (Seattle: University of Washington Press, 2007), 34–37; Neil, *White Clouds*, xiii–xiv.

51 Dant, "Making Wilderness Work," 261; Steve Bunk, "The Great Gospel-Hump Compromise," *Idaho Heritage* 12 (August 1978): 24. Although the committee called for a wilderness area of 220,000 acres, the final decision of Congress was for 206,000 acres; see Endangered American Wilderness Act of 1978, Public Law 95–237, U.S.

Statutes at Large 92 (1980): 43–46, available at http://www.wilderness.net/NWPS/documents/publiclaws/PDF/95–237.pdf.

52 Mike Crapo, "Owyhee Canyonlands Bill Sets New Standard for Land Management," *Idaho Statesman*, March 20, 2007; Omnibus Public Land Management Act of 2009, Public Law 111–11, 111th Cong., 1st sess. (March 30, 2009).

53 Cecil D. Andrus and Joel Connelly, *Cecil Andrus: Politics Western Style* (Seattle: Sasquatch Books, 1998), 19.

54 Dant, "Making Wilderness Work," 251–52.

IDAHO VOICES
Environmental History

Conservationist Ernie Day chronicles Idahoans' roles in
wilderness activism beginning in the 1960s.

INTERVIEWER: Who would you say was your core group here in Idaho?

DAY: Well, as far as preservation and protection, it was the hunters and
the fishermen. And that's not really surprising, because many of them, for
a long time, realized a good habitat is essential for good game. Also the
hunters and the fishermen were more knowledgeable on it. This was their
bailiwick. The fishing is good, the hunting is good, and the Idaho Wildlife
Federation was the first large group to back the Wilderness Bill in 1960, I
guess it was, maybe '59. And there was a small core of people who realized
that we had to get help from the East. And we kind of served as a beacon
that these eastern people honed in on.

INTERVIEWER: Who was the small group? Who were these people that
were putting—probably putting their good names on the line?

DAY: Well, one of them, probably the most outstanding, was Bruce Bowler,
a local attorney, and a fellow by the name of Frank Jones, who was a printer.
They were all kind of self-employed, because that didn't play too well with
the corporations even then. And a little bit later, Ted Trueblood, who was a
writer. He wasn't part of the original few for the Wilderness Act itself, but
he was one of the main players in the Frank Church River of No Return.
And I guess you might have to say I was too. We had a little group we called
the Idaho Wilderness Users Committee, and that's what the thing stemmed
from. And we actively sought help from the national Wilderness Society
and got it, and, thank God, Frank Church. And that's one of the real, kind
of, anachronisms of history, I think, is the fact that Frank Church, with the
same electorate, the same constituency, that Steve Symms has, could feel
that he could champion wilderness. In the last days of the Wilderness Act,
when Clinton Anderson was ill, Church carried it to its completion. In 1964
it was signed. And to this day that was a window to me, in history, that,

thank God, it happened. Because we did get the Wilderness Act. We had to wait twenty years for it to click in before it was really solid. Because the act was passed in '64. And '84, why, then it was closed to mining entry and a few other things, but not closed as much as a lot of people would like you to believe. So, that was—with the exception of the Sawtooths.

Now the Sawtooths is a different story, and since we're sitting here, I'll take the liberty to point that out. We pushed for wilderness for the Sawtooths. It had been a primitive area for some time. To get it in a wilderness status very early—and when the act passed, this area didn't have to wait the twenty years because a few years prior to that, we were successful in getting a 10-carat, sterling, 100-proof bottled-in-bond wilderness that by the terms of the act, made it what the rest of it was and twenty years later. So this was true wilderness before anything else in Idaho, with the exception of Selway-Bitterroot perhaps.

* * *

Jerry Cobb explains some of the cleanup efforts in the Silver Valley after decades of mining pollution.

It's one of the richest and largest mining districts in the country. And with that have come some of the problems associated with heavy industry. But at the same time, Bunker Hill in the 1920s, I think around 1928, had one of the first tailings impoundments in the area. Also the mining companies had put in a small detention area down on the Smelterville Flats for trying to keep materials from washing downstream. They weren't totally successful at that, of course. There's materials moved all the way down into Coeur d'Alene Lake. In the 1960s, mid-'60s, the EPA [Environmental Protection Agency] required central impoundment areas or mine tailings ponds be developed, tailings ponds be developed for all the mines, and that their [effluents] and discharge come out of the river, and they did that all the way up the valley, you'll note, large tailings, impoundment areas that have been very successful in removing the solid material from the rivers. In the early days it was called the Lead Creek, South Fork of the Coeur d'Alene River was, and it ran the color of milk. And after they pulled the mine tailings out, everybody said, "Well, the river will still run the color of milk forever." And I think within about two years, you couldn't visibly notice the tailings in the river anymore. There'd been so much bedload movement of materials on the bottoms of the stream that most of its fine tailings had been scoured and were gone, and, of course, now we've gone from an area that was pretty well sterile to rivers that now we begin to see fish moving through in the high-water times of the year. In fact, they fish the South Fork all the way down through to Big Creek. One of the larger problems that is still remaining is some of the acid mine drainage coming from this tailing pond behind us. Still leaches some zinc out into the creek and, of course, zinc is very toxic to fish. Even in the high—even now, though, in the high-water times of the year, it's my understanding that fish do move through, so things are much better.

Note

Ernie Day was interviewed by Barbara Pulling, October 10, 1989, Stanley Basin, ID. Idaho Educational Public Broadcasting System, transcript (OH1033) Oral History Center/Idaho State Historical Society, 3–5. Used with permission of Idaho Public Television.

   Jerry Cobb spoke with an unknown interviewer, May 30, 1989, Wallace/Kellogg, ID. Idaho Educational Public Broadcasting System/Idaho Public Television, transcript (OH0988) Oral History Center/Idaho State Historical Society, 2–3. Used with permission of Idaho Public Television.

4

Idiosyncrasy and Enigma

Idaho Politics

KATHERINE G. AIKEN

WHILE IT SEEMS SIMPLE ENOUGH TO DESCRIBE IDAHO AS one of the most conservative states in the union, there are subtleties and exceptions that provide insights into Idahoans' views of themselves and their relationship with the rest of the country. Historian Carlos Schwantes has written that, in fact, "Idaho remains one of the least known and most puzzling American states."[1] Political journalist Randy Stapilus noted that Idahoans "desire not just rugged but aggressive independence" and that "as a group they display a colorful political perversity."[2] Taken together, these characteristics outline the challenge of analyzing Idaho politics.

Four themes permeate Idaho politics: sectionalism, a complex relationship with the federal government, the influence of the Church of Jesus Christ of Latter-day Saints, and a string of colorful individuals who populate the Idaho political landscape. This chapter interprets Idaho political history in terms of these four influences and their intersections. The centrality of these themes waxes and wanes, but at any given moment, each helps to define Idaho politics. To facilitate the discussion, Idaho's history is divided into four sections, roughly corresponding to broad periods—Idaho beginnings (approximately 1860–1920), Idaho embraces modernity (1920–45), Idaho in a post–World War II America (1945–80), and Idaho on the right (1980–present).

IDAHO BEGINNINGS

As one of the last of the continental areas to become a state, Idaho was constituted from what was left over after other state boundaries had been drawn, making its geography a study in contrasts. Among the forty-eight contiguous states, only Texas and California have a longer distance between their northern and southern boundaries. Idaho encompasses 83,557 square miles of land. More than eighty mountain ranges dominate the Idaho land-scape, giving it the fifth-highest topography of any state. Immense physical barriers separate the north from the south, and this physical separation is mirrored in Idaho politics.[3]

Most Idahoans view the Salmon River as the dividing line between northern and southern Idaho, a border both geographic and political that has been reinforced throughout Idaho's historical development. The discovery of precious metal deposits, especially gold and silver, defined development in northern Idaho. Beginning with a gold rush in the Clearwater drainage in 1860, new discoveries in the northern part of the state during the remainder of the nineteenth century added to Idaho's population. While fortune hunters streamed into Idaho, members of the Church of Jesus Christ of Latter-day Saints began settling what is now southern Idaho. Thirteen Mormon colonists founded Idaho's first town, Franklin, on April 14, 1860, and other Mormon settlements followed. Although the Organic Act for Utah Territory (1850) established the forty-second parallel as Utah's northern boundary, no one knew exactly where that was at the time. Consequently, the early Franklin and Bear Lake settlers thought they were in Utah and paid taxes there until 1872, when an official survey publicized their error. President Abraham Lincoln signed the Organic Act creating Idaho Territory on March 4, 1863.[4]

The territorial period (1863–90) coincided with the American Civil War and the Gilded Age, and as was common during that age, the territorial governors were a rather lackluster group. Sixteen men were confirmed as governor during the twenty-seven years of Idaho's territorial status. Six resided in Idaho for less than a year. Only eight served a full year or more. Their incompetence and economic irresponsibility added to Idahoans' conviction that the government in Washington, D.C., did not have the best interests of Idaho uppermost in its mind.[5]

Lewiston became the capital, but on December 7, 1864, the second territorial legislature voted to move the capital to Boise. Lewiston boosters were enraged and sought judicial intervention. They succeeded in obtaining a temporary injunction forbidding the removal of the territorial seal and archives; meanwhile, the Lewiston sheriff deputized local citizens to guard these items in case of a Boise-based attempt to seize them (which Boiseans did try to do on December 31). Lewiston residents still claim that the state capital was stolen from them, and it is possible to purchase an Idaho license plate bearing the catchphrase "Lewiston: Idaho's First Territorial Capital."[6]

The 1860 Republican Party platform railed against the "twin evils of barbarism"—slavery and polygamy. Throughout the Idaho territorial period, anti-Mormonism was a recurring theme. Tension between members of the Church of Jesus Christ of Latter-day Saints and nonmembers was perhaps the most significant conflict during Idaho's transition from territory to statehood, as also described in chapter 5 in this volume. That church leaders were also political leaders certainly contributed to the discord: Mormons tended to vote in blocs for Democratic candidates during this period. More than anything else, the Mormon practice of plural marriage raised the ire of those who were not church members.[7]

When the U.S. Congress passed the Edmunds Act in 1882, it became illegal for polygamists to vote, hold public office, or serve on juries in litigation involving plural marriage. Idaho's U.S. marshal Fred T. Dubois was determined to enforce the law and used his anti-Mormon record as a platform for his own political ambitions, becoming the territorial delegate to Congress and a proponent of Idaho's attempt to gain statehood. The territorial legislature adopted the Idaho Test Oath in 1884, which required people to swear under oath whether or not they were members of the Church of Jesus Christ of Latter-day Saints and believed in its doctrines. The test oath, therefore, affected not just those who practiced plural marriage but all Mormons. All of this helped Idaho Republicans who were seeking to replace Democrats as the majority party. It also had a significant impact on the Idaho constitutional convention in 1889. Delegates from both political parties agreed that the Church of Jesus Christ of Latter-day Saints posed a threat to Idaho and voted to include the test oath as part of the constitution, thus inscribing religious discrimination into the state's founding document.[8]

Mormons challenged the test oath all the way to the U.S. Supreme Court, which ruled in *Davis v. Beason*, on February 3, 1890, that the oath was constitutional. Church president Wilford Woodruff ordered all Mormons to comply with civil law regarding marriage in September 1890, thus ostensibly eliminating a major roadblock to Idaho citizenship for Mormons. None-theless, Idaho's first legislature continued to bar church members from the polls. Although the Idaho legislature did end most restrictions on Mormon civic activity and repealed the test oath in February 1893, these changes were not reflected in the Idaho constitution until 1982.[9]

Sectional differences animated politics from the first, as the legislature could not decide on the requisite two U.S. senators. Both political parties had promised northern Idaho residents that one senator would be from that part of the state. Dubois asked the Senate Judiciary Committee if Idaho could elect three senators—one who would serve a full term and two who would split a term. Dubois received one of the senate seats, and George L. Shoup and William McConnell were to split the other. Upon their arrival in Washington, D.C., the two drew lots. When McConnell drew the first, ab-breviated term, northerners concluded that they had again come out on the short end. The Idaho legislature then elected William Claggett to Dubois's seat. Claggett went to Washington, D.C., but was unable to convince the Senate to unseat Dubois. Shoup ended up serving from 1890 to 1900. The first state legislators further recognized the continued sectional animosity by making other attempts to ameliorate it. Most notably, they confirmed that Boise would serve as the state capital and that Moscow would be the site of the state university.[10]

Along with the desire to create political stability, a major motivation for seeking statehood was the economic ties that would result. Timber, min-ing, and agriculture all relied on railroad transportation and connections to markets in other parts of the country. Idaho's links to the larger U.S. economy were especially evident in the Coeur d'Alene mining district, where metal production was crucial to the industrial revolution. Eastern investors in both mining companies and railroads wielded considerable influence. And entrepreneurs influenced politics in both Washington, D.C., and Boise.

Events in the Coeur d'Alenes, as the northern Idaho mining region was then known, brought Idaho national attention. When dynamite destroyed Kellogg's Bunker Hill Company concentrator in 1899, Governor Frank Steunenberg declared martial law, and federal troops from Fort Sherman in Coeur d'Alene incarcerated miners in makeshift jails called "bull pens." On December 30, 1905, former governor Steunenberg returned to his Caldwell home, opened his gate, and was blown apart by a homemade bomb. Current governor Frank Gooding hired Pinkerton detectives to investigate, and they focused on officials of the militant Western Federation of Miners. In what some call Idaho's trial of the century, "Big Bill" Haywood, George Pettibone, and Charles Moyer were charged with conspiracy in relation to the murder. William E. Borah was a special prosecutor; Clarence Darrow led the defense team. Americans throughout the country followed the deliberations, and the Boise-area jury found Haywood not guilty. Steunenberg's statue graces the front of the Idaho state capitol and carries an inscription that expressed Idahoans' views of radicalism: "When in 1899 organized lawlessness challenged the power of Idaho, he upheld the dignity of the state, enforced its authority and restored LAW AND ORDER within its boundaries, for which he was assassinated in 1905." A majority of Idahoans would echo those sentiments today.[11]

Changes in agriculture were also significant, as Kevin Marsh indicates in chapter 3 in this book. The federal Carey Act of 1894 gave participating states federal land, as much as one million acres, if they produced plans for irrigating it. By 1902, the federal Newlands Act (also known as the Reclamation Act), along with various private enterprises, did even more to expand Idaho's irrigated agriculture. Between 1895 and 1930, Idaho boasted sixty-five reclamation projects, and more than six hundred thousand acres had been patented.[12]

Despite economic development, farmers and miners faced continued economic stress and frustration. They became core supporters of the People's Party, or the Populists. The Populist platform included a graduated income tax, government ownership of telephone and telegraph lines and railroads, and the "free" and unlimited coinage of silver by the Treasury Department. Proponents of the platform were convinced that this silver production would result in an inflationary economic environment that would favor farmers and other debtors, not to mention the silver miners. In 1896, Idaho voters supported Populist and Democratic candidate William Jennings Bryan for president, and Populist voting delivered the governorship to Frank Steunenberg. However, the Coeur d'Alene mining wars sped the decline of the Populist Party, as many Americans linked silver miners with labor radicalism and therefore abandoned their advocacy of free silver.[13]

Still impatient with the lack of change, rural Idahoans later joined another political reform movement. The Nonpartisan League began with farmers in North Dakota in 1915, and by 1917, it had become an important important part of Idaho politics. By 1919, the league claimed twelve thousand members in Idaho, and its socialistic platform had broad appeal. Farmer-Labor candidates defeated Democrats in primary elections in 1918; however, by the time of the general election, the reform party appeared to have lost steam. Nonpartisan League members did well because of Idaho's direct primary rule, but when that was overturned in 1919, the only alternative for league supporters was to formally create a third party.[14]

Eventually many Idahoans who had supported the Nonpartisan League became advocates for the Progressive Party. Progressivism dominated much of American politics in the early twentieth century; Progressives supported a number of reforms at the local, state, and national levels. No Idaho politician is more closely associated with progressivism than William Borah. He came to be one of the most prominent Republican members of the U.S. Senate, elected in 1906, and certainly the leading Republican in Idaho. He remains perhaps the best-known Idahoan in history, and his statue is one of two that represent Idaho in the U.S. Capitol Statuary Hall. As the chair of the Senate Foreign Relations Committee, he was the most powerful elected official dealing with foreign policy issues. Known as the Lion of Idaho, he remains a first-rate example of the importance of independence to Idaho voters and politicians. Historian LeRoy Ashby referred to him as a "Spearless Leader," a man who tried to follow his conscience regardless of the directives of the Republican Party. For instance, although he prosecuted Haywood in the infamous "trial of the century" for the murder of Governor Steunenberg, he often backed labor in the U.S. Congress. Faced with episodes of censorship during World War I, , he advocated for civil liberties. He became a national, even international, figure as one of the most vehement opponents to the Treaty of Versailles. He earned a reputation for his position on the "outlawry" of war, the Kellogg-Briand Pact, and as a vocal proponent for diplomatic recognition of the Soviet Union. On the domestic front, he worked for farmers and miners. True to his maverick reputation, he favored some of Franklin D. Roosevelt's New Deal policies and adamantly opposed others. He knew well what other politicians had to

FIGURE 4.1. Senator William E. Borah arguably was Idaho's most influential
politician. He is seen here fishing on Big Creek, near Edwardsburg, Idaho, in what was
then known as the Idaho Primitive Area, an archetypal setting, August 2, 1927. Photo
courtesy of Idaho State Historical Society, 63–219.10.

learn—that maintaining close ties to his Idaho constituents was necessary
for any Idaho political figure.[15]

By no means was Borah the only idiosyncratic politician at the time.
Although Idaho seems an unlikely state to boast the nation's first Jewish
governor, Moses Alexander, a Boise Democrat, achieved that honor in 1915.
He is noted in Idaho politics for two initiatives unrelated to his religious affiliation. Prohibition was arguably the most important political issue in the
pre–World War I years, and as governor, Alexander determined to make it
a reality. In fact, both Alexander and his opponent, incumbent Republican
governor John Haines, favored Prohibition. House Bill 142 made it illegal
to manufacture, transport, or possess intoxicating liquor. Despite threats
to his life, Alexander signed the bill into law on March 1, 1915. Idahoans ap-

proved the prohibition amendment to the state constitution on November 7, 1916, presaging national prohibition.[16]

The United States' entry into World War I soon became the dominant concern for Alexander and Idahoans. Along with the Bolshevik Revolution in Russia, the war combined to create another political episode in Idaho related to labor. The Industrial Workers of the World (IWW), or the Wobblies, were a prominent labor organization in Idaho. "Big Bill" Haywood (of Steunenberg trial fame) was a founder of the IWW, which made significant inroads among timber and mining workers in the northern part of the state. In 1917, timber workers advocating the eight-hour day nearly shut down the timber industry; according to some estimates, more than three-fourths of the loggers in heavily timbered Benewah County were IWW members. Idahoans—and not for the first time—decried the radicalism of the IWW, feared that they were undermining the nation's ability to combat Germany, and urged Governor Alexander to act. Idaho was the first state to pass a criminal syndicalism act. In response to an IWW attempt to free one of its members from the St. Maries jail, Alexander requested federal troops to restore order. Prosecutions under the state's criminal syndicalism law destroyed the IWW. Haywood himself was convicted in 1918 of violating the federal Espionage Act.[17]

Sectionalism was a defining element in Idaho's progress from territorial status to statehood. National politics affected the role of the Church of Jesus Christ of Latter-day Saints in Idaho's early period and also was a driving force in Idaho politics. "Big Bill" Haywood and William Borah exemplify the colorful characters who helped to shine a national spotlight on the state.

IDAHO BECOMES MODERN

During the 1920s, Idaho's agricultural industry fell on hard times. Increased production during the war resulted in overproduction. Farmers who had borrowed during World War I to expand their landholdings and purchase equipment found that they could not make their payments. In part as a reflection of these hardships, Idaho politics moved from Progressivism to a more conservative approach. Republicans gained ascendancy in Idaho, as they did at the national level.

Republicans owed part of their sucess to political manager Lloyd Adams. A sometime newspaper man, attorney, and lobbyist, Adams served one term in the Idaho state senate but for the most part was content to work behind the scenes. During the 1920s, his Gooding-based political machine wielded considerable power, and he was sometimes referred to as the Idaho Republican Party's personnel officer. Republican control of state offices was due in no small part to Adams's efforts, and he continued to be influential until his death at the end of the 1960s. Adams is one of a handful of Idaho politicos who played the role of powerbroker without holding office.[18]

Idaho politicians in Boise and Washington, D.C., worked to stem the costs of agricultural problems. For example, in the U.S. Senate, William Borah sought to improve farm prices and advocated that the federal government support farmers with direct payments.[19] In 1922, Idahoans elected Charles C. Moore to the governorship. He characterized himself as a "dirt farmer" and was known for his penury. As a colorful example, he used all of his predecessor's stationery before ordering his own. In response to the agricultural economy's predicament, he supported high tariff duties, low freight rates, and more irrigation projects. Despite the efforts of Moore and Borah, the agricultural crisis continued and was exacerbated by the onset of the Great Depression in 1929.[20] The economic downturn coincided with a severe drought in the Snake River Plain that echoed conditions in the so-called Dust Bowl. The combination of financial and environmental crises devastated farmers. A pound of potatoes that sold for $1.51 in 1919 was worth only $0.31 in 1922 and just $0.10 by the time of the Depression, in 1932. Average farm income dropped from $686 a year in 1929 to $250 three years later. Overall, Idahoans saw their incomes reduced by almost half, much more than the approximately one-third drop posted by wealthier states. Things were so bad that in 1931 arsonists set fire to Idaho forests so that they could seek employment as firefighters.[21] By winter 1932–33, more than twenty thousand Idahoans were unemployed, and banks had foreclosed on more than a thousand mortgages. Dust Bowl refugees came anyway, and Idaho's population actually increased during the 1930s, stretching the government's ability to meet demands for relief.

In response to challenging times, Idahoans made a 180-degree political turn in 1930 and elected a Democrat as governor—Pocatello mayor Charles Benjamin Ross. Two years later, Ross was reelected, James P. Pope became

the first Democratic U.S. senator from Idaho in fourteen years, and Democrat Franklin D. Roosevelt carried every Idaho county except Bear Lake on
his way to defeating incumbent president Herbert Hoover. In 1928, when
Hoover had received 64 percent of the popular vote in Idaho, only Freemont
County had failed to support him. However, even in the midst of the Depression, Idahoans demonstrated their independence. When Ross challenged
William E. Borah for his U.S. Senate seat, he received 74,444 votes to Borah's
128,723. In the presidential contest that year, Roosevelt defeated Republican
Alf Landon 125,683 to 66,232 among Idaho voters. Ross advocated a one-cent
sales tax as a solution to some of the state's financial problems. Opponents
decried this "penny for Benny," voters ended the sales tax via referendum
in 1936, and Ross lost his bid to regain the governorship in 1938.[22]

The New Deal marked a sea change for Idahoans in terms of their relationship with the federal government. Despite their reliance on Washington, D.C., residents had been wary of federal interference, but the years
1932–45 marked an onslaught of federal initiatives and involvement. Idaho,
like the rest of the West, was transformed from a hinterland to a focus
of attention from the nation's capital. In 1933, Idahoans paid $904,000
in internal revenue taxes, and the state received $39.9 million in relief.
From 1933 to 1939, Idaho ranked fifth in the nation in per capita New Deal
expenditures.[23]

Agricultural programs were at the forefront of this transformation.
Roosevelt and his advisers sought to stabilize farm prices through the
Agricultural Adjustment Administration, and farmers were compen-
sated for reducing the number of acres they planted. The Farm Security
Administration loaned $76 million to help nearly twenty thousand Ida-
ho residents save their farms from foreclosure. Meanwhile, the Taylor
Grazing Act of 1934 assured western cattle producers access to federal
grazing lands at low fees—this is still a mainstay of the Idaho cattle and
sheep industries.[24]

Agriculture was not the only economic sector in Idaho to receive federal
support. In the U.S. Senate, William Borah, along with Key Pittman of Nevada and Montana's Burton K. Wheeler, supported silver miners and aided
in passing the Silver Purchase Act of 1934, which required the Treasury Department to purchase silver until it either reached a price of $1.29 an ounce

or accounted for one-fourth of the federal monetary reserve. A subsidy for the western mining industry, the Silver Purchase Act was a considerable help to Idaho metal producers.[25]

Other New Deal programs had an impact on various localities in Idaho. For instance, Civilian Conservation Corps (CCC) projects altered the state's landscape. Heyburn State Park, Idaho's only state park at the time, became a chief beneficiary of CCC efforts and funds. CCC workers also battled blister rust, a disease that was devastating northern Idaho's white pine forests. Idaho was home to 163 CCC camps, second only to California.[26] However, even the economic crisis and the federal dollars that flowed into the state did not lead to total acceptance of an expanded role for the federal government. Senator James P. Pope sponsored a bill to create a comprehensive Columbia Valley Authority (CVA), modeled after the Tennessee Valley Authority. The new agency would oversee the management of the Columbia River and Snake River systems. However, Idaho Power Company and other private utility companies successfully opposed the law. The majority of Idahoans favored private power over public, a reflection of long-held fears of government control and a deep-seated dedication to capitalism and free enterprise. Idahoans feared that public ownership was a precursor to socialism or even communism.[27]

While large federal programs could shape political and economic developments, local factors could also make a difference. One Idaho family had particular influence during the 1930s and early 1940s. Brothers Barzilla and Chase Clark came to Idaho in 1885 from Indiana. Barzilla served as Idaho Falls mayor for five terms. Chase was a mining attorney in Mackey and later was also mayor of Idaho Falls. Both were interested in public service. Barzilla was elected governor in 1936 and Chase governor in 1940 (Chase's daughter, Bethine, married Frank Church). Their nephew C. Worth Clark served in U.S. House of Representatives and in the U.S. Senate for one term beginning in 1938.[28] They came close to creating an Idaho political dynasty.

While the twin crises of the Depression and World War II generated significant changes in Idaho's politics, Idahoans valued their independence and their individualism, and this produced enigmatic political patterns. From the progressive Republican Borah to the overwhelming support of President Roosevelt and the homegrown dynasty of the Clark family, Idahoans in the modern era showed themselves willing and able to shift loyalties, priorities, and strategies. Beginning in 1938, Idahoans began to question the federal control that accompanied the New Deal and turned to Republicans, at least for awhile.

IDAHO IN A POST–WORLD WAR II AMERICA

Although it is difficult to imagine today, Democrats usually represented Idahoans in Washington, D.C., between 1945 and 1980, while Republicans tended to control the state legislature. Since 1980, the state has become increasingly conservative politically, with Republicans controlling national offices and the statehouse. Lyndon Johnson was the only Democratic presidential candidate to carry Idaho during this period, and even in that Democratic landslide year (1964), he received only .92 percent more of Idaho's popular vote than Barry Goldwater.

Idaho politics during the second half of the twentieth century continued to be based on personal and social relationships in ways that might appear provincial to outsiders. When Republican James McClure first ran for a seat in the U.S. Congress in 1966, one of his most successful campaign tactics was to give postcards to friends and supporters that they could use to promote him to others.[29] Democratic organizer Verda Barnes was legendary in terms of cultivating personal connections. According to newspaperman and 2004 gubernatorial candidate Jerry Brady, "Verda Barnes could make 10,000 votes in a week."[30] Republican leaders and their Democratic counterparts interacted on a regular basis, and were often friends, and much of the business of politics took place during face-to-face meetings.

Two structural changes altered the political scene. First, Idaho governors originally served two-year terms, which resulted in constant shake-ups in Boise and made state government an uncertain career. The four-year gubernatorial term came into being in 1946 and allowed for a more modern approach to government and policy on the state level. Second, there are only two U.S. congressional districts in Idaho. The First District is five hundred miles north to south and two hundred miles east to west at the widest point. Much of the terrain is mountainous, and travel is difficult, with only the treacherous Highway 95 connecting northern Idaho and southern Idaho. In 1966, redistricting placed all of Boise in the First District, to the benefit of Republicans.[31] While these structural changes had far-reaching effects, the individual career paths of Idaho politicians continued to illustrate the state's "colorful political perversity."

Glen Taylor, a Democrat, may be the most colorful Idaho politician to date. Known as the singing cowboy, he brought his band, the Glendora Ranch Gang, on his campaign junkets. When crowds gathered to hear the music, Taylor would present his political platform of near socialism and world peace. Although he ran for office eight times, he was elected only once and served in the U.S. Senate from 1945 to 1951. He voted for civil rights legislation and spoke in favor of better relations with the Soviet Union. He is perhaps best known for sitting on the steps of the U.S. Capitol attired in cowboy hat and boots, singing to the tune of "Home on the Range" to protest the wartime housing shortage in Washington, D.C.:

> Oh, give us a home
> Near the Capitol dome
> With a yard where the children can play—
> Just one room or two,
> Any old thing will do.
> We can't find a pla-a-ce to stay

Taylor joined Henry Wallace on the Progressive presidential ticket in 1948. From that point onward, most Idahoans saw him as a dangerous left-wing fanatic, and Wallace and Taylor received only five thousand votes. Taylor lost in the Democratic primary when he ran for reelection to the Senate in 1951, but he was a major player in a pivotal election in 1956. (He retired to California and manufactured wigs known as "Taylor Toppers.")[32]

Following the Glen Taylor debacle, Idaho Democrats were in disarray, and Tom Boise (the Democratic counterpart to Lloyd Adams) played a key role in their reorganization. A Lewiston businessman, Boise was a major force in the Democratic Party for thirty years. Most Democrats who succeeded in Idaho owed at least a portion of that success to him.[33]

The 1956 U.S. Senate race was one of the most pivotal elections involving national office in the post–World War II period and is emblematic of the complex nature of Idaho politics. A three-way battle pitted Republican incumbent Herman Welker against former senator Taylor and the young newcomer to politics Frank Church. Church had beaten Taylor in the primary by a mere 170 votes, so Taylor launched a write-in campaign (perhaps funded by Republicans).[34]

Welker's alliance with Senator Joseph McCarthy (Welker led the fight against McCarthy's censure in 1954) was so strong that people knew him as "little Joe from Idaho." He embraced strident anti-communism and used McCarthy's tactic of tarring opponents with the pro-communist brush. By 1956, McCarthy had been discredited, and Welker's behavior was often erratic. (At the time, the rumor was that he had a drinking problem, but it later became known that he was suffering from a brain tumor.) Nonetheless, Welker was the incumbent senator and remained a political force.[35] During the election, he focused his attacks on the fact that the National Committee for an Effective Congress supported Church, and Welker claimed that the group was a communist organization.[36]

Church defeated Welker in forty-one of Idaho's forty-four counties, in part because of the three-way nature of the race. By 1956, Taylor's brand of liberalism was anathema to many Idahoans. While his support for civil rights and civil liberties was often lauded, he was vocal in his criticism of Idaho corporations, especially Idaho Power Company. Taylor claimed that Church had been subsumed by corporate power, while Welker branded Church a communist. Church argued that it was difficult for both statements to be true, and Idahoans agreed. Church's effective use of television also contributed to his success as he was virtually the only Idaho candidate to utilize the medium. As late as 1953, there were no television stations in Idaho, and only a handful were operating in 1956.[37]

Although the senatorial election of 1956 may have been momentous, it was not the only important political race in the 1950s. Idaho voters made Gracie Bowers Pfost the first woman the state had elected to national office. She won the race in the First District in 1952 and was one of only twelve women who served in the Eighty-Third Congress. Pfost was from Nampa, the first person from south of the Salmon River to represent the First District, and she won even though her opponent was a Republican incumbent in a year when Dwight Eisenhower carried Idaho by about twenty-five thousand votes. She served through the 1950s, a decade known for traditional ideas about women and certainly a period when Idaho was not at the cutting edge of gender equality.

Pfost is best known for her tireless efforts to prevent Idaho Power Company from constructing three dams in Hells Canyon, a campaign that earned her the sobriquet "Hell's Belle." Pfost supported the federal government's proposal that one high dam in Hells Canyon would better serve Idahoans in terms of electrical power, irrigation, flood control, and recreation. As Kevin Marsh recounts in chapter 3 of this book, the resulting political battle was one of the most hotly contested in the post–World War II Pacific Northwest and had important ramifications for both Idaho and the larger environmental movement. Some Idahoans viewed the proposed federal dam-construction project as a sign of a burgeoning federal government and a challenge to a capitalistic economy. Pfost worried that Idaho Power Company would profit unduly from the construction of the three dams, and all at the expense of Idahoans. Although Idaho Power prevailed and constructed Oxbow, Brownlee, and Hells Canyon dams, the conflict was a significant turning point. Interests that are now considered environmentalists—the Sierra Club, for example—supported the federal government's high dam against the private Idaho Power Company construction. Their defeat was a bitter one and led them to establish a new environmental paradigm. Before the Hells Canyon controversy, even so-called environmental stalwarts would seldom have thought a moratorium on dam construction might be an option. After the loss, the idea became much more prominent.[38]

Idaho enjoyed years of economic growth from 1945 until the late 1970s. During the same period, Idahoans in general, and the Idaho Republican Party specifically, moved to the right. Len Jordan, a Grangeville businessman, represents this shift. (His wife, Grace Edgington Jordan, wrote one of the great Idaho later pioneer tales, *Home on Hells Canyon*.) He was vocal in his support of Idaho Power in the Hells Canyon controversy. Jordan was elected to the Idaho state legislature in 1946, became governor in 1951, and was appointed to the U.S. Senate in 1962 following the death of Henry Dworshak. He eventually proposed a moratorium on dam construction in Hells Canyon, and his old homestead became part of a national recreation area managed by the Forest Service.[39]

By 1964, Idaho Republicans found themselves divided, with some backing Governor Robert E. Smylie, a more liberal Republican and three-term Idaho governor who supported New York governor Nelson Rockefeller's campaign for the Republican presidential nomination, while many others favored Barry Goldwater's more conservative approach. Goldwater's book *Conscience of a Conservative* resonated with James McClure and Don Samuelson, among others. An emphasis on limiting both taxation and government control over citizens was crucial to the success of both men and the state's expanding conservative forces.[40]

No one epitomizes this conservative trend more than Governor Don Samuelson, elected in 1966. He advocated what he referred to as an "undiluted" form of Republicanism that emphasized lower taxes, less government interference, and a decided distrust of the federal government. His proclamation of "Kick a Beatnik in the Seatnik" Week resonated with some Idahoans, although it was generally ridiculed outside the state. The presidential election of 1964, the shifts in Republican officeholders, and the Samuelson governorship mark the triumph of the conservative branch of the Idaho Republican Party. When Len Jordan surprised almost everyone by deciding to retire, McClure won election to his Senate seat. His Democratic opponent, Idaho State University president "Bud" Davis, alienated Idaho voters when he endorsed Cesar Chavez and the United Farm Workers' grape boycott. McClure, a Payette attorney, served in the Senate for three terms that were marked by a conservative agenda, a spotless record of personal integrity, and an industrious and workmanlike approach to congressional assignments. A reputation as a leader in energy policy and in Middle East policy making marked his career.[41]

Ironically, Samuelson's reelection campaign was noteworthy for bringing Cecil Andrus to the fore of the Idaho Democratic Party. In 1970, Andrus challenged Samuelson again, having lost in 1966, and an environmental controversy dominated the campaign. A battle between development and conservation interests centered on the White Clouds area of the Sawtooth Mountains about twenty-five miles northwest of Sun Valley, an area noted for its pristine beauty. In 1968, prospectors for the New York–based American Smelting and Refining Company (ASARCO) found considerable deposits of molybdenum. This alloy was in demand for the space industry and others that required steel with resistance to high heat. ASARCO filed mining claims and requested Forest Service permission to construct roads into the area. The company planned a 740-acre open-pit mine that would eventually employ 350 people. Opponents noted that the area included 11,820-foot-high Castle Peak as well as fifty-four high glacial lakes. They thought that development would jeopardize critical fish runs. Conservation groups such as the Sierra Club and the National Wildlife Federation feared that the construction of roads would open the land to a variety of misuses or end the possibility of wilderness designation. In Governor Samuelson's view, ASARCO had filed a legal mining claim, and he took the Forest Service to task for delaying road construction. He did not recognize how widespread and well organized opposition to the White Clouds development had become. Statements such as "They aren't going to tear down mountains. They are going to dig a hole," did not endear him to environmentalists. The dispute received national attention, including a January 1970 *Life* magazine article, "Whose Wilderness?" Governor Samuelson was inundated with letters. Many of his constituents viewed the controversy as a case of eastern mining interests working against the interests of Idahoans. Samuelson's supporters noted, however, that the Sierra Club was also primarily an outside group.[42]

Andrus made the White Clouds controversy a major campaign issue, noting, "The most important long-range issue is the protection of our magnificent Idaho environment." Samuelson pointed out that without economic development activities, Idahoans would be relegated to minimum-wage jobs. The governor tried to mitigate the damage with campaign ads showing him fishing and stating, "I want to make two things clear. . . . Idaho's air and water." But it was not enough, and he lost a close election to Andrus. Although Andrus carried only fifteen of forty-four counties, he won by 10,896 votes. Twenty-four years had passed since a Democrat had been elected Idaho's chief executive.[43]

Cecil Andrus, along with Frank Church, had reshaped the Idaho Democratic Party in the post–World War II period, making it more liberal than some other branches of the party. They were staunch supporters of civil rights, advocated government social welfare programs, and favored organized labor. Andrus remains the most prominent Idaho Democrat of the post–World War II period. Natural resource issues were at the forefront during his administration. He received 71 percent of the vote in his reelection campaign in 1974. Later, he became U.S. Secretary of the Interior in the Jimmy Carter administration, the first Idahoan to serve as a member of the president's cabinet.[44] He won the governorship again in 1986 and in 1990, for an unprecedented fourth term.

As the Hells Canyon and White Clouds issues demonstrate, environmental concerns had risen to the forefront of Idaho politics. In the past fifty years, they have often been debated in terms of "wilderness." This is a particularly critical concept in Idaho, where 34 million acres, nearly two-thirds of the state's territory, is federal land. While historians and commentators paint this as primarily a big business and Republicans versus Democrats and the general population kind of battle, that is not the case in Idaho. It is possible to argue that while Democrats have received the most credit for advances in the area of wilderness protection, collaborations among individuals from both parties have in fact been responsible, and every discussion of "wilderness" rouses some of Idahoans' most deeply held sentiments. Idahoans are attached to their landscape and desire to keep the state pristine and protected from outsiders of any ilk, and hunting and recreation are dear to the hearts of Idahoans of both parties. At the same time, resource-based industries have dominated the Idaho economy. This makes for strange bedfellows but also has placed the state on the cutting edge of wilderness legislation. The Sawtooth National Recreation Area is a good example.

The Sawtooth region continued to be a focus of dispute. Some advocated that the area become a national park, but many Idahoans viewed the National Park Service as a rigid bureaucracy more concerned with compliance than common sense. They preferred the U.S. Forest Service, a government agency that Idahoans had dealt with for years. Congressman James McClure, a Republican, worked with Senator Church, a Democrat, and Senator Jordan, a Republican, to pass legislation that created the Sawtooth National Recreation Area. It became law in 1972.[45]

Idaho sectionalism and the role of the Church of Jesus Christ of Latter-day Saints are clearly evident when analyzing politics in the state's two congressional districts.[46] While Democrats often held the First District congressional seat, the Second District was primarily Republican. George

Hansen, one of the most interesting Idaho political figures of the past fifty years, was elected to the position seven times. A member of the Church of Jesus Christ of Latter-day Saints, he grew up in Tetonia, near Pocatello. He had ties with the archconservative John Birch Society, opposed the Panama Canal Treaty, fought against the Occupational Safety and Health Administration (a federal bureaucracy that residents throughout Idaho distrusted), and campaigned vigorously. When Jordan was appointed to fill the Dworshak seat, Hansen ran for the U.S. House of Representatives. He ignored the advice of most Republican leaders and ran unsuccessfully against Church in 1968; he also ran for an open Senate seat in 1972 and lost. However, in 1974, he defeated Orval Hansen and regained the Second District seat. Hansen solidified his political legacy in the aftermath of the 1976 Teton Dam disaster that devastated Rexburg and the surrounding area. Without a doubt, the most effective relief activities were those the Mormon Church conducted, and Hansen benefited as the only church member in the Idaho congressional delegation.

Still, Hansen was not immune to controversy. Financial scandal constantly plagued him as he struggled with both campaign and personal debts. He was the first federal official indicted under the 1978 Ethics Law. He and his wife, Connie, were involved in financial dealings with the notorious Nelson Bunker Hunt, the House voted 354 to 52 to reprimand him, and Hansen was eventually convicted on four felony charges. Through most of his troubles, the Republican Party hierarchy stuck by him, and he continued to win elections. Even in 1984, in the wake of the House reprimand and his legal difficulties, Richard Stallings defeated Hansen by only a few hundred votes in an election in which the returns were questioned.

The post–World War II period of Idaho politics was a harbinger of the more decisive move to the right that is the hallmark of recent Idaho political history. Many talented and dedicated Democrats served the state in the postwar era, but the party's influence was waning. Moreover, despite the ubiquitous presence of the federal government, distrust of it and insistence on independence became synonymous with Idaho politics.[47]

IDAHO ON THE RIGHT

Just as it dramatically altered the national political scene, the 1980 election was a turning point for Idaho politics. Church sought his fifth term in the

Senate. A critic of some parts of U.S. foreign policy, including the Vietnam War, he chaired a committee that investigated the FBI and CIA. The so-called Church Committee concluded that U.S. intelligence and law enforcement agencies had sometimes overstepped their constitutional bounds, a conclusion that many Americans found troubling.[48] From the powerful position of chair of the Senate Foreign Relations Committee, he oversaw the United States' withdrawal from the Panama Canal Zone. Both of these actions met with little approval from Idaho voters.

However, Church's environmental policies put him at odds with a number of Idaho constituents and provided fodder for challenger Steve Symms. The Gospel-Hump region, located in north-central Idaho, includes about five hundred acres between Buffalo Hump Mountain and Gospel Peak. Hoping to broker an agreement between developers and conservationists, Church held a meeting to this end in Grangeville, where anti-environmentalists had hanged him in effigy. Following almost three months of meetings, the two sides agreed on a 220,000-acre wilderness that would be part of the Endangered Wilderness Act signed into law by President Carter. Congressman Symms advocated for a different view; he thought that adding the Gospel-Hump region to the National Wilderness Preservation System would create a "division of Idaho" and sought to prevent this. Symms and Church also disagreed on the proposed River of No Return Wilderness, and Symms used both topics in his campaign against Church in 1980.[49]

Veteran campaign organizer Phil Reberger ran Symms's campaign against Church. By Idaho standards, it was an expensive campaign—about $5 million between the candidates, or more than $5 for each Idaho resident. The campaign received national attention as a classic liberal-versus-conservative competition. Symms's campaign literature often showed him taking a bite out of an apple from the Symms family orchards, symbolizing his goal of taking a bite out of what he saw as a too large and powerful federal government. Although Symms battled charges that he was a womanizer, and some Mormon voters objected to the Symms family's ownership of the Ste. Chapelle winery at Sunnyslope, Ronald Reagan's victory in the presidential race aided Symms. While Reagan beat Carter by a two-to-one margin in Idaho, Symms defeated Church by less than 1 percent of the vote. No Idaho Democrat has held a seat in the U.S. Senate seat since then. Republican dominance was confirmed in 1986, when it looked like Democrats might rebound, with Cecil Andrus running for governor, Governor John Evans (a Mormon) seeking a Senate seat, and Richard Stallings, a Mormon Democratic incumbent in the second congressional district, running for reelection. Only Andrus and Stallings were successful, and Andrus is the only Democrat to have campaigned successfully for statewide office since.[50] In 1990, Larry Craig replaced Steve Symms in the House and later followed him to the Senate.

Underscoring much of this Republican ascendance was the Sagebrush Rebellion, a regional movement that began in 1979 when Nevada passed a law insisting that the federal government "return" forty-nine million acres of land it managed within the state. The movement gained a following in other public land states such as Idaho, as it appealed to rural westerners opposed to conservation laws and environmental groups that were perceived as outsider-dominated, such as the Idaho Conservation League and the Sierra Club. Sagebrush Rebellion sentiments lasted into the 1990s. Symms had close ties with it, as did Representative Helen Chenoweth, from the First District. Only the second woman elected to national office from Idaho, she epitomized the more conservative elements that have come to characterize the state. She served in Congress from 1994 to 2000, one of the insurgents in the Republican Revolution that swept the Democrats out of power in 1994. She had served as state executive director of the Idaho Republican Party and was chief of staff for Congressman Symms.[51]

Chenoweth is remembered for her strident opposition to the United Nations. She claimed that the United Nations used black helicopters to spy on Idahoans and that it was a foreign entity seeking to curtail the liberties of Americans. Many Idahoans shared her distrust of that international organization on the grounds that it put U.S. sovereignty in jeopardy. Chenoweth sponsored legislation that would have made it illegal for Americans to wear foreign uniforms and/or serve under officers from other countries in an attempt to end American participation in U.N. peacekeeping efforts. Following Chenoweth's statement that salmon could not be an endangered species because she could purchase canned salmon at any Albertson's supermarket, bumper stickers proclaiming "Can Helen, Not Salmon" appeared.

Meanwhile, Chenoweth joined Republicans in promoting family values and denouncing the Democrats' alleged unwillingness to do the same. According to many Idaho pundits, she won a close election in 1994 in part because her opponent, incumbent Democrat Larry LaRocco, admitted to an extramarital affair with a coworker. Four years later, in response to the scandal involving President Bill Clinton and Monica Lewinsky, Chenoweth ran advertisements declaring, "Personal conduct does count, and integrity matters." These campaign ads prompted the *Idaho Statesman* to investigate rumors about Chenoweth herself. She had to admit that fourteen years earlier, she had had an affair with her married business partner Vernon Ravenscroft (onetime Republican gubernatorial candidate). Despite considerable press attention, Chenoweth easily won reelection in 1998, a testament to the strength of a Republican incumbent in Idaho by that time.[52]

Aside from personalities, politics has also revolved around salient issues. Gambling and taxation are two recurring issues in Idaho politics at the state level. Idahoans' preoccupation with these concerns affected the second half of the twentieth century. Gambling is somewhat a north-south issue, since the south, where the Church of Jesus Christ of Latter-day Saints is predominant, opposed gambling, while northern Idahoans often took a different position. In March 1947, the legislature passed a bill that allowed for slot machines with a $500 licensing fee—half of which went to the county and half to the city. Some places located on the outskirts of metropolitan areas (Garden City outside of Boise, for example) used the law as a moneymaking tool. During the 1950s, the gambling issue was often a critical component of state legislative campaigns. Governor Len Jordan worked to outlaw slots in 1951. Democrats Allen Derr and Vernon Smith were interested in legalizing gambling. (Derr argued the precedent-setting women's rights case *Reed v. Reed* before the U.S. Supreme Court, and Smith defended the "Boys of Boise," a group of gay men who were persecuted in Boise in the 1950s and whose case became a cause célèbre in the gay community.)[53] Many argued that gambling would make tax increases unnecessary. So Derr ran for governor on a local option platform in 1958, as did Vernon Smith in 1962; Robert Smylie defeated them both. In 1988, Idaho voters approved a state lottery, and in recent years, much of the debate around gambling has focused on Indian tribes and gambling on reservations, the consequences of which are discussed by Rodney Frey and Robert McCarl in chapter 2 in this volume.[54]

FIGURE 4.2. Robert E. Smylie served as governor from 1955 to 1967. Here, reflecting an earlier age, he is typing a speech in the governor's office. Photo courtesy of Idaho State Historical Society, 77–163.46.

Taxes were easier. Simply put, Idahoans hate taxes; for Idahoans, taxes represent the intrusion of government into private lives, as well as a financial burden. Ironically, Republican Robert Smylie's tenure as governor represents a turning point for Idaho's tax policy. Under Smylie, Idaho experienced a huge increase in the cost of state government—from $74.7 million in 1953 to $140.1 million in 1961. According to the state constitution, the government's books must be balanced, so financing this increase was a challenge for lawmakers. The sales tax seemed to be a solution, although many Idahoans were strongly opposed, particularly in northern Idaho, where the lack of a sales tax allowed merchants to compete with neighboring Spokane,

Washington. In an example of the unpredictable nature of the Idaho electorate, Idahoans approved a 3 percent sales tax in 1966 by almost sixty-four
thousand votes, the same election that saw Don Samuelson defeat Cecil
Andrus. In 1967, the Idaho Supreme Court ruled that all property had to be
taxed equally at 20 percent of its appraised value and had to be reappraised
by 1982. In response, the Idaho Property Owners Association proposed the
One Percent Initiative—a cap of 1 percent of market value on property taxes
(similar to California's Proposition 13). It passed by about 60 percent in
1978 but was not put into effect because the Idaho Supreme Court ruled it
unconstitutional. The state legislature brokered a compromise to keep taxes
at 1978 levels, which led to dramatic cuts in state government growth.[55]

The Church of Jesus Christ of Latter-day Saints continues to be a major
force in Idaho politics, as Jill Gill shows well in chapter 5. In some ways,
Mormon dominance is a regional phenomenon. In 1920, five counties were
at least half Mormon in population—Bear Lake, Franklin, Oneida, Madison,
and Teton. By 1970, eleven of fourteen counties in eastern Idaho were half
Mormon, and in the other three, at least one-third of the people belonged
to the church. In 1982, when a statewide election determined whether to
eliminate the old anti-Mormon amendment from the state constitution,
100,113 Idahoans voted against allowing Mormons to vote in the state; a
majority of these voters resided in the north. When Ralph Harding defeated
Homer Budge for the Second District congressional seat in 1960, it was a
race between two Mormons, and the Democrat won. Harding demonstrates
that the church is not the monolith that many believe it to be; he even
criticized Mormon leader Ezra Taft Benson, a member of the Council of
the Twelve Apostles and secretary of agriculture under Eisenhower. However, Harding is certainly an anomaly, and while it is impossible to discuss
Idaho politics without examining the impact of the Church of Jesus Christ
of Latter-day Saints, for the most part, its influence is wielded within the
Republican Party.[56]

This impact has informed Idahoans' approach to the so-called family
values issues that have played a role in recent Idaho politics as well: abortion and same-sex marriage are examples. Idaho's abortion laws are among
the strictest in the United States. In November 2006, Idahoans passed a
gay marriage ban that is likewise one of the nation's most restrictive: "A

marriage between a man and a woman is the only domestic legal union that shall be valid or recognized in the state." It was approved by 67 percent of the voters.[57]

Idaho in the twenty-first century is very much one of the red states, a popular designation for states with a Republican majority. In 2008, of the 105 seats in the Idaho state legislature, Democrats held only 26. William "Bill" Sali, who represented Idaho's First District in the House of Representatives from 2006 to 2008, was certainly one of the most conservative Republicans in Congress, a far cry from the historically Democratic bent of that district. Idaho governor Butch Otter was an executive at Simplot Corporation—one of Idaho's preeminent corporate entities (he married Gay Simplot, J. R. Simplot's daughter, in 1964 and divorced her in 1992). A gifted politician and campaigner, he is an advocate for free enterprise and entrepreneurship. He lost a campaign for the governorship in 1978, but in 1986, he was elected Idaho's lieutenant governor, a position he held from 1987 to 2001. Otter represented the First District for three terms in Congress before his successful gubernatorial campaign in 2006.[58]

Republican complacency was shattered in August 2007, when *Roll Call* revealed that Idaho senator Larry Craig had been arrested for lewd contact in a men's bathroom in the Minneapolis airport and pleaded guilty to a lesser charge of disorderly conduct. Craig had been elected to the Idaho state senate in 1974 and to the First District congressional seat in 1980. He won the Senate seat formerly held by James McClure in 1990. Craig was a sharp critic of President Clinton during the Monica Lewinsky debacle, referring to the president as a "bad boy—a naughty boy." At the time of his arrest, he was a member of the Senate Appropriations Committee and held other influential committee assignments. Craig stepped down from those positions but served the remainder of his term amid considerable discussion in Idaho as to whether or not this was appropriate.[59]

Election year 2008 will forever elicit images of Barack Obama, the first African American president of the United States. In Idaho, Jim Risch won the Senate seat Larry Craig had held and continued the Republican Party's control of the position. Democrat Walt Minnick defeated Bill Sali in a close race—Minnick received 50.6 percent of the vote to Sali's 49.4 percent. While at first glance Minnick's election might appear to mark a shift in Idaho politics, in fact, as a part of the so-called Blue Dog Coalition of conservative Democrats, Minnick's votes in Congress reflect Idaho's conservative outlook. He was one of only eleven House Democrats to vote against President Obama's economic stimulus package and did not win reelection in 2010.[60] His successor, Raul Labrador, boasts close connections to the ultra-conservative Tea Party Movement.

* * *

Enigma and idiosyncrasy continue to define Idaho politics. Will Democrats ever regroup? Will Republicans continue their conservatism? In the meantime, the nature of Idaho politics is changing dramatically due to the pressures of growth and the increasing numbers of outsiders, topics covered in several of the chapters in this volume. Boiseans often note that in days past, a meeting of the chief executives of J. R. Simplot Company (J. R. Simplot may have been Idaho's wealthiest individual, was on the board of Idaho Power Company, and helped to establish Micron), Albertsons, Morrison-Knudsen, Boise Cascade, Idaho First National Bank, and Idaho Power (perhaps at the legendary Arid Club) could resolve issues or shape policies. Since the corporate seats of power are no longer in Idaho, this is no longer the case. As is true of other places, television means that the geographic challenges that once were a defining element in Idaho politics are not so daunting. The Church of Jesus Christ of Latter-day Saints remains a force in state politics. As astute political commentators have pointed out, "The percentage of Mormons in Idaho has grown (roughly doubling in the last half century), and LDS Church members are overwhelmingly Republican."[61] As the major controller of land in Idaho, the federal government will always have a voice in Idaho policy making. Idahoans remain stalwart in their independence, their attraction to quirky politicians, and their self-identity as westerners.

NOTES

1   Carlos Schwantes, *In Mountain Shadows: A History of Idaho* (Lincoln: University of Nebraska Press, 1991), 253.
2   Randy Stapilus, *Paradox Politics: People and Power in Idaho* (Boise: Ridenbaugh Press, 1988), 2.
3   Katherine G. Aiken, "Idaho," in Benjamin F. Shearer, ed., *The United States: The Story*

of Statehood in the Fifty United States (Westport, Conn.: Greenwood Press, 2004), 1:325–65.

4   Katherine Aiken, Kevin R. Marsh, and Laura Woodworth-Ney, *Idaho: The Heroic Journey* (Encino, Calif.: Cherbo Publishing Group, 2006), 21; Merle W. Wells, "The Creation of the Territory of Idaho," *Pacific Northwest Quarterly* 40 (April 1949): 106–13.

5   Robert C. Sims and Hope A. Benedict, eds., *Idaho's Governors: Historical Essays on Their Administrations* (Boise: Boise State University, 1992), 211–22; Ronald Limbaugh, *Rocky Mountain Carpetbaggers: Idaho's Territorial Governors, 1863–1890* (Moscow: University of Idaho Press, 1988).

6   Merle W. Wells, "Unexpected Allies, Fred T. DuBois and the Mormons in 1916," *Idaho Yesterdays* 35 (Fall 1991): 27–33.

7   Merle W. Wells, *Anti-Mormonism in Idaho, 1872–1892* (Provo, Utah: Brigham Young University Press, 1978).

8   Robert H. Blank, *Individualism in Idaho: The Territorial Foundations* (Pullman: Washington State University Press, 1988), 54–57.

9   Dennis C. Colson, *Idaho's Constitution: The Tie That Binds* (Moscow: University of Idaho Press, 1991), 105–6, 110–11, 148–59, 220–23.

10   Keith C. Petersen, *This Crested Hill: An Illustrated History of the University of Idaho* (Moscow: University of Idaho Press, 1987), 16–21.

11   Schwantes, *In Mountain Shadows,* 49–76; Aiken, Marsh, and Woodworth-Ney, *Idaho,* 21–26; Katherine G. Aiken, *Idaho's Bunker Hill: The Rise and Fall of a Great Mining Company, 1885–1981* (Norman: University of Oklahoma Press, 2005); J. Anthony Lukas, *Big Trouble: A Murder in a Small Town Sets Off a Struggle for the Soul of America* (New York: Simon and Schuster, 1997).

12   See Hugh T. Lovin, "The Carey Act in Idaho, 1895–1925: An Experiment in Free Enterprise Reclamation," *Pacific Northwest Quarterly* 78 (October 1987): 122–33; Leonard J. Arrington, *History of Idaho* (Moscow: University of Idaho Press, 1994), 1:476–85; Mark Fiege, *Irrigated Eden: The Making of an Agricultural Landscape in the American West* (Seattle: University of Washington Press, 1999).

13   James B. Weatherby and Randy Stapilus, *Governing Idaho: Politics, People and Power* (Caldwell, Idaho: Caxton Press, 2005), 38; William J. Gaboury, "From Statehouse to Bullpen: Idaho Populism and the Coeur d'Alene Troubles of the 1890s," *Pacific Northwest Quarterly* 58 (January 1967): 14–22.

14   Schwantes, *In Mountain Shadows,* 196–97; Hugh Lovin, "The Nonpartisan League and Progress Renascence in Idaho," *Idaho Yesterdays* 32 (Fall 1988): 2–15.

15   Claudius O. Johnson, *Borah of Idaho* (Seattle: University of Washington Press, 1936); and especially LeRoy Ashby, *The Spearless Leader: Senator Borah and the Progressive Movement of the 1920s* (Urbana: University of Illinois Press, 1972).

16   David L. Crowder, "Moses Alexander," in Sims and Benedict, *Idaho's Governors,* 78–87.

17   Schwantes, *In Mountain Shadows,* 184–89; Aiken, Marsh, and Woodworth-Ney, *Idaho,* 44–46; Robert Sims, "Idaho's Criminal Syndicalism Act: One State's Response to Radical Labor," *Labor History* 15 (1974): 511–29.

18   Weatherby and Stapilus, *Governing Idaho,* 40.

19   F. Ross Peterson, *Idaho: A Bicentennial History* (New York: W. W. Norton & Company, 1976), 143.

20 Leonard Arrington, *History of Idaho* (Moscow: University of Idaho Press, 1994), 2:33–35.

21 Schwantes, *In Mountain Shadows*, 201–10; Aiken, Marsh, and Woodworth-Ney, *Idaho*, 51–56.

22 Michael Malone, "C. Ben Ross," in Sims and Benedict, *Idaho Governors*, 116–17.

23 Leonard J. Arrington, "Idaho and the Great Depression," *Idaho Yesterdays* 13 (Summer 1969): 2–8.

24 Arrington, *History of Idaho*, 2:59–62.

25 David M. Kennedy, *Freedom from Fear: The American People in Depression and War, 1929–1945* (New York: Oxford University Press, 1999), 198.

26 Judith Austin, "The CCC in Idaho," *Idaho Yesterdays* 27 (Fall 1983): 13–17.

27 See Michael P. Malone, "C. Ben Ross," in Sims and Benedict, *Idaho's Governors*, 112–19; Michael Malone, *C. Ben Ross and the New Deal in Idaho* (Seattle: University of Washington Press, 1970); Schwantes, *In Mountain Shadows*, 210–18; Aiken, Marsh, and Woodworth-Ney, *Idaho*, 61–67; Karl Boyd Brooks, *Public Power, Private Dams: The Hells Canyon High Dam Controversy* (Seattle: University of Washington Press, 2006).

28 Robert C. Sims, "Chase Clark," in Sims and Benedict, *Idaho Governors*, 132–37; Willard Barnes, "Brazilla Clark," in ibid., 120–25.

29 Senator James McClure and Louise McClure, conversation with the author, Boise, January 17, 2008.

30 Troy Reeves, "Verda Barnes: Powerbroker," *Idaho Yesterdays* 47 (Spring–Summer 2006): 57.

31 See Boyd A. Martin, "The Sectional State," in Frank H. Jonas, ed., *Politics in the American West* (Salt Lake City: University of Utah Press, 1969), 196.

32 See LeRoy Ashby, *Fighting the Odds: The Life of Senator Frank Church* (Pullman: Washington State University Press, 1994), 50–52; Schwantes, *In Mountain Shadows*, 236–42; Carlos Schwantes, *The Pacific Northwest: An Interpretive History* (Lincoln: University of Nebraska Press, 1989), 36–61; Ross Peterson, *Prophet without Honor: Glen H. Taylor and the Fight for American Liberalism* (Lexington: University Press of Kentucky, 1974).

33 Stapilus, *Paradox Politics*, 85–87, 127–29, 131–33; Weatherby and Stapilus, *Governing Idaho*, 46–48.

34 Ashby, *Fighting the Odds*, 58–59; Stapilus, *Paradox Politics*, 91.

35 Joe Miller, "The Battle of Idaho: Welker vs. Church," *The Reporter* 15 (1 November 1956): 16–17.

36 Peterson, *Prophet without Honor*, 168–69.

37 Ashby, *Fighting the Odds*, 47–70; Schwantes, *In Mountain Shadow*, 236–42; Stapilus, *Paradox Politics*, 88–92.

38 Katherine G. Aiken, "Gender and the Political Career of Idaho's Gracie Pfost," *Journal of the West* 42 (Summer 2003): 44–51. For a discussion of Hells Canyon, see Brooks, *Public Power, Private Dams*; William Ashworth, *Hells Canyon: The Deepest Gorge on Earth* (New York: Hawthorne Books, 1977), 69–120; Susan M. Stacy, *Legacy of Light: A History of Idaho Power Company* (Boise: Idaho Power Company, 1991); Adam M. Sowards, *The Environmental Justice: William O. Douglas and American Conservation* (Corvallis: Oregon State University Press, 2009), 120–22.

39 Weatherby and Stapilus, *Governing Idaho*, 46.

40 See Robert Smylie, *Governor Smylie Remembers* (Moscow: University of Idaho Press, 1988).

41 Neil R. Peirce, *The Mountain States of America: People, Politics, and Power in the Eight Rocky Mountain States* (New York: Norton, 1972), 137–39.

42 J. M. Neil, *To the White Clouds: Idaho's Conservation Saga, 1900–1970* (Pullman: Washington State University Press, 2005).

43 Cecil Andrus and Joel Connelly, *Cecil Andrus: Politics Western Style* (Seattle: Sasquatch Books, 1998).

44 Katherine G. Aiken, "Don Samuelson," in Sims and Benedict, *Idaho's Governors*, 176–81; Stephan Shaw, "Cecil Andrus, 1971–1977," in Sims and Benedict, *Idaho's Governors*, 182–89; Stapilus, *Paradox Politics*, 122–24, 135–36, 140–44.

45 Kevin Marsh, *Drawing Lines in the Forest: Creating Wilderness Areas in the Pacific Northwest* (Seattle: University of Washington Press, 2007), 35, 72, 118, 137–38.

46 This paragraph and the following paragraph are derived from William L. Smallwood, *McClure of Idaho* (Caldwell, Idaho: Caxton Press, 2007), 240–315 passim; Stapilus, *Paradox Politics*, 171–86.

47 Individualism and independence have been part of Idahoans' self-concept throughout the state's history. Merrill D. Beal and Merle W. Wells, *History of Idaho* (New York: Lewis Historical, 1959), 1:440–54.

48 Katherine G. Aiken, "Senator Church and His Constituents," in Russell A. Miller, ed., *U.S. National Security, Intelligence and Democracy: From the Church Committee to the War on Terror* (London: Routledge, 2008), 76–95.

49 Ashby, *Fighting the Odds,* 561–606; Schwantes *The Pacific Northwest*, 377–79.

50 Ronald L. Hatzenbuehler and Bert W. Marley, "Why Church Lost: A Preliminary Analysis of the Church-Symms Election of 1980," *Pacific Historical Review* 56 (February 1987): 99–112; Ashby, *Fighting the Odds*, 531–60; Stapilus, *Paradox Politics*, 214–18.

51 Weatherby and Stapilus, *Governing Idaho*, 48, 175–76.

52 Betsy Z. Russell, "Women's Issues: Say What?" *Spokesman Review* (Spokane, Wash.), January 19, 1996.

53 John C. Gerassi, *The Boys of Boise: Furor, Vice and Folly in an American City* (Seattle: University of Washington Press, 2001).

54 Stapilus, *Paradox Politics*, 70–78.

55 Ibid., 258–61.

56 Ibid., 148–49.

57 Constitution of the State of Idaho, State of Idaho, http://legislature.idaho.gov/idstat/IC/Title003.htm (accessed July 12, 2010).

58 "About Governor C. L. 'Butch' Otter," http://gov.idaho.gov/our gov/otter_bio.htm.

59 Erika Bolstad, "Craig's Fall from GOP Favor Was Meteoric," *Idaho Statesman* September 9, 2007.

60 Claire Suddath, "A Brief History of Blue Dog Democrats," *Time*, July 28, 2009.

61 Weatherby and Stapilus, *Governing Idaho*, 55.

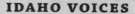

IDAHO VOICES
Political History

Charles Gossett, a Democrat who was active in politics in the 1930s and 1940s, describes Governor C. Ben Ross's sales tax and some Idahoans' opposition to taxes.

INTERVIEWER: Well, I guess the story was, and again, it may be inaccurate information, the story was that Ross through the sales tax was trying to raise money to match what the government was offering and that was the basis of the issue.

GOSSETT: Well, that could have been, that could have been. That could have been true. Yeah. But he didn't. He only had it for two years. And the people then, they voted it out, see, and it was out until it went in here, oh, let's see, when did it go in the last time? In the '60's, wasn't it? Late '50's or '60's. It was out for twenty years or more. About that.

INTERVIEWER: Yeah.

GOSSETT: So we got along without it for that length of time. We might have been better off if we had it, I don't know. But we didn't have it. It was a kind of a vicious thing. . . . I think probably Ben had a pretty good deal, but it didn't give the merchants any consideration, see. And they just fought it teeth and toenail. And when you'd go in and buy your groceries, you'd pay for your groceries and they'd say, "Now give me a penny for Benny." A penny for Benny. And that's the way they killed the sales tax, see. [Every time] you bought some groceries, "Give me a penny for Benny!" That was pretty vicious.

INTERVIEWER: You thought it was fairly effective?

GOSSETT: Oh, it was effective. You bet. Yeah, it was effective, "a penny for Benny." And they played it. The merchants haven't been, you know, they're not so pure in the state of Idaho. And that's one thing that if I got into this legislation, that I would say. You take it over the years, the merchants and the timber industry of the state of Idaho have never been . . . well, they've always had their hand out for something. Now you take the mining industry, they're very different, they've always been willing to pay their fair share of taxes. We have a, we have a tax on the net profit of mines in the state of Idaho. Well, you couldn't get a tax on the net profits of a merchant or a timber company in the state of Idaho to save your soul.

* * *

Bethine Clark Church, Senator Frank Church's wife, tells stories of campaigning in Idaho in the postwar years.

INTERVIEWER: What kind of trade, what kind of secrets did you have to campaign[ing] in Idaho, which itself is large enough to travel around?

CHURCH: Well, we used to be very careful with our schedule, and that is one way when I came in, even in the presidential race, I said, "You can't go [too] far. You can't flip back and forth from one end of the state to another." People in this state campaigning take awful risks in little planes in bad weather. You just can't get, can't get yourself scheduled so tightly that you don't have a little flexibility, if something good comes up that you should be present for. And you should try, if you possibly can, to do like we did that first time, make a swing, through a whole area. And cover it as well as you can, then swing through another. If you have to peel off and fly some time to cover something, try to make [it] so that you can do it at the beginning or the end of one of those swings, and then you don't, you don't flit away your time. So many people, people I have seen campaign in this state, they just seem to run restlessly from [one] thing to another. And it keeps them from getting a feel for the area they're in, and for the people. We used to go up to Green Creek for their big dinner; we used to go down to Montpelier. You know, it was good, but we hit each part of the state as a separate entity. I remember a funny story. Frank never used to tell jokes, Frank never used to tell jokes; what he used to do is tell real happenings, things that happened to him. And when we were on the campaign trail and he got bitten in the nose by a dog, down in Malad, and he said, he told the story about leaning over to the dog, and petting him, and it turned out it was a Republican dog, and it bit him, soon as it could see him. And we used to, he used to tell things like that, actual things that happened to him as he'd go through campaigning.

NOTE

Charles Gossett was interviewed by Diane Alters, November 27, 1973, Boise, ID, Idaho Bicentennial Commission/Idaho State Historical Society, transcript (OH0109) Oral History Center/Idaho State Historical Society, 12–13. Used with permission of Idaho State Historical Society.

Bethine Clark Church spoke with an unknown interviewer on September 4, 1989, Payette Lake, ID. Idaho Educational Public Broadcasting System/Idaho Public Television, transcript (OH1028) Oral History Center/Idaho State Historical Society, 10–11. Used with permission of Idaho Public Television.

5
The Power and the Glory
Idaho's Religious History

JILL K. GILL

IDAHO'S PUBLISHED RELIGIOUS HISTORY LOOKS MUCH LIKE the state itself: bottom-heavy and abundantly Mormon. Historians have concentrated their research on nineteenth- and early twentieth-century religious stories, many of which involve the Church of Jesus Christ of Latter-day Saints (LDS). The amount of research thins considerably for the period between 1920 and 1970, just as the middle of the state does in population. One finds small clusters of studies on particular sociopolitical religious topics between the 1970s and 2000, particularly those related to modern-day culture wars, just as one encounters scattered population centers when reaching Idaho's panhandle. For anyone interested in religious history, therefore, Idaho is still a frontier; it contains vast areas of uncharted terrain, especially with respect to twentieth-century religious subjects. This presents an opportunity for anyone seeking fresh research ideas but poses a challenge for those attempting to analyze the state's full religious past.

Compounding this problem, the religious novelties of Idaho's western and southern neighbors have drawn more scholarly attention, leading researchers either to ignore Idaho or to base generalizations about Idaho's religious character on that of its neighbors. For example, Oregon and Washington have become famous as the nation's official "none zone," the area with the fewest religious adherents. Only 36.7 percent of Washingtonians and Oregonians subscribe to an organized religion.[1] Of those, Catholics are the largest religious group, constituting about 11 percent of each state's population. Mormons account for a mere 3 percent, and Protestants for about 20 percent. By contrast, 50 percent of Idahoans claim a religious affiliation, a figure little changed from the 46.1 percent of Idaho's population who declared so in 1906. While the Mountain West contains the second-lowest number of religious adherents in the nation, Idaho cannot be included easily with the "none zone" in terms of religion. With the exception of its panhandle, which has rates of religious unaffiliation that rival Washington's and Oregon's, it makes an awkward fit.[2]

Idaho's southern neighbor, Utah, also has drawn more interest than Idaho due to its unique Mormon hegemony that has functioned almost like a state religion. Fully 76.5 percent of Utahans are religious adherents, 86.8 percent of which are Mormons; Mormons compose 66.4 percent of Utah's population. Conversely, Idaho's Latter-day Saints make up 48.1 percent of its religious adherents and 24.1 percent of its total population. While the Saints are by far Idaho's largest religious group, they do not wield the kind of statewide dominance as in Utah. Only Idaho's most southeastern counties approximate Utah's religious makeup; as one travels west and then north, the numbers of Saints decrease, while those of Protestants, Catholics, and the unaffiliated grow. Catholics are the second-largest religious group in Idaho, encompassing about 20 percent of the state's religious adherents and 10 percent of its population. Together, various Protestant groups represent 31.5 percent of Idaho's religious adherents, or 15.8 percent of the population. Therefore, throughout Idaho's history, the Saints have contended with non-Mormons numerous enough to have made turf, economic, and political struggles quite heated.[3]

Despite the gaps in published works on Idaho's religious history, enough exists to draw a few thematic conclusions about the nature of religion's influence on the state. First, as in most of the West, nearly all religious groups played critical roles in transforming Idaho from what white settlers deemed "frontier" into permanent communities. In addition to dotting the countryside with missions, churches, and temples, religious organizations built much of the state's infrastructure of hospitals and schools, while serving as centers of social activities, networking, and critical services. They aimed to help civilize, settle, and root western people.

Second, Idaho's unique religious makeup and sectional distinctions exacerbated explosive economic and political conflicts. Some used religious differences as tools for dividing and conquering rivals. With the exception

TABLE 1. Approximate percentages of religious adherents in sample counties from three sections of Idaho, 1990

	Bannock County (southeastern Idaho)		Ada County (southwestern Idaho)		Kootenai County (northern Idaho)	
	Percentage of county's population	Percentage of county's religious adherents	Percentage of county's population	Percentage of county's religious adherents	Percentage of county's population	Percentage of county's religious adherents
Catholics	5.7	8.9	7.6	17.7	6.7	20.8
Mormons	48.2	75.9	15.8	36.9	5.1	15.9
Mainline Protestants	4.5	7.1	8.8	21.0	6.5	25.2
Non-mainline Protestants	5.0	7.8	10.1	23.6	12.2	38.0
Other	0.2	0.3	0.3	0.8	0.0	0.0
Unaffiliated	36.5	—	57.2	—	68.0	—

Source: Approximated from figures reported in Martin Bradley, Norman Green Jr., Dale Jones, Mac Lynn, and Lou McNeil, *Churches and Church Membership in the United States, 1990* (Atlanta: Glenmary Research Center, 1992).

of a few pacifist sects and Jehovah's Witnesses, rarely did Idaho's religious groups treat religion as a purely "transcendent," private, spiritual matter. Rather, Idahoans thrust it into the public square repeatedly to serve worldly purposes. From the 1970s onward, when the West became central to religiously driven political battles over social issues, Idaho's fast-growing conservative religious organizations propelled it into the thick of them and transformed the state into one of the most Republican in the nation.

Finally, religion in Idaho has operated as both a cultural divider and a uniter, helping to determine which of its citizens should be treated as part of an in-group or an out-group by including and excluding according to religious determinations. While this is largely true in much of the nation, Idaho's reputation as a sanctuary for religious dissenters and experimenters, combined with its mix of religious libertarians and activists, has added some unique elements to its story.

RELIGION AS "CIVILIZER," "SETTLER," AND "SERVER"

Protestants and Catholics saw Idaho's nineteenth-century frontier as part of a vast western mission field. Offices back east sent missionaries, clergy, and funds for saving the heathen (both Native American and Euro-American), while expanding their own influence. Mormons considered Idaho an extension of their Utah homeland and believed its Native populations (called "Lamanites") to have descended from one of the lost tribes of Israel. All three groups built missions to "civilize" and "Christianize" Indians, requiring them to convert and adopt white cultural ways. As demonstrated also by Rodney Frey and Robert McCarl in chapter 2 in this book, Indians proved open to new faith ideas but resistant to full-scale cultural change, blending Native and Christian religious ideas in ways suited to their own preservation.

Catholics arrived in the 1840s, answering what they perceived to be an invitation from the Coeur d'Alenes to teach them Catholic ways of worship. Father Pierre-Jean DeSmet established the Jesuits' rather successful Northwest mission network. With Indian labor, he built the Mission of the Sacred Heart in 1850, now known as the Cataldo Mission. Father Joseph Cataldo succeeded DeSmet, expanding the system with several schools and Indian-run farms. Funded largely by a wealthy Pennsylvania benefactor, Katherine Drexel, he established orphanages, hospitals, and a novitiate in which to train clergy. The mission became a lively social and religious center for residents and travelers. Coeur d'Alenes worshipped there for more than twenty years until they were moved to a reservation in 1877. Their adoption of Christianity and farming had failed to satisfy whites hungry for their lands.[4] The mission remains the oldest building in Idaho. It became a state park in 1975 when the Catholic Church simultaneously deeded the mission to the Coeur d'Alenes. The tribe celebrates the Catholic Feast of the Assumption there every year.[5]

The Presbyterians entered Idaho in 1836 when Henry and Eliza Spalding began missionizing the Nez Perce. Resistant Indians noticed that those who converted received preferential status and jobs, although their lands were diminished by whites regardless of their willingness to Christianize and assimilate. Sue McBeth took charge of the mission after Spalding's death in 1874, creating Indian Presbyterian churches, training many Native clergy, and beginning a camp meeting ceremony that Nez Perce practiced annually until the 1930s. Although women technically were not "clergy," McBeth served as such in all but name. The Indian Presbyterian Church in Kamiah,

FIGURE 5.1. Missionaries brought Christianity to Idaho Native Americans, who made selective use of the imported religion. The Indian Presbyterian Church in Kamiah, Idaho, was completed in 1874 and remains the oldest Protestant church in the state. Photo courtesy of Idaho State Historical Society, 63-221.90d.

Idaho, retained the Nez Perce language and key aspects of tribal culture.[6] Ironically, it even became a medium for preserving and passing these on.

Latter-day Saints began missionizing among the Shoshones and Bannocks in 1855 under Brigham Young's direction. With easy requirements for baptism, they ushered several tribal members into their faith, although many later fell away. Young promoted intermarriage with the "Lamanites," but few Saints did so. Like their Protestant and Catholic counterparts, the Saints required cultural assimilation and had few qualms about taking Indian land when they wished to expand. In 1858, Bannocks attacked the mission, killed several LDS missionaries, and stole their cattle. The Saints then excommunicated their former converts and abandoned the mission. A powerful Bannock prophet, who warned against white expansion, likely influenced the attack.[7]

The Bannocks used Native syncretic faiths to maintain key aspects of their culture amid white pressure and to forge a pan-Indian identity among other oppressed tribes in the Great Basin. In 1867, Shoshones and Bannocks were pushed onto the Fort Hall reservation in southeastern Idaho. They drew on spiritual traditions to resist cultural destruction, maintain hope, and develop intertribal ties. The Numu (northern Paiute) prophet Wodziwob inspired a form of the Ghost Dance faith among Bannocks in the 1870s, urging Indian unity and religious power as a means of restoring Native strength; the Paiute prophet Wovoka developed these basic beliefs further in 1889. The Bannocks became perhaps the most influential proselytizers of the Ghost Dance. Indians from the Great Basin and Great Plains traveled to Fort Hall to learn its principles and create bonds, both before and after the Seventh Cavalry slaughtered ghost-dancing Sioux at Wounded Knee, South Dakota, in 1890. The Shoshones and Bannocks still practice it.[8]

White missionaries received warmer receptions from the white miners, farmers, and ranchers, although they, too, resisted the lifestyle changes, such as temperance, that the clergy urged. Rather, frontier people welcomed what clergy and church construction brought by way of social interaction, charity, education, and a sense of town permanence. Whether one was religious or not, rising steeples signified maturity, and church edifices provided places where people could meet and network. Religious organizations also often tapped eastern as well as local sources for donations for raising schools, colleges, and hospitals. These helped prevent frontier towns from going bust after they boomed. And when disasters devastated areas, people trusted clergy to distribute charitable gifts.[9]

Miners in northern and southwestern Idaho, especially the Irish and Italians, embraced the Catholic priests who built some of their first churches. In 1863, they constructed St. Joseph's in bustling Idaho City, the earliest in the basin. Priests were well liked, for unlike Protestant clergy, they raised money for church construction through dances, lotteries, and music, all popular among the gruffest rowdies. Miners gave generously whether Catholic or not. Italian miners welcomed St. Anthony's chapel in Priest River in 1915. Priests also followed Basque shepherds into the Jordan Valley, building St. Bernard's in 1917 and, later, the Church of the Good Shepherd in Boise when Basques urbanized.[10] The Catholic Church selected Boise as a diocese headquarters in 1893, allowing its first bishop to build St. John's Cathedral. The city enjoyed the distinction. Such structures symbolized permanence and status, which helped fuel economic growth.

Denominations raced to establish a prominent presence in the state's young capital city. First United Methodist Church rose in 1872; it would morph after World War II into Boise's grand Cathedral of the Rockies. The stately First Presbyterian Church appeared blocks away in 1878. The Episcopal Church purposefully built its cathedral, Saint Michael's, behind Idaho's capitol building in 1902 in order to exercise influence with the powerful. Christian groups also competed to build schools and colleges, not only to educate their young, but to indoctrinate others and spread their worldviews. Catholics constructed parochial schools wherever they went; even during the 1960s, when a chronic shortage of priests and nuns forced several closures, Bishop Sylvester Trienen built Boise's Bishop Kelly High School, which has been a state star ever since.[11] In part to rival the Catholics, the dynamic pioneer Bishop Daniel Tuttle urged Episcopalians to create academies, many of which drew the children of Idaho's most distinguished citizens. St. Margaret's, an academy for girls (1892), developed such a high academic reputation that the finest eastern women's colleges courted its graduates. It became Boise Junior College in 1932 and eventually Boise State University.[12] The Catholics and Episcopalians established premier hospitals, too, with Catholics constructing St. Alphonsus (1894) and the Episcopalians St. Luke's (1902) medical centers in Boise. Catholics also built hospitals in Cottonwood, Jerome, Lewiston, and Nampa.

Presbyterian missionary Sheldon Jackson was one of the West's most prolific church planters, riding the rails using free passes, creating congregations out of small family clusters, and ordering prefabricated church buildings from back East paid for with eastern money. Presbyterians also erected many schools, including the College of Idaho in 1891; Caldwell Reverend William Judson Boone ran it for years, teaching many of the classes and transforming himself into an expert on local botany.[13] Nearby, the Nazarenes raised an elementary school in 1913 that eventually became Northwest Nazarene University.

In the 1870s and 1880s Presbyterians also targeted Mormon areas, building schools where the Saints had few, seeking to influence their children. Rigby, Franklin, Malad City, Preston, Montpelier, Paris, and Samaria each boasted at least one. Mormons resented the invasion. Children used the term *Presbyterian* when they wanted to offend someone. Nevertheless, the schools' high quality drew students, and the Presbyterians' savvy use of female teachers engendered less resistance. The Presbyterians helped "Americanize" LDS youth, introducing them to national rituals and holidays not yet practiced in Deseret. When the Presbyterians' presence inspired the Saints to build their own school and college system in the 1880s, Protestants reduced their southeastern effort.[14]

The Mormons built academies, stakes, tabernacles, and temples as rapidly as their growth allowed. In 1888, they celebrated the first classes at Bannock Stake Academy, which later became Ricks College and is now Brigham Young University–Idaho. They completed the Rexburg Tabernacle, which served as a religious and social center for the area, in 1911. LDS Hospital opened its doors in Idaho Falls in 1923, and a temple followed in 1945. The Boise temple was completed in 1984 and the Twin Falls temple in 2008.[15]

Religious groups also founded towns. A group of pacifist evangelical Quakers, who, unlike Pennsylvania's traditionalists, used music and a paid clergy, established Greenleaf, Idaho, and erected the stone Friends Church around 1906. They also built a school, Greenleaf Friends Academy, where they could teach their worldview. In a move that stunned eastern Quakers, Greenleaf passed a law in 2007 advocating gun ownership. The pastor of Friends Church, who owned several shotguns, explained that gun ownership was a western norm, even for Quakers.[16]

Religious organizations not only enhanced town development but also provided oppressed groups with critical sources of strength, hope, connection, assistance, and community. For example, religious work often became the only socially approved means of public leadership for women. When a church, hospital, or orphanage needed building, women administered the local fund-raisers. They created Ladies Aid or "Mite" Societies and hosted bazaars and other "socials" that brought in contributions. Dynamic women's societies within nearly every religious body gave women the opportunity to perform organizational functions that not only provided critical community services but also fed their own desires for greater access to public leadership.[17]

Jews came to Idaho in the late nineteenth century, often as merchants and shopkeepers to supply miners and farmers. Small Jewish communities emerged in Lewiston, Idaho City, Boise, and Pocatello. Jews created many of the most used and recognized stores in Idaho and helped other Jews get into business. Leo Falk of Boise not only managed a chain of Falk stores but also constructed the Owyhee Plaza Hotel and Egyptian Theater, which became city landmarks. Moses Alexander, a German Jew, launched a successful line of clothing stores from Weiser to Twin Falls before becoming Boise's mayor (1897–99, 1901–3) and the nation's first Jewish governor (1914–18). Wherever Idaho's Jews lived, they became engaged civic leaders.

They also worked hard to create Jewish congregations and preserve their distinctive rituals amid a largely Christian population. Alexander and Falk helped build Temple Beth Israel in 1896, the oldest continually used synagogue west of the Mississippi River. The congregation merged with the more traditional Adath Israel founded in 1912 by eastern European Jews, to form Ahavath Beth Israel in the mid-1980s. Jews in southeastern Idaho built Pocatello's Temple Emanuel in 1946. (They joked that "Mormon country" was the only place in the world where a Jew could be considered a "gentile.") All operated with lay leadership until 1994, when Ahavath Beth Israel hired the state's first full-time rabbi. Jewish congregations became vital educational, social, and spiritual centers. Idaho's Jews encountered little overt anti-Semitism; sheer ignorance was more common. They did notice, however, that elite social clubs like the Elks failed to extend membership invitations to them, which was atypical for the West.[18]

As Laurie Mercier also explores in chapter 7 in this book, Idaho's tiny black population eagerly sought to build black churches to help members fortify their spirits and create support networks in a state where overt systemic racism reigned. Pocatello's African Americans built the Colored Baptist Church and an African Methodist Episcopal Church (AME) in 1908. African Americans constructed Boise's St. Paul's Baptist church in 1921; the original building now serves as Idaho's Black History Museum. Later Baptist, AME, and Church of God in Christ congregations emerged, including one in Idaho Falls.[19]

As Boise's population grew more diverse, especially after the city became a refugee relocation center in the mid-1970s, so did its religious makeup. Hindus built Krishna Temple in 1999, and Muslims completed the Boise Mosque and Islamic Center in 2002. Many of its first attendees had emigrated from Bosnia.

FIGURE 5.2. Jews arrived in Idaho in the late nineteenth century and built a thriving community. Temple Beth Israel in Boise, Idaho, is the oldest continuously used synagogue in the American West. Photo courtesy of Idaho State Historical Society, 71-189.19.

Idaho's ethnic churches regularly offered entertaining programs and festivals to educate their neighbors about their traditions. Boise's black congregations have shared their music with the broader community through their annual Gospel Workshop. Boise's Greek Orthodox Church has hosted a yearly Greek Food Festival and offered tours of its sanctuary; Ahavath Beth Israel likewise has sponsored annual Deli Days for more than two decades, including guided tours of the synagogue and Jewish music by groups like the Moody Jews.

Even Idaho's more unconventional religions helped build towns and communities. Frank Bruce Robinson founded Psychiana in Moscow in 1929, perhaps the most successful mail-order religion in the world. Like many "new thought" religions, it advocated positive thinking, rationalism, and inner spirituality as a path to prosperity. Anyone who sent in twenty dollars received twenty lessons, with satisfaction or a refund guaranteed. The business boomed, employing more people than any other private company in Latah County. It opened invaluable jobs to women during the tight Depression years. The volumes of mail even earned tiny Moscow first-class post office status. Although local Christians held Robinson at arm's length, he made considerable donations to town charities and gave the county a park. He even helped found the area's leading newspaper, the *Daily Idahonian*. Robinson's death in 1948 hastened Psychiana's demise, and it ceased operations in 1953. But the town benefited for years, and Psychiana pioneered new ways for religious organizations to use mass mailing and media.[20]

Religious organizations not only founded churches, temples, schools, and hospitals; they supplied key services to communities. Groups needing space, from Alcoholics Anonymous to the Boy Scouts, found church buildings open to them. Religious groups have sponsored educational lectures, events, day care centers, and summer camps. They have also functioned regularly as polling centers at election time and generated extensive local charity, relief, and social justice programs.

For example, during World War II, the Mennonites largely funded Camp Downey, in Downey, Idaho, for religious conscientious objectors who performed essential farm, irrigation, repair, and firefighting work in southeastern Idaho in lieu of military service.[21] When the war and the nation's bracero program drew Mexican workers into Idaho's shabby farm labor camps, as discussed in detail by Errol D. Jones in chapter 8 of this volume, the Southern Idaho Migrant Ministry (which would become one of the nation's largest and most successful migrant ministry programs) founded the Idaho Council of Churches (ICC). Launched in 1956, before Cesar Chavez helped expose the farmworkers' plight to the world, this program provided education, health services, food and nutrition assistance, sewing groups, films, citizenship classes, job training and placement help, teen recreation centers, child care, citizenship and language classes, and community action initiatives. In a hostile racist environment, churches became critical sites for consciousness-raising among whites on behalf of farmworkers. In the 1960s, the ICC tackled the social justice issues of poverty, labor rights, and empowerment of Latino cultures. Federal budget cuts in the late 1960s ended its run, but not before it had established a foundation for future migrant worker organizations.[22] A prominent social justice ministry sprang from St. Paul's black Baptist church, too. The Treasure Valley Council for Church and Social Action Community Ministries Center, founded by Reverends H. Lincoln and Mamie Oliver, has provided poor valley residents with food, clothing, counseling, and medical assistance since 1980.[23] Continuing in that tradition, in 2005, an interfaith coalition of mainline Protestant, Jewish, Unitarian Universalist, Catholic, Mormon, and Hindu congregations opened their sanctuaries and pooled their resources to provide sleeping space and dinners for Boise's homeless population through the harshest winter months. Taking the name Sanctuary, the coalition opened a permanent shelter in 2007 that accommodates all people without religious proselytizing and regardless of faith tradition, gender, or family situation.

Throughout Idaho's history, religious communities have enhanced the state's growth, quality of life, and citizen care, contributing significantly to its infrastructure, development, health, culture, educational base, and social services.

RELIGION'S ROLE IN ECONOMIC AND POLITICAL BATTLES

Many religious organizations prefer to see themselves as being in but not of the world. They aim to emphasize transcendent divine truths while remaining uncorrupted by the society that they seek to transform spiritually. With rare exceptions, however, Idaho's religious communities have thrust their faiths into the muck and mire of economic and political battles, sometimes allowing religion to become a tool for economic and political gain and, in more recent years, using religion to drive political realignments and issues. Despite a few significant exceptions, religion in Idaho has been a rather worldly thing.[24]

The battle over polygamy presents a clear early example. It inspired non-Mormons (called "gentiles" by Latter-day Saints) to strip LDS citizens of key political rights in 1884 and then entrench these discriminatory policies in Idaho's constitution (1890), as Katherine G. Aiken shows in chapter 4 in this volume. Painted as a moral struggle to preserve Christian monogamous marriage, religious arguments justified actions designed, at base, to swing political and economic advantages toward gentiles in general and the Republican Party in particular.

Idaho's non-Mormons resented the Saints for reasons other than their religious beliefs. When Mormons moved into southeastern Idaho, they practiced a type of economic communalism called the United Order. Seeking self-sufficiency, they discouraged interactions with gentiles and kept Saint resources securely within the tribe. Saint social networks and activities also cut out non-Mormons. These practices helped build strong LDS communities, which made sense given past persecution in the Midwest, but left neighbors of other faiths resentful and economically vulnerable. To those on the outside, LDS insularity violated frontier values of economic individualism and hospitality. The Saints also practiced near-unanimous voting, meaning that they bloc-voted for parties and candidates, giving them huge power in swaying elections.

Mormons came to Idaho as Democrats, for the national Republicans threatened to end the "twin evils" of slavery and bigamy. Since many of Idaho's earliest non-Mormon settlers were Democrats from Confederate states, Saints and gentile Democrats ensured that the Democratic Party wielded local power from the mid-1860s to the early 1880s. Idaho's Republicans sought to break the Democrats' electoral advantage by driving a wedge between Mormons and non-LDS members. The polygamy issue proved an effective tool for splitting the party. As Republicans in the east passed a national anti-polygamy statute in 1882, which permitted the arrest and imprisonment of active polygamists and denial of their voting rights, and later added limitations on LDS church economic holdings, Idaho's Republicans whipped up a virulent moral crusade against polygamy that drew Protestant and Catholic Democrats to their side. Together they elected officials who would stop the Mormon "menace." Republican anti-Mormons won statewide elections in 1884 and then persuaded anti-Mormon Democrats to pass a "test oath" law that banned anyone belonging to a group that endorsed polygamy from voting, running for office, or serving on a jury.[25] They justified it by arguing that Mormons put loyalty to church beliefs above federal and state laws when it came to prosecuting polygamy and that therefore they should lose certain legal and political rights in order to ensure enforcement of the law. The test oath knocked LDS leaders from elected seats in southeastern Idaho, where they constituted a majority, allowing non-Mormons to make economic laws advantageous to themselves, and it eliminated the possibility that the LDS voting bloc could swing elections to the Democrats.

Idahoans then ushered test oath bans into their constitution. Unlike Midwestern LDS-Protestant battles during the 1830s and 1840s, which ended in violence, Idaho's took place in the courts and legislature. While still questionable on legal and ethical bases, the relative nonviolence of the conflict is significant given the earlier history.

When the LDS church ended polygamy in 1890, it did so in negotiation with national Republicans who demanded the concession in exchange for Utah's statehood. Idaho's non-Mormons did not remove the test oath immediately after polygamy ended, for polygamy had never been the Republicans' primary concern. Idaho Republicans let local LDS officials know that if the Saints would switch their votes to the Republican Party or, at minimum, stop bloc-voting Democrat, they would end test oath restrictions. Given that LDS officials felt they had been abandoned by Idaho's non-Mormon Democrats during the test oath fracas, and given that the Republicans had captured power, Idaho's southeastern Saints swung toward the Republicans. The Bear Lake County newspaper, which had been Democratic, publicly switched its allegiance to the Republicans, signaling this change. The state Republican Party then removed the test oath in 1892, and Idaho Republicans warmly welcomed their former LDS adversaries into their new party home. The test oath provisions remained, even if unenforced, in the state constitution until 1982, when Idahoans voted to delete them. Still, one hundred thousand citizens voted against the change (34 percent of the state's voting population), illustrating how strained LDS–non-Mormon relations remained one hundred years later.[26]

The Saints also used religion to their economic advantage. In an effort to help restore economic solvency and turn a profit after the polygamy fight and 1893 depression, the church entered the sugar beet industry. It invested heavily in the creation of the Utah and, later, in 1903, Idaho Sugar Companies, owned significant shares of their stock, and placed church leaders in top management. At one point, church president Joseph F. Smith also served as president of Utah Sugar. The same officers ran both the Utah and Idaho Sugar Companies. In the dog-eat-dog world of Gilded Age industrialism, in which unfair monopolistic business practices became the norm, the Utah and Idaho Sugar Companies employed those same expedient profit-making strategies. Idaho Sugar crushed competitors in southern Idaho by imploring LDS members to grow beets for, invest in, assist, buy, or do business with only Idaho Sugar, even if this went against their personal best interests. A few Saints who failed to do the company's bidding received church sanctions. Idaho Sugar, which merged with Utah Sugar, had a monopoly in Idaho, with factories in Fremont County, Lincoln, Blackfoot, Idaho Falls, Nampa, and Payette, bringing large profits to the church and its top leaders, who owned considerable stock. Its business practices provoked several federal investigations in the early twentieth century. Years later, the church began obliging its top leaders to terminate their business entanglements.[27]

Business profit mingled with religious values in other instances, too, sometimes trumping them when politicized. For example, in the 1890s, Boiseans praised women's persuasive efforts to make the city more "moral," but when the Women's Christian Temperance Union (WCTU) sought to move from persuasion to legislation placing prohibitions on alcohol, it ran into community resistance. At that time, Boise's saloons outnumbered all other businesses. Many Boiseans, including several city leaders, owed their salaries to the liquor trade. Boise's WCTU chapter thus quieted down somewhat, enraging female reformers from other parts of the state. Idaho eventually passed prohibition in 1916, when it was tied to a patriotic crusade and drew in coalitions of other groups.[28]

Idaho's Protestant and LDS churches generally supported women's prohibition work. But Protestants were more reluctant than the Saints about endorsing another women's issue: suffrage. Protestants feared that the measure would advantage the Saints. Back then, many non-Mormon voting-age males were single, whereas most LDS males had wives. Nevertheless, Idaho's women received the right to vote with bipartisan support in 1896, with more Saints than Protestants in favor.[29]

Economic concerns also fueled the moral panic known as the "Boys of Boise." In 1955, Boise advertised itself as a quiet, clean, Christian community, with little crime, strong businesses, and seventy thriving churches—a place where families could escape the degenerate urban areas of Seattle or San Francisco. This image, projected in *Time* magazine, promoted business, settlement, and tourism. But a story about illegal homosexual sex, printed by the *Idaho Statesman* under the headline "Crush the Monster," threatened all of this. The newspaper turned the incident into a moral panic that gained nationwide attention and falsely painted the town's young boys as targets of a huge predatory homosexual ring—this during the McCarthy era when the government deemed homosexuals national security risks and when conformity, domesticity, and purging communists was in vogue. Hoping to save the town's image, church and city leaders led an overzealous campaign to imprison suspects and drive all gay "perverts" from the state. Boise's ministerial association contributed to this atmosphere, praising the arrests and helping pay for a special investigator to cleanse the city. The panic proved to be out of proportion to reality, giving Boise a bigger public black eye than the actual crime likely would have.[30]

In the 1950s, no solid correlations existed between conservative Protestantism (including LDS) and the Republican Party in the Intermountain West. However, political scientists argue that, from the early 1970s into the early twenty-first century, not only did religious conservatives shift firmly into the Republican Party but a large in-migration of evangelical Protestants during those years drove a political realignment in the state, making it one of the nation's most conservative. As evangelical Christians joined forces with the Republican Party, they also became more politically activist, pushing social legislation in line with their moral values. Idaho's rising numbers of religious conservatives have led it to the forefront of America's culture wars. The main counterforce to this trend has been the state's growing Latino population (whether Catholic or Protestant), which has voted Democratic.[31] Mormon scholar Kathleen Flake described the LDS church as "the most single-party religious institution in the nation," with 55 percent firmly Republican. Collectively, evangelical Protestants also vote Republican about 55 percent of the time. Idaho's traditionally high numbers of independent voters (at times, a third of its population) means that the state has a relatively small number of dedicated Democrats. Given that 78 percent of religious people generally register to vote, compared to 67 percent of the unaffiliated, and given the growing numbers of religious conservatives, those churchgoers have turned Idaho elections.[32]

The Saints' percentage of adherents has held fairly steady in Idaho over the past decades, but conservative evangelical Protestants have boomed while their more liberal mainline brethren have declined. For example, in 1980, mainline Christians composed a slight majority of Idaho's Protes-

TABLE 2. Approximate percentages of Idaho religious adherents who are mainline Protestants or non-mainline conservative Protestants

	1980	1990	2000
Mainline	17.3	11.7	9
Conservative	16.3	18	20

Source: Kathleen Flake, "The Mormon Corridor: Utah and Idaho," in Shipps and Silks, Mountain West, 96–97; and Jan Shipps, "Conclusion: Sacred Landscapes in Transition," in ibid., 146–47. Calculating for the entire Mountain West region, Shipps states that 42 percent of white Catholics vote Republican, and 20 percent vote Democratic; about 15 percent of white evangelicals and 17 percent of Mormons vote Democratic.

tants; by 2000, fully 64.4 percent of all Idaho Protestants were non-mainline conservatives.

In 1952, the Southern Baptist Convention declared the American West its new home mission field, seeking to stretch out of the South. Southern evangelicals spread across the Sun Belt states, especially into southern California (already a bastion for Pentecostals), and, beginning in the 1970s, many religious conservatives emigrated from there to Idaho, producing what some have called the "southernization" of the state. Southern Baptists have more than tripled their numbers in Idaho since 1971.[33] Rising conservative Protestant percentages and a steady dominance of Saints, all strongly affiliating with the Republican Party, have colored Idaho politics.

The Equal Rights Amendment (ERA) presents a clear example. In 1972, Idaho quickly ratified the ERA along with a cluster of other states. As the movement gained steam, conservative evangelicals organized against it. Seeing the proposed constitutional amendment as an attack on traditionally defined gender roles and the family, the LDS church declared its formal opposition in 1976, pouring sizable church resources into national "Stop ERA" efforts and insinuating that ERA support connoted heresy. It even excommunicated Mormon ERA advocate Sonia Johnson. LDS officials declared the ERA a "moral" rather than a "political" issue, compelling church involvement. (By contrast, both the LDS church and evangelical Protestants had deemed the earlier civil rights movement for racial equality merely a "political" issue and thus urged churches officially to stay out.) By 1975, only Idaho's Catholics overwhelmingly supported the ERA, with 74 percent approval. In February 1977, with newly mobilized evangelical voters and LDS opposition, Idaho rescinded its earlier ERA ratification. This also shows that when the LDS church wanted to flex its political muscles in Idaho, it could.[34]

It did so again in 1990 to help pass state legislation outlawing abortions in all but the rarest cases. At that time, Saints made up one-third of the state legislature, giving them greater legislative representation than their 26.6 percent of the population. LDS and several conservative Protestant legislators strongly supported the bill (Catholics split evenly over it, and a majority of Protestants opposed it), securing its passage. Democratic governor Cecil Andrus vetoed the measure, so it never became law,[35] but conservative religious power had made its statement.

The 1994 battle over Proposition 1 illustrates both the assertiveness and the strength of Idaho's Christian evangelicals, as well as the lingering tensions between Protestants and Saints. Pushed onto the ballot by the evangelical Idaho Citizens Alliance, the proposition aimed to deny Idaho's homosexuals civil rights protections, prevent any positive representations of homosexuality in public schools, and force public libraries to block children under eighteen from accessing materials on homosexuality. The divisive campaign engulfed the state. Many conservative church reader-boards urged "yes" votes, while several of the state's liberal churches publicly opposed the measure. In the end, the proposition failed by a mere 2,800 votes out of more than 400,000 cast. On top of the fact that the measure's opponents waged a savvy campaign that painted it as "Too Much Government, Not Enough Idaho," Mormon voters in the southeastern counties helped kill it. They had learned that Proposition 1's evangelical ICA proponents had also authored noted anti-Mormon media, leading many to vote "no." Celebrating the narrow defeat, "No on One" workers sang a round of the Christian spiritual "Kumbaya" at their election night rally.[36] In 2006, however, evangelical activists turned the tables when their new group, the Idaho Values Alliance (IVA), succeeded in its three-year effort to amend Idaho's constitution to ban any state recognition of relationships (including civil unions) other than marriage between a man and a woman. This time they had secured LDS support.

During that same 2006 election, the IVA lost another tenaciously waged "moral" battle to have a Ten Commandments monument returned from private land owned by St. Michael's Episcopal Church to public property in Boise's Julia Davis Park. It had stood obscurely in a corner of that park from 1965 to 2004, when the city moved it to avoid a lawsuit by Reverend Fred Phelps, of Kansas, who lobbied to place his own religious monument (bashing homosexuals) in the same park. Most Boiseans had never noticed the monument and were surprised to learn that it existed. The move infuriated area evangelicals who deemed it an assault on God. Boise's Interfaith Alliance disagreed and supported the city's decision. Boiseans soundly defeated the IVA measure, affirming the monument's relocation to what actually proved to be a more visible spot.

In recent years, Idaho's evangelical community has sponsored most of the culture war measures that have reached the ballot. Since Idaho's Saints have often united to wield enough power to make a decisive political difference, winning has usually rested on evangelicals gaining LDS support, although evangelicals historically have dubbed the Saints a dangerous cult. Both groups in concert have empowered Idaho's Republican Party, which expanded its legislative monopoly in the lower house from 76 to 87 percent, and in the upper house from 62 to 91 percent between 1986 and 2000.[37]

RELIGION AS A CULTURAL DIVIDER AND UNITER

Religion has drawn Idahoans into debates over the nature and identity of their communities, determining who might be considered mainstream and who marginal. It has sometimes divided and at other times united people depending on whether the religion stressed broad connective spiritual themes or emphasized the need to remain "pure," "clean," and "separate" from the "un-chosen." The following occurrences forced Idahoans to publicly address questions of religious representation, diversity, belonging, and image.

The Table Rock cross controversy highlighted Idaho's assumed homogeneity within perhaps its most diverse city. In 1956, the secular Junior Chamber of Commerce (Jaycees) erected a prominent illuminated cross on publicly owned Table Rock mesa, just above downtown Boise. There were other such crosses in Twin Falls and Jerome, often placed on sites where churches held Easter sunrise services. According to one Jaycee member, the Table Rock cross was designed to "symbolize the faith of all people in the Boise Valley."[38] He saw it as an inclusive icon, a common 1950s-era notion.

However, since crosses identify one particular faith, some experienced it as exclusionary. To them, the cross expressed Christian cultural hegemony and reminded residents of who had cultural power and who did not.

Privileging Christianity in such a visible way on public land did not inspire overt dissent in the 1950s, but critical voices rose later. When the U.S. Supreme Court began ruling such structures unconstitutional, the state's land board sought to head off a lawsuit by quickly selling the Jaycees the small strip of property on which the cross stood for $100 in 1972. State leaders suppressed news of the public auction in order to prevent competing bids and scuttle resistance. The American Civil Liberties Union questioned the sale's legality and integrity but never took a case to court. Those who interpreted the symbol as disrespectful of the city's growing diversity asked the Jaycees to remove it but did not take action. As time passed, the Jaycees needed funds to repair and maintain the cross. They held major fund-raisers in 1993 but received few donations, and only fourteen people participated in a walk for the cross. The town's apathy evaporated in 1999, however, when a Chicago atheist promised to sue the city, bragging that he had "jerked down" crosses nationwide and would do so in Boise. Whether it was religious inspiration or aversion to an outsider's threats, suddenly ten thousand Boiseans followed aroused evangelicals in a Save the Cross march to the capitol. The march was one of the state's largest for any issue or event. Bumper stickers appeared on cars, and Republican governor Dirk Kempthorne declared Table Rock Cross Day. The Chicagoan suspended his court action. Quiet local grumbling continued, but the cross remains, currently unchallenged. Some now defend its presence there for historic preservation purposes rather than spiritual ones, seeing it as a relic and reminder of Boise's 1950s-era culture.[39] It will likely remain controversial.

Nothing inspired more impassioned dialogue about the nature of Idaho's religious and racial culture than the efforts of white supremacist groups to transform the state into an Aryan homeland. Remote and libertarian, northern Idaho has long provided sanctuary for fringe religious groups seeking privacy. Schismatic Catholic sects protesting the 1960s Vatican II reforms gravitated there, one of which became quite anti-Semitic.[40] Polygamous families calling themselves "orthodox Mormons," who split from the LDS church over its termination of polygamy, live near the Canadian border in Boundary County.[41] In the early 1970s, seeking to escape southern California, Richard Butler bought twenty acres near Hayden Lake, establishing a new headquarters for the Church of Jesus Christ, Christian, also known as the Aryan Nations. Racist Christian Identity ideas, which infused groups like the Aryan Nations, sprang up originally in the Deep South and moved to southern California as part of the broader conservative religious migration across the Sun Belt. As a Christian Identity minister, Butler preached a hyperpatriotic, antimodern, anti-Semitic, anti-Catholic message that called nonwhites "mud people." Protecting white American Christian purity was the goal.[42]

Butler was not alone in northern Idaho. Bo Gritz launched his Almost Heaven community for antigovernment tax protesters nearby; so, too, did America's Promise Ministries, a fellow Christian Identity group. White supremacist Christian patriots, like Randy Weaver, built homes in the vicinity. A white supremacist mail-order business, 14 Word Press, set up shop in St. Maries. Another white supremacist Christian patriot group called 11th Hour Remnant Messenger was located near Sandpoint. Butler hoped that his compound would operate as a central unifying base for all such groups, not only in Idaho but around the nation. Every year, he held major conferences at his compound to unite like-minded operations. Neighboring communities frequently found Aryan-Christian leaflets on their doorsteps.[43]

In 1980, twenty-eight religious leaders, including Father Bill Wassmuth, a Catholic priest in Coeur d'Alene, repudiated Butler's skewed uses of Scripture. Wassmuth had just moved north from Boise's Catholic diocese, where he had run its religious education programs. He had imbued them with a social justice thrust that became statewide Catholic policy. In northern Idaho, Wassmuth felt that it was morally imperative that people of faith project a different spiritual message and ethic than those flowing from Butler's compound, challenging Butler's religious rationalizations for injustice head-on with their own biblical interpretations. A small group formed what soon became the Kootenai County Task Force on Human Relations, which met at Wassmuth's church. Yet, as distasteful as the Aryan Nations' ideas were to many northern Idaho residents, the motto of "live and let live" bred a type of apathy. The word "Christian" in the name of Butler's church also made people wary of challenging him, until a terrorist group affiliated with the Aryan Nations, the Order, began staging violent attacks throughout Idaho and the greater Northwest.[44]

The Aryan Nations had called for a racial holy war. Christian patriots began burning crosses in yards and plastering swastikas on doors. The Order bombed a Boise synagogue in 1984, murdered a Denver talk show host, and committed a string of robberies to finance the purchase of guns and one hundred acres of land near Priest River that would serve as a militia training facility. Boise's Jewish community began inspecting worship areas for bombs and vandalism before every service. Mormon buildings in Idaho Falls and Meridian were defaced, while Catholics discovered their cars plastered with hate literature after Mass.[45]

Wassmuth became head of the Kootenai task force because the Order had proved that it would kill opponents, and he was the only member without a spouse and children. People connected with the Aryan Nations bombed Wassmuth's rectory in 1986. Interfaith coalitions of people came together to pledge their active support and resistance. Butler and those like him forced Idaho's residents to address their communities' racism, cultures, and homogeneity. Religious beliefs motivated those like Wassmuth; Butler's negative effect on Idaho's image, reputation, tourism, and business communities motivated others, like Coeur d'Alene's Chamber of Commerce. Wassmuth became the visible face of a growing human rights community in northern Idaho. Several counties soon formed their own human rights task forces, made up largely of citizens moved by spiritual values. The task forces, along with many religious communities, lobbied for passage of the Malicious Harassment Law, the Uniform Hate Crimes Reporting Act, and the Explosive Devices Act, and got them. They also helped convince the state government to recognize Martin Luther King Jr. Day as a holiday, beginning in 1990. Wassmuth said that "being a follower of the Gospel is building a just world" and that "working as a priest . . . was a way to make a difference."[46]

Wassmuth helped Bonner County create a human rights task force to deal with the 11th Hour Remnant Messenger organization, which declared whites to be a chosen lost tribe of Israel. Each of the task forces visibly countered every public move that the white supremacists made, defying attempts at intimidation and pressing the motto coined by Ada County's group, "Idaho Is Too Great for Hate." Wassmuth urged religious communities to focus as well on the proactive work of nurturing respectful diverse communities instead of just reacting against racist Christian Identity groups. He spoke out against Proposition 1 and tried unsuccessfully to get protection for sexual orientation added to Idaho's hate crimes law. Wassmuth won many awards, including Idaho's Citizen of the Year, before moving to Seattle to head a Northwest human rights group he helped found.[47]

Idaho residents, especially those up north, battled the Aryan Nations for twenty years before one of its violent acts led to a lawsuit that bankrupted it in 2000. Butler left the state, and in 2001, his compound was bulldozed; Greg Carr, a businessman and Idaho native, purchased the land and then donated it to North Idaho College for possible development into a Peace Park.[48]

In 1995, several religious persons and human rights advocates brought the internationally renowned exhibit *Anne Frank and the World* to Idaho for a month; it drew forty-six thousand visitors and inspired Reverend Nancy Taylor, of Boise's First United Church of Christ, to establish a permanent human rights memorial in Boise. Drawing together a large interfaith coalition as well as business leaders and city officials, and with financial help from Greg Carr, Boise completed the Anne Frank Human Rights Memorial in 2002. Sixty quotations about human rights from diverse voices along with the entire Universal Declaration of Human Rights cover a stone wall and several tablets that surround a waterfall and teaching circles, where visitors may engage in discussions and reflection. Taylor hoped the memorial would "inspire each of us to contemplate the moral implications of our civic responsibilities."[49] Unitarian Universalist minister Elizabeth Greene saw it, in part, as an inclusive counterbalance to Boise's Table Rock cross, for Unitarian Universalists do not identify with the cross symbol. The Anne Frank Memorial functions, therefore, as a place of diverse spirituality. The state embraced it as a step toward dispelling the racist image it had earned as the Aryan Nations' self-selected homeland. Like the Table Rock cross, it became part of Idaho's religious and moral debates over identity, inclusion, culture, and values.

Discussion of Idaho's religious history must also address the approximately 50 percent of the state's population that has consistently declared itself "religiously unaffiliated." While some call themselves atheists or agnostics, most are spiritual seekers who have left established religious organizations and may still feel loosely tied to them or who have created syncretic beliefs of their own. In a state teeming with natural beauty, many find spiritual meaning through an earth-centered focus, such as the growing Deep Ecology movement. People like Nelle Tobias, along with the Idaho Earth Institute, have spread Deep Ecology's spiritual ideas throughout local communities for years. Idaho's mountains have also attracted gatherings of groups like the Rainbow Family of Living Light, which urges human connections, alternative lifestyles, peace, love, and caring for the earth.[50]

Environmentalism may be the newest and most compelling ecumenical glue holding together formerly unlikely coalitions of conservative and liberal religious bodies in Idaho. Boise's Vineyard Church, a conservative evangelical group that spawned some IVA leaders, took a bold step recently in embracing what it calls "Creation Care," joining liberals in the moral and spiritual tasks of environmental preservation. Its controversial leap to the so-called left made national news.[51] Environmental work, the Anne Frank Human Rights Memorial, struggles against the Aryan Nations, and the Interfaith Sanctuary for the homeless have all helped Idaho's diverse religious groups find periodic common ground amid sharp culture-war arguments over religious monuments, diversity, homosexuality, and the Table Rock cross, among other things. Religion continues to prod Idahoans to ponder questions of inclusion and identity.

CONCLUSION

Wedged between the "none zone" and Utah's prominent Mormon influence, Idaho's religious history defies simple analysis. Research gaps invite further scholarship, but what exists illustrates that faith groups have strongly shaped Idaho's infrastructure, economics, politics, and cultures. They have not functioned simply as ethereal, soul-focused, otherworldly forces in people's lives; rather they have been publicly engaged, often controversial, and forceful. Idaho's blend of religious communities led to particular historical clashes, conflicts, progress, and questions that profoundly affected Idahoans' "secular" culture. Therefore religion must be integrated into scholarly studies that seek to understand and explain the state.

Notes

1   Patricia O'Connell Killen and Mark Silk, eds., *Pacific Northwest: The None Zone* (Walnut Creek, CA: AltaMira Press, 2004).

2   Walter Nugent, "The Religious Demography of an Oasis Culture," in Jan Shipps and Mark Silks, eds., *Mountain West: Sacred Landscapes in Transition* (Walnut Creek, CA: Alta Mira Press, 2004), 39–41. Percentages are for 2000; see information gathered from the 2000 Religious Congregations and Membership Survey, conducted by the Glenmary Research Center, at the Polis Center's Digital Atlas of American Religion, http://www.religionatlas.org (accessed July 7, 2007).

3   Percentages in the text are for 2000; those in the table are for 1990.

4   For more information about why the Coeur d'Alene accepted Christianity, see Laura Woodworth-Ney, *Mapping Identity: The Creation of the Coeur d'Alene Indian Reservation, 1805–1902* (Niwot: University Press of Colorado, 2001).

5   Wilfred Schoenberg, S.J., *A History of the Catholic Church in the Pacific Northwest 1743–1983* (Washington, DC: Pastoral Press, 1987), 722–25; Robert C. Carriker, "Direct Successor to DeSmet: Joseph M. Cataldo, S.J., and the Stabilization of the Jesuit Indian Missions of the Pacific Northwest, 1877–1893," *Idaho Yesterdays* 31 (Spring–Summer 1987): 3–7; Richard Etulain, "Saint Joseph's Church in Idaho City," *Idaho Yesterdays* 11 (Spring 1967): 32–36; Thomas Cox, "Tribal Leadership in Transition: Chief Peter Moctelme of the Coeur d'Alenes," *Idaho Yesterdays* 23 (Spring 1979): 2–9, 25–31; Bill Scudder, "Preserving the Cataldo Mission," *Idaho Yesterdays* 47 (Fall–Winter 2006): 61–62. Catholics also established missions among the Nez Perce and Flatheads.

6   Lawrence G. Coates, "The Spalding-Whitman and Lemhi Missions: A Comparison," *Idaho Yesterdays* 31 (Spring–Summer 1987): 38–46; Allen and Eleanor Morrill, "Talmaks," *Idaho Yesterdays* 8 (Fall 1964): 2–15; Ferenc Szasz, *Protestant Clergy in the Great Plains and Mountain West 1865–1915* (Lincoln: University of Nebraska Press, 2004), 177–90; Allen P. Slickpoo, Sr., "The Nez Perce Attitude toward the Missionary Experience," *Idaho Yesterdays* 31 (Spring–Summer 1987): 35–37.

7   Coates, "Spalding-Whitman and Lemhi Missions"; Gregory Smoak, "Fort Hall and the Ghost Dance," *Idaho Yesterdays* 47 (Fall–Winter 2006): 7–27.

8   Smoak, "Fort Hall and the Ghost Dance."

9   Szasz, *Clergy*, 39–49.

10 Etulain, "Saint Joseph's Church"; Schoenberg, *History of the Catholic Church*, 392, 487–89.

11 Schoenberg, *History of the Catholic Church*, 662–67.

12 Szasz, *Clergy*, 41–58; Betty Derig, "Pioneer Portraits: Daniel Sylvester Tuttle," *Idaho Yesterdays* 12 (Winter 1968): 13–22.

13 Ferenc Morton Szasz, *Religion in the Modern American West* (Tucson: University of Arizona Press, 2000), 48–56.

14 Szasz, *Clergy*, 133–74.

15 Aaron McArthur, "Building Zion," *Idaho Yesterdays* 47 (Fall–Winter 2006): 47–59; Szasz, *Modern American West*, 106.

16 Heath Druzin, "Greenleaf," *Idaho Statesman*, June 26, 2007, A1.

17 Szasz, *Clergy*, 52–51; Suzanne Sermon, "'Beyond Simple Domesticity,' Organizing Boise Women, 1866–1920" (MA thesis, Boise State University, 1996), 32–37.

18 Nancy Schoenburg, "The Jews of Southeastern Idaho," *Western States Jewish History* 18 (July 1986): 291–314; Alan Minskoff, *Keeping the Faith: A Centennial Celebration of Organized Jewish Life in Boise, Idaho* (Boise: Ahavath Beth Israel Congregation, 1997).

19 Mamie Oliver, *Idaho Ebony: Boise's Black Baptists: Heritage, Hope and Struggle* (Boise: Idaho African American Heritage Society, 1995); Mamie Oliver, *Idaho Ebony: The Afro-American Presence in Idaho State History* (Boise: printed by the author, 1990).

20 Keith Peterson, "Frank Bruce Robinson and Psychiana," *Idaho Yesterdays* 23 (Fall 1979): 9–15, 26–29; Szasz, *Modern American West*, 80–81.

21 Patricia Ourada, "Reluctant Servants: Conscientious Objectors in Idaho during World War II," *Idaho Yesterdays* 31 (Winter 1988): 2–14.

22 Szasz, *Modern American West*, 134–39; Errol Jones and Kathleen Hodges, "Writing the History of Latinos in Idaho," in Robert McCarl, ed., *Latinos in Idaho Celebrando Cultura* (Boise: Idaho Humanities Council, 2003), 25–26. Szasz states that the ICC created the migrant ministries program; Errol Jones, whose research specializes in this subject, argues that the ICC emerged from the migrant ministries program and that this was unique. Errol Jones, discussion with author, October 2008. See also Errol D. Jones, "MS 99 Collection Titled 'Southern Idaho Migrant Ministry' (SIMM): An Initial Index," Idaho State Historical Society Digital Index.

23 Oliver, *Idaho Ebony: Boise's Black Baptists*; Oliver, *Idaho Ebony: The Afro-American Presence*; flyer, TVCCSA Community Ministries Center.

24 For example, Jehovah's Witnesses remain largely disengaged from politics, and they reject nationalism; Idaho's traditional Mennonite populations are also rather insular.

25 See Merle Wells's extensive body work on this subject, including "Origins of Anti-Mormon Antagonism in Idaho, 1872–1880," *Idaho Yesterdays* 44 (Winter 2001): 47–58; "Law in the Service of Politics: Anti-Mormonism in Idaho Territory," *Idaho Yesterdays* 25 (Spring 1981): 33–43; "The Idaho Anti-Mormon Test Oath, 1884–1892," *Pacific Historical Review* 24 (August 1955): 235–52; "Unexpected Allies: Fred T. DuBois and the Mormons in 1916," *Idaho Yesterdays* 35 (Fall 1991): 27–33. These sources were used for the following paragraphs on Idaho's test oath. On the larger political context of this struggle, see chapter 4 in this volume.

26 E. Leo Lyman, "A Mormon Transition in Idaho Politics," *Idaho Yesterdays* 20 (Winter 1977): 2–11, 24–29; see also the essays by Merle Wells cited in n. 25.

27 Matthew Godfrey, *Religion, Politics and Sugar: The Mormon Church, the Federal Government, and the Utah-Idaho Sugar Company, 1907–1921* (Logan: Utah State University Press, 2007).

28 Sermon, "'Beyond Simple Domesticity.'"

29 T. A. Larson, "Women's Rights in Idaho," *Idaho Yesterdays* 16 (Spring 1972): 2–15, 18–19.

30 Seth Randal, *Fall of '55* (film), Boise premiere, September 30, 2006; and discussions with Alan Virta, the film's historical consultant. For more about the scandal, see John Gerassi's *The Boys of Boise: Furor, Vice and Folly in an American City* (1966; repr., Seattle: University of Washington Press, 2000), which ironically misses the religious aspects of it.

31 John Kevin Olson and Ann C. Beck, "Religion and Political Realignment in the Rocky Mountain States," *Journal for the Scientific Study of Religion* 29 (June 1990): 198–204;

Gary Moncrief, "Idaho: The Interests of Sectionalism," in Ronald J. Hrebenar and Clive Thomas, eds., *Interest Group Politics* (Salt Lake City: University of Utah Press, 1987), 67–74; Nugent, "Religious Demography," 19–48; Robert H. Blank, *Regional Diversity of Political Values: Idaho Political Culture* (Washington, D.C.: University Press of America, 1978), 157–79; Szasz, *Modern American West*, 132–62; Stephanie Witt and Gary Moncrief, "Religion and Roll Call Voting in Idaho: The 1990 Abortion Controversy," *American Politics Quarterly* 21 (January 1993): 140–49.

32 Kathleen Flake, "The Mormon Corridor: Utah and Idaho," in Shipps and Silk, *Mountain West*, 96–97. Shipps, "Conclusion: Sacred Landscapes in Transition," in ibid., 146–47. Calculating for the entire Mountain West region, Jan Shipps states that 42 percent of white Catholics vote Republican, while 20 percent vote Democratic; about 15 percent of white evangelicals and 17 percent of Mormons vote Democratic.

33 Szasz, *Modern American West*, 139–62; Nugent, "Religious Demography," 30; Szasz, "How Religion Created an Infrastructure for the Mountain West," in Shipps and Silk, *Mountain West*, 61; Douglas Johnson, Paul Picard, and Bernard Quinn, *Churches and Church Membership in the United States, 1971* (Washington, DC: Glenmary Research Center, 1972); Quinn et al., *Churches and Church Membership in the United States, 1980: An Enumeration by Region, State, and County, Based on Data Reported for 111 Church Bodies* (Atlanta: Glenmary Research Center, 1982); Bradley et al., *Churches and Church Membership.*

34 O. Kendall White Jr., "Mormonism and the Equal Rights Amendment," *Journal of Church and State* 31 (Spring 1989): 249–68; Blank, *Regional Diversity*, 157–79; Flake, "Mormon Corridor"; Witt and Moncrief, "Religion and Roll Call Voting."

35 Witt and Moncrief, "Religion and Roll Call Voting."

36 Clare Muller and Daniel Gallagher, *Our Private Idaho* (London: Devil's Avocado, 1998), film; Chris Collins, *Kamikaze Summer* (San Francisco: Hawk Films, 1996), film.

37 Shipps and Silk, *Mountain West*, 148; see also Makeup of Legislature 1986–1996, Lily Wai, University of Idaho, http://www.webs.uidaho.edu/idstats/chapter17/17–14a .htm (July 7, 2007).

38 Statement paraphrased from Keith Gabriel, in "Cross Symbolizes Faith," *Idaho Statesman*, March 22, 1974.

39 See "The Cross for Tablerock," *Idaho Statesman*, November 27, 1955, 4; Reverend Roy C. Pieczulawski, "Yes: Boise's Brightest Landmark Must Remain," editorial, *Idaho Statesman*, June 13, 1993, 2F; Sidney Fleischer, "No: Responsible Citizens Must Be Aware of Others," editorial, *Idaho Statesman*, June 13, 1993, 2F; Anna Peterson, "Ada Commissioners Endorse Push to Save Table Rock Cross," *Idaho Statesman*, August 6, 1993, 2C; Sherry Squires, "Valley Has 2 Crosses to Bear," *Idaho Press Tribune*, April 14, 1995, A1; Dan Popkey, "Outside Threat Spurs Thousands to Stand Up for the Table Rock Cross," *Idaho Statesman*, December 5, 1999, 1A; Tim Jackson, "Officials' Thoughts May Rule Fate of Cross," *Idaho Statesman*, December 5, 1999, 1A.

40 One was the Tridentine Latin Rite Church (formerly the Fatima Crusade) in Coeur d'Alene, led by Francis Konrad Schuckardt. The other, located at Post Falls, was the Immaculate Conception Church, founded by Father Edward DeBusschere in 1971. See Schoenberg, *History of the Catholic Church*, 725–29; Andrea Vogt, *Common Courage: Bill Wassmuth, Human Rights, and Small-Town Activism* (Moscow: University of Idaho Press, 2003), 75–90.

41 Andrea Dearden, "Polygamous Sect Moving into North Idaho," *Idaho's NewsChannel 7*,

May 10, 2005, http://www.rickross.com/reference/polygamy/polygamy346.html (August 7, 2007).

42 James Aho, *The Politics of Righteousness: Idaho Christian Patriotism* (Seattle: University of Washington Press, 1990); Vogt, *Common Courage*. See also Tom Alibrandi and Bill Wassmuth, *Hate Is My Neighbor* (Moscow: University of Idaho Press, 1999); David Neiwert, *In God's Country: The Patriot Movement and the Pacific Northwest* (Pullman: Washington State University Press, 1999).

43 Vogt, *Common Courage*.

44 Ibid.

45 Ibid.; Minskoff, *Keeping the Faith*, 64–92.

46 Vogt, *Common Courage*, 124.

47 Vogt, *Common Courage*.

48 Ibid.

49 This quotation is inscribed on the wall itself. Other information comes from my own involvement with the Ada County Human Rights Task Force and Boise First United Church of Christ, which both assisted with the memorial project.

50 More than ten thousand members gathered in Idaho's mountains in 2001. For more information, see the Rainbow Family official website, http://www.welcomehome .org/ (July 7, 2007); Szasz, *Modern American West*, 67. The Idaho Rainbow Family is currently constructing a website.

51 Journalist Bill Moyers included a story about the Boise Vineyard Church in a *Moyers on America* segment called "Is God Green?" on PBS, October 11, 2006.

Religious History

Clara Miller describes a polygamist's warning system.

INTERVIEWER: How many brothers and sisters did you have?

MILLER: We had seven, Mother had.

INTERVIEWER: And then your father married twice more, did he not?

MILLER: Yeah, Father married Carolyn Rudby, and they had about thirteen, I believe, children. And when Father was a polygamist, you know, the sheriff used to come and get him, and while they would go in the house to eat[,] us children had to be out watching the trails to see whether any of the sheriffs would come. He had a nice place where he could a hid if we could a got him in that in time. Then our neighbor—Father and his brother, they sleep together in the willows, and whenever they'd come in the house, why, us children, we'd watch the trails. And they made an agreement that—we could just see across the valley, Uncle Chris was living against the sidehill and Father was living, I guess, about three miles this side, so they said we will make a fire whenever they came, the sheriff, to Uncle Chris, he was going to make a fire so Father could go hide. And the night the sheriff was up on the mountain, we saw a big fire by Uncle Chris, and we knew that the sheriffs were up. And Uncle Chris told us, he says, "I have never made no fire and I've never saw the sheriffs; they never stopped at my place." So, some good spirit made a fire to warn Father, but he didn't take the warning. It was in the morning. Father was just going down to get a little cream out of the dairy house, and while he was in there, the sheriff rode down on him and took him. And if he could a got in the house, we had a double wall built. No one would have known that it was a double wall, and he could a went down the cellar and just pushed up a board, and no one would have known anything better than that. And they'd a never found him, but he wasn't there at the time that happened, so the sheriff took him and we all cried—and our dad, he have to go six months to jail.

* * *

Political activist Genie Sue Weppner analyzes the Latter-day Saints' role in defeating Proposition 1.

INTERVIEWER: I'm wondering what comments or memories or stories you have about the importance or maybe the lack of importance of the LDS church particularly in east Idaho?

WEPPNER: I think that was the reason we defeated it. What we did with the campaign was have small house parties, small group meetings where friends would invite friends, neighbors would invite neighbors, and then individuals would go there and speak about the issue. I think that allowed some candid discussion that might not have occurred in other situations. . . .

My memory is, is we had a discussion at one point at which somebody said, "You know the church leaders have an understanding of what this really is all about. It's not really about gays and lesbians. It is about denying specific rights to people who are not deemed Christian." And they had experienced similar discrimination early on in the formation of the church with Joseph Smith and the kind of things that they experienced there. And I think that they were able to make the leap between "this is not really about what we believe is the right thing to do and what we believe about homosexuality. But it is about denying rights to a group of people. And we've experienced that, and we don't want to have that happen again. And we believe that if this happens, then there will be more opportunities for those kinds of things to happen in the future." That's the discussion I remember going on.

NOTE

John and Clara [Henry] Miller were interviewed by Harold Forbush, November 2, 1959, Cedron, ID, transcript (OH0311) from Idaho Oral History Center/Idaho State Historical Society, 11–13. Used with permission of Idaho State Historical Society.

Genie Sue Weppner was interviewed by Troy Reeves, Boise, ID, October 13, 2006, transcript (OH 2449) from Oral History Center/Idaho State Historical Society, 2–3. Used with permission of Idaho State Historical Society.

6
Defying Boundaries

Women in Idaho History

LAURA WOODWORTH-NEY AND TARA A. ROWE

A STUDENT OF IDAHO HISTORY, SURROUNDED AT HER DESK BY the classic histories of the state, might conclude that women—but only white women—played an almost imperceptible (if supportive) role in establishing and developing the state of Idaho. Intimidating in attention to detail and printed on heavy paper housed between gilt leather bindings, the works of Hiram T. French, John Hailey, Cornelius J. Brosnan, James H. Hawley, Byron Defenbach, and William J. McConnell feature the political machinations of the state's male founders, primarily themselves. If they mention women at all, these hefty books make only passing reference to white women pioneers, wives, and/or suffragists.[1] Our student, skimming through hundreds of two-column pages of elite names and political events in French's *History of Idaho*, might come upon this passage in the only chapter to address women, "Women of Idaho—Equal Suffrage—The Columbian Club—Women's Clubs—A Tribute": "The history of equal suffrage in Idaho does not disclose a long, determined struggle such as characterizes this movement in the eastern states and in other nations. This right was given to the women of Idaho with comparatively little urging on their part. Probably the untrammeled spirit of the West was a dominating factor."[2]

Hiram's opening sentence seems more like a criticism of Idaho's women than a tribute. It sets the tone for a chapter that dismisses the hard work of female activists such as Idaho's Abigail Scott Duniway. While it privileges the position of white pioneer women who "had borne an arduous part in the development of the Northwest," it gives them little agency, since it was the "leading men" who "not only chivalrously acknowledged, but they desired to have the further co-operation and interest of the women."[3] Even in this "tribute" to women's suffrage, the book finds a way to glorify male politicians.

Native American women are rarely if ever mentioned within these pages, nor are Asian women, migrant Hispanic women, or individual Mormon women mentioned, let alone highlighted. Native Americans appear as either perpetrators of war or the inevitable victims of non-Indian so-called progress. Political history dominates this book and the other works that compose the state's early twentieth-century historiography. This trend was in keeping with the discipline of history's then narrow definition of which topics were worthy of study. In Idaho's youthful state, and in other similarly juvenile institutions in the West, political history also dominated because of the political motivations and aspirations of the individual men who wrote these histories. Certainly, women were also writing the history of statehood, but their writings often occurred outside the historical, literary, and political establishment. By contrast, Hailey, French, Defenbach, and McConnell each enjoyed political careers that collectively spanned decades. All were highly instrumental in the development of Idaho in the early years of statehood. Their historical writings served a dual purpose, seen in other western states as well: they established a historical record of Idaho's founding, written by the founders, and they romanticized Idaho and the West in an effort to draw people, financing, and publicity to the state. Boosterism and the past came together in a romantic mix—minus women and nonwhites. Since political topics dominated early Idaho history and white men dominated the state's politics, the result was a gendered state history model that influenced all Idaho state history.

Our student might wander up to the stacks, or down to the special collections area of the library (invariably in the basement), to peruse additional books on the state of Idaho. She would find that works about Idaho history written after the early booster period fall into two main categories: amateur and independent scholarly histories of towns, regions, and "pioneer days"; and general histories written by specialists, often commissioned by the Idaho State Historical Society (ISHS) or by its employees, usually salaried state historians. Examples of the former include Betty Meloy Thiessen's *Past Days of the Tammany-Waha Area* (1982) and Mary Jane Fritzen's *Idaho Falls: City of Destiny* (1991). Examples of the latter include Merle Wells and

Arthur A. Hart's *Idaho: Gem of the Mountains* and Leonard J. Arrington's monumental *History of Idaho*.[4] If she went searching online for source material, our student would most likely find ISHS's Idaho Reference Series, a collection of short histories of important places, people, and events in Idaho history. The reference series remains dominated by men and male-dominated topics, including mining, agriculture, and commerce. The "biographical series"—a subheading of the entire reference series—contains only the biographies of the male founders: Norman B. Willey, William John McConnell, Frank Steunenberg, John T. Morrison, Frank Robert Gooding, James Henry Hawley, John Michener Haines, Charles Calvin Moore, Charles Benjamin Ross, and Clarence A. Bottolfsen, all governors, businessmen, and/or politicians; "Teton" Jackson, a fur trapper turned criminal; and Carl Buck, a mythical crack-shot frontier figure.[5] There are several biographies of women in ISHS's reference collection, including those of Mary Hallock Foote, Idaho's most well-known nineteenth-century author and illustrator, and Grace Jordan, the wife of Idaho governor Len B. Jordan, but they appear not under the "biography" heading but only in the master list of all the reference publications, making them difficult to locate.[6] Unlike the biographies of men in the reference series, which were written from the inception of the series in the mid-1960s, the biographies of women were written during the 1990s.[7]

If our student looked for volumes expressly about the history of women in Idaho, she would find a small grouping of biographical accounts, M.A. theses and Ph.D. dissertations, and a scattering of thematic works and federally funded reports. Theses and dissertations include Cynthia S. Powell's 1994 M.S. thesis "Beyond Molly B'Damn: Prostitution in the Coeur D'Alenes, 1880 to 1911" (Central Washington University) and Yixian Xu's "Chinese Women in Idaho during the Anti-Chinese Movement before 1900" (M.A. thesis, University of Idaho, 1994). Scholarly biographies of Idaho women include Dick D'Easum's *Dowager of Discipline: The Life of the Dean of Women* (1981), a biography of the University of Idaho's influential dean of women students, Permeal French (1869–1954), for whom the university's French Hall is named. French became one of Idaho's first female elected officials in 1898 when she won the position of state superintendent of public instruction, a post held by women for the next thirty-five years.[8] Our student would also likely find books and articles about Abigail Scott Duniway. One of the Pacific Northwest's most active woman's suffrage leaders and owner of an Idaho ranch in the Lost River area, Duniway established her reputation in Portland, Oregon, as editor of the Pacific Northwest's most prominent pro-suffrage newspaper, *The New Northwest*. She also wrote novels aimed at promoting women's rights, including a trilogy of stories set in Idaho: *Edna and John: A Romance of Idaho Flat* (1876), *Blanche LeClerq* (1886), and *Margaret Rudson* (1896). Duniway's strong female characters follow the early development of the state of Idaho. *Edna and John* is set in a woman-hating, barren Idaho mining town where the protagonist, Edna, never fully realizes her ambitions due to legalized restrictions on women's civic freedoms. The female characters in *Blanche LeClerq* fare better, as their lives parallel Idaho statehood, but it is the heroine Margaret Rudson who achieves enfranchisement. Duniway's Rudson is a "New Woman of the New West," a woman with the vote, education, and the ability to take advantage of Duniway's idealized American West, where agriculture paves the way for an enlightened future.[9] Duniway's own Idaho agricultural experience was less than ideal. She purchased her Lost River ranch in 1887, but returned to Portland in 1894 after a series of devastating winters that killed entire herds of cattle, especially at higher elevations.[10]

Our student may find the name of Grace Jordan, the wife of former Idaho governor and U.S. senator Len B. Jordan, on the spines of several volumes. Grace Jordan's works include *Home below Hell's Canyon*, an autobiographical account of her life on a rural ranch during the Depression; *Canyon Boy*, a dark, fictional account of rural life with a realistic western backdrop; *The Unintentional Senator*, the story of her husband's rise in politics and her role as a politician's wife; *The King's Pines of Idaho*, the story of an eastern family's trek to rural oblivion in McCall, Idaho; and *Country Editor: A Novel of the Early 1900s*, written largely from her own perspective as a female editor in a male-dominated trade. Jordan had edited the *Idaho Reader* for a time and wrote a syndicated column for the Idaho newspapers.[11] Annie Pike Greenwood, another female writer from Idaho, has also received a fair amount of scholarly attention, beginning with the publication of her detailed memoir *We Sagebrush Folks* (1934). Greenwood's harrowing narrative remains the best firsthand account of homesteading on an irrigated farm in southern Idaho during the 1910s.[12]

Outside of this biographical smattering, our student would not find many books and articles expressly about women in Idaho history. As the former editor and student editorial assistant of ISHS's peer-reviewed journal *Idaho Yesterdays*, we know what our student might encounter because we ourselves set out to discover what it is, if anything, about state and regional history that limits publications and submissions about women. Articles expressly about women or women's history in Idaho have appeared only twenty-nine times in *Idaho Yesterdays*, the peer-reviewed journal of record for Idaho history, since it began publication in 1957.[13] Many of these take as their subjects the biographies of elite women, the pioneering experience during a narrow slice of the nineteenth century, and the literary works written by Idaho women. Featured prominently in these articles are the lives and works of Mary Hallock Foote, the prominent author-illustrator who came to the Boise Basin during the 1880s with her engineer husband, Arthur Foote, and ended up creating a Local Color writer's market for her stories about the state, as Richard Etulain describes in chapter 9 of this book; Annie Pike Greenwood; and other women who wrote letters and memoirs. Biographical approaches such as these are limited by what they can, and cannot, contribute to a more holistic understanding of gender and state history. Most biographers must rely heavily on the writings of the women themselves.[14] Women who left significant writings tended to be white elites whose experiences tell us little about the majority of Idaho women. Educated, elite nineteenth- and early twentieth-century women were reticent about providing intimate details of their lives and would have avoided any public dissemination of information that they perceived as potentially harmful to their reputations. But as the *Idaho Yesterdays* articles about Idaho women show, it is elite women writers, politicians, clubwomen, and activists who have received historical attention. Women employed in the frontier sex trade are the exception to this rule. Prostitutes have received historical attention disproportionate to their numbers and their influence. Propertied madams in mining communities such as Helena, Montana, wielded a certain amount of economic and political influence for several decades during the late nineteenth century, but it was ultimately snuffed out when Protestant, white elite women exercised their cultural power—through writing, club activity, and sheer numbers—by the turn of the twentieth century. Indeed, elite women's groups used anti-vice campaigns to define what it was to be white and upper-class in western places like Boise, Rupert, and Caldwell.[15]

In consulting secondary sources to try to understand the history of women in Idaho, our student would be confronted with several significant historiographical barriers: state histories, by their very nature, subsume women's experiences; state and regional history has often been rejected by academic historians and the academy as illegitimate and provincial; and the obvious requirement that state histories pay homage to their own boundaries is a nearly impossible—and contradictory—limitation for women's and gender historians to follow. Academics often ignore state history, women's history often ignores state boundaries, and state histories often ignore women.

IDAHO STATE HISTORICAL SOCIETY, GENDER, AND PROFESSIONALIZATION

The Idaho legislature designated the Idaho State Historical Society a state agency in 1907, only seventeen years after Idaho became a state. The agency's first fifty years were spent in the basement of the capitol building, where an appointed secretary-librarian presided over the society's collections. As the longest-standing organization devoted to preserving and providing access to state history, the early ISHS was linked to state politics and boosterism. John Hailey served as the society's first secretary-librarian, and Ella Cartee Reed, who had been his assistant, followed him in the position. Her appointment ushered in decades of control by women connected to the history of the state and to Idaho's financially and socially prominent families. Reed, for example, came to Idaho in 1867 with her father, Lafayette Cartee, who was then Idaho Territory's surveyor general. She eventually married George H. Reed, an attorney who served several terms in the territorial legislature. The Reeds lived in Caldwell, which allowed Ella to become connected with Boise's vibrant turn-of-the-century women's club movement. She became the first librarian for the state's most prominent federated women's club, the Columbian Club, in 1894. The club later instituted a very popular traveling library for rural communities throughout the state, and Reed became its librarian in 1901. The Columbian Club advanced a variety of municipal housekeeping reforms, including parks, public drinking fountains, public sanitation, nurses in public schools, playgrounds, and 6:00 P.M. closing ordinances for drinking establishments. By the time she became secretary-librarian at ISHS in 1921, she had served as Hailey's assistant for about ten years. Her appointment linked the state historical society to women's club work, a tie that would remain until the 1950s. Her connections also linked the early ISHS to Boise's elite families. Reed's father had been instrumental in establishing Idaho Territory; her husband served in the Idaho legislature; her brother Ross married John Hailey's daughter Leona; and her son George W. Reed, Jr. served as assistant and archaeologist for the Idaho State Historical Society.[16]

Idaho's elite culture of founders, bankers, lawyers, politicians, and engineers was maintained through marriage and perpetuated through the shaping of the founding story, or the history of the state. A string of seven women appointees—Althea E. Fouch (appointed 1931), Claudia Ross (1937), Alice Beath Nash (1939), Ora B. Hawkins (1941), Margaret S. Roberts (1943), Flora Mason Foster (1945), and Gertrude McDevitt (1947)—followed Reed as the historical society's secretary-librarian (the title of the agency's director was changed to "state historian" in 1939). All had the benefit of formal educations: Ross graduated from the Red River Valley University in Wahpeton, North Dakota; Nash graduated from Miss Hill's School in Philadelphia and served as an Episcopal Church missionary in Wyoming; Hawkins held a degree from the State Teachers College in Lock Haven, Pennsylvania. The wives of lawyers, postmasters, ministers, and physicians, all of these women were active in social causes and club work in Idaho. Roberts, for example, is credited with founding the state's first kindergarten and served as the first Idaho chairwoman of the League of Women Voters.[17]

The historical profession of the early twentieth century, however, often viewed untrained women historians in state historical societies and libraries with some disdain. Throughout the early twentieth century, history professors worked to legitimize themselves within the academy and, in so doing, emphasized university training and official academic positions as essential elements of the professional historian. The result, in Idaho and elsewhere, was a double divide, between women's history and women historians and the official academic community and between academic historians and historians of state and local organizations. Women and early Idaho state history were intrinsically linked, but they were also tied to a nonacademic perception. As Ian Tyrrell has argued, after the 1930s, the profession of history in the United States split "between nationally and internationally oriented academic history on the one hand and specialized professional historians in state historical societies on the other." Furthermore, professionalization "pushed" amateur groups, local history organizations, genealogists, women librarians, and antiquarians "out of the orbit of academic history almost entirely."[18]

Professionalization came to ISHS in 1956 when Gertrude McDevitt resigned the directorship due to poor health. The board of trustees hired Holman J. "Jerry" Swinney, who brought to Idaho a background in museum management. Changes occurred within months. The society began to invite memberships, started a genealogical library, and made Merle Wells, a faculty member in history at the College of Idaho, in Caldwell, an official "consultant historian."[19] With a professional historian at the helm of ISHS, the focus of the organization shifted from boosterism and women's club activism to the professionalization of the state's history. The term *professional* equated with political history, which therefore continued to dominate the writings of the state historians. Economic history also enjoyed significant attention, but no mention of women's economic participation can be found in these professional histories, which were written mostly during the mid- to late twentieth century (ironically, during a time of unprecedented female participation in the official economy of the World War II era). The founder of the Idaho State Archives and founding editor of *Idaho Yesterdays*, Merle Wells, became an icon of Idaho history. Wells and Merrill Beal, at the time a faculty member at Idaho State University, cowrote the first ISHS history of the state, *History of Idaho*, which was also the first state history published since the end of the booster period of Idaho history. Wells and Beal, however, referred to women even less than their predecessors: not a single chapter or heading contains a reference to women, a woman's name, or even mention of women's suffrage. Merle Wells and Arthur Hart's 1985 publication *Idaho: Gem of the Mountains,* ISHS's second commissioned history, does acknowledge the historical role of women. It contains numerous photographs of women and ordinary Idahoans at work and at home, as well as analysis of women's economic and political statuses. Notably, one of the book's sidebars details the lives of three female ranchers: Abigail Scott Duniway, Polly Nathoy Bemis, and Kitty Wilkins, also known as the "Horse Queen of Idaho."[20] This dramatic turnaround reflects the changes in the historical profession introduced by 1960s social movements and the increase in available secondary source material. Still, while the mention of these historically prominent women represented a move forward, they remained corralled in the margins, banished to sidebars while men conquered territory and politics in the text's main narrative.

The most recent historical work commissioned by ISHS is its fifty-year anniversary revision of Wells and Hart's *Idaho: Gem of the Mountains*. The authors of the new book (one of them a coauthor of this chapter) used a crossroads theme—that Idaho sits at a cultural, geographic, and historical crossroads—to create a narrative that pays homage to its predecessors but that also includes women, Native Americans, immigrants, and ethnic and multicultural groups to an unprecedented degree. Despite this decision and the resulting expansive narrative, late in the production process, the publisher changed the title of the book to *Idaho: The Heroic Journey*, a title reminiscent of pioneer glorification histories and male-dominated narratives.[21]

As state history became professionalized during the mid-twentieth century, male professionals replaced local female librarians and historians. Women did not begin to show up in state history narratives or as professionally recognized historians until late in the twentieth century. As shown below, contradictions between the state and gender analysis remain.

CONTRADICTIONS BETWEEN STATE AND WOMEN'S HISTORY

The contradictions faced by women historians of state and regional history have had an impact on the memberships of regional and state organizations that support Idaho and western United States history. Many scholars of women's history find that their work fits best in other categories, including cultural studies, American studies, women's studies, gender studies, borderlands studies (Canada and Mexico), transnational studies, and other interdisciplinary fields. The defection of feminist scholars from professional organizations based on state and regional history reflects the broader trends in the discipline of western United States history, leading away from the tradition of Frederick Jackson Turner to multicultural and other interpre-

tations. The Western History Association, founded in 1961 as an organization devoted to the promotion and "study of the North American West in
its varied aspects and broadest sense," has often struggled to attract and
retain women members.[22] The 2005 membership survey revealed that the
organization was still dominated by men; only 30.9 percent of respondents
were women, while only 3.7 percent of respondents listed "women" as their
first choice in the category of "topical area of scholarly interest."[23] Its official
refereed publication, the *Western Historical Quarterly*, recently published a
special issue devoted to gender and women's history in order to encourage
and sustain submissions about women and gender.[24]

Other contradictions involve the nature of women's history and the
field of western women's history. Women's western history is a relatively
new subdiscipline, and its dedication to the concept of the American West
as a place bounded by cultural, historical, and social boundaries, but not
necessarily state boundaries, has limited its applicability to state history.[25]
Indeed, western women's history has functioned largely in opposition to
the architecture of state history. Gender analysis, as noted women's historian Susan Armitage recently argued in an essay about women and Pacific
Northwest history, is often at odds with regional history.[26] The term *region*
is used to refer to places of commonality, according to geographic definitions, and tends to subsume inhabitants within a bordered area and assume
that those who live there have more in common with one another than with
those who live in a different region. Women and men within regions may
have less in common with others in the region than they do with those of
the same gender, class, race, or socioeconomic status outside it. The concep-
tualization of space encapsulated by regional boundaries creates the false
idea of containment: that there are insiders and outsiders, fixed boundaries,
and clear demarcations.

Yet in women's history, there are never fixed boundaries and clear demarcations. One of the main themes of women's history is fluidity and
porous boundaries. Rigid adherence to boundaries of region—not to mention boundaries of social behavior—obfuscate the tracks of generations of
women who moved in and out of those spaces, whose voices were not heard
in the marking of the territory, and whose associations, connections, and
ties to place create unmarked and often conflicting subregions and female-

centered spaces. The conflict between region and gender is less significant, however, than that between state and gender. Our student would find that the very structure and function of state histories have often been at odds with the goals of women's history. The function and form of state history have worked to minimize the history of women and gender, while the historical construction of state boundaries, state institutions, and municipalities have created gendered landscapes and gendered inequities based on spatial boundaries and the economic, social, and aesthetic privileging of public over private—and rural over urban—spaces.

Regional boundaries may take cultural and social history into account, but state boundaries are political lines historically negotiated by men and maintained by male-dominated political entities. Political boundaries ignore—or contradict—Native American, social, cultural, or natural boundaries, especially in the Rocky Mountain region, where competition over mining resources and political votes influenced the formation of state lines. Congress carved states out of territories using political and resource-allocation considerations, not social/cultural definitions, and occasionally did so in a fickle and sporadic manner. In the western territories, state boundaries emerged from gendered political interests that ignored female spaces and conceptions of region based on family and social connections. Idaho's awkward boundaries were drawn not because of a grassroots effort within the boundaries as they exist today but from outside them as forces in what was then Washington Territory jockeyed for political position with one another and with the neighboring state of Oregon. Idaho's odd shape—the result of perhaps the most counterintuitive state boundaries in the country—were, according to historian Carlos Schwantes, "a product of the cavalier manner in which politicians often treated territorial matters."[27]

Idaho's boundaries reflect the political interests of territorial leaders in western Washington who desired a more compact territory. As Dorothy O. Johansen and Charles Gates put it in their now classic history of the Pacific Northwest region, "the movement for the organization of Idaho Territory originated in western Washington and was assisted by Oregon."[28] Washington's leftovers included all of what is now Idaho and portions of Montana and Wyoming. The unwieldy territory claimed Lewiston as its capital, but it was nearly impossible for legislators to travel from the Upper Missouri

to the confluence of the Clearwater and Snake Rivers. When the Idaho territorial legislature asked to be divided into more manageable sections, the
panhandle was created and most of northern Idaho was given to Montana.
As a result, the boundaries divided female Native spaces, such as the camas
fields straddling northern Idaho and eastern Washington that held significant cultural meaning and a source of the food, and created the seeds of
future divisiveness based on lack of transportation, communication, and
social networks. Idaho's boundaries have also made it a difficult place in
which to live. The panhandle has been cut off from the rest of the state's
transportation networks, and much of the state's communities have lacked
transportation and infrastructure, limiting female networks and associations and negatively impacting access to health care.[29] The political forces
in the northern panhandle and the southern Snake River Plain have seldom
agreed about the state's economy, politics, or social and cultural beliefs as
shown in chapters 3 and 4 in this volume.

Idaho's geographically confused boundaries mean that historical analyses based on cultural or social arguments necessarily ignore parts of the
state line, since the state crosses many cultural and social boundaries. Our
student would find little help from historical geographers, who have disagreed about Idaho's boundaries and region. Geographic and historical definitions of the region place Idaho in several overlapping geographic regions.
Joel Garreau's widely cited 1981 map of the Nine Nations of America made
the point that state boundaries were essentially meaningless. On his map,
Idaho appears in the area designated "The Empty Quarter," along with the
remainder of the Rocky Mountain West and most of the American Southwest.[30] In scholarly works, Idaho has been considered part of the Rocky
Mountain West region and part of the Pacific Northwest region. Students
taking college-level courses on the history of Idaho at Idaho State University, located in the southeastern Idaho community of Pocatello, are often
baffled by textbook definitions of Idaho as part of the Pacific region, an
area with such a strong connection to the Pacific Ocean and a cultural and
economic reliance on fish, particularly salmon. They feel a much stronger
geographic and cultural affinity to Utah, Wyoming, and the metropolitan
region of the Wasatch Front. Students taking the same class at the University of Idaho, however, find it strange that a definition of Idaho's region

would include Utah and Colorado, places that have little in common with western Washington.

Historical geographers of the western North American region have offered very different interpretations of where Idaho fits into the concept of region, but they have said very little about how regional and the state boundaries influence gender constructions and the lives of women. Gary J. Hausladen's anthology of historical geography essays about the American West contains few references to the interplay of gender and region in part, Hausladen points out, because the concepts are often viewed as mutually exclusive: "Because questions of race, ethnicity, gender, and class have proliferated in late-twentieth-century historical inquiry, it is at times argued that the concepts of 'regional' or 'sectional' division are in danger of obsolescence."[31] Race, ethnicity, and gender are concepts that are often explored outside regional constraints; their ascendance in academic studies can be viewed as postregional, anti-regional, or transregional, to use the term employed by Richard Etulain in chapter 9 in this volume. Linda McDowell's survey of feminist geography highlights the problem: feminist geography simply does not address American states, boundaries, and statehood issues. Feminist geographers grapple with community, suburbia, cities, localities, gender and space, nation-states, and the space of the female body, but they do not wrestle directly with the geographic boundaries/spaces of states within the American federal system.[32]

The origins of state history in the American West tend to obliterate difference and highlight commonality. As noted above, the state history and state historical society movement in Idaho and elsewhere was linked to the boosterism of early settlement communities, a nostalgic reminiscence of the pioneering experience and a desire to glorify the unique history of individual states. From the perspective of women's history, the state history movement contained a fundamental contradiction: state and local history was often supported by women and women's organizations but often did little to advance the history of women. One reason for this was the marginalization of state and local history by academic historians and the academy generally, leading to the feminization of state history and the perception, in male-dominated academic settings, that state and local history lacked rigor and professionalism. Thus, while some state and local historians might have been delving into nontraditional topics such as women and Native Americans, these efforts went largely unnoticed or were directly challenged and diminished by the academic establishment.[33]

In addition, women's organizations and some of the women historians writing about state history did so within the booster archetype, which supported the linear, male-dominated, political structure of state history. Boosterism and patriotism have formed cores of what could be termed "traditional Idaho state history," as the state has long struggled with its historical identity and its place in the history of the nation. During the twentieth century, Idaho historians, boosters, and pioneer organizations worked to find an important place for Idaho, while historical societies in neighboring states laid claim to some of Idaho's more well-known historical events and individuals, such as Sacagawea and the Nez Perce Conflict. While many of the groups most interested in the state's history were women's organizations, early statehood history excluded the role of women and the standard of living—socioeconomic and legal—of the state's female residents. It also completely ignored any recognition of gendered analysis. White female pioneers were featured, but the narrative structure of state history was not challenged, and little was said about the role of nonwhite men and women or the role of elite women in constructing the ideas of "whiteness" functioning in Idaho.

SACAGAWEA, POLLY BEMIS, AND WOMEN'S SPACE

The trajectories of written history about Idaho's two most prominent historical women, Sacagawea and Polly Bemis, illustrate the contradiction of state history and women's history. By any definition, Sacagawea was an Idaho woman: she was born in what became Idaho; her actions influenced state history; her people, the Lemhi Shoshone, remain in their ancestral homeland in what is now Idaho; and her story has made its way into every textbook about Idaho. Sacagawea, along with another Native American woman, Pocahontas, is one of the most recognizable women in United States history, due in large part to the efforts of women historians early in the twentieth century. But her story provides a clear example of how state and gender history are often at odds. Despite the many books written about Sacagawea, little is known either about her life outside the Lewis and Clark

Expedition or even about her role in it, and national sources often fail to link Sacagawea to Idaho, a source of contention and controversy among the Lemhi Shoshone even today. "Even this highly celebrated indigenous woman," Virginia Scharff has written, "has left a surprisingly faint trail."[34]

The efforts of women state historians and club activists writing within the booster model obscured Sacagawea's life as much as they illuminated it. As geographers Michael Heffernan and Carol Medlicot have argued, "Sacagawea as a historical model for modern American womanhood was assiduously cultivated" by suffrage activists, including Abigail Scott Duniway, a suffragist who lived in both Idaho and Oregon; Eva Emory Dye, a prominent Oregon clubwoman; and Grace Hebard, an activist woman historian in Wyoming. Dye's *The Conquest: The True Story of Lewis and Clark* sought to place Sacagawea into the history of the Pacific Northwest.[35] Describing her as the "Madonna of her race," Dye attributed much of the expedition's success to Sacagawea's role as "female guide."[36] Alternately, suffrage activists appropriated Sacagawea for their own goals in their own states and created a popular narrative that continues to be replicated in history texts at all levels, despite serious inaccuracies, including the argument that Sacagawea functioned as an official "guide." The appropriation of Sacagawea by women's organizations for the purposes of Idaho state boosterism cries out for further study of the gendered construction of state identities.

Polly Bemis, an Asian immigrant woman born Lalu Nathoy, has also received significant historical attention. Ruthanne McCunn's 1981 novel *Thousand Pieces of Gold* introduced Bemis's story in fictionalized form because, as McCunn has noted, she could not find enough historical material available about Nathoy/Bemis to piece together a coherent historical narrative.[37] Interest in Nathoy expanded the reach of Idaho history and led to the historic preservation of the Bemis ranch on the Salmon River, but that interest did little to inform historical understanding of Chinese American women in Idaho. As McCunn has stated, the historical record is silent on whether or not Polly Bemis had contact with the Chinese American community in Warren, Idaho. Even less clear is the route Bemis took to arrive in Idaho, thus obscuring the connections between Bemis and the routes covered by other Chinese American women. What is apparent is that her experience was not typical. Lalu Nathoy escaped indentured servitude, married a white

FIGURE 6.1. Chinese immigrants constituted a prominent community in nineteenth-century Idaho mining camps. Lalu Nathoy, better known as Polly Bemis, represents the rare and exceptional Chinese woman whose experiences have not been entirely lost to history. February 6, 1910. Photo by Charles Shepp. Photo courtesy of Idaho State Historical Society, 62-44.7.

man, and lived most of her life among whites, not Chinese. Most Chinese immigrant women in Idaho and in the American West have been—through intent or neglect—lost to history. Many first-generation Asian immigrants did not speak English, did not leave behind textual records, and did not hold jobs or positions that created official documents that archivists could save. Moreover, the pervasive connection between prostitution and Chinese immigrant women has created historical stereotypes that have distorted history. During the nineteenth century, Chinese men immigrated to the western United States in much larger numbers than did Chinese women, creating a dramatically skewed gender ratio in western boomtowns. Chinese male immigrants found work building the transcontinental railroads and in burgeoning mining camps. Because mining communities had so few women, Chinese men often took jobs held by women in other communities in the United States, including as providers of laundry services, as cooks, and as boardinghouse managers.[38] While many immigrant Chinese women became prostitutes in the American West—often by force—the representation of Chinese women in the West as sex objects, exotics, and deviants marginalized their role in the written history of the American West, particularly in the histories of states like Idaho that experienced high relative numbers of Chinese immigrants.[39] "The actual numbers of Chinese prostitutes were small," Shirley Hune has written, "compared to those of women of other nationalities on the U.S. frontier."[40]

Opportunities for many groups of women were limited in the American West, but the Chinese woman prostitute became the focus of anti-prostitution and anti-immigration campaigns in male-constructed nineteenth-century histories of the West. By the mid-twentieth century, the bitter anti-Chinese rhetoric had disappeared from the historiography of the American West, and Chinese men appeared as laborers and community builders, but Chinese women remained invisible or marginalized in Idaho state histories until very recently. The state's history is now influenced by revisionist histories of Asian women in the United States that have reinterpreted Chinese American history by incorporating feminist and gender scholarship and utilizing new methodologies to tease information from fragmented sources, such as photographs. A photograph of a Chinese immigrant family in Idaho City in 1902, housed at the Denver Public Library, shows women as clearly part of a larger family community of wives, daughters, mothers, and sisters.[41] Idaho history needs more accessible and published history of how these women interacted with their communities, how they affected the economy, how they made choices about work and home, and how they acted as agents of their own lives.

Several new avenues of research show promise for changing the structure of state history. The role of white women's literature and elite women's clubs in defining western spaces, territories, and towns has emerged as an important area of research. New approaches go beyond an analysis of the social and political power of women's organizations, though women's clubs

FIGURE 6.2. Elite women exerted political influence through their clubs and
organizations. Nettie Chipp, president of the Boise Women's Christian Temperance
Union, is shown in the state headquarters in the Empire Building in Boise, Idaho,
about 1916. Photo courtesy of Idaho State Historical Society, 60-114.7.

undeniably possessed and exercised such power.[42] Women writers and
women club members—sometimes the same individuals, sometimes not—
in Idaho were responsible for creating some of the definitions of space,
and of physical and social boundaries, of the state and its municipalities.
Ideas about state and region were often important tools in constructing and
maintaining borders and boundaries.

Idaho's National Federation of Women's Clubs organizations had an
interest in facilitating ideas about Idaho's uniqueness, its economic and
business climate, and its cultured maturity. Members of groups such as
the Pocatello Women's Club, Rupert Culture Club, Twin Falls Syringa Club,
and Boise Columbian Club were the spouses of the state's first small-town
bankers, doctors, lawyers, dentists, and real estate speculators.[43] They also

viewed themselves as part of a western elite class that defined itself by Protestantism, hard work, civic-mindedness, and whiteness (as opposed to nonwhite immigrants, Hispanic migrants, or Native American residents). In defining what it meant to be white and elite, they influenced the social structure of frontier communities and of the Rocky Mountain West. They based their notions of progress on Progressive ideals. These women were committed to resurrecting the Idaho of the Old West as the Idaho of the New West. Suspicious of unruly mining communities, supportive of the arts and culture in agrarian communities, women like Elizabeth DeMary of the Rupert Culture Club, Minnie Howard of the Pocatello Women's Club, Mary Ridenbaugh of the Boise Columbian Club, and Francena Kellogg Buck of the Lewiston Women's Christian Temperance Union and Tsceminicum Club significantly influenced the literary, cultural, and architectural landscapes of early Idaho communities.[44]

WOMEN IN TWENTIETH-CENTURY IDAHO

Twentieth-century topics promise great strides forward for Idaho women's and gender history. For instance, Idaho women's economic contributions—at home and at work—are the great neglected topics of the twentieth-century history. As women's historians have shown, women's domestic labor was essential to family survival throughout the farm depression of the 1920s and the Great Depression of the 1930s. Idaho's women contributed to the Depression economy in numerous ways. They took in knitting, grew gardens, tended orchards, canned vegetables and fruit, made clothing, milked cows, made cheese and butter, and taught their children to read. They took jobs in town and nursed their neighbors back to health. They fed the children of families in misfortune. During World War II, they worked in munitions factories, but most Idaho women stayed home, rationed meat and other foods, and made do. Women's participation in Japanese internment locally, and the role of Japanese women within the internment system, link Idaho women to the world. After the war, some Japanese families remained in Idaho, as internment had obliterated their opportunities elsewhere, and founded businesses—the Manhattan Café in Shoshone and George K's in Twin Falls and Burley—where women worked alongside their husbands. George K's Chinese restaurants were favorites for dance dates and family outings until they closed in the 1980s and 1990s, but few diners had any idea that the original owners and founders were Japanese.[45] We need to know more about these women, their circumstances, and the value of their economic participation.

By the 1970s and 1980s, Idaho's women, like women in the rest of the nation, were involved in the massive transitions rocking America's rural and urban communities alike. Idaho's only urban center, Boise, experienced rapid growth during this period, although its city center faltered. More Idaho women joined the workforce, straining the state's developing child-care system and inadequate preschool systems. Drugs and alcohol plagued many Idaho towns, as well as Indian reservations, during these tumultuous decades. Young people struggled to find their place in a shifting and unpredictable economy, at a point in Idaho's history when higher education was only starting to become more accessible. "I complained bitterly about there being nothing to do in the mill town we called home," award-winning writer and Idaho resident Kim Barnes recalled of her hometown, Lewiston, in the late 1970s. Jobs were limited: "You worked at the mill, the bullet factory, the stockyards, the Hilltop Café. You were a parts runner for Napa Auto, a tire grunt for Les Schwab. Summers you worked the peas—a backbreaking, money-making job, twelve hours a day, seven days a week—for as long as the annual harvest and processing of legumes would last."[46]

Without education and opportunity, Barnes languished at her relatively good bank teller job and eventually quit, beginning a dependent, drug-ridden, "hungry" existence with an abusive man. Leaving him behind with nothing but the clothes on her back, Barnes was able to extricate herself with the help of female friends, find low-paying work, and enroll for credits at Lewis-Clark State College. Other women facing the desolation of the late 1970s in Lewiston, Boise, and Pocatello were not so lucky and spent years as the dependents of abusive, drunken men or lived in shelters and trailer parks with their small children. Analysis of rural recipients of Aid to Families with Dependent Children during the mid-1990s confirmed that homeless people in rural areas tended "to be younger, more highly educated, less likely to be disabled, and more likely to be women with children than their urban counterparts" and that "poverty among female-headed families in rural areas" exhibited persistence "owing to fewer employment options,

minimal public housing, and the lack of public transportation."[47] Throughout the 1980s and 1990s, single mothers, whose ranks were growing, were
politicized with the dismissive term "welfare mothers," but little historical
literature has focused on the socioeconomic structures that created the
problem of poverty for mothers and children, especially in the small towns
of northern Idaho, where extractive economies gave way to desperation,
unemployment, and—for the lucky—low-paying service jobs.[48]

Some Idaho farmers also struggled during the last few decades of the
twentieth century, as corporate farms swallowed family farms and com-
modity prices plummeted, while farm families were buried in debt during
the 1980s. For corporate farmers, the concept of the "farm wife" as defined
by Annie Pike Greenwood in *We Sagebrush Folks* ceased to exist. Employees of corporate farms—men and women—often lived in town. Modern
"farm wives" supplemented the family income by working at the bank or
the grocery store. Women living on small farms and tenant farmers experienced significant hardship as the farm economy struggled throughout
the 1980s and early 1990s. Despite many works on the farm crisis in the
Midwest, little scholarly attention has focused on the farm family during
Idaho's late twentieth-century agricultural crisis. With existing resources,
our student could set out to answer critical questions about the experiences of Idaho farm families during the crisis years of the 1980s, but those
questions have yet to be asked and answered in modern scholarship.[49]
How did women contribute to the farm economy during this period? How
did women's labor—domestic, farm, migrant, managerial—support the
growth of corporate farming, and which women found opportunity within
this transition in Idaho?

The notion of regionalism and gender becomes more difficult—as if
it did not already suffer from the contradictions outlined here—after
1990, as the nation as a whole experienced declining regional differences.
Northerners, southerners, and westerners live predominantly in cities
and suburbs with the same retail chains, hotels, and theme restaurants.
They watch the same cable news channels and surf the same Internet
sites. They have access to national papers like *USA Today* and the *New
York Times*. These are, however, surface similarities, and great discrep-
ancies continue to exist. Women's access to education, health care, and

basic services in Idaho continues to lag. Nearly 57 percent of families in Idaho without health insurance had children under eighteen, according an Idaho Department of Health and Welfare study.[50] The state of Idaho does not, moreover, have a systematic junior college system, which can inhibit the ability of working parents to seek higher educational opportunities. These problems are accentuated for Idaho's significant Hispanic and Native American communities, where access to health care and other services can be limited by language barriers and geographic isolation. Generations of Mexican immigrants have created cultural enclaves in places like Rupert and Caldwell (as explored by Errol Jones in chapter 8 in this book), where agricultural labor provided opportunity for first-generation immigrants. Rupert's town square is dotted with Spanish-speaking businesses, where Anglos and Mexican Americans alike stand in line for hours for a taco during Fourth of July celebrations. Successive immigrant generations in these quasi-borderland communities have founded small businesses, corporate farms, and professional practices, yet we know very little about gender and women's roles within these social networks.

Twenty-first-century Idaho women include those like MaryJane Butters, a northern Idaho organic farmer and entrepreneur. Growing up as one of seven children in an Ogden, Utah, Mormon family, Butters acquired a love of the country and outdoor work. After years of jobs in roofing and on ranches, Butters joined the thousands of women who have become a movement in the United States in favor of organic and sustainable agriculture. In 2003, Random House predicted that her outdoor-living, chemical-eschewing farming lifestyle would have national appeal, when its division, Clarkson Potter, offered her a $1.35 million advance to write two illustrated books. Since that entry in 2003, Butters has launched a brand—MaryJanesFarm: Simple Solutions for Everyday Organic—complete with its own magazine, mail-order catalog, bed-and-breakfast, chat room, and blog, where city-bound farm enthusiasts can order everything from note cards to garlic seedlings. "These days, women are seeking common-sense remedies that rely on classic values," notes Butters. "There is a new interest in domesticity that includes the resurrection of forgotten arts like canning and crocheting. When we gather together, we share our talents, tell what we long for and talk about what is missing in our lives.

Creating a trail counter to market-driven cultural models can be lonely—
and loony—territory."[51]

* * *

Perhaps our student will take on the challenging task of writing a more
comprehensive history of women in Idaho, one that departs from the traditional narrative of western history, informs state history, and includes
the stories of women like MaryJane Butters. As women's historian Susan
Armitage has noted, "the most common unit of economic survival and adaptation was not the solitary man but, rather, the family."[52] A history that
fully incorporates women and gender would necessarily need to depart from
traditional topics such as statehood and resource allocation and look more
closely at motivations for statehood and actual resource use. It would also
need to draw on interdisciplinary inquiries, such as the work of feminist
scholars.[53] Women's and gender history offer ways of viewing state history
as the development of a political, cultural, and social construct, rather than
as the rigid linear expression of conquest and territorial acquisition. We
need to move beyond the biographies—what we know and don't know—of
Sacagawea, Polly Bemis, and Abigail Scott Duniway and look, instead, at
their world of connections and associations, and the ways in which those
associations shaped and defined Idaho boundaries of all kinds. We need to
examine the roles and interactions of Mexican immigrant women and their
professional daughters. In order to fully incorporate women and all peoples,
state history must finally move beyond the models created by white male
boosters at the time of statehood.

Notes

1   Hiram T. French, *History of Idaho: A Narrative Account of Its Historical Progress, Its
    People and Its Principal Interests* (Chicago: Lewis Publishing Company, 1914); John
    Hailey, *History of Idaho* (Boise: Syms-York Company, 1910); C. J. Brosnan, *History
    of the State of Idaho* (New York: Charles Scribner's Sons, 1918); James H. Hawley,
    History of Idaho: The Gem of the Mountains (Chicago: S. J. Clarke, 1920); Byron De-
    fenbach, *Idaho, the Place and Its People: A History of the Gem State from Prehistoric
    to Present Days* (Washington, DC: American Historical Society, 1933); William J.
    McConnell, *Early History of Idaho* (Caldwell, ID: Caxton Printers, 1913).
2   French, *History of Idaho*, 515.
3   Ibid., 515.

4   Betty Meloy Thiessen, *Past Days of the Tammany-Waha Area* (Lewiston, ID: printed by author, 1982); Mary Jane Fritzen, *Idaho Falls: City of Destiny* (Idaho Falls: Bonneville County Historical Society, 1991); Merle Wells and Arthur A. Hart, *Idaho: Gem of the Mountains* (Northridge, CA: Windsor Publications, 1985); Leonard J. Arrington, *History of Idaho* (Moscow: University of Idaho Press; Boise: Idaho State Historical Society, 1994).

5   Idaho State Historical Society, Reference Series, http://www.history.idaho.gov/reference-series (accessed June 27, 2011).

6   Guila Ford and Elizabeth Jacox, "Grace Edgington Jordan, 1892–1985" and "Mary Hallock Foote," Idaho State Historical Society Reference Series, nos. 1143 and 1139, January 1996.

7   The Reference Series is listed in thematic or numerical order. The first reference essay in numerical order, "Canoe Camp Site," was written in August 1964. See http://history.idaho.gov/sites/default/files/uploads/reference-series/0001.pdf (accessed October 25, 2013).

8   See also Arrington, *History of Idaho*, 1:438.

9   As quoted in Debra Shein, preface to *Edna and John: A Romance of Idaho Flat*, ed. Debra Shein (Pullman: Washington State University Press, 2000), xvii.

10 Also see "Abigail Scott," *Women of the West Museum*, http://theautry.org/explore/exhibits/suffrage/abigail3_full.html (accessed June 27, 2011).

11 Susan H. Swetnam, *Western Writers Series: Grace Jordan* (Boise: Boise State University, 2005).

12 Annie Pike Greenwood, with a foreword by JoAnn Ruckman, *We Sagebrush Folks* (Moscow: University of Idaho Press, 1988).

13 Only one issue, *Idaho Yesterdays* 41, no. 3 (1997), guest edited by Linda Morton-Keithley, was devoted to the topic of women's history.

14 Susan Armitage discussed the deficiencies of women's biographies in "Western Women's Biographies," *Western American Literature* 41, no. 1 (2006): 66–72.

15 An example of this type of organization is the Boise-based Anti-Saloon League of Idaho, a branch of the Anti-Saloon League of America.

16 French, *History of Idaho*, 519–20; Marjorie Williams, "Directors and Secretaries of the Idaho State Historical Society," *Idaho History Reference Series*, no. 882 (1989): 1–4, http://www.history.idaho.gov/sites/default/files/uploads/reference-series/0882.pdf (accessed October 25, 2013).

17 For this material, we have relied on Williams, "Directors and Secretaries," 1–6. See also Sandra Haarsager, *Organized Womanhood: Cultural Politics in the Pacific Northwest, 1840–1920* (Norman: University of Oklahoma Press, 1997), esp. 195–206.

18 As quoted in Ian Tyrrell, *Historians in Public: The Practice of American History, 1890–1970* (Chicago: University of Chicago Press, 2005), 209.

19 Williams, "Directors and Secretaries," 4.

20 Merle Wells and Arthur A. Hart, *Idaho: Gem of the Mountains* (Boise: Idaho State Historical Society in conjunction with Windsor Publications, 1985). The "Idaho's Independent Ranchers" sidebar appears on pp. 70–71. Philip Homan, associate professor and catalog librarian at Idaho State University's Oboler Library, is writing a book-length biography of Kitty Wilkins. See also Philip A. Homan, "Queen of Horses: Little-Known Now, Kittie Wilkins in Her Day Was America's Most Famous Western Woman," *Idaho Magazine*, October 2008, 19–23.

21 Katherine Aiken, Kevin Marsh, and Laura Woodworth-Ney, *Idaho: The Heroic Journey* (Encino, CA: Cherbo Press, for the Idaho State Historical Society, Boise, 2006). When the authors requested an alternative title, the response was that the authors "were too close" to the writing and that the story of Idaho was clearly the story of "accomplishment." E-mail correspondence in Woodworth-Ney's possession, December 2005–April 2006.

22 The purpose statement of the Western History Association (WHA) was taken from the WHA website, http://www.westernhistoryassociation.wildapricot.org/ (accessed October 25, 2013). The disparities that limited women's participation have eased during the past five years. Virginia Scharff, a historian of women and currently the Women's West Chair at the Autry Center in Los Angeles, served as president of the organization during 2008. Coauthor Laura Woodworth-Ney is a member of the organization.

23 Jonathan Foster, "WHA 2005 Membership Survey, Statistical Summary," *Western Historical Quarterly* 38 (Autumn 2007): 351.

24 Of the nearly 106 articles published in the *Western Historical Quarterly* between spring 2001 and spring 2008, approximately 34 were written by or about women (in some cases, by women, about women). The winter 2005 issue (vol. 36, no. 4) concentrated on gender and women's western history with articles by leading western historians, including Virginia Scharff, Peter Boag, and others.

25 Ironically, the field of western women's history was inaugurated in Idaho at a series of women's West conferences held in Sun Valley, during the early 1980s.

26 Susan Armitage, "From the Inside Out: Rewriting Regional History," *Frontiers: A Journal of Women Studies* 22 (2001): 32–47.

27 Carlos A. Schwantes, *In Mountain Shadows: A History of Idaho* (Lincoln: University of Nebraska Press, 1991), 63.

28 Dorothy O. Johansen and Charles M. Gates, *Empire of the Columbia: A History of the Pacific Northwest* (New York: Harper and Brothers, 1957), 327.

29 The issue of inadequate access to health care in rural Idaho remains of great concern to the Idaho legislature. Recently, Idaho instituted a rural health care access program and the Idaho Code states: "The public policy of this state is to encourage and facilitate voluntary provision of health care services" (39–7701). However, rural health care clinics are disproportionately distributed between northern and southern Idaho, and more than 75 percent of Idaho residents are part of either a medically underserved population or a medically underserved area. (These figures are available from the Idaho Department of Health & Welfare.) The United Health Foundation's eighteenth annual published report, "America's Health Care Rankings: A Call to Action for People and Their Communities" (2007), ranks each of the state health care systems. Idaho ranks forty-third in access, thirty-ninth in quality, and forty-fifth in equity. Suicide rates in Idaho are also among the highest in the United States, ranking in the top ten.

30 See the Garreau Group, http://www.garreau.com/main.cfm?action=book&id=3 (accessed June 27, 2011).

31 Gary J. Hausladen, ed., *Western Places, American Myths: How We Think about the West* (Reno: University of Nevada Press, 2003), 2.

32 This argument has benefited from many conversations with our historical geographer consultant, Dr. Sarah Hinman, at Idaho State University. Her wise counsel has

aided this paper, but our mistakes are entirely our own. Linda McDowell's *Gender, Identity, and Place: Understanding Feminist Geographies* (Minneapolis: University of Minnesota Press, 1999) includes the chapters "Home, Place, and Identity," "Community, City, and Locality," and "Gendering the Nation-State."

33 Examples from another state, Oklahoma, include the work of Muriel Wright, Angie Debo, and Alice Marriott. Wright's scholarship with the Oklahoma State Historical Society, Debo's pioneering efforts in highlighting Native American history in Oklahoma, and Marriott's experimental ethnography with Oklahoma tribes went relatively unnoticed, or unrecognized, within academic circles until much later. Wright, Debo, and Marriott "illustrate various degrees of this literary invisibility," writes Patricia Loughlin in *Hidden Treasures of the American West: Muriel H. Wright, Angie Debo, and Alice Marriott* (Albuquerque: University of New Mexico Press, 2005), xix.

34 Virginia Scharff, "Seeking Sacagawea," in Virginia Scharff, ed., *Twenty Thousand Roads: Women, Movement, and the West* (Berkeley: University of California Press, 2003), 12.

35 Michael Heffernan and Carol Medlicot, "A Feminine Atlas? Sacagawea, the Suffragettes and the Commemorative Landscape of the American West, 1904–1910," *Gender, Place and Culture: A Journal of Feminist Geography* 9 (June 2002): 109–31, quoted on 109.

36 Eva Emory Dye, *The Conquest: The True Story of Lewis and Clark* (Chicago: A. C. McClurg and Company, 1902), 290; Heffernan and Medlicot, "A Feminine Atlas?" 113.

37 Ruthanne Lum McCunn, "Reclaiming Polly Bemis," *Idaho Yesterdays* 46 (Spring–Summer 2005): 22–39.

38 See Susan Lee Johnson, *Roaring Camp: The Social World of the California Gold Rush* (New York: Norton, 2000), 464. For more on the Chinese in Rocky Mountain mining communities, see Liping Zhu, *A Chinaman's Chance: The Chinese on the Rocky Mountain Mining Frontier* (Boulder: University Press of Colorado, 1997).

39 Shirley Hune, "Chinese American Women in U.S. History: Explaining Representations of Exotic Others, Passive Objects, and Active Subjects," in S. Jay Kleinberg, Eileen Boris, and Vicki L. Ruiz, eds., *The Practice of U.S. Women's History* (New Brunswick, NJ: Rutgers University Press, 2007), Kindle ed. (n.p.).

40 Ibid.

41 This image (X-21517) is part of the Western History and Genealogy Digital Image Collection accessible through the Denver Public Library, http://digital.denverlibrary .org/u?/p15330coll22,21621 (accessed June 27, 2011).

42 Mary Ann Irwin's "'Going About and Doing Good': The Politics of Benevolence, Welfare, and Gender in San Francisco, 1850–1880," in Mary Ann Irwin and James F. Brooks, eds., *Women and Gender in the American West* (Albuquerque: University of New Mexico Press, 2004), 236–58, explores the work of women's charity societies in San Francisco; Karen J. Blair's *The Clubwoman as Feminist: True Womanhood Redefined, 1868–1914* (New York: Holmes and Meier, 1980) is the classic general work on the women's club movement; and Lori D. Ginzberg offers a national perspective on women's benevolence in *Women and the Work of Benevolence: Morality, Politics, and Class in the 19th-Century United States* (New Haven, CT: Yale University Press, 1990).

43 The Pocatello Women's Club consisted of a large number of elite women, many the

wives of prominent men in southeastern Idaho, including Dr. Minnie F. Howard, a physician; Nellie Cline Steenson, a member of the Idaho House of Representatives and the first woman to serve in the state senate; and Eva Kasiska, the daughter of W. F. Kasiska, a prominent physician. The Pocatello Women's Club is featured prominently in the papers of Dr. Howard, located at Idaho State University (Minnie F. Howard Papers, 1890–1957, Idaho State University Oboler Library Special Collections Department, MC 001, Pocatello, Idaho, 1890–1957). An electronic link to the Minnie F. Howard Papers description can be found at http://www.isu.edu/library/special/mc001t.htm (accessed June 27, 2011).

44 For an analysis of Elizabeth Layton DeMary's Culture Club, see Laura Woodworth-Ney, "Elizabeth Layton DeMary and the Rupert Culture Club: New Womanhood in a Reclamation Settlement Community," in Dee Garceau-Hagan, ed., *Portraits of Women in the American West* (New York: Routledge, 2005), 232–59; for more on the activities of women's clubs in Boise, see Suzanne Sermon, "Early Women's Organization in Boise," *Idaho Yesterdays* 41, no. 3: 20–26. For more on Buck, see Haarsager, *Organized Womanhood*, 84–87. Some records of the Twin Falls Syringa Club are available at the Twin Falls Public Library, http://twinfallspubliclibrary.org (accessed June 27, 2011).

45 Jim Gentry, *In the Middle and on the Edge: The Twin Falls Region of Idaho Twin Falls: College of Southern Idaho* (Twin Falls: Twin Falls Centennial Commission, 2003), 309.

46 Kim Barnes, *Hungry for the World* (New York: Random House, 2000), 83.

47 Moreover, in a 1990s study conducted in Maine for Aid to Families with Dependent Children (AFDC), employment and/or education did not ensure "an escape from poverty" in rural areas where jobs were scarce and the economy tenuous. Sandra Sue Butler, "Homelessness among AFDC Families in a Rural State: It Is Bound to Get Worse," *Affiliate Journal of Women and Social Work* 12 (Winter 1997): 427–28; quoted material from unpaginated online version, http://aff.sagepub.com/content/12/4/427 (accessed June 27, 2011).

48 See Ellen Reese, *Backlash against Welfare Mothers: Past and Present* (Berkeley: University of California Press, 2005).

49 Congressional manuscript collections, like that of former congressman Richard H. Stallings at Idaho State University, contain casework and requests from constituents for congressional intervention with government agencies such as the U.S. Department of Agriculture that chronicle the plight of Idaho farm families during the farm debt crisis of the 1980s and early 1990s.

50 "Health Status among Idaho Adults in 2004 and 2005," Idaho Department of Health and Welfare, http://www.healthandwelfare.idaho.gov/portal/alias_Rainbow/lang_en-US/tabID_3457/DesktopDefault.aspx (accessed June 27, 2011).

51 MaryJane Butters's article about her books and philosophy of farming appeared in "Diary: A Weeklong Electronic Journal," *Slate Magazine*, posted November 10, 2003, http://www.slate.com/id/2090894/entry/2091037/ (accessed June 27, 2011). Her website and mail-order company is at http://www.maryjanesfarm.org (accessed June 27, 2011).

52 Susan Armitage, "Women and the New Western History," *Organization of American Historians Magazine of History* 9 (Fall 1994): 22–27.

53 See Linda McDowell, *Gender, Identity & Place: Understanding Feminist Geographies* (Minneapolis: University of Minnesapolis Press, 1999).

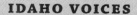

IDAHO VOICES
Women's History

Henrietta C. Dunbar explains some
social activities of a clubwoman.

On April 11, 1939, the *Statesman* sponsored a class in electric cooking. As
president of the Columbian Club, I was asked to introduce the speaker, and
I said, "I have been invited to introduce Miss Emily Conklin, who is [to] present this series of lessons in the art of cookery. As you perhaps know, one
of the objectives of the club movement in America is the betterment of the
American home, and since the preparation and serving of food play such an
important part in that home betterment program, any effort that can help
the housewife . . . to perform this important duty more effectively should
certainly be regarded as a civil contribution. And so, I am sure that you will
agree that the *Idaho Daily Statesman* should have an expression of appreciation from us for affording us this opportunity each year of becoming better
informed in regard to this important art, the art of cookery, which includes
not only the preparation of better food but also the serving of it more at-
tractively. And so, I feel that it is not only a privilege and an opportunity but
also a very real pleasure to present Miss Emily Conklin, who is to conduct
this series of lessons for us.

* * *

Magdalena Fritchle Lukens, wife of Idaho secretary of state Fred Lukens
(1927–33), describes her social roles and political ideas.

INTERVIEWER: Did you take an active part in the political life that your
husband had to lead?

LUKENS: Yes. You know, when Mrs. Baldridge and I—she was the governor's wife—we decided that it might be a good thing; the members of the
legislature brought their [wives] quite often, and they were entertained—

but we decided that it might be a good thing if we organized the women, the wives of the legislators, into a group. So, Mrs. Baldridge had a tea—a luncheon—and we did just that. And we organized, and from then on— once every two weeks—we had a dinner dance at the Owyhee Hotel. And the women once a week—once every two weeks—the opposite week, had a luncheon together, and I think they still continue to do that.

INTERVIEWER: Did the women get involved in the political issues, like did they with Prohibition?

LUKENS: No, no, we didn't at all. We were Democrats and Republicans together, and it made no difference. It was a social thing. So there wasn't any politics in any of the women's groups.

INTERVIEWER: Did you sometimes have a desire to get into politics more?

LUKENS: No, really I—no really. You know, being a part of a party is some- thing—My father, as I remember it, voted the Democratic ticket. I remem- ber he voted for silver. Well, that was an issue once. I wish it still were! And so, when I came to Idaho to teach, which I did and met my husband, Idaho had suffrage and women had the vote, but no Eastern states did. And so the Western women—I remember voting, and President Wilson was running, and there was a war situation again. They were both good men, but Wilson said he'd keep us out of the war, and I remember voting for Wilson.

Note

Henrietta C. Dunbar was interviewed by Esther F. Gibson, January 27, 1971, place unknown, transcript (OH0026), Oral History Center/Idaho State Historical Society, 21. Used with permission of Idaho State Historical Society.

Magdalena Fritchle Lukens was interviewed by Diane Alters, September 15, 1972, place unknown, transcript (OH 0120), Oral History Center/Idaho State Historical Society, 2–3. Used with permission of Idaho State Historical Society.

7

Confronting Race and Creating Community

Idaho's Ethnic History

LAURIE MERCIER

IN THE NATIONAL MIND, IDAHO IS SET APART FROM OTHER
states for the lack of diversity in its population. It is perceived to be
white, Anglo, and—based on high-profile cases of Aryan Nations strong-
holds—hostile to ethnic and racial diversity.[1] Although its foreign-born and
nonwhite populations have been small in comparison to the rest of the nation, closer examination of Idaho's history reveals that it has been shaped
by dozens of ethnic groups who have settled in the state, usually drawn by
economic opportunities.[2] Of course, Shoshone, Coeur d'Alene, Nez Perce,
and other Native Americans had carved out distinct communities and cultures for thousands of years before the first Latin American, African American, and European American explorers ventured to the Pacific Northwest
as Rodney Frey and Robert McCarl describe in chapter 2 in this volume. In
the nineteenth century, French Canadian fur traders, Italian missionaries, miners from Cornwall and China, Scottish sheep ranchers, Mormon
farmers from England, African American and Mexican cowboys, and Jewish
merchants were among those who trickled into Idaho Territory. They were
followed by Scandinavian homesteaders and southern European railroad
workers in the decades after statehood. Mexican agricultural workers and
Southeast Asian refugees moved to Idaho and shaped new communities in
the latter half of the twentieth century.

A combination of factors determined how these ethnic groups fared in
Idaho: economic opportunities, kinship networks, the presence and size
of ethnic enclaves, reception by others, and ideologies about "race." How
did Idahoans' ideas about race and residency, reflected in everything from

individual prejudice to systematic discrimination, shape Idaho's ethnic communities and influence whether people stayed or left? As the United States became increasingly rigid in applying hierarchical categories from white to black and from superior to inferior, the degree to which a migrant group could define itself as "white" appeared to tilt it toward success.[3] As Elliott Barkan explains, the issue of whiteness in the West "frequently determined whether [individuals] were welcomed or excluded, well treated or mistreated, equitably rewarded or simply exploited, tolerated, or killed."[4] This reception determined a community's size, and the relatively small population proportion of most migrant groups made forging a community difficult. There often were not enough people to support the institutions necessary for an ethnic community to emerge. Yet ethnic ties did persist, despite and sometimes because of discrimination and hardship. Some communities formed by choice, others—because of racism—by necessity.

This chapter compares five ethnic groups that settled in Idaho during the period of great American immigration and migration, from 1870 to 1950. The economic, social, and political foundations laid during this period affected the persistence or evolution of more recent communities. How did they emerge and sustain themselves over time? In many ways, the experiences of Idaho's Chinese, Japanese, Basque, and Italian immigrants and African American migrants parallel the larger history of the region and nation. Mostly male migrants were pulled to Idaho for economic opportunities. Once they found particular economic niches where their services were needed, they began a chain migration, with relatives and neighbors following them. For example, in the mining county of Shoshone, in northern Idaho, immigrant miners beckoned their kin to join them in the grueling but lucrative work underground. Mining, agriculture, and other industries initially attracted migrants to this inland mountain state. Their labors built Idaho and made their employers wealthy, yet many found establishing a "home" to be challenging.

After the 1920s, fewer foreign-born whites, Chinese, Japanese, and African Americans moved to Idaho. Rising nativism following World War I and restrictive national immigration legislation significantly reduced immigrant numbers via a quota system that privileged northern Europeans and categorically excluded Asians. Supreme Court decisions and the

Johnson-Reed Immigration Act of 1924 affirmed racial requirements for citizenship, curbing Italian, Basque, and Japanese migration to Idaho. Discrimination and lack of economic opportunity discouraged African Americans from moving to the state. State laws, such as an antimiscegenation law that prohibited Asians, blacks, and multiracial people from marrying whites, also reminded people of color of their second-class status.[5]

At the same time, the expansion of irrigated and large-scale agricultural production in the American West required a large, mobile, and seasonal workforce, and businesses pressured Congress to exempt the western hemisphere from quotas.[6] Idaho employers looked south for a new source of labor: Mexican Americans from the Southwest and immigrants from Mexico.

CHINESE IMMIGRANTS

Gold strikes in Idaho in the early 1860s attracted Chinese miners from California, and by 1870, about a third of the territory's population was Chinese, the highest percentage in any state or territory.[7] Although this statistic may be well known among students of western and mining history, it warrants further examination because of the rapid decline of the numbers of Chinese in Idaho in subsequent decades. This decline, and the enormous challenges faced by Chinese immigrants in Idaho, speak to the specific racial and gender characteristics of the state's ethnic communities.

Mining communities in the American West were among the nation's most diverse, attracting people from all over the world and across the United States to seek fortunes or a better living.[8] But anti-Chinese sentiment swept the mining West before the first Idaho gold strikes and led to legislation that denied the Chinese equal treatment and limited their economic opportunities. In 1864, the Idaho Territorial Legislature prohibited their entrance unless they paid a monthly tax of four dollars; two years later, it raised the tax to five dollars.[9] Yet limited opportunities elsewhere and the recruitment of some Chinese to revitalize mining camps continued to lure Chinese immigrants to Idaho. Even three violent massacres of Chinese in 1866 as they traveled to the Boise Basin from California and Nevada did not stop Chinese miners from migrating to Idaho.[10]

Chinese placer miners, both individually and in groups, dug in the mountains and canyons of Idaho, worked as laborers for mining ventures, and sometimes owned their own companies. Bigotry and perceptions of labor competition drove many Idaho mining camps to restrict or prohibit Chinese from working claims until white miners believed that most precious metals were gone. As placers yielded less by the late 1860s and 1870s, white miners were anxious to sell to Chinese, who added significantly to the wealth of the state by successfully working near-exhausted river bars in this second phase of mining. However, labor unions made certain that they were excluded from the capitalized and more stable mining taking place in the north in the Coeur d'Alenes.[11]

In assessing Chinese mining and entrepreneurial successes, many observers reinforced stereotypical notions that the immigrants could survive on little and needed fewer calories than their white counterparts. As Liping Zhu discovered, however, Chinese miners were more successful, despite discriminatory laws and taxes, because they secured a balanced diet and had superior health care, giving them a mortality rate only half that of white miners in Idaho and other mining states. Chinese miners also brought skills and knowledge to diggings thought to be exhausted. For example, recruited from California to revive mining in the Boise Basin, Chinese immigrants built elaborate water ditches and flumes that enabled them to extend the mining enterprise and increase their profits.[12] As the diggings played out in Pierce in the mid-1860s, white miners encouraged Chinese to purchase their claims, resulting in a large community of 445 Chinese men and 8 women in 1870. The vast majority mined, but a few dozen were gamblers, hotel cooks, restaurateurs, blacksmiths, gardeners, laundrymen, merchants, and doctors. The women worked as prostitutes.[13]

The relatively few Chinese women who immigrated to the United States were concentrated in mining areas of California, Idaho, and Nevada, and their numbers were frozen by the 1882 exclusion laws, which prevented most Chinese men and women from entering the United States. Bachelor sons and married men without their wives and families accommodated new gender roles, and some found domestic work in mining camps and cities, washing clothes, cooking, and waiting on families.

Since few Chinese women could immigrate to the United States and anti-miscegenation laws prevented Chinese men from marrying white women, the men created a measure of community in their segregated bachelor "Chinatowns" in Idaho. For example, Silver City, with a Chinese population of seven hundred in 1874, had a Chinese Masonic temple, two joss houses, several restaurants, two laundries, four stores, two lotteries, five gambling houses, and several warehouses. Businesses along Idaho Street in Boise's Chinatown provided social networking sites as well as critical goods, such as special foods, and services, including medical care, not available elsewhere.[14] Even after its move to Front and Seventh Streets in 1900, the Boise Chinatown retained its identity into the twentieth century. In fact, in 1902, about four hundred Chinese Masons dedicated a three-story hall, and three years later, political activists constructed the headquarters for the Chinese Empire Reform Association.[15] Family clan associations, expanded in the United States to include all persons with the same surname, formed to protect and support their members and mediate disputes. Two district associations, Sze-yap and Yung-wa, from the Six Companies that served throughout the country, offered labor contracts to Idaho Chinese. Other groups, including the tongs and Masons, provided organization, networks, and support in Chinese communities.[16] Despite isolation and hardship, Chinese immigrants came together in everyday moments of joy and sadness and perpetuated important traditions. For example, newspapers frequently reported on Chinese New Year celebrations, which continued into the twentieth century in some Idaho communities. Funerals also brought large numbers of people together. When Elk City merchant To Quong died in 1887, hundreds gathered in Lewiston to view the deceased in an elegant casket and mourn in ceremonies led by Chinese Masons, who marked the occasion with a feast and then marched to the Chinese cemetery for the burial.[17]

White workers had long resented Chinese competition, even though the threat was more perceived than real. Stories spread about white workers being victimized because of employer "preferences" for Chinese, as was the case of one female domestic who wrote to a newspaper to complain about Chinese men usurping her job prospects: "The Chinese barbarians have captured Boise and will soon rule the whites. . . . I went to . . . try and get employment but the answer at each house was, 'We've got a Chinaman.' . . . I left them disgusted, and subsequently met a friend, Mrs. — [;]

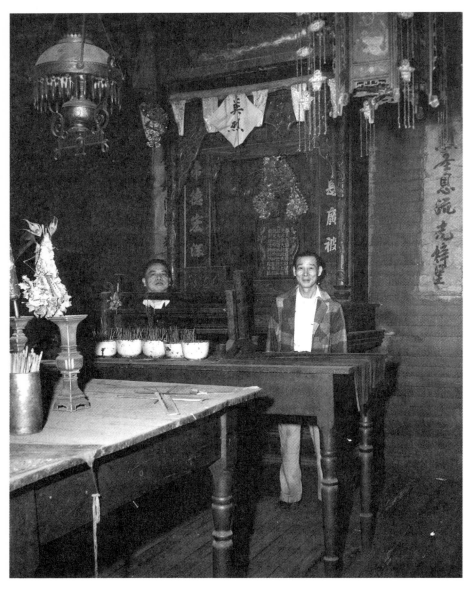

FIGURE 7.1. The Chinese community created spaces for maintaining cultural practices. Here Quon Lee (on the left) and Owen Eng are seen in the Buck Eye Mao Joss House in Lewiston, Idaho. Photo courtesy of Idaho State Historical Society, 2965.

... she said she had given her Chinaman $7, but he was much better than a white woman. I bade her good day, with a tear in my eye, wishing I was a Chinaman."[18] Southern Europeans, who had also been racialized, strove to establish their "whiteness" in contrast to Asians in order to gain greater acceptance. One Moscow business, the Delimonco (sometimes Delimonico) Restaurant, tried to pull business away from Chinese restaurants by advertising "We cook in a good [w]holesome style and by a white woman. White cooks, white waiters and white prices." Other Moscow businesses ran ads in the 1880s that noted "white" labor and "no Chinese employed."[19]

Just as gendered characterizations of Chinese men rationalized their persecution, sympathetic accounts of Chinese women sometimes permitted them better treatment. Lalu Nathoy, who became well known as Polly Bemis, was a chattel laborer owned by a Chinese gambling hall owner in Warren, Idaho, who was befriended by (and later married) the white entrepreneur Charlie Bemis. She became a celebrated resident of north-central Idaho during her lifetime and the subject of numerous books, articles, and a film. She ran a popular boardinghouse and later farmed with Bemis along the Salmon River. Her gender also made her the object of much attention. The 1924 immigration law made it impossible for Chinese wives to join Chinese husbands in the United States, so a Chinese female was an unusual sight. Because of her status, Bemis escaped the anti-Chinese terrorism inflicted on many other immigrants in late nineteenth-century Idaho.[20]

As critical as Chinese laborers were to American industrial expansion, rising racist fears led to the passage of the 1882 Exclusion Act, which prohibited further Chinese immigration. But instead of reassuring whites, the law, in formalizing the Chinese as "other," actually helped rationalize and accelerate acts of brutality directed at Idaho Chinese communities. Earlier, hostile acts and brazen demonizing of the Chinese in the Idaho press had been common, but communities such as Hailey, Ketchum, Clarks Fork, and Bonners Ferry began openly threatening Chinese residents, telling them to leave or face violent expulsion. In 1885, vigilantes hanged five Chinese men in Pierce for a suspected murder. The Anti-Chinese Congress met in Boise in 1886 to organize a wholesale boycott of Chinese labor. The worst anti-Chinese violence in the history of the West occurred in the Snake River canyon in 1887, when a gang of seven horse thieves murdered thirty-four

Chinese miners, sent their bodies downstream, and fled with their gold. Only three were apprehended, and none was convicted of the murders.[21]

Other Chinese residents struggled to maintain their place in Idaho, and some asserted themselves in the courts, defending their rights and seeking protection and justice when other remedies failed in the face of mounting hostility. They rarely won their cases, since the 1882 Exclusion Act forbade Asian citizenship, leaving them with no rights to mining claims or other property.[22] Some Chinese, especially those with prominent connections in the capital city of Boise, were able to negotiate acceptance in the larger community. Dr. C.K. Ah Fong practiced his medical trade for more than twenty years, beginning in 1889. When Idaho became a state in 1890, the Board of Medical Examiners denied Fong his credentials. He sued and won his case before the state supreme court, winning the right for himself and other Chinese doctors to practice medicine.[23]

Idaho's Chinese population declined rapidly as the state grew, from the much-vaunted high of 4,272 in 1870 to about 1,500 in 1900. It is not clear where these immigrants moved. Some, seeking community and social and economic security, migrated to Chinatowns in the larger West Coast cities of San Francisco, Seattle, and Vancouver, British Columbia, but some believe that most of the Chinese men returned to China.[24] Situated in the state's largest urban area, Boise's Chinese community, even if small, persisted when others disappeared. As Arthur Hart notes, attempts to boycott and drive out the Chinese were largely unsuccessful, since they played a vital economic role in the city. Nearby Garden City was named for the Chinese gardeners who provided much produce for Boise city dwellers. Boise's Chinatown actually grew from 131 residents in 1890 to 523 in 1900, as Chinese left other parts of the state.[25] Repeal of the Chinese Exclusion Act in 1943, the Walter-McCarran Act of 1952, and the Immigration Act of 1965 further eased restrictions on Chinese immigration. A new wave of immigrants finally began to mitigate the unbalanced sex ratio of Chinese men to women in the United States and started a transformation of Chinese American communities. Few moved to Idaho, however; its once vibrant Chinatowns remained a historical curiosity with only some buildings, artifacts, and oral histories left to document their memory.

AFRICAN AMERICAN MIGRANTS

Just as mining strikes attracted many Chinese to Idaho, several dozen en-
terprising black single men, women, and families came to the territory in
search of economic opportunity. They faced intimidation and hostile legislation and were often included in statutes that limited Chinese mining. In
1863, Boise County passed a law to exclude blacks and Chinese from pros-
pecting, and the territorial legislature introduced a bill to prohibit black
migration to the region in 1865. In 1869, a black miner in Silver City wrote
to the *San Francisco Elevator* to complain about the level of prejudice he
encountered. By 1870, Idaho Territory had but sixty African Americans; ten
years later, their numbers had dropped to fifty-three, the lowest number
in the American West, less than 15 percent the number in the neighboring
states of Montana, Washington, and Oregon.[26]

The desire to escape segregation and discrimination in southern, eastern, and some midwestern states motivated African Americans to migrate
west. Many believed that the racial atmosphere in the Pacific Northwest
was much more tolerant, although many were disappointed. Racial prejudice in Idaho led many pioneer blacks to seek community in certain mining
and urban areas. For a time, a cluster of African Americans settled in both
Custer and Silver City, finding opportunities as domestics, barbers, and
laundresses as well as miners.

Some miners successfully navigated around the barriers of racism to
achieve a measure of success and acceptance. Because of his skill in finding
ore in the Clearwater country of northern Idaho, William Rhodes secured
a grubstake from Lewiston backers. He accumulated thousands of dollars
from a claim that became known as Rhodes Creek near Pierce. George Washington Blackman became a successful miner in the Hailey area beginning
in 1879. Blackman Peak in the Sawtooth National Recreation Area bears his
name, and one local historian claimed he "was loved and respected by all
who knew him."[27] William C. "Doc" Hisom also became somewhat of a local
celebrity, mining along the Snake River in Canyon County from 1906 until
his death in 1944. He received a steady stream of curious visitors, including
one local resident who recalled his fascination with Hisom: "To see a colored

man, why, that was really kind of exciting to us. We really appreciated it. . . .
[H]e was a mystery man."[28] The comment reveals how individual African
Americans who lived outside a larger black community had to endure treat-
ment as "characters" and cultivate community support.

Other African Americans managed to cross racial boundaries to succeed
on homesteads and farms and become part of the white rural communities
where they settled. Joe and Lou Wells homesteaded near Deary in Latah
County in 1889, and they were included in community affairs and social
gatherings. Joe Wells supplemented his family's farm income as a gyppo
logger for the Potlatch mill, as a blacksmith, and as a carpenter.[29] Eugene
Settle migrated with his parents and siblings from Oklahoma to Latah
County in 1898 because his father wanted to homestead and heard that
there was "very little prejudice" in the Northwest. The Settles bought and
rented land and earned the respect of neighbors, who sometimes helped
with planting. The family also sold raspberries and strawberries in Moscow. The Settles and Wellses represented two of the less than dozen African
American farm owners in Idaho in the early twentieth century,[30] but few
children of these farm families remained in the area, lured to cities after
World War II for jobs and less social isolation.

Despite some success stories among black pioneers, by the early twentieth century, far fewer African Americans lived in Idaho than in the neighboring states of Montana, Oregon, and Washington, and the relatively
small number in the state was concentrated in the cities of Boise and Pocatello.[31] Excluded from most occupations, African Americans migrated to
cities, where they could find employment in the service and manufacturing
sectors or become entrepreneurs. The 1910 census revealed that a quarter of black males in Idaho labored as waiters, servants, and barbers; 20
percent worked as farm, railroad, or general laborers; and only 9 percent
were farmers or miners. The Boise Owyhee Hotel alone employed fourteen
black waiters. Most important, the city provided safety in numbers and
some social networks. Similar to the black female workforce throughout
the West, 81 percent of black women in Idaho worked as domestics.[32] Some
black women managed to escape domestic work by developing small businesses. For example, Mamie Greene was a well-known caterer in Boise for
more than thirty years. The percentage of urban African Americans in Idaho

would grow through the twentieth century. In 1920, 70 percent of the 920 blacks living in Idaho were classified as urban, compared to 28 percent of white residents.[33]

Jobs with the Union Pacific Railroad attracted many African Americans to Pocatello. Blacks labored in railroad yards, on section gangs, and as porters, and they created a thriving community. Although Idaho's black population never rose above 0.5 percent of the total population, in 1920, a significant 2.4 percent of Pocatello's population was black. Its 366 African American residents far surpassed Boise's 63. Edward and Mary Noble left their home in Tyler, Texas, in 1917 in response to Union Pacific job advertisements. Kinship ties brought others to the area. Two of Mary Noble's sisters, Hattie Washington and Ophelia Bairfield, joined the Nobles a few years later. Listoria Smith came to Pocatello from Dennison, Texas, to live with her older, married sister, Lena Edwards. Joseph Taylor "J.T." Jones left his Fulton, Arkansas, home in 1918 to join his brother Chauncey, who was then working as a porter at the Bannock Hotel. Jones shined shoes at the hotel and later became a porter for the Union Pacific.[34]

In Idaho, African Americans experienced discrimination in employment, housing, and public accommodations such as restaurants, hotels, and other public places. Even as late as the 1950s, African Americans in Pocatello were denied service in some local hotels and restaurants. When the Ink Spots performed at the Moore Inn, the bartender refused to serve band members. Yet, like the Chinese, African Americans countered this treatment by developing strong associations, churches, and businesses. Many African American residents noted that being segregated in neighborhoods on the east side of the city aided the formation of a tight-knit community. Joe Hamilton established the Porters and Waiters Club on South First to provide accommodations for traveling blacks who were turned away elsewhere, and residents established lodges and social clubs for men and women. The black American Legion Post No. 120 and the Elks Lodge No. 558 frequently held dinners and dances for the black community. Rosa Tigner recalled that families on the east side created an "atmosphere of togetherness" and shared with one another during hard times, creating a buffer against the harsh realities of a racist society.[35]

In Boise, segregation also had the effect of pulling black families closer together. Many lived south of the railroad tracks, on East Bannock, River, and South Fourteenth Streets. Yet that closeness came at a high social cost. Erma Madrey Hayman recalled that when she moved to Boise in 1927, blacks could not rent in most parts of town and were refused service in most restaurants, including at the bus depot. Even in death, blacks and Chinese were segregated, laid to rest in their own sections of Rose Hill cemetery.[36] Boise's African American community found other outlets for socializing, through their churches, jobs, lodges, clubs, and friends. Different groups organized events at the Grand Army of the Republic Hall from the early 1900s through the 1940s. The Rosebud Women's Club had high turnouts for its functions, which included house parties, luncheons, and card parties.[37]

Churches in particular catalyzed black social, political, and spiritual life. In 1908, African Americans founded the Colored Baptist Church and Allen Chapel African Methodist Episcopal Church (AME) in Pocatello. Both erected churches in the 1920s. Gloria Hines recalled that both churches brought area blacks together and jointly sponsored political rallies, educational events, and social gatherings.[38] Matching Pocatello's timing, African Americans in Boise founded two churches in 1908, including St. Paul Baptist Church. After meeting in homes for years, the congregation built St. Paul in 1921, and it remains one of the oldest buildings constructed by Idaho African Americans. The church's first pastor, Reverend William Riley Hardy, a skilled carpenter, not only helped construct the church but remained pastor for two decades.[39] Historian Mamie Oliver notes that the church played an even more critical role in Idaho than in other regions of the country because it was "an environment with fewer people interested in their welfare." St Paul's, for example, offered temporary housing and social networks for emotional and job support. Mary Sanders Watkins remembered that the Bethel Baptist Church in Pocatello provided the one space where blacks were autonomous and could escape the oppression of white society.[40]

Racial harassment and discrimination did not daunt black leaders and organizations in their struggle to end discrimination in housing, employment, education, and public accommodations. The Ku Klux Klan (KKK), which enjoyed a revival in Idaho as in the rest of the nation in the 1920s, held rallies and parades in Pocatello in 1922–23 and, according to Shelley Hale, had significant influence in city politics. But African American residents fought back. "Yellowstone Jack," the city's noted black policeman, who joined the force after World War I, rounded up several men to defend the AME Church, deterring a planned KKK attack. Beginning in the early twentieth century, Boise's black community asserted its concern for equal rights by sponsoring regular celebrations, plays, and speeches. In May 1926, the community presented a musical drama depicting the story of black soldiers. Held at the high school under the direction of Madame Lena L. Johnson of Tacoma, Washington, the drama was a moving entreaty for equality. The *Idaho Daily Statesman* reported, "There was evidence of feeling and sincerity in their portrayal of the plea for recognition of their race's contribution to America's greatness."[41]

Despite general population growth in the state between 1920 and 1940, the numbers of African Americans dropped dramatically, from 920 to 595, due partly to inflamed racial bigotry and declining economic opportunities during the Depression.[42] Following World War II, the African American population rebounded. The new migrants revived cultural and political institutions, including the Boise and Pocatello chapters of the National Association for the Advancement of Colored People.[43]

JAPANESE IMMIGRANTS

The same racial barriers that limited opportunities for African Americans and Chinese also shaped Japanese American communities in Idaho. Japanese immigrants first came to the Pacific Northwest in the 1880s, when federal legislation that excluded further Chinese immigration created demands for new immigrant labor.

Railroads in particular recruited Issei, or first-generation immigrants, from Hawaii and Japan. Thousands of Japanese workers helped construct the Great Northern, Northern Pacific, Oregon Short Line, and other railroads in the region. Like other laborers at the turn of the twentieth century, Japanese railroad workers organized and struck to demand wage increases or to protest cuts. These workers commanded higher wages from railroad companies as the sugar beet industry began competing for their labor.[44] During the early 1900s, as new irrigation projects expanded sugar beet production in the West, employers such as the Utah and Idaho Company actively recruited Issei to work on farms and in refineries in the Snake

River Valley, often trading seasonal labor with railroads. Migrations to Idaho increased the Japanese population to more than 1,500 by 1910.[45]

Most Japanese immigrants came from farming backgrounds, and many viewed independent farming as the way to move up the economic ladder and form communities. Often unable to purchase land because of discrimination, many Issei eventually leased land so that they could work for themselves. Hajimu "Henry" Fujii's story illustrates the struggle many immigrants went through to acquire land. After arriving in the United States, he worked in a Seattle restaurant, in sugar beet fields near Billings, Montana, and in a "muscle-straining job" for a railroad in Montana before joining a sugar beet crew near Emmett, Idaho. The crew, mostly Japanese workers, thinned beets with a short-handled hoe, "the kind of work to break not only backs but spirits too." At the end of the beet season, Fujii joined 1,500 other Japanese on a railroad crew near Nampa. In 1908, he formed a partnership with his brother and a friend, and they leased an eighty-acre farm near Emmett.[46]

In the early twentieth century, despite the Issei's hard work, envy and racial prejudice led to increasing anti-Japanese attitudes in Idaho and the West Coast, much as feelings had hardened against perceived Chinese competition. White residents of Coeur d'Alene, Nampa, Caldwell, and Mountain Home threatened or drove out Japanese workers. Articles from the *Idaho Daily Statesman* of July 1892 report that "Mountain Home people try to abate the nuisance. . . . Japs . . . are no more desirable than the Chinese, being just as miserly and much filthier."[47]

Yet despite the racism, Idaho may have presented more openings for Japanese Americans than neighboring West Coast states. A 1910 Senate report on Japanese businesses in Idaho noted that "unlike the white residents of the Pacific Coast states, those of Idaho give no evidence of any hostile feeling" toward the Japanese.[48] Like other western states, Idaho sought to block Japanese immigrants from owning and renting property with anti-alien land laws, but Idaho's Issei successfully fought anti-Japanese legislation for a number of years through the lobbying efforts of the 150-member Japanese Association of Western Idaho, the United Japanese Association Council, the sugar industry, and churches. In 1921, the Idaho Senate defeated the Alien Land Measure, which would have denied aliens the right to own or lease lands in the state. Japanese Americans considered their efforts somewhat successful; while legislation prohibiting land ownership finally passed in 1923, it allowed renewable leases, making Idaho the only state in the West where Issei could lease land.[49] The Issei also circumvented discriminatory state laws by subleasing land from citizens or registering land in the names of their Nisei (meaning "second generation") children, who were American citizens by birth. Nonetheless, because of alien land laws, farmers like Toji Fujimoto had to wait thirty-five years until his American-born son Masayoshi could purchase 120 acres for the family in 1937.[50]

After 1908 and the passage of the so-called Gentleman's Agreement between the United States and Japan, more Japanese women were able to immigrate, contributing to more stable communities.[51] Nonetheless, many Issei women were disappointed with their new homes, far from families and friends, where they had to endure discrimination and hard work in order to survive. Henry Fujii had saved enough money to return to Japan to marry and brought his new wife to Idaho. Fumiko Mayeda Fujii encountered a crude cabin on the Emmett farm that her new husband leased, which she had to share with his partner, Henry Hashitani, and Hashitani's family. In addition to facing crowded living conditions and hard labor on the farm, she had to learn a range of new skills, including baking bread, sewing, and speaking English.[52]

Although they may have initially come to the United States to earn and save money and then return to Japan, the birth of their children persuaded many Issei to remain in their adopted country and strengthen their communities. By the 1920s, the numbers of Japanese American families had grown significantly, and a high percentage had moved from performing migratory work to owning businesses or farms. But the National Origins Act of 1924, which limited European immigration by establishing quotas, upheld the racialization of Asians by essentially excluding any further Japanese immigration.

While struggling for a place in American society, the Issei sought to retain ties to Japan and teach their American-born children, the Nisei, their cultural traditions. They formed chapters of the Japanese Association of America, which maintained official links with Japan, to fight discriminatory legislation, and provided mutual aid and social activities for its members.

The Nisei hoped to realize their immigrant parents' dreams of finding success in the United States through American citizenship and its benefits, including the right to own land. Beginning in the 1920s, intent on promoting Americanization as well as pursuing their civil rights, they formed Japanese American Citizens League (JACL) chapters. A JACL chapter in Pocatello fought the Alien Land Law of 1923.[53] The Issei also sought to educate their neighbors and to ease discrimination by promoting their Japanese heritage, trade, and friendship. In response to a friendship project initiated by the Federal Council of the Churches of Christ, the Japanese Committee on International Friendship among Children formed and sent Japanese doll messengers to all of the states before Christmas 1927. Miss Nara was displayed in store windows throughout Idaho before being donated to the Idaho State Historical Society for safekeeping.[54] Immigrants and their children also embraced American traditions, even if segregated. Baseball teams brought together Issei and Nisei and Japanese American communities scattered throughout the Northwest. The annual Japanese Northwest Fourth of July Baseball Tournament attracted thousands from Washington, Oregon, and Idaho.

Despite their attempts to prove their "Americanness," both Nisei and Issei were targeted in the anti-Japanese hysteria that swept the country with the onset of World War II. The military and federal government initially called for Japanese Americans to voluntarily relocate away from the West Coast, but politicians such as Governor Chase Clark of Idaho vigorously opposed such a plan. Clark blocked California Japanese families from purchasing land in Idaho and actively discouraged others from relocating. Idaho JACL presidents, fearing for their community's safety, felt pressured to pledge that their members would discourage relatives from relocating to Idaho. Ultimately only three hundred Japanese Americans moved to Idaho to escape forced evacuation.[55]

On February 19, 1942, President Franklin D. Roosevelt issued Executive Order 9066, which ordered the removal of 120,000 persons of Japanese descent from the West Coast to ten concentration camps in isolated inland areas in seven states. Despite Governor Clark's hostility, his state soon became home for 10,000 West Coast Japanese and Japanese Americans who were removed from their real homes and sent to Minidoka internment camp. The Minidoka camp, located north of Twin Falls near Hunt, opened in August 1942 and housed Issei and Nisei internees mostly from lush western Washington and Oregon. Two-thirds of those interned were American citizens. Japanese Americans living in Idaho, eastern Oregon, and east of the Columbia River in Washington escaped incarceration. As one internee passed through Nampa, where he had once worked, he commented on "how ironic it was that we should see . . . Japanese who were free to do as they pleased while we, by trainloads, were being herded to camps."[56] Yet Japanese Americans living in Idaho were also the object of animosity and through necessity maintained a low profile during the war; some moved to safer havens in Spokane, Washington, and Ontario, Oregon.

The Minidoka desert camp became the second-largest "city" in Idaho. Despite their illegitimate persecution and the harsh, cramped, unsanitary conditions of the camp, residents tried to reconstruct their lives behind barbed-wire fences and guard towers. Minidoka internees cultivated flowers in the dry soil, formed musical groups, published a newspaper, played on sports teams, developed crafts, and seized opportunities to leave the camp. Almost immediately, by May 1942, south-central Idaho farmers and sugar beet companies turned to evacuees as a solution to their labor shortages.[57]

The camp experience destroyed many community ties, while others persevered, albeit in different forms. Camp residents sustained the popular prewar Japanese American baseball teams. Inmate Herb Iseri remembered that "there was nothing else to do" in the harsh, isolated environment.[58] In 1943, Hunt (Minidoka) High School formed a baseball team, played area white teams, and became a member of the Idaho High School Athletic Association. In 1944, area male and female teams entered the camp to compete in a tournament hosted by the Nisei players. Some Minidoka players even created a semipro baseball team that joined the Southern Central Idaho League and routinely attracted thousands of fans to its games. And the older Issei, who had suffered most from the internment experience as they lost their patriarchal authority, embraced softball as an outlet.[59]

The war represented a turning point for Japanese American communities in Idaho and the West. As a result of their internment, Japanese Americans lost homes, jobs, businesses, friends, and savings. The mass incarceration represented one of the most serious violations of civil liberties in U.S.

FIGURE 7.2. Japanese Americans were interned in southern Idaho during World War II. Despite hardship and violations of civil rights, internees found creative and recreational outlets. This orchestra is from the Minidoka Relocation Center near Hunt, Idaho. Photo courtesy of Idaho State Historical Society, 76-28.1mmm.

history. Yet no Japanese American committed any act of espionage or sabotage or was ever charged with a crime. The government suppressed its own evidence that there was no military necessity for incarcerating Japanese Americans. Racial prejudice, pressure from the army, and West Coast agricultural interests motivated the government's actions. The War Relocation Authority closed all but one of its internment camps in 1945, and a number of former internees apparently chose to remain in Idaho rather than return to their former West Coast homes; the state's Japanese population grew by eight hundred between 1940 and 1950. As historian Robert Sims notes, however, most internees left, and significant numbers moved to Malheur County in eastern Oregon and Spokane County in Washington. Recognizing that Japanese American labor had been critical to the sugar beet industry during the war, Ontario mayor Elmo Smith invited former internees to help fill service and farm jobs in the southeastern Oregon farming community. By the end of the war, one thousand Japanese Americans had settled there, giving Malheur County the largest percentage of Japanese Americans in Oregon.[60]

In the years following the war, Japanese Americans worked successfully to remove discriminatory state legislation and restore full citizenship
and land ownership rights. The 1952 passage of the Walter-McCarran Act
allowed Japanese immigrants to become naturalized citizens of the United
States. In 1955, Idaho's Japanese Americans successfully obtained the repeal
of the Alien Land Law, and in 1962, a constitutional amendment granted
them full citizenship rights.[61] Communities formed anew, revived older institutions, acknowledged the past in public ways, and embraced Japanese
American cultural traditions. Japanese American Buddhists from southwestern Idaho joined the larger community in Ontario, Oregon, to establish
a temple in 1947 and built a new one in 1957. In 1991, the Snake River chapter
of the JACL raised funds to launch construction of a $10 million cultural
center in Ontario to honor those who had been relocated or interned.

SOUTHERN EUROPEANS: BASQUES AND ITALIANS

Southern Europeans composed 25 percent of the 20 million immigrants
who poured into the United States between 1890 and 1924. Although most
of these immigrants headed to coastal, industrial, and urban areas, several
thousand moved to Idaho in the early twentieth century. The largest number came from Italy and the Basque country of the northern Spanish Pyr-
enees. Although Italians settled in many parts of the United States, Basques
found an economic niche in the sheep ranches of southwestern Idaho and
northern Nevada and California. As with the other ethnic groups discussed
here, southern Europeans were also racialized and concentrated in low-
wage work. Most of the immigrants were male, and many returned to their
homelands after some time in the United States. This immigration essentially ended in 1924, when anti-immigrant sentiment led to legislation that
established limited quotas for immigrants from southern and eastern Europe. But where Japanese, Chinese, and African Americans met exclusionary legislation and racism that hindered the formation of communities, the
very success of European immigrants made ethnic cohesion more difficult.

Italians came to Idaho to mine, farm, ranch, build railroads, and start
businesses. They heard about jobs or joined relatives already in the state,
often migrating from within the United States rather than directly from
Italy. In 1890, for example, sixteen-year-old Louis Sala, encouraged by his

father, who had earlier made a small stake in the Montana mines, worked in mines in Michigan and Wisconsin in an effort to secure funds to travel to Burke, Idaho, where his uncle was a blacksmith in the Poorman Mine. Sala worked in the Coeur d'Alene mining district until his death in 1954.[62] Mines in northern Idaho excluded Asians and African Americans but eagerly hired new southern European recruits. In the 1890s, Italians made up 8 percent of the workforce at the Bunker Hill Mine, and by World War I, they had created enclaves in Kellogg and Wallace.[63]

By 1900, 779 Italians had moved to the state, and in 1910, their numbers tripled to 2,627. This jump in Italian migration to Idaho reflected new jobs in expanding railroad service. Many Italian immigrants lived in the state temporarily, while they laid track, repaired sections, and constructed bridges. Italians lived in almost every town in Idaho with rail service.

Although most Italians who sought to farm immigrated to California, some who worked for railroads in Idaho managed to purchase farmland. A center for producing railroad ties, Priest River attracted many Italian workers, and later their families, as tie cutters. After the railroad was completed, dozens of immigrants remained and acquired homesteads east of Priest River or purchased land from the Great Northern, creating a community known as "the Italian settlement" by the 1890s.[64] As in other agricultural communities, women's labor was critical to family enterprises. Women helped clear thick timber for garden plots, where they grew vegetables that they harvested and then hauled in gunnysacks slung across their backs to sell in town.[65]

A significant Italian community formed near Lewiston, where some families developed vegetable and fruit enterprises along the Clearwater River. Phoebe Paffile remembered tending asparagus, onions, strawberries, cherries, and other fruits and vegetables and helping her husband, John, pack, load, and deliver boxes of produce in Lewiston and Moscow, as well as Pullman, Washington. Frank Speno and his mother and stepfather, Mike Pecora, raised fifteen acres of strawberries and twelve acres of vegetables. They often relied on Nez Perce Indians to harvest crops.[66]

Although some historians have concluded that Italians received warmer treatment in the West than in eastern cities, Kathy Vitale discovered that this was not always the case in Idaho. She found that newspapers in northern Idaho and Pocatello frequently used negative stereotypes, lumped Italians with other ethnic groups, and misspelled surnames. Italian Americans remembered frequent verbal attacks by townspeople and disparaging labels such as "Wop" and "dago." The condescending terms Dago Point and Dago Peak marked where Italian workers had built roads and railroads. Italians in Potlatch did not feel comfortable attending the local Catholic church, recalled Arthur Sundberg, because "these other snooty women that went to church there ... didn't want to mingle with 'em." Even the Potlatch Company mill was reluctant to hire Italians. One superintendent commented, "If you cannot get White men for Common Labor you may send five or six good Greeks or Italians." Towns often intentionally segregated the immigrants in the poorest housing in sections called "Dago Town."[67]

Just as with other groups, discrimination often led to community solidarity and the development of cultural institutions. By far the largest Italian community in the state was in Pocatello, where railroad jobs, and potential businesses serving workers, attracted many. For example, Sam Guido, Vito Cuoio, Tony and Aldemo Colianni, Ferdinand and Maria Lombardi, and Gaetano Valentine operated grocery stores that stocked familiar Italian staples such as olives, olive oil, pastas, tomato sauces, meats, and grapes for winemaking.[68] For more than twenty years, Italians in Pocatello nurtured a vibrant culture. They formed a chapter of the Cristobal Columbus lodge and built a lodge hall and bocce court, held an annual celebration of the feast day of Saint Anthony on June 10, and sponsored other activities at St. Anthony Church. Residents concentrated on the city's east side, which was known as the "League of Nations" for its diverse neighborhood housing Greeks, Hispanics, and African Americans as well as Italians.[69]

As in Idaho's African American communities, churches became the glue for ethnic communities, especially in northern Idaho, where Italians struggled to maintain ethnic cohesion. In Priest River, community members dedicated the St. Anthony's Mission Church in 1915. The settlement's schoolhouse also gathered area Italian families for picnics, weddings, and dances as well as children for classes. The loss of the church and school—the school in 1939, when county consolidation sent children to the Priest River school, and the church in 1951, when the congregation joined St. Catherine's Church in town rather than invest in expensive repairs—marked the fading away of the close-knit Italian community, as children identified less with their parents' heritage.[70]

Community solidarity was also reflected in work life, and Italian immigrants found labor traditions from the old country helped them improve wages and working conditions. Italian workers supported unionizing efforts in Idaho, and the press frequently portrayed them as leading strikes at mines and construction sites across the state.[71] Kathy Vitale discovered that almost half the Italians in Pocatello left the state after workers lost the nationwide railroad strike in 1922. Many of the Pocatello workers were blacklisted and unable to return to their jobs, so they moved to Oakland, California, in search of work.[72]

Following the crushing of the 1922 railroad strike and 1920s immigration restrictions, Idaho's Italian communities declined. Pressures to Americanize led parents to push their children to speak English only. The children also were able to succeed as "whites" in a place where race was the line between obtaining and not obtaining advantages. Families who remained in the state, no longer part of ethnic enclaves as were their counterparts in larger American cities, parted with their traditions in the effort to attain economic and social mobility.

Whereas the strength of Italian communities in Idaho diminished by the 1930s, Basques created an enduring ethnic stronghold in the state. Although they did not compose a large percentage of southern Europeans who came to the United States in the early twentieth century, they concentrated in southwestern Idaho and actually surpassed the number of Italian-born immigrants by 1910.

Many Idahoans have mistakenly assumed that Basques initially brought their sheepherding skills from the Basque country, or Euskal Herria, of northeastern Spain. The immigrants actually knew little about sheep but instead found and developed an economic niche. With the expansion of mining in the late nineteenth century, ranchers in California, Nevada, and Idaho found markets, expanded their herds, and needed workers. Basque immigrants, having few English skills, endured the isolation and proved themselves capable, and their relatives followed them into herding jobs. The kin and village networks are reflected in the fact that 96 percent of Basque immigrants to Idaho hailed from the province of Bizkaia.[73]

Like many other immigrants, Basques hoped to find work and return to their homeland with a bit of wealth. In the early twentieth century, one young Basque man wrote home describing Idaho as "a sad country to live in forever" but "good for earning a little money for a few years to return to Spain . . . and look for a girlfriend."[74] There were a number of early success stories, including Joe Bengoechea and Juan Archabal, who became wealthy after amassing large herds and ranches of their own. But Victor Otazua believed that the biggest percentage of Basques returned to Spain; like many other immigrants, they came to Idaho "always with the idea they wanted to go home."[75] Many herders never earned the money they anticipated, and the physical and mental demands of sheepherding took their toll. Basques left the sheep industry as soon as they could find other work.

Sheepherders were often held in low regard, and the immigrants were racialized much like the other ethnic groups discussed in this chapter. As cattle came to compete directly with sheep, ranchers helped fuel anti-Basque sentiment. The *Caldwell Tribune* ranted in 1909 that the work and culture of "the Bascos are on par with those of the Chinaman," which they described as "clannish and undesirable" and could soon "make life impossible for the white man."[76] Ranchers and cowboys frequently harassed and even attacked Basque sheepherders in the first decades of the twentieth century.

Just as churches and ethnic associations became central to other ethnic communities, the Basque boardinghouses became homes away from home and social centers for the Basque immigrant community. Boardinghouses provided a temporary residence for new arrivals, who often had little money, until they found employment. During the winter, herders came down from the mountain grazing zones and filled boardinghouses in Boise and southern Idaho towns, where they found the company of others who spoke the same language and shared the same customs, traditional cuisine, and family atmosphere. Patrick and Mark Bieter note that "sheepherding helped Basques get started in Idaho, but boardinghouses helped keep them there."[77] Juan and Teresa Yribar opened one of the first Basque boardinghouses at 118 South Seventh Street in 1900, and the southeastern section of Boise became the largest urban center for Basques in the United States, with boardinghouses, bars, clubs, and jai alai courts.[78]

Although more than 75 percent of the Basque immigrants were single males, an increasing number of women found employment operating or working in the boardinghouses. Many immigrant domestics found husbands in the boardinghouses, reinforcing ethnic enclaves and discouraging exogamy. Marriages, and later children, rooted more Basques in Idaho, and family settlements grew. Often, women remained in town while their husbands trailed sheep to mountain pastures, and many found they could stretch family budgets by operating boardinghouses. By the 1920s, Basque boardinghouses could be found across southern Idaho in Hailey, Shoshone, Twin Falls, and Mountain Home. Pia Unamuno Arriaga and Maria Epifania Inchausti operated boardinghouses in Hailey, and Florentina Yrazabal opened the first boardinghouse, the Posada, in Twin Falls in 1920. Santa Guisasola Bilbao, who came to Idaho in 1905, opened a boardinghouse in Twin Falls in 1924 and operated it for twenty-five years. Basque women often treated boarders like their sons or brothers. Marion Oneida remembered how her mother-in-law pampered her boarders at breakfast: "She would cook the breakfast individually for each boarder the way they wanted it, whether they wanted ham and eggs, bacon and eggs, or pancakes." Julie Pagoaga Lucerta added, "That's the way the boardinghouses started . . . a helping hand."[79]

Basque immigration virtually ceased under the immigration quota law of 1924. As the sheep business declined during the 1920s and 1930s, Basque herders, camp tenders, and shearers scrambled to find work. New ranchers such as Joe Pagoaga had to find other work, for "the railroad, the canal and whatever came along."[80] Boise's tight-knit Basque colony began to decline in the 1920s, as more Basque Americans became educated and affluent and moved to other parts of the city, and few new immigrants arrived.[81] Their "whiteness" and success brought them greater acceptance than Chinese, Japanese, and African Americans experienced.

The Basque story is different because Basque immigrants were accepted by the white community and because the arrival of a new generation of immigrants reinvigorated Basque communities and traditions in Idaho. By the outbreak of World War II and new labor shortages, the sheep industry in Idaho and Nevada was allowed to recruit and import Basque immigrants to work as sheepherders. In the postwar era, when most European immigrants and their children had assimilated, some Basque Americans began to take interest in the preservation of Basque culture and customs, as Richard Etulain explains in chapter 9 in this volume. They were able to focus more freely on social advancement and cultural preservation because they did not experience discrimination to the same degree as some other immigrant and ethnic groups. Unlike many other early twentieth-century ethnic communities, a hundred years later, the strength of the Basque community is still reflected in thriving cultural events and the Basque Museum and Cultural Center, established in a former Boise boardinghouse.[82]

CONTINUITY AND CHANGE IN ETHNIC COMMUNITIES

The history of these five ethnic groups in Idaho parallels the history of other immigrant and migrant groups in the nation and the American West. The entrenched racism of the period, affirmed by pseudoscience, law, and popular ideologies, led to Jim Crow segregation, Chinese and Japanese exclusion, and restrictions on immigration from southern Europe. The intersections of class, race, gender, and region are reflected in Idaho's ethnic history. Economic opportunities and kin networks used to obtain jobs and homes have been paramount in attracting groups of people to any particular region in the United States. As migrants found jobs and established homes; they created community—the institutions, networks, and social and cultural traditions that sustained and enriched lives. Ethnic discrimination paradoxically was both barrier and aid to the creation of those communities.

Early on, race was a significant factor in shaping the experiences of Idaho ethnic groups. Even during the territorial period mining boom, fewer African Americans found opportunities in Idaho than in the gold fields of California. George Blackburn and Sherman Ricards found in their study of Owyhee County mining camps that race and gender determined economic and social achievement. Opportunities were limited for blacks and Chinese, who were segregated and pushed into service jobs or were mining exhausted claims. They were excluded from more lucrative quartz mining and from owning property.[83] Impediments to accessing wealth in the early years of Idaho's growth only continued in later decades. When economic opportunities did not beckon, there was little to hold people in or induce them to stay in the state, as the declining population figures for African Americans, Chinese Americans, and Japanese Americans in table 7.1 reveal. And those

TABLE 3. Race and immigration in the state of Idaho, 1880–1950

	Total population	Foreign-born white (percentage of total)	African American (percentage of total)	Chinese (percentage of total)	Japanese (percentage of total)
1880	32,610	6,599 (20.2)	53 (0.2)	3,379 (10.4)	—
1890	88,548	15,464 (17.5)	201 (0.2)	2,007 (2.3)	—
1900	161,772	21,890 (13.5)	293 (0.2)	1,467 (0.9)	1,291 (0.8)
1910	325,594	40,427 (12.4)	651 (0.2)	859 (0.3)	1,363 (0.4)
1920	431,866	38,963 (9.0)	920 (0.2)	585 (0.1)	1,569 (0.4)
1930	445,032	31,303 (7.0)	668 (0.2)	335 (0.1)	1,421 (0.3)
1940	524,873	24,116 (4.6)	595 (0.1)	208	1,191 (0.2)
1950	588,637	19,407 (3.3)	1,050 (0.2)	244	1,980 (0.3)

Source: U.S. Bureau of the Census, *Seventeenth Census of the U.S.* (1950), table 14, "Race by Sex for the State, 1880 to 1950" (Washington, DC: Government Printing Office, 1951), 12–25.

who remained were concentrated in the state's urban areas. At the same time, the growing acceptance of Basque Americans as "white" helped increase their opportunities in Idaho.

In the twenty-first century, Idaho's ethnic population is growing. The steady increases of Latinos in urban and rural areas bring Idaho into the general expansion of Latino residents in the American West and the nation as a whole. Changes in immigration laws since 1965 have increased the Asian-Pacific American population. Many residents have actively fought against and defeated racist groups in their communities. The Center for Public Policy and Administration at Boise State University found in a 1999 survey that racial prejudice had declined and attitudes toward ethnic and religious minorities had improved since a previous 1988 survey.[84] A significant number of residents in the 2000 census self-identified as German or English, reflecting growing pride or interest in their immigrant heritage, albeit a white, northern European heritage. And many ethnic groups and communities have sought to honor their heritage, establishing in recent years the Black History, Basque, and Ontario multiethnic cultural museums. These institutions and a growing interest in ethnic celebrations, foods, and festivals highlight both the enduring legacies and the new contributions of Idaho's ethnic groups.

NOTES

1   *Ethnicity* is a fluid term that refers to one's self-identity or association with a particular group of people who share a common language, history, place of origin, religion, and/or customs. Ethnic identity changes from place to place and over time and also can be based on economic and social class, gender, race, sexuality, region, age, and national legislation. *Race* is also a fluid term whose meaning varies across time and space, but there is rarely an element of choice in the designation.

2   The Pacific Northwest—including the states of Idaho, Washington, and Oregon—has historically had a greater proportion of white residents in comparison with the rest of the United States. Philip L. Jackson and A. Jon Kimerling, eds., *Atlas of the Pacific Northwest*, 9th ed. (Corvallis: Oregon State University Press, 2003), 27.

3   As many scholars have noted, race is a category of power. It is based not on biology but rather on how societies have protected privilege by delineating particular groups of people as "lesser" and undeserving of full economic and social equality. See, for example, Paul Spickard, *Almost All Aliens: Immigration, Race, and Colonialism in American History and Identity* (New York: Routledge, 2007).

4   Elliott Robert Barkan, *From All Points: America's Immigrant West, 1870s–1952* (Bloomington: Indiana University Press, 2007), 7.

5   The nation's first immigration and citizenship laws—including the naturalization law of 1790 that granted citizenship only to free white men and, a century later, the Chinese Exclusion Act of 1882—were race-based. For more on the 1920s restrictive legislation, see Roger Daniels, *Guarding the Golden Door: American Immigration Policy and Immigrants since 1882* (New York: Hill and Wang, 2005), and Mae M. Ngai, *Impossible Subjects: Illegal Aliens and the Making of Modern America* (Princeton, NJ: Princeton University Press, 2004).

6   For an excellent summary of 1920s race-based immigration and citizenship legislation, see Mae M. Ngai, "Nationalism, Immigration Control, and the Ethnoracial Remapping of America in the 1920s," *OAH Magazine of History* 21 (July 2007): 11–15.

7   Carole Simon-Smolinski, "Idaho's Chinese Americans," in *Idaho's Ethnic Heritage: Historical Overviews*, ed. Laurie Mercier and Carole Simon-Smolinski (Boise: Idaho Centennial Commission and Idaho State Historical Society, 1990), 1:7–8; Mario Compean, "Chinese Americans in the Columbia River Basin," Columbia River Basin Ethnic History Archive (CRBEHA), http://www.vancouver.wsu.edu/crbeha/ca/ca.htm.

8   On mining camp diversity, see Susan Johnson, *Roaring Camp: The Social World of the California Gold Rush* (New York: Norton, 2000).

9   Mark Wyman, "Mining Law in Idaho," *Idaho Yesterdays* 25 (Spring 1981): 14–22.

10 Elmer Rusco, "The Chinese Massacres of 1866," *Nevada Historical Quarterly* 45 (March 2002): 3–30.

11 Simon-Smolinski, "Idaho's Chinese Americans," 8; Priscilla Wegars, "Entrepreneurs and 'Wage Slaves': Their Relationship to Anti-Chinese Racism in Northern Idaho's Mining Labor Market, 1880–1910," in *Racism and the Labour Market: Historical Studies*, ed. Marcel van der Linden and Jan Lucassen (New York: Peter Lang, 1995), 463–79.

12 Liping Zhu, "No Need to Rush: The Chinese, Placer Mining, and the Western Environment," *Montana: The Magazine of Western History* 49 (September 1999): 42–57.

13 Simon-Smolinski, "Idaho's Chinese Americans," 12, 18. Chinese women who la-
    bored as prostitutes were almost always held as chattel by masters who had bought
    them. Ruthanne Lum McCunn, "Reclaiming Polly Bemis: China's Daughter, Ida-
    ho's Legendary Pioneer," *Frontiers: A Journal of Women Studies* 24 (2003): 78.
14 Compean, "Chinese Americans"; Aminda M. Smith, "Choosing Chinese Medicine:
    Idaho's C.K. Ah Fong and the Turn of the Century Apothecaries in the American
    West," *Journal of the West* 46 (Summer 2007): 25.
15 Simon-Smolinski, "Idaho's Chinese Americans," 13, 37.
16 Ibid., 34–35; Compean, "Chinese Americans."
17 Compean, "Chinese Americans"; Simon-Smolinski, "Idaho's Chinese Americans,"
    32–33; Arthur A. Hart, *Chinatown: Boise, Idaho, 1870–1970* (Boise: Historic Idaho,
    2002), 18.
18 From *Idaho Avalanche* (Silver City), March 31, 1877; quoted in Li-hua Yu, "Chinese
    Immigrants in Idaho," (Ph.D. diss., Bowling Green State University, 1991), 130.
19 Quoted in Priscilla Wegars, "Chinese in Moscow, Idaho, 1883–1909," *The Historian*
    52 (November 1989): 96.
20 For more on Bemis, see Kathleen Whalen Fry, "Rendering Polly: the Romantici-
    zation, Manipulation and Decontexualization of One Chinese Woman's History
    in the American West," (M.A. thesis, Washington State University, 2006); Walter
    Hesford, "Thousand Pieces of Gold: Competing Fictions in the Representation
    of Chinese-American Experience," *Western American Literature* 31 (Spring 1996):
    49–62.
21 Simon-Smolinski, "Idaho's Chinese Americans," 22–25; R. Gregory Nokes, "'A Most
    Daring Outrage': Murders at Chinese Massacre Cove, 1887," *Oregon Historical Quar-
    terly* 107 (Fall 2006): 326–53; Nokes, *Massacred for Gold: The Chinese in Hells Canyon*
    (Corvallis: Oregon State University Press, 2009).
22 Ronald L. James, "Why No Chinamen Are Found in Twin Falls," *Idaho Yesterdays*
    36 (March 1993): 14–24.
23 Simon-Smolinski, "Idaho's Chinese Americans," 16.
24 Grant Yee, oral history interview by Jackie Day, March 16, 1976, Idaho Historical
    Society; Yixian Xu, "Chinese Women in Idaho during the Anti-Chinese Movement
    before 1900" (M.A. thesis, University of Idaho, 1994), 26.
25 Hart, *Chinatown*, 93, 119.
26 Quintard Taylor, Jr., "A History of Blacks in the Pacific Northwest, 1788–1970"
    (PhD diss., University of Minnesota, 1977), 81; population comparisons in Quin-
    tard Taylor, *In Search of the Racial Frontier: African Americans in the American West,
    1528–1990* (New York: Norton, 1998), 104, 135.
27 Quoted in Laurie Mercier, "Idaho's African Americans," in Mercier and Simon-
    Smolinski, *Idaho's Ethnic Heritage*, 1:4–6.
28 Kathy Hodges, "The People of the Cove," December 1986, Idaho State Historical
    Society (ISHS) Oral History Collection, 8–9, 12–18.
29 Eugene Settle, interview by Sam Schrager, Latah County Historical Society col-
    lection.
30 Ibid.; census figures in Taylor, *In Search of the Racial Frontier*, 152.
31 For example, in 1900, Idaho counted just 293 African Americans compared to 1,523
    living in Montana.

32 Mercier, "Idaho's African Americans," 10–11, 18; Lawrence de Graaf, "Race, Sex, and Region: Black Women in the American West, 1850–1920," *Pacific Historical Review* 49 (May 1980): 298; US Census, 1900 and 1910.

33 Mercier, "Idaho's African Americans,"17.

34 Ibid., 21–23.

35 Ibid., 25; Rosa Tigner, interview by Mateo Osa, Boise, ID, Feb. 6, 1981, ISHS Oral History Collection.

36 Erma M. Hayman, interview, December 17, 1980, ISHS; Mercier, "Idaho's African Americans," 31.

37 Mercier, "Idaho's African Americans," 18–19.

38 Ibid., 23.

39 When the St. Paul congregation moved to a new church in 1993, a preservation committee formed to save and restore the seventy-two-year-old building and founded the Idaho Black History Museum in 1995. It is the only African American history museum in the Pacific Northwest. See http://ibhm.org/ (accessed December 10, 2008).

40 Mamie O. Oliver, "Black Culture: Ethnic Community Experience in Boise, Idaho," in *The Black Church and Kinship Networks* (Boise: printed by author, 1982), 2–5; Sam Hanson, "Racial Discrimination in City Was Confusing for Black Girl," *Idaho Journal*, January 27, 1985.

41 Mercier, "Idaho's African Americans," 27–28; *Statesman,* September 18 and 24, 1907; August 15, 1914; May 2 and 12, 1926.

42 James W. Loewen notes that by 1930 Idaho had one of the highest number of counties in the nation with few or no blacks, even though the general population of those counties had expanded; see *Sundown Towns: A Hidden Dimension of American Racism* (New York: The New Press, 2005), 56, 455.

43 For more on Idaho's postwar black history, see Mercier, "Idaho's African Americans," 32–44.

44 Robert T. Hayashi, *Haunted by Waters: A Journey through Race and Place in the American West* (Iowa City: University of Iowa Press, 2007), 54.

45 US Census, General Characteristics, 1950, table 14, "Race by Sex," 12–25.

46 Henry Fujii, oral history interview by Annbelle Alexander, August 23, 1971, ISHS; Mercier, "Japanese Americans in the Columbia River Basin," CRBEHP; Mary S. Henshall, "Pioneer Portraits: Henry and Fumiko Fujii," *Idaho Yesterdays* 19 (March 1975): 22–26. Similarly, Toji Fujimoto came to Idaho in the early twentieth century to work as a beet laborer for the Utah and Idaho Sugar Company. He saved his wages to rent 180 acres on which to grow his own beets, and his father, brothers, and picture bride soon joined him. Mercier, "Japanese Americans," CRBEHP.

47 Carole Simon-Smolinski, "Idaho's Japanese Americans," in Mercier and Simon-Smolinski, *Idaho's Ethnic Heritage*, 1:44–89, 54.

48 Quoted in Simon-Smolinski, "Idaho's Japanese Americans," 66–67.

49 Eric Walz, "From Kumamoto to Idaho: The Influence of Japanese Immigrants on the Agricultural Development of the Interior West," *Agricultural History* 74 (Spring 2000): 404–18; Simon-Smolinski, "Idaho's Japanese Americans," 65–66.

50 Walz, "From Kumamoto to Idaho," 413–14.

51 Tensions led to the 1908 agreement that limited the numbers of laborers who could

emigrate from Japan but allowed wives and brides to join earlier male immigrants in the United States, changing the gendered character of the immigrant community.

52 Fujii interview.

53 Simon-Smolinski, "Idaho's Japanese Americans," 72.

54 "Japanese Americans," CRBEHA.

55 Robert C. Sims, "The 'Free Zone' Nikkei: Japanese Americans in Idaho and Eastern Oregon in World War II," in *Nikkei in the Pacific Northwest: Japanese Americans and Japanese Canadians in the twentieth Century*, ed. Louis Fiset and Gail M. Nomura (Seattle: University of Washington Press, 2005), 237, 243.

56 Ibid., 236.

57 Ibid., 87.

58 Quoted in Michael L. Mullan, "Sport, Ethnicity and the Reconstruction of the Self: Baseball in America's Internment Camps," *International Journal of the History of Sport* 16 (January 1999): 8.

59 Ibid., 12–16.

60 US Census, General Characteristics 1950, table 14; Sims, "'Free Zone' Nikkei," 249.

61 Simon-Smolinski, "Idaho's Japanese Americans," 71, 88. In the 1970s, Japanese Americans and their supporters began a decades-long redress movement that ultimately succeeded in getting legislation through Congress providing a formal apology and monetary compensation to the surviving internees; President Reagan signed the bill in 1988.

62 Richard G. Magnuson, *Coeur d'Alene Diary* (Portland, OR: Binfort & Mort, 1983), 87–88.

63 Mercier, "Idaho's Southern Europeans," in Mercier and Simon-Smolinski, *Idaho's Ethnic Heritage*, 1:4.

64 Marilyn Cork, "The Settlement—the Italians at Priest River," in *The First Home Town Primer* (Sandpoint, ID: Bonner County Historical Society, 1974), 12.

65 Marilyn Cork, in Mercier, "Idaho's Southern Europeans," 11.

66 Nez Perce County Historical Society (NPCHS) Oral History Committee, "Reflections of East Lewiston 1920s," NPCHS *The Journal* (Winter 1981–82), 4.

67 Kathy Vitale, "The Italians of Idaho," unpublished manuscript, ISHS, 4–6; Lysle Mulkey Selway, *Place Names of Lemhi County, Idaho* (MA thesis, University of Idaho, 1970); James Carl Dahl, *Bonner County Place Names* (Boise: Idaho State Historical Society, 1969); quotations in Keith Petersen, *Company Town: Potlatch, Idaho, and the Potlatch Lumber Company* (Pullman: Washington State University Press, 1987), 119–21, 143.

68 Vitale, "Italians of Idaho," 12–13; Juanita Rodriguez, "Railroads Brought Italians to Pocatello," *Idaho State Journal*, June 21, 1982.

69 Vitale, "Italians of Idaho," 14.

70 Cork, in Mercier, "Idaho's Southern Europeans," 12–13; ibid., 8–11.

71 See, for example, "Strikers Are Quiet," *Spokesman Review*, May 4, 1899; "Uprising of Italians Employed on the State Wagon Road," *Idaho Daily Statesman*, Nov. 16, 1894; *Pend d'Oreille Review*, May 12, 1917.

72 Vitale, "Italians of Idaho," 12.

73 John Bieter and Mark Bieter, *An Enduring Legacy: The Story of Basques in Idaho* (Reno and Las Vegas: University of Nevada Press, 2000), 30.

74 Quoted in ibid., 34.

75 Quoted in Mercier, "Idaho's Southern Europeans," 27.
76 Quoted in Bieter and Bieter, *Enduring Legacy*, 39.
77 Ibid., 43.
78 Mercier, "Idaho's Southern Europeans," 19.
79 Mercier, "Idaho's Southern Europeans," 20, 24–26; quotes from Robert McCarl and JaNene Buckway, eds., *Shoshone and Idaho Perspectives* (Boise: Idaho Commission on the Arts, 1989), 21. For more on Basque women's work, see Jeronima Echeverría, *Home Away from Home: A History of Basque Boarding Houses* (Reno: University of Nevada Press, 1999).
80 Quoted in Mercier, "Idaho's Southern Europeans," 22.
81 John B. Edlefsen, "Enclavement among Southwest Idaho Basques," *Social Forces* 29 (December 1950): 155–58.
82 For more on the postwar Basque community, see Mercier, "Idaho's Southern Europeans," 28–31; Compean, "Basque Americans"; and Bieter and Bieter, *Enduring Legacy*, 2–3.
83 George M. Blackburn and Sherman L. Ricards, "Unequal Opportunity on a Mining Frontier: The Role of Gender, Race, and Birthplace," *Pacific Historical Review* 62 (February 1993): 19–38.
84 Center for Public Policy & Administration, "Survey of Racial and Religious Prejudice in Idaho," Idaho Public Policy Survey 10 (Boise: Boise State University, 1999), 3–4.

Farmer Henry Fujii discusses discriminatory land laws in Idaho in the 1920s.

INTERVIEWER: Everyone got along fine?

FUJII: Yes. But [in] 1915 agitators come from California tryin' to make anti-Japanese land laws in Boise.

INTERVIEWER: Were they Japanese men?

FUJII: No.

INTERVIEWER: White men?

FUJII: White men. They wanna make [sure] the Japanese can't own that land. That's what they wanted. Anti-Japanese land law they call it.

INTERVIEWER: Did they get away with it?

FUJII: They did. They done that from California way, then come to Idaho and Oregon, all western states.

INTERVIEWER: What did the Japanese people do then?

FUJII: In Idaho, we [were] prohibited [from] owning the land, but we had to lease under five-years land lease allowed to us, so we farmed leased land, most of 'em. I already owned a land at the time. Finally this land . . . law went through Idaho Legislature, 1923, but I bought this land in 1918 so we didn't have no trouble.

INTERVIEWER: Oh, well then what happened to the other Japanese people that they wanted to buy land?

FUJII: They leased the land.

INTERVIEWER: They leased it?

FUJII: That's the only way they can farm after this law pass.

INTERVIEWER: How long was that law in effect?

FUJII: Until after the war.

INTERVIEWER: I've never heard that before.

FUJII: I think . . . 1948 or '49 they refused that. It was an unfair, unfair law. That would [have] stood in California too until they repealed. Oregon same way; they couldn't hold the land and they couldn't lease the land in California and Oregon. Washington too. Utah, Arizona.

INTERVIEWER: Well, did all the states repeal that law then?

FUJII: Um-hm. But children born in the United States, they're citizens, so they can buy the land, lease the land for their own help, and older Japanese, they can buy land and keep on farming.

* * *

Rosa Lee Tigner describes discrimination in Boise against African Americans.

INTERVIEWER: Did you have any problems in Boise getting services, like perhaps in Pocatello, some of those places you mentioned, were there places like that in Boise?

TIGNER: Was there. Boise we was thought—I don't know about northern Idaho, I've never lived in northern, but Boise is worse than Pocatello.

INTERVIEWER: It was?

TIGNER: Yeah, because Boise had in their Greyhound bus station "We do not cater to colored persons." That was on the Greyhound bus. Going from Pocatello to Grand Coulee, Washington, and I got off—I used to be crazy about a ham and egg sandwich, and it choked me to death when I happened to look up and see—I couldn't eat another bite because that sign right there—it was just choking me—I couldn't eat no more. I went and got back on the bus. But they had service—they couldn't refuse the service because I was Black.

INTERVIEWER: They'd lose a lot of customers. Was that pretty common around Boise?

TIGNER: It was then, I found out. And I found out that not until—it hadn't been too many years that Boise had kind of changed their attitude, and really there's a little undercurrent yet.

INTERVIEWER: Still?

TIGNER: Yeah.

NOTES

Henry Fujii was interviewed by Robert Alexander and Cecil Hungerford, August 23, 1971, Nampa, ID, transcript (OH0037), Idaho Oral History Center/Idaho State Historical Society, 13–14. Used with permission of Idaho State Historical Society.

Rosa Lee Tigner was interviewed by Mateo Osa, February 6, 1981, Boise, ID, transcript (OH0560), Idaho Oral History Center/Idaho State Historical Society, 21–22. Used with permission of Idaho State Historical Society.

8

Latinos in Idaho

Making Their Way in the Gem State

ERROL D. JONES

IDAHOANS ARE KEENLY AWARE THAT THE LATINO POPULATION in their state has increased dramatically over the past quarter century.[1] The 2010 U.S. Census counted 175,901 who claimed Latino heritage out of a state total of 1,567,582, or 11.2 percent. Most of that growth is attributed to immigration. Latinos are the state's largest minority. It is also presumed that more than 25,000 undocumented immigrants, mostly Mexicans or other Latin Americans, live in the Gem State.

For the past thirty years, Latino immigration to Idaho has mirrored national trends. The 1980 U.S. Census recorded 36,560 Latinos in a total Idaho population of 944,000. Of these Idaho "Hispanics," 80 percent or more were Mexicans or of Mexican descent. In the 1980s, the Latino population grew to almost 53,000, an impressive increase of 16,367, or about 5.3 percent of the state's total of 1,004,000. Despite a significant numerical increase, Latinos still constituted a small percentage of the total population. But from 1990 to 2000, their numbers almost doubled, from a little less than 53,000 to 102,901, an astonishing increase of 95 percent, or 8 percent of the total population of 1,293,953.[2]

In the past quarter century, at least until 2008, Idaho experienced phenomenal economic growth and with it great population increase. Since the 2000 census, the overall population expanded by 21.1 percent, putting Idaho in a similar category as its neighboring states: Utah, 24 percent; Washington, 14.1 percent; Oregon 12 percent; and Nevada, 32 percent. In all of these states, the Latino population increased, contributing significantly to rapid overall population and economic growth. Latinos in each of the above states in 2011 constituted 11 percent or more of the population total, with Nevada reaching almost 25 percent.[3] Idaho and surrounding states historically have been racially homogeneous but always counted on cultural and racial minority groups like Chinese, Greeks, Italians, and Latinos to labor in their fields, toil in the mines, harvest timber, build railroads, and contribute to the economic development of the region, as described by Laurie Mercier in chapter 7 in this volume. This chapter presents a saga still in the making of a people who, like other identifiable minorities, have had to struggle to overcome adversity, discrimination, and racism.

EARLY LATINO PRESENCE

Mexicans and Mexican Americans have been in Idaho at least since the 1860s, if not earlier, and played a role in the state's development. Seldom recognized, they made significant contributions to the state's economy, culture, and history. With the news in 1860 that gold had been discovered, Mexicans and thousands of other fortune seekers rushed to Idaho Territory. Some were experienced miners from the Mexican state of Sonora who, along with Chileans and Peruvians, flocked first to California in the late 1840s and 1850s and then to Idaho. Introducing mining technology adopted by other miners regardless of their origin, Mexican miners in 1863 used *arrastras* in Spanish Town near Rocky Bar. Large, heavy stone wheels dragged by horses or mules around a circular pit lined with smooth rocks, *arrastras* crushed softer quartz placed beneath them. These devices were used widely throughout the area.[4]

The 1870 territorial census found sixty Latinos living in Idaho, most of Mexican descent. A small group numerically, they nevertheless played an important economic role, bringing with them Mexican traditions of handling horses and livestock. Some worked as mule packers, ranchers, and cowboys, while others were miners and laborers. A few landed in Idaho Territory as soldiers in the U.S. Army. Counted in the early census, they also appeared in occasional newspaper stories. Soon, those who stayed, like Jesús Urquides and Manuel Fontes, became solid members of Idaho's pioneer communities. Spanish words, along with Mexican techniques and equipment, informed the cowboy and ranching cultures of southwestern

Idaho, eastern Oregon, and northern Nevada. Their influence continues to this day.[5]

On rare occasions, Idaho's early territorial history yields a glimpse of a richer more diverse culture, like the glint of gold in a rocky stream, than standard accounts portray. Mexican vaqueros broke horses and herded cattle on isolated ranches in southwestern Idaho and eastern Oregon. Some succeeded in buying spreads of their own. Skilled Mexican muleteers (*arrieros*) packed supplies over dangerous trails into Idaho's isolated mountain mines. At times, the U.S. Army depended on them for necessities as it campaigned against the Nez Perce and other Idaho Native Americans. Along with Mexican men who came to Idaho as miners, muleteers, and cowboys were women and children—of the sixty Latinos counted in the 1870 territorial census, fourteen were women and children.

Mexican American families like the Urquides, Valdez, Galindo, Fontes, Ortiz, Ruiz, Amera, Ursino, and Escaso prospered and earned respect and acceptance in their Idaho communities. The late nineteenth and early twentieth centuries brought change to Idaho's economy. An emergent expansive agricultural and livestock industry edged out the short-lived gold rush. Railroads penetrated the territory, bringing thousands of settlers to lands opened up by large-scale government-financed irrigation projects. Southern Idaho's arid Snake River plateau blossomed with sugar beets, potatoes, and other market crops. Before long, Utah-Idaho Sugar Company had built a rendering plant at Lincoln in eastern Idaho and recruited Mexican workers to plant and harvest sugar beets. Mexico's 1910 revolution aided recruitment efforts as many fled north into labor-starved markets in the western United States. When the U.S. government entered World War I in 1917, it signed a contract labor agreement with Mexico, sometimes called the first bracero program. Faced with labor shortages, employers could hire Mexican workers at recruiting centers where they agreed to wage rates, contract length, work description, and worker accommodations. A "multitude of problems" and broken agreements ended the program on December 31, 1919.[6]

Idaho sugar and railroad companies recruited some of those early twentieth-century braceros to work the fields and rail lines in southern Idaho.

State labor commissioner William J. A. McVety, investigating accusations of abuse against Mexicans in the summer of 1918, estimated that about 1,500 had been brought to southeastern Idaho, 500 of them women and children.[7] In the Twin Falls, Burley, and Paul area, another 200 Mexicans worked as field hands in an arrangement with Amalgamated Sugar Company. Commissioner McVety found no complaints there, but in Idaho Falls, Shelley, and Blackfoot, he encountered numerous grievances regarding wage agreements, living quarters, and lack of winter clothing. His investigation revealed that Utah-Idaho Sugar Company's contracted braceros suffered many of the abuses alleged in the accusations. "Too much is left to the supervision of the Sugar Company," McVety concluded. The contracts gave the company great power over workers. Labor abuses, he warned the governor, jeopardized the company's future survival as well as that of the industry.[8]

Termination of this early bracero program did not end Mexican immigration to the United States and to Idaho. Immigrants continued to come despite company abuse, hard work, long days, miserable pay, unscrupulous labor contractors, and horrid living conditions. Idaho's growers and out-of-state agribusinesses shamelessly exploited desperate people. U.S. immigration policies of the 1920s excluded Chinese and Japanese and limited southern and eastern Europeans but not Mexicans. Even the immigration head tax was often waived as a gesture to the farm lobby. Local Idaho newspapers reported large numbers of Mexicans arriving to work in the fields in the 1920s.[9]

Railroad expansion opened up opportunities for Mexicans, Mexican Americans, and other immigrants. Pocatello became the regional headquarters for Union Pacific Railroad, which, along with other railroads, hired workers from Mexico before World War I. After the war and throughout the 1920s, companies continued to employ Mexican immigrants. By decade's end, nearly 60 percent of the section crews on Idaho's railroads were Mexican.[10] Mexican Americans like Mike Rivera in Pocatello coveted jobs with the railroads even though working track maintenance (called *traqueros* in Spanish) was not the best job available. Like many others, Rivera worked in the beet, potato, or pea fields before hiring on with the railroad. Railroad work, no matter how menial, usually meant steady employment, in a permanent place, with higher wages than fieldwork. Farm labor was seasonal.

FIGURE 8.1. Mexican Americans provided a significant labor force for Idaho's agricultural economy. Here, men and women migrant laborers harvest crops in the fields. Photo courtesy of Idaho State Historical Society, 76-102.61i.

Workers followed the crops, living in tents, lean-tos, or deplorable camps. It took a heavy toll on families; school-age children were pulled from their studies in early spring and returned in late fall.[11]

From their consulate in Salt Lake City, Mexican officials, then as now, attempted to advocate for their citizens in disputes over wages or for better working and living conditions. They investigated incidents in which Mexican citizens were injured or lost their lives. One such tragedy occurred in Burley on July 4, 1920. Two Mexican beet workers were shot (one fatally), when Burley police burst into a shack near the sugar beet factory where the men played poker with other workers. The coroner's inquest revealed that both men were shot in the back as they fled the game, but a jury exonerated the two Burley police officers of any wrongdoing. Despite blatant injustices and nagging questions regarding the event, the Mexican consul could do little to guarantee fair treatment and justice for his country's citizens. Mexicans in Idaho faced the same kind of callous and unjust treatment in the legal system that they experienced in Texas, California, and Arizona at that time.[12] Another remarkable incident that occurred a year later yielded a more favorable outcome. Mexican president Alvaro Obregón sought and won clemency for a Mexican sentenced to death by an Idaho tribunal.[13]

Where significant numbers of Mexican nationals had taken up permanent residence in Idaho—such as in and around Pocatello by 1922—the Mexican consul appointed a government-sponsored *comisión honorífica*. Among other things, the *comisiónes* attempted to promote cultural patriotism for the fatherland and foster self-help organizations in the Mexican community. As U.S. citizens, Mexican American migrants working in Idaho, often regarded as foreigners in their own country, merited no special protection; none was forthcoming from government officials.

The 1920s brought more Mexican Americans and Mexican nationals to Idaho. Unfortunately, they met discrimination and human rights abuses. Idaho in the 1920s exhibited the same kind of xenophobia that defined American society at that time. In June 1924, the Ku Klux Klan rallied a gathering of five hundred in Boise to hear a Payette minister praise the Klan's mission to end Jewish economic monopoly, prevent mixed marriages, bar Catholics from political office, and dry up the "flood of undesirables" pouring into the country.[14]

Reports in the *Twin Falls Daily News* during the summer of 1924 show a clear bias against people of Mexican heritage, who were accused of criminal activity and vilified for low morality and unacceptable customs such as smoking marijuana. Authorities concluded that idle Mexican migrants increased crime and moral turpitude. Mexicans who were unable to show visible means of support were arrested for vagrancy and run out of town.[15]

During the 1920s and 1930s, large out-of-state produce companies contracted Idaho farmers to grow green peas for export to markets on the Eastern Seaboard. At harvest time, these companies hired labor contractors to supply a small army of skilled pea pickers, most of whom were Mexican and Mexican Americans, to reap the crop. Soon complaints poured into the Salt Lake City Mexican Consulate alleging wage disagreements, terrible living conditions, and other abuses. Prompted by these allegations, Vice Consul Elias Colunga traveled to Driggs in the summer of 1931 to investigate. The reports of abuse were validated by his visits to migrant camps (where conditions proved so shocking that he took photographs and sent copies to state officials) and interviews with workers, labor contractors, and company representatives. Colunga's own report emphasized that conditions were worse than he had expected.[16]

Migrant workers found themselves at the mercy of labor contractors who, then as now, exercised great control and frequently abused their power. Colunga learned that contractors made deals with company managers to sell "whiskey and marijuana to the Mexicans and provide them with prostitutes." Contractors set up "company stores" in camps and sold food and other items at inflated prices and deducted the cost of purchases from workers' pay. They even controlled leisure activities like card games, with the "house" collecting 20 percent of all winnings, to be split between contractor and company manager. It was a system designed to coerce workers to spend what little they earned. Arrangements like these were common throughout the West at this time.[17]

Promises of $1.25 for every one hundred pounds of peas picked plus a bonus if they worked every day until the harvest ended enticed workers to Driggs. They were furious when they learned on arrival that they had been duped. Without written contracts, who could say if they had been misled or not? Lack of signed contracts plagued migrant workers in Idaho and elsewhere. It was a perennial source of conflict between laborers, contractors, and growers.[18]

From 1931 to 1935, conditions and wages in Teton Valley's pea fields saw no improvement, and they grew worse in Depression times. Moreover, farmers in the upper Snake River Valley suffered through the second year of a severe drought, and competition for limited water resources caused tempers to flare. On August 13, 1935, seeking to prevent violent solutions to water disputes, Governor C. Ben Ross sent Idaho's adjutant general, Brigadier General M. G. McConnel, to Driggs. McConnel's arrival coincided with a strike of migrant pea pickers over wages.[19] The strike arose out of earlier conflicts between workers and San Diego Fruit and Produce, one of several big companies that bought peas from local farmers and directly hired harvesters. Strike leaders pulled about 1,500 workers out of the pea fields when the companies refused their wage demands. The Teton County sheriff told McConnel that most workers were willing to work for what the companies offered, but a small minority had bullied them into striking.[20]

Angry farmers warned McConnel and local authorities to restore order and end the strike or they would do it themselves. Convinced that local police could not handle the situation, the county prosecuting attorney
urged the governor to intervene.[21] Without hesitation, Governor Ross declared martial law in Teton County and sent Idaho National Guardsmen to
Driggs on the morning of August 15. Media accounts, citing official reports,
blamed a few American and Mexican agitators for the strike. No evidence
indicates that anyone talked to strikers directly or that public officials, military officers, or journalists tried to understand the workers' point of view or
questioned the veracity of the company and official explanations of events.
No one contacted the Mexican consul, who could have informed state authorities of the legitimacy of worker complaints and the history of abuses
they had suffered at the hands of contractors and company managers. The
picture emerges distorted and incomplete without these voices. Only the
brief recollection of a young Mexican witness fifty-five years later provides
a worker's version of the story.[22]

Governor Ross preferred a military solution to negotiations with union
officials. On August 15 and 16, troopers arrested about 125 Mexicans from
the labor camp and plucked another 30 from the streets of Driggs. They
were paid the wages owed them, loaded into trucks or forced into their own
vehicles, escorted to the county line, and warned not to return to Teton
County.[23] The next day, the remaining workers returned to the fields. The
strike was over. The workers lost, and their civil rights were trampled. Governor Ross came under fire from the Nampa and Boise Trades and Labor
Councils, and the Idaho State Federation of Labor officially opposed using
the National Guard to end strikes.[24]

Most Americans endured hardship and suffering during the Great Depression. No record exists, however, of an official policy to force Mexicans or
Mexican Americans out of Idaho during that time, but some communities
near Twin Falls pressured farmers to "hire whites only."[25] Local residents
complained bitterly when the Idaho Sugar Beet Growers Association hired
Mexicans for spring thinning in 1935. Growers shrugged off the criticism,
preferring to hire the cheaper, faster, and more efficient Mexicans.[26] Intended to discourage migrants, signs on roads entering the state warned
nonresidents that they would be denied state social services. Rita Perez of

Idaho Falls lamented that, for "Mexicans . . . there was no relief" during the Depression.[27] Ironically, high demand for Mexican migrant labor in sugar beet production may have brought more Mexican and Mexican American migratory workers to the state during the 1930s.

WORLD WAR II AND THE SECOND BRACERO PROGRAM

The 1941 mobilization for war renewed demand for farm labor as domestic migrants and local agricultural workers found better-paying jobs in wartime industries. Farm federations pressured the United States Employment Service to import thousands of Mexican contract workers. Labor unions and the Farm Security Administration lobbied against a new bracero program, fearing it would depress wages for local and migrant farmworkers. Like many who oppose current efforts to bring in guest workers from Mexico, they contended that labor shortages would cease if growers paid higher wages. During the Depression, large commercial growers in California and other states unleashed violence and intimidation to defeat attempts by union organizers to increase worker pay. Growers wanted a steady, controllable surplus labor pool to keep wages low.

Caving in to growers' demands, the U.S. government signed the bracero agreement with Mexico on September 27, 1942. Six months later, Mexican braceros arrived in the Pacific Northwest. From then until 1948, 15,600 Mexican "guest workers" came to Idaho to fill agricultural needs. Unfortunately, discrimination and abuse of braceros and violation of contracts in some parts of the state forced the Mexican government to withdraw them in 1948. Nevertheless, national growers' organizations lobbied to extend the agreement in other states until 1964. By then, 4.5 million Mexican men had entered the country to work as braceros.

The contract under which braceros arrived in Idaho and other states stipulated that workers not be discriminated against in any way, they were to be guaranteed living expenses and transportation from Mexican recruitment centers to the U.S. job site and back home at the end of the contract, and they were not to displace domestic labor or reduce prevailing wages.[28] None of these basic protections applied to American migrant workers regardless of race or ethnic origin.

Many Idaho farmers preferred to obtain their workers through labor contractors as they always had and showed great antipathy toward these rules, ignoring them when they could. Nothing in the braceros' agreement gave workers the right to strike, but faced with contract violations, wage disputes, and poor food and working conditions, they struck anyway. Braceros in Preston struck twice over wages and other abuses in 1944. Farmers used violence to end the second strike. Wage disputes drove about four hundred Mexicans in Nampa to strike on June 17, 1946. They were joined by other workers from the Marsing, Franklin, Upper Deer Flat, and Amalgamated Sugar Company camps. The Mexican consul in Salt Lake City ended the walkout by arranging a hearing where workers could air their grievances. Still, Idaho's wages were the lowest in the Pacific Northwest, and strikes were longer and more intense. Some Canyon County residents openly discriminated against Mexicans, barring them from stores and saloons. Others, however, denounced this kind of behavior: the Notus Farm Labor Committee rightly predicted that Idaho growers could lose their labor supply. Shortly thereafter, the Mexican government removed Idaho from eligibility for contract workers.[29] Discrimination and overt racism were not universal, however. Many communities welcomed braceros and celebrated Mexican holidays with them.

War's end did not lessen Idaho's need for agricultural labor. Most of these jobs were seasonal, paid low wages for long days and harsh conditions, and did not attract locals who sought better opportunities elsewhere. Deprived of braceros, Idaho growers turned increasingly to braceros who had broken their contracts. As before the war, farmers came to rely more on local Mexican American families, Indians, and others who journeyed north on a migrant stream to Idaho and the Pacific Northwest.

The bracero program, which was changed and extended several times after 1948, had an important impact on Idaho. These post–World War II extensions supplied large numbers of contracted Mexicans to agribusinesses in the Southwest and elsewhere, and growers came to depend on this governmentally supported, institutionalized source of cheap labor. Although contrary to law, braceros earned less than the prevailing wage in those areas, forcing local farmworkers, mostly Mexican Americans, to accept lower wages or pursue higher-paying jobs and expanding opportunities elsewhere. In 1955, the U.S. Public Health Service recorded more than

8,000 migrant workers and 13,500 of their family members in Idaho. Ten years later, the numbers doubled; 80 percent came from Hidalgo and Maverick Counties in southern Texas. The large number of migrants proved a godsend for Idaho growers and the state's political leaders. Migrants came with their own transportation, were skilled and experienced agricultural workers, worked for low wages, demanded little of the state's social services, and generally vanished when the work was done. They proved essential to Idaho's agricultural prosperity.[30]

LEAVING THE MIGRANT STREAM AND JOINING THE MAINSTREAM

From 1950 through the 1970s, most migrants who came to Idaho were families from rural backgrounds with little or no experience other than farming. Once farmworkers embarked on a migrant way of life, it was almost impossible to escape. Migrants had little or no education, were unorganized and disfranchised, and found themselves struggling in a chaotic market. Not included in the ranks of protected labor, they were forced to do backbreaking stoop labor, use short-handled hoes for weeding sugar beets, and drink and wash in contaminated water. Moreover, they were exposed to dangerous pesticides and denied private toilet facilities in the fields. Their grievances fell on deaf ears. The federal Fair Labor Standards Act did not apply to them, and the Labor Relations Board offered no protection. In addition, constant travel endangered families, disrupted schooling for children, and exposed families to inconvenient and unsanitary housing. Family relationships often deteriorated, voting privileges evaporated along with dependable incomes, and local health and welfare services were denied them. Migrants' circumstances offered few chances to develop feelings of belonging to a stable community. Despite these odds, many migrant families managed to create their own internal community by traveling with friends and relatives over the years.[31]

A number of factors motivated migration, but most migrants took to the road out of desperation; it was migrate or starve. The personnel director of an industrial farm candidly declared that those who migrate and work on farms are the "people who are the hungriest. Who wants to work that hard for that little money?"[32]

Migrants who followed the crops faced constant housing problems. In response to this pressing need, the Farm Security Administration (FSA) began constructing and operating a series of model farm labor camps in the mid-1930s. In an effort to assist states in meeting the urgent health and housing needs of growing Anglo migrant populations, the FSA built twenty-six camps in California, Arizona, and the Pacific Northwest, among them, Idaho's Twin Falls and Caldwell labor camps. Federally administered camps not only provided basic housing for some migrant families but also addressed educational, health care, social, and spiritual needs. The Caldwell camp (currently Farmway Village) included a central utility building with hot and cold running water, laundry, toilets, and showers; a social hall for meetings, day care, church services, and dances; a children's playground; a clinic; sewage disposal system; a mattress shop; and a cannery. Fifty small, single-family wood-frame houses offered permanent shelter for migrant families, and wooden platforms for tents housed 350 more. An elected camp council represented resident migrant families before management and kept order in the camp. Unfortunately, there were never enough of these camps. Migrants not fortunate enough to stay in the Twin Falls or Caldwell camps had to settle for whatever was available at prices they could afford. They slept in cars or in tents pitched at the side of a farmer's field. In the late 1940s, however, the FSA liquidated or sold the camps. In nearly all cases, once the camps were under private local control, housing and sanitation standards, clinics, schools, and recreational facilities evaporated along with the self-governing camp councils.[33]

On August 26, 1954, President Dwight Eisenhower appointed the cabinet-level President's Committee on Migrant Labor. The new committee extended Social Security to cover farm labor and migrants, regulated transportation of farmworkers over more than seventy-five miles and across state lines in privately owned trucks and buses, and set up the Farm Placement Service's Annual Worker Plan for utilizing domestic labor more efficiently. By 1960, twenty-eight states, including Idaho, had migratory labor committees based on the federal pattern. These in turn stimulated a variety of legislative measures related to migratory labor.

Pressured by the President's Committee on Migrant Labor, local Protestant churches affiliated with the National Council of Churches Migrant Ministry, the Catholic Diocese of Boise, and various labor organizations,

Idaho's legislature created the Governor's Migratory Labor Committee in 1955. The committee oversaw modest attempts to improve housing conditions and issued annual reports. Camps in Twin Falls and Caldwell provided adequate housing, but others were intolerable, with little or no running water and dangerously unsanitary conditions. Arrangements ran the gamut from one- and two-room wood-frame shacks that sugar companies had built near rendering plants to spaces for tents and temporary shelters provided by individual farmers and farmers' associations. Such wretched living conditions attracted widespread attention from state officials, the press, and religious groups.[34]

Most migrants of Mexican heritage were Catholics, and the church in Idaho had ministered to their needs since 1949. But many migrants gravitated toward Protestant (mostly Pentecostal) churches, and in 1956 the Southwest Idaho Migrant Ministry (SIMM) began providing them spiritual and community services. A primary concern for SIMM, affiliated with the National Council of Churches Migrant Ministry, was to improve living conditions in the labor camps and pressure the governor's committee to establish and enforce health regulations for migrant camps. After lengthy study, the governor's committee called a public hearing on April 30, 1959, to present its new health and sanitation regulations for migrant labor camps. Marked by contention and acrimony, the hearing revealed that Idaho's migrant agricultural workers faced ignorance, prejudice, fear, and a preoccupation with cost over human needs.[35]

The Governor's Migratory Labor Committee conducted annual on-site inspections of the camps and issued public reports. Federally insured loans enabled many farm labor camp associations to comply with state health regulations by 1965, and the committee reported that most of the seventy-three camps inspected "have a healthful atmosphere, and the buildings are generally well constructed and properly maintained." Conditions at a few, however, continued to be unbearable. After issuing repeated citations, inspectors recommended that the American Falls labor camp be rebuilt or closed. When camp owners stalled, a frustrated official lamented that it was like "butting your head against a stone wall."[36]

Conservative Republican governor Don Samuelson disbanded the Governor's Migratory Labor Committee in 1969, and migrant camp standards

lapsed. The State Department of Health stopped enforcing health regulations in the camps, leaving this responsibility to regional health districts
whose oversight was limited to water and sanitation. As a recruiter for out-
of-state migrant farm labor, the State Department of Employment was sup-
posed to "guarantee adequate housing and healthful labor camp conditions
at the job site," but by 1976 it no longer inspected camps. The Idaho Migrant
Council, a private nonprofit organization formed in 1971, took up migrant
housing problems and made efforts to improve and advocate for adequate
health standards in the camps.[37] From this point forward, except in the case
of workers brought to Idaho under H-2A temporary agricultural labor visas,
the state abdicated its responsibility for migrant camps, leaving it to the
Migrant Council, local communities, and the owners of private labor camps.

Idaho's economy after World War II provided new economic opportunities for its growing population and for migrants as well. When possible,
migrant seasonal workers took advantage of a chance to break out of the
migrant stream and settle permanently, but those who tried to do so faced
enormous difficulties. Poor, unskilled, with little or no education, and unable to speak, read, or write English well, they had trouble adapting to the
demands of the majority society. Idaho was unlike the communities they
had left behind in Texas's Rio Grande River Valley. There, they were the majority in their barrios, and everyone spoke or understood Spanish. In Idaho,
extended networks of family and friends protected them from a harsh environment, but the desire to hold onto their culture insulated Mexican Americans from economic and educational opportunity.

Small permanent communities of Mexicans and Mexican Americans
that had survived in Idaho cities since the early twentieth century expanded
as more year-round jobs became available for former migrant workers. Public institutions and attitudes in Anglo communities accustomed to the migrants' transitory nature were slow to adapt to a changing situation. The
Anglo community failed to distinguish between permanently employed
Mexican American citizens and new arrivals working the fields. To the
majority, they seemed the same: poor, unable to speak English, living in
labor camps, and transient. Mexican Americans who wanted to be accepted
into mainstream Idaho society would have to overcome the language and
education obstacles that characterized migrant life. But their language and

cultural trappings were continually reinforced by increasing numbers of recent arrivals (many undocumented) from other states and Mexico. This was not a problem unique to Idaho's Latino community but a phenomenon that prevailed throughout the United States.[38]

As more migrant workers of Mexican heritage found permanent work, they organized community activities such as parades, fiestas, and dances that expressed their cultural identity. Idaho's first such fiesta, organized in 1957 and designed to show appreciation to migrant agricultural workers, was put on by the workers themselves with some funding from the Department of Employment. It drew crowds of Mexican Americans and Anglos from the Twin Falls area. Featuring music, dances, speeches, and a baseball game, the fiesta intended "to show that the workers are more than just laborers on our farms."[39] Other communities imitated the Twin Falls gala, and now such fiestas are part of Idaho's annual cultural landscape everywhere that Latinos have a significant presence. Idahoans, regardless of race or ethnic origin, attend Cinco de Mayo (May 5) and September 16 (Mexico's Independence Day) fiestas and delight in sharing the music, food, dances, games, and handicrafts of Mexican American culture. In 1998, supporters of migrant workers revived the practice of showing gratitude by celebrating Farm Worker Appreciation Day in Caldwell every August. Burley recently implemented a similar event for its farmworkers.

For migrant families and especially those attempting to settle permanently, education of their children took priority. The Governor's Migratory Labor Committee and religious leaders encouraged school districts to integrate migrant children into regular classes and provide summer school programs to help with overcoming deficiencies. State legislation authorized local school districts to levy a small tax for migrant education programs, but some were opposed to the tax, and few took advantage of the programs. Lack of school personnel with an understanding of and sensitivity toward children from Mexican American culture proved an obstacle. Recognizing this, the National Council of Churches Migrant Ministry developed a program to bring volunteer teachers from the border region of Texas to teach in the Caldwell labor camp's summer remedial program. From 1956 to 1966, the Migrant Ministry facilitated remedial school programs, vacation Bible schools, recreational activities, sewing classes, and other services for mi-

FIGURE 8.2. By the late 1950s, Mexican Americans were publicly sharing their unique cultural heritage. A parade float from the Wilder Labor Center celebrates Mexican American historical traditions. Photo courtesy of Idaho State Historical Society, 76–102.63q.

grant camps in southwestern Idaho and southeastern Oregon. The Mennonite Church placed a family at the Caldwell camp to help migrants negotiate social and economic issues. The sheer numbers of migrant children under age sixteen—4,870 during July 1964 in southern Idaho—overwhelmed these efforts. The Catholic Church had for some time ministered to the spiritual needs of migrants but also took an active role in educating youth.[40] Despite the compelling interest migrant parents had in their children's education and the increasing numbers enrolled in secondary schools, a 1966 Employment Security Agency report concluded that "short-sighted citizens and some educators purposely 'overlook' [these migrant] children. . . . Obviously this is no solution."[41]

Nationwide changes in the 1960s and 1970s held great promise for Idaho's Mexican Americans. The civil rights movement inspired legislation that enabled minorities to participate in the transformation of their own destiny through such antipoverty programs as Head Start. Laws required that those served be represented on the advisory committees or boards of service organizations receiving federal funding, so in 1965 the Southwest Idaho Migrant Ministry established Idaho Farm Workers Services, Inc., which briefly ran a Head Start program. Two years later, El-Ada, Inc., a joint community action agency, opened a Head Start program in Glenns Ferry.[42]

In 1967, however, Treasure Valley Community College in Ontario, Oregon, gained management of most federally funded antipoverty programs for southwestern Idaho and southeastern Oregon. Leadership was drawn primarily from college administrators. When Mexican American community activists sought control of some of the programs, a struggle erupted in 1970. The conflict gave birth to the Idaho Migrant Council as Lucy Peña Hunt, Humberto Fuentes, Pedro López, and Tony Solis attempted to take over the Migrant Education Program from the community college administrators.[43]

With the help of the Utah Migrant Council, Fuentes and the others channeled Office of Economic Opportunity funds into a new organization, the Idaho Migrant Council, run by and for farmworkers. Incorporated in 1971, the Idaho Migrant Council (now Community Council of Idaho) spent the next forty years, most of that time with Fuentes at the helm, serving Idaho's poorer Mexican Americans in the areas of health, education, and housing. The catalyst that motivated Chicano activists was a farmworkers' strike in Canyon County during the summer of 1970. Accounts differ as to the cause of the strike, but it is clear that local strike leaders sought to organize farmworkers into a union that could possibly be affiliated with César Chávez's United Farm Workers. Growers characterized the organizing effort as "being instigated by a bunch of outside organizers," while it was obvious that strike leaders hailed from Caldwell.[44] Despite the local nature of the organizing effort and the clear desire of Mexican American farmworkers to have some say in their wages and working conditions, growers rushed to lobby state political leaders to pass a law preventing strikes during harvest season. One local newspaper reported that "efforts to obtain safe working conditions" were characterized by the bill's advocates as "unfair labor practices."⁴⁵ The legislature passed the temporary Agricultural Labor Law in 1971, but growers feared yielding to farm labor. One farmer expressed his concern to Senator Frank Church, writing, "I wonder how anyone can doubt the serious situation the subversives have planned for our nation."⁴⁶ The following year, Governor Cecil Andrus signed a compromise bill granting collective bargaining rights to agricultural workers but placing restrictions on strikes and boycotts.⁴⁷

Some in the Anglo community who had worked to create and run Head Start and migrant education programs resented being excluded as farm-workers attempted to take charge of their own future. President Lyndon Johnson's War on Poverty changed things everywhere, not least in Idaho, where migrant labor and poor Mexican Americans and others were con-cerned. Legislation creating the Office of Economic Opportunity required that 50 percent of the advisory committees of federally funded nonprofit organizations working with the poor had to be drawn from those meant to benefit from the programs. The other 50 percent should be made up of com-munity members interested in helping the poor. Humberto Fuentes framed the issue clearly, emphasizing that "farm workers need a voice." They should control their own destiny. They should have "the power and the ability to organize and have a say so in the way things are run."⁴⁸

From its inception, the Idaho Migrant Council faced enormous chal-lenges. The 1970 census counted 18,476 Idahoans whose first language was Spanish. About 4,800 were children under age sixteen enrolled in school. Almost a quarter of the adults had fewer than five years of education, and only 27 percent had graduated high school. Barely 4 percent were college graduates. Only seventy-nine Latino teachers could be found among the ranks of the state's nine thousand teachers. More than 60 percent of Latino workers were farm, nonagricultural, and blue-collar laborers compared to about 30 percent of Anglos in similar occupations. More than 25 percent of Latinos lived below federal poverty lines compared to 10 percent of the general population. Ten years later, conditions had not changed much for the state's Latinos except that their numbers had almost doubled, to 36,350. Still, 21 percent had only five years of schooling, 38.7 percent had graduated from high school, and 5.5 percent had four or more years of college. These were slight improvements, but still far below the accomplishments of Anglos and other ethnic groups. Half the Anglo workforce had management and professional jobs, but less than a quarter of Latino workers held these positions. Moreover, Latinos suffered an 11 percent unemployment rate.[49]

Civil rights legislation and affirmative action programs provided opportunities for Latinos to leave the migrant stream and achieve better-paying and higher-status jobs. Most who took these jobs, however, were from nonmigrant families or were two or three generations removed from being migrants. Nevertheless, Latinos could now be seen in positions that had previously been the exclusive domain of Anglos. Activists working in government formed the statewide advocacy group Image de Idaho, which worked to promote improvements in the Latino community. Affiliated with Image groups in other states, Pocatello activists formed their own local Image del Sudeste. Every year, Image de Idaho sponsored an annual conference in either Boise or Nampa to focus attention on social and economic issues confronting Latinos. The program of the 2006 conference, for example, examined the growing problem of Mexican youth gangs in Idaho.[50] Image del Sudeste, Community Council of Idaho, the Hispanic Business Association (formed in 1991), and the state's colleges and universities all raise scholarship funds for talented and accomplished Latino students.

THE EDUCATION CHALLENGE

Despite promoting education and raising funds for college scholarships, Latino leaders worried about the high proportion of their community's children who were failing and dropping out of an educational environment deemed unresponsive to their needs. In 1978, the Idaho Migrant Council studied six school districts in southern Idaho and learned that between 80 and 90 percent of the Mexican American students dropped out before graduating. Alleging that education officials had failed to comply with state and federal laws protecting the rights of limited English proficient (LEP) students, the council sued the State Board of Education and local school districts. Citing a 1974 Supreme Court decision, *Lau v. Nichols*, and the Equal Education Opportunity Act of the same year, council lawyers contended that the board of education was doing little to help students overcome language barriers.

After the suit was dismissed by the Idaho courts, Idaho Migrant Council

lawyers appealed to the Ninth District Circuit Court of Appeals, which re-
versed the decision. The appellate court noted that federal law imposed requirements on the state "to ensure that plaintiffs' language deficiencies are
addressed." By 1983, the courts had hammered out an agreement between
the two litigants requiring each school district to identify LEP students and
submit a plan to ensure their participation in the schools' standard curriculum. If necessary, districts had to provide instruction in the students'
native language to keep them at grade level while simultaneously pursuing
English-language development. Idaho State Department of Education annual reports between 1985 and 1988 found monitored school districts in
compliance. Still, evidence showed that LEP students lagged behind their
peers. In 1989, of the fifteen LEP programs surveyed, "six . . . were criticized
for not making the curriculum accessible" either because they failed to provide language assistance or because they mainstreamed students before
the students' language skills merited it. The following year showed little
improvement. LEP students continued to function far below grade level
and dropped out long before their graduation dates. While it was clear that
some districts had failed to comply with the court's mandate, the department applied no sanctions.[51]

In June 1990, the State Board of Education Task Force on Hispanic Education discovered that 40–60 percent of Latinos still dropped out of school.
It recommended that the state use money from its general funds to meet
the needs of LEP students rather than rely solely on federal funds. The legislature complied, appropriating $1 million in 1993 and bumped up funds for
LEP students to $2.25 million four years later. Unfortunately for the more
than 13,000 LEP students, increased funding and additional efforts failed
to produce expected results. A 1995 report from the U.S. Department of
Education Office for Civil Rights charged that Nampa, Caldwell, Twin Falls,
Idaho Falls, and several other school districts had failed to fulfill state and
federal mandates. Estimated dropout rates still stood at over 43 percent.
Some feared it might take another lawsuit to resolve the problem.[52]

A 1999 study of a junior and senior high school in Nampa found that of
the seventy-five teachers interviewed, 95 percent had little or no training
in dealing with minority students. Most had no understanding of Mexican
American culture, lacked time to help students who needed special atten-

tion, and expected Latino students to assimilate to mainstream societal norms. The study cited these as reasons for the high dropout rate. Institutions needed to address cultural differences and foster a truly pluralistic environment, or the problem would continue.[53]

A decade later and despite the federal mandates of the No Child Left Behind Act, many of Idaho's Latino children are left behind. Minidoka School District administration, for example, decided to discontinue a successful bilingual program at Minico High School that had raised standard achievement test scores substantially over the two years it was in place. When the program was eliminated, Minico's students (40 percent Latino) lost their only Latino teacher. Moreover, some teachers have been accused of devaluing the cultural heritage of their Mexican students. Other districts, such as American Falls and Blaine County, however, support progressive bilingual-education approaches to addressing the needs of their LEP students.[54]

Statewide, great educational challenges remain for the Latino community, but the 2012 *Hispanic Profile Data Book for Idaho* reveals improvement. By grade ten, 87.2 percent of non-Latino students were reading at or above grade level, but Latino students were catching up, with almost 74 percent proficiency. Latino students showed improvement in math by grade ten as well; 62.5 percent proficiency versus 78.5 percent for all others. Latinos' levels of proficiency in all tested areas would be much higher if migrant and LEP students were not included; these two groups continue to score poorly on tests. Another bright spot in Latino education is the decreasing dropout rate. From 1993–94 to 2009–10, the rate has been cut from almost 13 percent to less than 2 percent. But when it came to college readiness, only 10 percent of Idaho's Latinos were considered college-ready versus 26 percent of non-Latinos. About 54 percent of Idaho's adult Latinos over age twenty-five have graduated from high school, but only 7 percent hold bachelor's degrees or higher. For non-Latinos, 88.3 percent graduated from high school, and 24.4 percent earned bachelor's degrees or higher.[55]

Federally funded programs at Boise State University, such as the High School Equivalency Program and the College Assistance Migrant Program, established in 1983 and 1984 respectively, have helped overcome the educational obstacles faced by Latinos, especially those from migrant families. As their names imply, these two programs provide aid and academic support to students whose migrant backgrounds have prevented them from obtaining a high school education in a timely fashion or eliminated the possibility of pursuing a college education. The Boise State University college assistance program accepts forty students each year, and by 2010 it had served almost 1,200 students. Both the University of Idaho's college assistance program, which opened in 1999, and Boise State's program enable disadvantaged youth from migrant families to realize their educational goals and move into more rewarding occupations. Many Idahoans, however, have voiced complaints about the High School Equivalency Program for recruiting high school dropouts from migrant families whose children may not have legal residency status. Similar objections have been raised to the failed attempts of the Idaho Community Action Network and other advocacy groups to advance legislation allowing undocumented students who have graduated Idaho high schools to pay in-state university tuition.[56]

FIGHTING DISCRIMINATION AND BIGOTRY

Discrimination and hostility toward braceros in Idaho moved the Mexican government to cancel the program in the state in 1948, but Latinos continue to encounter such problems to the present day. Although some migrants found conditions in Idaho superior to what they had known in Texas, they could not escape prejudice. Anglos inclined to discriminate did not distinguish between citizens of the United States or of Mexico. To them, a Mexican was a Mexican. Isidro "Blackie" López, whose family migrated to Nampa in 1941, remembered the respect local residents showed him when he came home after the war dressed in his military uniform. However, "when I put on civilian clothes," he told Maria Salazar some years later, "Anglos saw me as just another Mexican, worthless in their eyes." Fortunately, this was not the case in all Idaho communities.[57]

Well-known and widely admired Nampa community activist Antonio Rodriguez Sr. recalled encountering signs in various Treasure Valley businesses in the late 1950s warning Mexicans, Negroes, Jews, Indians, and dogs to stay out.[58] Angered by such blatant displays of bigotry and ignorance, Rodriguez joined others to combat prevailing attitudes of racial and ethnic intolerance. They formed the Idaho Citizens Committee for Civil Rights and secured passage of the state's first antidiscrimination law. House

Bill 217 prohibited discrimination in employment practices and made it il-legal to bar anyone from public places on the basis of race, religion, national origin, color, or creed. Opponents argued that the bill "was not needed in a state like Idaho," yet it passed by an overwhelming margin (44–10) and became law on March 14, 1961.[59]

Recent migrants and many permanent residents of Mexican descent, however, knew nothing of Idaho's new law and feared that complaining about abuse would end in reprisals. For undocumented Mexican nation-als, the idea of voicing dissatisfaction to anyone in a position of authority seemed like sheer lunacy. Making sure that businesses and employers hon-ored the law fell to the people who had urged its passage in the first place, or to the few who felt safe in filing complaints. Studies show that laws of this type were ineffective in guaranteeing individual civil rights. Civil actions in other western states proved "slow, chancy and expensive," especially if victims were poor. Local prosecutors were reluctant to prosecute, and "charging local businessmen with crimes was not politically palatable." After ninety-three years with such a law, Colorado had not prosecuted anyone under its criminal provisions.[60]

After the assassination of Martin Luther King, Jr., in April 1968, the state government refused to keep official flags at half-mast until King was buried. In December of that year, angered by this affront, Citizens for Civic Unity, a broad-based group of civil rights activists, drafted a bill creating the Idaho Human Rights Commission. Phil Batt, a Republican senator known as a champion of minority rights, agreed to push SB 1221 through. Citizens for Civic Unity found the new agency a disappointment. Underfunded and with no "statutory assurance" allowing for "effective complaint processing procedures," the commission lacked direct enforcement and subpoena pow-ers. A year later, legislative attempts to increase its powers proved unsuc-cessful. With little chance of bringing criminal charges against violators of the recent antidiscrimination act, the commission placed heavier emphasis on "conciliation of complaints and achieving immediate relief for the com-plainant." In time, "minority communities in some parts of the state . . . expressed a lack of confidence in the county advisory committees," costing the commission the support "of a significant portion of the community it was designed to serve."[61]

Jesse Berain's appointment as a commissioner and subsequently a full-time investigator gave Mexican Americans a voice on the commission, but he was unable to do much to resolve the serious civil rights violations that his community suffered. Migrant labor camps, while improving, still reminded farm laborers that some Idaho growers did not value their contributions enough to provide decent housing or even portable toilets in the fields. Many employers dragged their feet in hiring qualified minorities. Cases brought before the Idaho Human Rights Commission in the early 1970s revealed that owners of some eating and drinking establishments continued to refuse service to people of Mexican heritage or demanded that they speak English on the premises.[62]

Discrimination and scapegoating of Mexicans and other Latinos were not limited to the southern region of the state but seemed to be everywhere. Gregg Olsen reported its troubling existence in his award-winning book *The Deep Dark*, on the disastrous Sunshine Mine fire in Kellogg, Idaho, in May 1971. Joe Armijo, who died deep in the bowels of the mine, was the son of Mexican immigrants, a tough and scarred survivor of an earlier accident at Bunker Hill. In their search for an explanation for the fire that killed ninety-one miners, five of them Latinos, Sunshine executives were more than willing to believe that a disgruntled miner had set it. When Armijo's deranged wife blamed the fire on her husband, "those who needed a scapegoat pounced." Mine superintendent Al Walkup was not one of them. "I know the man. He didn't do it." Walkup blamed racism for making Armijo a target: "*Mexicans are always getting blamed for everything around here, even if it isn't their fault, they get blamed.*"[63]

In the 1980s, increasing racial tensions between Latinos and government officials in Canyon County, as well as a host of unresolved problems, spurred the Idaho Migrant Council, Image de Idaho, and Latino leaders to pressure the legislature to create the Idaho Commission on Hispanic Affairs. After three years of intense lobbying to obtain the desired legislation (1984–87), Rudy Peña became the commission's first executive director.[64] The commission provides a forum for addressing the changing needs of Idaho's Latino community. In 2008, Governor C. L. Otter wrote that it "offers a crucial perspective on the issues and opportunities facing Hispanic Idahoans. Its responsive, data-driven recommendations are an invaluable asset for Idaho policy makers." Despite the governor's high esteem for the work of the commission, when the state faced a severe budget crisis in 2010, Otter recommended that both the Commission on Hispanic Affairs and the Idaho Human Rights Commission be disbanded.[65]

Idaho lagged far behind other western states in providing protection to its farmworkers. Change finally occurred as agriculture lost its place as the driving force behind Idaho's economy. First, farmworker advocates won small concessions with the passage of a law in 1981 to place portable toilets in fields where people worked. Then, after eight unsuccessful attempts between 1917 and 1996, farmworker supporters pressured the state legislature into extending workers' compensation coverage to farm labor. Idaho was one of the last states in the nation to pass such a law. Aided by this momentum, numerous advocacy groups fought acrimonious battles with Idaho agricultural interests to apply the minimum wage to farm labor and to force labor contractors to register and post bonds. They won both battles; the former passed into law in 2001 and the latter in 2002.[66]

The Immigration Reform and Control Act of 1986 provided a process for about ten thousand undocumented workers in Idaho to become legal residents eligible for citizenship. The act provoked intense conflict when it was passed, and the immigration issue continues to agitate many Idahoans who are outspoken in opposition to similar proposals debated by Congress since that time. Other Idahoans, chiefly those in agriculture and most in the Latino community, favor fewer restrictions on the flow of international labor. Former senator Larry Craig's AgJobs bill re-created a program of guest workers for agribusiness but raised the ire of many of his constituents, who heckled and booed him at one Canyon County town hall meeting. His critics claimed that the bill would grant amnesty to illegal immigrants who should be punished and deported.[67]

In April 2006, a national Latino effort attempted to influence Congress to reform the policy of border interdiction and forced deportation of undocumented workers. Marches and protests took place across the country. In Treasure Valley, various Latino advocacy groups organized a march of more than five thousand. Leaders rallied the crowd at the state capitol with speeches. They called for laws allowing increased legal migration, unification of families, protection from exploitation for workers lacking legal status, and an earned "pathway to citizenship." Speakers urged reforms to enable law-abiding but undocumented workers to continue in their jobs without fear.[68]

Itself a reaction to strong anti–illegal immigrant sentiment, the march provoked an immediate backlash. Responding to an unfounded perception that undocumented Mexican immigrants were overwhelming Canyon County's law enforcement and social services, County Commissioner Robert Vasquez sent a bill to the Mexican government demanding payment of $2 million for these "extra costs." He also sought federal assistance to defray health costs for indigent immigrants. Vasquez's commission then brought charges under the federal Racketeer Influenced and Corrupt Organizations Act against four Canyon County corporations and the Idaho Migrant Council for recruiting, hiring, and protecting unauthorized workers from Mexico. The courts threw out the initial case and a subsequent appeal.[69] The Idaho Association of Counties joined the issue when it asked the legislature to deny use of county indigent funds for illegal immigrants. County officials claimed that they spent $1.5 million a year on illegal residents' health care costs. A coalition of religious groups, advocates for the poor, business leaders, and others succeeded in killing the bill.[70]

The April 2006 march, however, goaded Vasquez and his supporters to harden their stance against unauthorized immigration. Vasquez declared himself a candidate for Larry Craig's U.S. Senate seat. Although defeated in the primary, he and his backers' anti–illegal immigrant stance added to a growing rift in the Idaho Republican Party. Conservative Republicans, aided by Governor Otter, tried again in the 2007 legislative session to block unauthorized immigrants' access to state benefits.[71] They also endorsed English as the official state language and rejected in-state tuition at the state's colleges and universities for children of undocumented immigrants who graduated from the state's high schools. In the 2008 legislative session, Meridian Republican senator Shirley McKague introduced a resolution calling on the president and Congress to end birthright citizenship for children of illegal immigrants, secure the nation's borders, reject any legislation that would extend amnesty to unauthorized immigrants, and end economic incentives to them. The legislature also barred undocumented workers from obtaining Idaho drivers' licenses and renewing licenses from other states.[72]

Editorials in the *Idaho Statesman* and other Treasure Valley and Magic Valley newspapers railed against undocumented immigrants and those who dared come to their defense. Boise State University's College Republicans added to the turmoil in March 2007 by inviting Commissioner Vasquez to speak on campus. Posters promoting his speech were insensitive and childish, further polarizing the issue.[73] Former U.S. representative Bill Sali attempted unsuccessfully to block the Mexican government from locating a consulate in Boise.

Many police forces around the country have been reluctant to question the legal status of Latinos, fearing that it would compromise effective police work in their communities, But Ada County's sheriff considered using a federal program to train and authorize officers on enforcing federal immigration laws. In September 2007, federal immigration officers aided by Blaine County Sheriff's deputies conducted predawn raids on immigrant homes in the Hailey-Ketchum area. Some questioned the tactics employed and the cooperation of the local police in the sweep, while others warned that the anti–illegal immigrant activity and attendant emotion could easily be directed toward the entire immigrant and Latino community. Idaho's Catholic bishop lamented the breakup of immigrant families.[74] After Barack Obama was reelected president in 2012 with such overwhelming Hispanic support, Idaho's Latino leaders are again organizing to renew their pressure on the state's political elite.

LOOKING AHEAD

In the twenty-first century, economic opportunities for Latinos have broadened, as the younger generation branches out into a variety of careers and businesses. The current edition of the Hispanic Business Directory shows that Hispanic-owned businesses expanded statewide by almost 40 percent between 2002 and 2007. Latinos have established professional careers in medicine, teaching, law, public administration, and engineering; their buying power continues to grow, but in 2010, 28.8 percent lived in poverty compared to 13.5 percent of non-Latinos. Agricultural workers, still largely Mexican or Mexican American, receive low wages for dirty, dangerous, hard work. Despite recent laws protecting farm laborers, enforcement is another matter. The Idaho Department of Labor encounters numerous attempts by labor contractors and farmers to hinder field inspectors, exploit loopholes, and circumvent the legislation intended to protect farm labor.[75]

Farmworkers take risks on a daily basis as exemplified by the following two incidents. In 1996, while digging post holes on a southeastern Idaho farm, Javier Tellez Juarez suffered the loss of both arms and a leg when a piece of his clothing caught in an auger and pulled him into the machine. This terrible accident spurred passage of the law that provides farm laborers with workers' compensation insurance. In June 2005, another accident near Caldwell demonstrated the need for heightened vigilance to protect farmworkers. Twenty-nine men and women were sent into onion fields that had recently been sprayed with a toxic brew of pesticides that made many of them violently ill and sent some to the hospital. No one had posted the necessary danger signs warning the crew to stay out of the fields.[76]

Since the 1970s, attitudes have changed and Idahoans have grown more accepting, but intolerance and bigotry toward Latinos still exist. Accustomed to a racially and ethnically homogenous society, many non-Latinos worry about the growing presence of the Latino culture and what they perceive to be its negative impact on their way of life. Fear of the unknown drives the virulent backlash against unauthorized immigrants and an unwillingness to seek workable solutions to that problem. Unfortunately, there is a tendency to identify hardworking, law-abiding, decent Latinos who are contributing to the economic prosperity and cultural richness of the state with criminals and gang members only because they speak the same language or have the same ethnic or racial heritage. Consequently, the number of hate crimes statewide has risen. In two May 2008 *Idaho Statesman* articles, Tim Woodward acknowledged his own ignorance and naïveté when he wrote about tolerance and goodwill as a Boise hallmark. So many letters and e-mails recounting acts of discrimination and racism flooded his mailbox that he was forced to write an apology and reeducate himself as to the reality faced by many of the city's and state's minorities.[77] Reports of discrimination, racist remarks, and inappropriate behavior toward minorities, even by public officials, have appeared in the state's newspapers with such frequency in the past twenty-five years that it is clear that Idaho, while improving in some ways, still has much to do to overcome its history of racial and ethnic discrimination.

NOTES

1   The term *Latino* describing people of Latin American heritage in Idaho is judged
    preferable to the government-coined term *Hispanic* and will be used as much as pos-
    sible throughout this chapter. For terminology, see Idaho Commission on Hispanic
    Affairs, http://www2.state.id.us/icha/menus/history.asp (accessed July 2, 2008).

2   See 2010 census results at Idaho QuickFacts at the US Census Bureau, http://
    quickfacts.census.gov/qfd/states/16000.html (accessed July 20, 2011); Errol D.
    Jones, "Invisible People: Mexicans in Idaho History," *Idaho Issues Online* (Fall 2005),
    http://www.boisestate.edu/history/issuesonline/fall2005_issues/1f_mexicans.
    html (accessed August 2, 2010); Jessie Bonner, "Hispanic Population in State Grows
    40 Percent," *Idaho Statesman*, May 1, 2008, Main 3; Idaho Commission on Hispanic
    Affairs, "Snapshot of Idaho Latino Community: Final Report, 2008," http://www2
    .state.id.us/icha/ (accessed June 26, 2008).

3   State and County QuickFacts, http://quickfacts.census.gov/qfd/states/ (accessed
    July 20, 2011).

4   "The Ethan Allen and Its Discoverer," *Idaho World*, March 11, 1865, 2; Maria Salazar,
    "Yo, Tambien, He Estado Aquí," unpublished manuscript, written for Idaho's cen-
    tennial celebration, 1991, 2–3; "Rocky Bar Spanish Legend," Reference Series no. 19,
    Idaho State Historical Society, Boise, ID; Merrill D. Beal and Merle W. Wells, *History
    of Idaho* (New York: Lewis Historical Publishing Company, 1959), 1:279.

5   Max Delgado, *Jesús Urquides, Idaho's Premier Muleteer* (Boise: Idaho State Historical
    Society and the Hispanic Cultural Center of Idaho, 2006), 5, 21–24, 49–56; Erasmo
    Gamboa, "The Mexican Mule Pack System of Transportation in the Pacific North-
    west and British Columbia," *Journal of the West* 19 (January 1990): 16–27; Todd
    Shallat, *Ethnic Landmarks: Ten Historic Places That Define the City of Trees* (Boise:
    Boise City Office of the Historian and Boise State University, 2007), 63–73. In 2013,
    Boise City commemorated Urquides and his home site with a monument located
    at 115 Main Street.

6   Juan Ramon García, *Operation Wetback: The Mass Deportation of Mexican Undocu-
    mented Workers in 1954* (Westport, CT: Greenwood Press, 1980), 21.

7   Errol D. Jones and Kathleen R. Hodges, "A Long Struggle: Mexican Farm Workers
    in Idaho, 1918–1935," in Jerry Garcia and Gilberto Garcia, eds., *Memory, Community,
    and Activism: Mexican Migration and Labor in the Pacific Northwest* (East Lansing:
    Julian Samora Research Institute, Michigan State University, 2005), 54.

8   William J. A. McVety file, Idaho State Historical Society, Library and Archives, MS
    307, box 1, folder 3.

9   *Idaho Farmer*, October 13, 1921, notes that Amalgamated Sugar brought in five hun-
    dred Mexican field hands to the Twin Falls area and was trying to recruit more; Jones
    and Hodges, "A Long Struggle," 52–56.

10 Erasmo Gamboa, "Mexican American Railroaders in an American City: Pocatello,
    Idaho," in Robert McCarl, ed., *Latinos in Idaho: Celebrando Cultura* (Boise: Idaho
    Humanities Council, 2003), 35.

11 Salazar, "Yo, Tambien," 8–9; Patricia Ourada, *Migrant Workers in Idaho* (Boise: Boise
    State University, 1980), 17.

12 Errol D. Jones, "The Shooting of Pedro Rodriguez," *Idaho Yesterdays* 46 (Spring–Sum-
    mer 2005): 40–55. A vast literature documents these injustices. See, for example,

Beatriz de la Garza, *A Law for the Lion: A Tale of Crime and Injustice in the Borderlands* (Austin: University of Texas Press, 2003).

13   President Alvaro Obregon to Governor David Davis, September 21, 1921, Idaho State Historical Society, Library and Archives, Penitentiary Records, 2561 AR42/200072432 Ramirez, Vincente [*sic*]. Thanks to Kathleen R. Hodges for bringing this document to my attention.

14   Ourada, *Migrant Workers*, 17, 20.

15   *Twin Falls Daily News*, July 19, 1924, 8; July 20, 1924, 8; and July 27, 1924, 5.

16   Jones and Hodges, "A Long Struggle," 70–74; Mexican Vice Consul at Salt Lake City Elias Colunga to Secretariat of Foreign Relations, September 1, 1931, Archivo Historico del Secretario de Relaciones Exteriores (Mexico City), file no. IV-193–22, exp.241.8/(73–54). Colunga's photos are attached to his report.

17   Numerous investigators have written accounts of the labor contract system in the American West. See, for example, Gunther Peck, *Reinventing Free Labor: Padrones and Immigrant Workers in the North American West, 1880–1930* (Cambridge: Cambridge University Press, 2000), and Daniel Rothenberg, *With These Hands: The Hidden World of Migrant Farmworkers Today* (New York: Harcourt Brace, 1998).

18   Colunga's report. One of the major grievances was the exploitation suffered by pea pickers under the labor contract system. Worker belief that contractors were unfairly profiting from their labor touched off a massive strike in pea fields in Alameda and Santa Clara Counties, California, in April 1933. Stuart Marshall Jamieson, *Labor Unionism in American Agriculture*, Bulletin no. 836 (Washington, DC: U.S. Department of Labor, 1945; repr., New York: Arno Press, 1975), 88–89.

19   M. G. McConnel to Governor C. Ben Ross, Driggs, ID, August 14, 1935, Governor Ross Papers, Idaho State Historical Society, Library and Archives, Boise, ID, AR2/15, box 1.

20   M. G. McConnel to Governor C. Ben Ross, Boise, ID, August 21, 1935, Governor Ross Papers. See also "Teton County Labor Strike Causes Martial Law Order: Troops Enroute to Driggs," *Idaho Daily Statesman*, August 15, 1935, 1; *Idaho Falls Post-Register*, August 15, 1935, 1. Salt Lake City Mexican consular files provide no information on this strike.

21   McConnel to Ross, August 14, 1935. Prosecuting attorney S. H. Atchley's telegram in Governor Ross Papers; "Teton County Labor Strike," 1.

22   J. Asunción Pérez, interviewed by Rosa Rodríguez, Idaho Falls, 1991, Idaho Oral History Center, Boise, ID, 38.

23   Charles W. Hope, Director, Regional Labor Board, telegram to Governor C. Ben Ross, Seattle, WA, August 15, 1935; Hermenegilro Robles, Consul of Mexico, letter to Governor C. Ben Ross, Salt Lake City, UT, August 16, 1935; Col. Frederick Hummel's report to the adjutant general, August 27, 1935; all in Governor Ross Papers.

24   "Governor Ross Draws Attack of Labor Group," *Idaho Daily Statesman*, August 27, 1935; C. Ben Ross letter to Nampa Trade and Labor Council, Boise, ID, August 27, 1935, Governor Ross Papers; Idaho State Federation of Labor, "Resolution No. 14," *Proceedings of the Idaho State Federation of Labor Convention*, 1935, 33–34.

25   Quoted in Jim Gentry, *In the Middle and on the Edge: The Twin Falls Region of Idaho* (Twin Falls: College of Southern Idaho, Twin Falls Centennial Commission, 2003), 269–70. Salazar, "Yo, Tambien," 11; Rita Perez interview, in Erasmo Gamboa, ed., *Voces Hispanas/Hispanic Voices of Idaho* (Boise: Idaho Commission on Hispanic Affairs and Idaho Humanities Council, 1992), 21–22.

26   Erasmo Gamboa, *Mexican Labor and World War II: Braceros in the Pacific Northwest, 1942–1947* (Austin: University of Texas Press, 1990), 14–15.

27   Gamboa, *Voces Hispanas*, 21.

28   Richard B. Craig, *The Bracero Program: Interest Groups and Foreign Policy* (Austin: University of Texas Press, 1971), 43; see agreement in Garcia, *Operation Wetback*, app. 1, 241–45.

29   Gamboa, *Mexican Labor and World War II*, 112.

30   Salazar, "Yo, Tambien," 15; Jones "Invisible People"; Louisa R. Shotwell, *The Harvesters: The Story of the Migrant People* (Garden City, NY: Doubleday & Company, 1961), 30.

31   Maria Gonzalez Mabbut, interview by the author, Nampa, ID, August 6, 1999, Idaho State History Society Public Archives and Research Library, Oral History Center, Boise, Idaho; and Jesse Berain, interview by the author, Boise, ID, July 20, 2008.

32   Shotwell, *Harvesters*, 39.

33   Ibid., 105; Ourada, *Migrant Workers*, 31. Mike Dittenber, *The Caldwell Labor Camp: A Place to Call Home* (Caldwell, ID: printed by author, 2012), 4–13.

34   Robin Peterson, "Idaho Migratory Labor Camps, 1930–1980" (M.A. thesis, Boise State University, 2000), 30–38.

35   Ibid., 39; "Migratory Labor Camp Betterment Urged at Hearing," *News-Tribune* (Caldwell, ID), April 30, 1959, 1; "Farm Labor Group Opposes Federal Action on Workers," *News-Tribune* (Caldwell, ID), February 28, 1959, 1.

36   Governor's Migratory Labor Committee report, 1965, cited in Idaho Advisory Committee to the United States Commission on Civil Rights, *A Roof Over Our Heads: Migrant and Seasonal Farmworker Housing in Idaho* (Washington, DC: U.S. Commission on Civil Rights, 1980), 12; "The Scar at American Falls: Despite Request That It Clean Up or Close, Migrant Labor Camp Is Getting Worse," *Intermountain Observer*, July 26, 1969, 2.

37   *A Roof Over Our Heads*, 12.

38   David Gutierrez, *Walls and Mirrors: Mexican Americans, Mexican Immigrants, and the Politics of Ethnicity* (Berkeley: University of California Press, 1998); Shotwell, *Harvesters*, 159–60; Tom Current and Mark Martinez Infante, . . . *And Migrant Problems Demand Attention* (Salem: Oregon Bureau of Labor, 1959), 115–35; Salazar, "Yo, Tambien," 19.

39   *Times-News* (Twin Falls), June 25, 27, 30, 1957.

40   Salazar, "Yo, Tambien," 18; *Southern Idaho Migrant Ministry Newsletter*, Spring 1963, 3; "Special School Conducted to Benefit Children of Migrant Workers in [Paul] Area," *Idaho Register*, October 23, 1964, 2.

41   *1955–1965: Ten Years of Progress in Idaho for Migrant Workers* (Boise: Employment Security Agency, 1966), cited in Salazar, "Yo, Tambien," 18.

42   Idaho State Historical Society Reference Series, "Hispanic Migrant Workers' Social and Educational Services in Idaho," no. 1092 (February 1995); "Head Start Program at Glenns Ferry," *Idaho Register*, September 8, 1967, 1–2.

43   "The Migrant Education Tug-of-War," *Intermountain Observer*, February 6, 1971, 6.

44   Danny O'Halloran, "The Chicanos Organize in Southwest Idaho," *Intermountain Observer*, September 5, 1970, 3; Stephen Hunt, "Historical Perspectives on a Treasure Valley Farm Labor Strike, 1970," unpublished paper, 2003, in author's possession.

45   "Fear versus Anger in the Legislature," *Intermountain Observer*, February 6, 1971, 5.

46   Marvin Jeppeson, to Senator Frank Church, March 1, 1971, Farm Labor File, Senator

Church Papers, Boise State University Special Collections, Boise, ID, box 77, folder 20.

47 Idaho Agricultural Labor Act, 1972, Idaho Code §§22–4101–22–4113; "New Farm Labor Law Spurs Demand for Potato Boycott," *Idaho Statesman*, March 24, 1972, A8.

48 Quoted in Errol D. Jones and Kathleen Rubinow Hodges, "Writing the History of Latinos in Idaho," in McCarl, *Latinos in Idaho*, 28; Santos Recalde, "Migrants in Idaho Get Help from Head Start," *Idaho Register*, July 24, 1970, 1, 7.

49 Statistics are from the 1970 and 1980 censuses, cited in Salazar, "Yo, Tambien," 19–20.

50 For more information about Image de Idaho, see http://www.imagedeidaho.org/ (accessed April 17, 2008).

51 Sam Byrd, "The Plight of Mexican-American Students in Idaho's Public Schools," in Errol D. Jones and Kathleen Rubinow Hodges, eds., *The Hispanic Experience in Idaho* (Boise: Boise State University, 1998), 108–31.

52 Ibid., 128–31.

53 Richard Baker, *Mexican American Students: A Study of Educationally Discounted Youth* (Dubuque, IA: Kendall/Hunt Publishing Company, 1999), 12–14.

54 Ben Reed (KFTM Spanish-language radio station in Rupert) and Ed Luker (former bilingual teacher at Minico High School), interviews by the author, June 24, 2008, and Sam Byrd, director of Centro de Comunidad y Justicia, interview by the author, June 27, 2008; Rich Greene, "'Minico Isn't Like This': Controversy over Minico Student's Flag Sparks Silent Protests at School, National Discussion about Racism," *Magic Valley*, http://www.magicvalley.com/articles/2008/05/08/news/top_story/136322.txt (accessed June 20, 2008); Hector Tobar, *Translation Nation* (New York: Riverhead Books, 2005), 148–86.

55 Idaho is below the national average for those who have earned bachelor degrees or higher whether Latino or non-Latino. Idaho Commission on Hispanic Affairs, *Hispanic Profile Data Book*, 3rd ed. (Boise: Idaho Commission on Hispanic Affairs, 2012), 62–77.]

56 Michelle Kelley, associate director, BSU HEP program, interview by the author, Boise, June 26, 2008; and Martha Salas, administrative assistant, BSU CAMP program, interview by the author, June 24, 2008; Program Summary—College Assistance Migrant Program, http://education.boisestate.edu/camp/.

57 Salazar, "Yo, Tambien," 14. The Ramos family found the area around Idaho Falls where they settled in 1946 a vast improvement over the Rio Grande Valley in Texas. Maria Ramos Galaviz, "A History of the Ramos Family," unpublished manuscript, 2000, 7.

58 Antonio Rodriguez Sr., interview by the author, Nampa, ID, January 12, 2000; Rodriguez, interview by Patricia McDonald, Nampa, ID, November 5, 10, 1991, Idaho State Library and Archive, Boise, ID.

59 *General Laws of the State of Idaho, 36th Session*, chapter 309 (H.B. 217) 1961, 573–75; *Journal of the House of Representatives of the Idaho Legislature, Thirty-sixth Session* (1961), 504; "A Civil Rights Bill Is Approved," *Lewiston Morning Tribune*, March 3, 1961.

60 Donald E. Knickrehm, "A Study of the Idaho Human Rights Commission," Boise, unpublished manuscript, 1971, 2.

61 Ibid., 10–26.

62 Jesse Berain, interview by the author, Boise, June 25, 2008; Records of the Human Rights Commission, AR 60, box 3, Idaho State Historical Society Library and Archives. These files subsequently were closed to the public.

63 Gregg Olsen, *The Deep Dark: Disaster and Redemption in America's Richest Silver Mine* (New York: Three Rivers Press, 2005), 123, Olsen's emphasis, 330.

64 *Idaho Statesman*, November 30, 1987; Richard Baker, *Los Dos Mundos: Rural Mexican Americans, Another America* (Logan: Utah State University Press, 1995), 98–101; Rudy Peña, interview by the author, Pocatello, ID, August 18, 2011.

65 Governor Otter's message is at http://www2.state.id.us/icha/ (accessed June 27, 2008).

66 Dale N. Duncan Jr., "The Struggle for Equal Coverage: The Battle for Workers Compensation in Idaho's Fields," in Jones and Hodges, *Hispanic Experience*, 136–54; Gregory Hahn, "Kempthorne Signs Farmworker Bill," *Idaho Statesman*, March 22, 2001, Main 1 (related *Statesman* articles can be found in January 9, 2001, Local 4; March 13, 2001, Main 1; and December 31, 2001, Local 4); Leo Morales, "Farm Labor Bill Will Aid Idaho," *Idaho Statesman*, January 31, 2001, Local 9; and Idaho Code, Title 44, chs. 15 and 16 respectively.

67 Shawna Gamache, "Hecklers Harass Sen. Craig in Caldwell," *Idaho Statesman*, July 6, 2006, Main 1; Dan Popkey, "Craig Standing His Ground," *Idaho Statesman*, August 20, 2006, Main 1.

68 Kathleen Kreller, "Unity Marks Rally for Immigrants," *Idaho Statesman*, April 10, 2006, Main 1; for the role of the Catholic Diocese of Boise in the immigration debate, see Errol D. Jones, "Latinos and the Churches in Idaho, 1950–2000," in Linda Allegro and Andrew Grant Wood, eds. *Latino Migrations to the U.S. Heartland: Changing Social Landscapes in Middle America* (Chicago: University of Illinois Press, 2013), 87–94.

69 *Canyon County versus Syngenta Seeds, Inc., Sorrento Lactalis, Inc., Swift Beef Company, Harris Moran Seed Company, Idaho Migrant Council, Inc., and Albert Pacheco*, I.2. Canyon County dropped its complaint against the Idaho Migrant Council, but not against its executive director. *Idaho Statesman*, September 8, 2005, Local 3.

70 Rebecca Boone, "Idaho Justices: Illegal Immigrants Entitled to Indigency Aid," *Idaho Statesman*, June 17, 2008, Main 1.

71 Gregory Hahn, "House Okays Ban on State Benefits for Immigrants," *Idaho Statesman*, March 23, 2007, Main 3. Other *Statesman* articles on this topic appeared on January 14 and March 1, 2007.

72 Gregory Hahn, "Legislature Grapples with Immigration Issues," *Idaho Statesman*, March 3, 2007, Main 3; *Idaho Statesman*, February 12, 2008, Main 3; *Idaho Statesman*, January 29, 2008, Main 3.

73 For examples, see *Idaho Statesman* editorial pages April 16, 19, May 4, 5, 8, 10, 11, 24, June 18, and October 7, 2006; June 8, 28 and July 8, 2007, February 27, 2008; letters in opposition to Senator Craig's AgJobs bill, June 1, 7, 2006, and April 17, May 27, and June 2, 2007; *Magic Valley*, http://www.magicvalley.com, January 10, June 6, 2007, May 19, 2008, (accessed June 1, 2008); *Idaho Press Tribune*, June 10, July 9, 2007. For a smaller sample of those who wrote in support of undocumented immigrants, see *Idaho Statesman*, June 30, July 2, 11, 2006, and March 23, 2007; Sandra Forester, "BSU Student Flier Angers Some Hispanics," *Idaho Statesman*, March 19, 2007, Main 2; Sandra Forester, "BSU Republicans Offer Apology to Restaurant," *Idaho Statesman*, March 20, 2007.

74 "Jail Deputies May Target Illegal Aliens," *Idaho Statesman*, December 17, 2007, Main
    3; Michael Brown, "A Community Living in Fear," *Idaho Catholic Register*, October
    5, 2007, 1; Michael Brown, "Bishop Barnes Calls Catholics to Solidarity with Immi-
    grants," *Idaho Catholic Register*, October 5, 2007, 1; Bill Roberts, "Crapo, Sali: Raids
    Point to Need for Reform," *Idaho Statesman*, September 22, 2007, Main 1.

75 Idaho Department of Labor official Regina Montenegro, interviews by the author,
    Boise, ID, August 8, 2007, July 15, 2009, and May 18, 2011

76 Duncan, "The Struggle for Equal Coverage," 148; Idaho State Department of Agricul-
    ture Case 06003; Idaho Community Action Network, "Protect Idaho Farm Workers
    from Harmful Pesticides," February 8, 2006; Sandra Forester, "Farmworkers Seek
    Answers in Apparent Pesticide Poisoning," *Idaho Statesman*, July 16, 2005; Sandra
    Forester, " Fines in Pesticide Case Could Total $42,000," *Idaho Statesman*, August 18,
    2005; Shawna Gamache, "Activists Take Requests to Statehouse," *Idaho Statesman*,
    January 17, 2006, "Farmworkers Need Pesticide Notices Proposed in Bill," *Idaho
    Statesman*, March 27, 2006.

77 Tim Woodward, "A Little Tolerance Would Become Us All," *Idaho Statesman*, May
    14, 2008; "Boise—City of Bigots," *Idaho Statesman*, May 28, 2008.

IDAHO VOICES
Latino History

Ayda Cortina, a former farmworker, recalls
the migratory life.

INTERVIEWER: When you first [got] to the labor camp, what was your
first impression of it, do you remember?

CORTINA: Well, yeah. I liked it, because there was a lot of people around
here from—at that time we were migrant people, you know. We used to
go—stay here during the summer and then go back to our place, you know,
where we came from, Texas, California, all those states, and warm weather,
then, and worked at the field in Texas or California. And, well, we liked it
here because, like I say, there was a lot of our friends; we met a lot of friends
here, made a lot of friends. And we liked to work out on the farm. And, you
know, we used to do the thinning of beets with small hoes, short-handle
hoes; we used to work all day. Boy, it was really hard 'cause your back would
hurt a lot. . . .

INTERVIEWER: What was the house like that you lived in, in Caldwell?

CORTINA: They were—well, right now what they have at the spaces where
we used to live, which are these block apartments, these are four-plexes.
Well, there were six rooms to—they called them barracks—there were
six rooms, and they were only single rooms. It was a living room, it was
a bedroom, it was a kitchen, it was all in one. It was a small one, and we
used to have a wood stove. We didn't have any other kind of stove at that
time. And we used to go to Meridian Wood, at that time that's what it was
called, now it's called Wood Grain, I think. And then we used to go and get
little pieces of lumber, and that's what we put in the stove, so you know, we
used it.

INTERVIEWER: Well, you did your cooking and all on that wood stove?

CORTINA: Yes, and we had a—I still remember we had a big bed, a double
bed, and then we had a bunk bed. So two of us would sleep on the top part

of the bunk bed, and then two on the bottom, and one on the floor, and my mom and dad on the double bed.

INTERVIEWER: All in one room?

CORTINA: All in one room.

* * *

A child of a migrant laborer, J. Asuncíon Perez, recollects school and field work in the 1930s.

INTERVIEWER: So then, you must have been going to school here the first part of your early years?

PEREZ: No. My father did not send me to school, because he had intended to return back to Mexico. My mother never resignated [resigned?]—she did not even want to come to the United States. And, incidentally, my mother had kept my father from going into agriculture for himself. Even though he was a very stern man—most of the old Mexicans were—he still catered to his wife like most men do [*laughter*]. And consequently, he never *did* go into agriculture for himself. So he done what best he could. Would you repeat your—

INTERVIEWER: Well, I wanted to know if you had gone to school here.

PEREZ: Oh, because of that, he never did put me in school. It was not until 1935, after we came back from California, that the truant officer for this district—I cannot recollect his name right now. When he had served in the Philippines—the occupation of the Philippines—and [he] knew Spanish quite well. He came to my father and asked him, he said, "Mr. Perez." I happened to be present. I did not understand English at the time, but I had a memory like an elephant. "Why aren't these little *muchachitos* not going to school?" And he spoke to him in English, but yet *muchachitos* he said in Spanish. My father told him, he said, "Mister," he said, "I don't have a means of dressing them fit for school." He said, "No, Mr. Perez," he said, "they don't have to be dressed fancy, as long as they're clean." He said, "The law requires that you send those little *muchachitos* to school." And my father sometimes would get hung up on the language, and so then he started speaking Spanish to him. My father told him, he said, "I have three of school age."

Consequently, Mrs. Rodriguez, I did not start school until the fall of 1936. And I was about four years behind my classmates—or my school-mates. I shouldn't say "my classmates," but my schoolmates of the same age. Therefore, I went to Riverside School from—oh, I would say that it was after Thanksgiving 1936, to about April—first days of April 1937. At that time the beet thinning started, and my father took us out of school. My brother George and myself were already helping him.

NOTE

Ayda Cortina was interviewed by Raymona Maddy, October 22, 1997, Farmway Village, Caldwell, ID, transcript (OH2009), Oral History Center/Idaho State Historical Society, 2–3, 3–4. Used with permission of Idaho State Historical Society.

J. Asuncíon Perez was interviewed by Rosa Rodriguez, ca. 1991, Idaho Falls, ID, transcript (OH1155), Idaho Hispanic Oral History Project/Idaho Oral History Center, 19–20. Used with permission of Idaho State Historical Society.

9
Shifting Currents

Cultural Expressions in Idaho

RICHARD W. ETULAIN

WHEN VARDIS FISHER, PERHAPS IDAHO'S BEST-KNOWN writer, returned to the state in 1931 after several years in the Midwest and East, he quickly became a revealing example of shifting transregional cultural trends. The embodiment of American interregional—and even larger—influences in his Idaho fiction and the twelve-volume Testament of Man series, Fisher also represented key ingredients in Idaho's cultural identity: it too was transitioning from a frontier to a definable region. Later, as in much of the West, Idaho writers and sometimes artists moved on to postregional emphases in their works. These "frontier," "region," and "postregion" stages illustrate transitions in Idaho culture from the earliest travelers' descriptions through an emerging regional consciousness and on to recent emphases on nonregional, or more than regional, subjects. Idaho has also often been an "in-between" culture. Like Arizona, which is surrounded by Mexican, Californian, New Mexican, and Mormon cultures, Idaho is bounded and influenced by regional and national cultures. Vardis Fisher's career illustrates these chronological shifts and inner and outer contexts that have frequently shaped the cultural history of Idaho.[1]

This chapter deals briefly with selected cultural currents in Idaho from 1800 to the present. The first section discusses writers, beginning with the earliest explorers and travelers who passed through Idaho headed elsewhere, and then treats authors such as Mary Hallock Foote, Vardis Fisher, and Marilynne Robinson, who lived and wrote during at least a decade of residence in Idaho. A second section focuses on art, specifically the work of painters, in Idaho. The stress is on frontier, regional, and postregional transitions and outside-in relationships that figure prominently in Idaho culture. For instance, consider the artistic travelers, including John Mix Stanley, George Catlin, and Thomas Moran, and the ideas and artistic techniques they brought from outside to their early paintings of the region. In addition, think of the important Local Color images that dominate the domestic artworks of Mary Hallock Foote, the best-known Idaho artist of the late nineteenth century. A brief discussion of Idaho art in the post-1900 era completes this section. The third part of the chapter touches on one example of ethnic culture in Idaho, that of the Basques, to show cultural expressions within a particular context. As this section suggests, ethnic influences can be more powerful than place in shaping cultural trends. The closing paragraphs provide a few concluding thoughts about cultural currents in Idaho. This final section raises questions about Idaho's cultural future and notes topics that ambitious writers interested in the state's cultural history could address.[2]

LITERATURE IN IDAHO

The first writers who visited Idaho from roughly 1800 to 1860 usually wrote about what they considered the unique—or at least unusual—qualities of the lands and humans they encountered. These emphases mean that on their routes to other places, explorers and travelers, their heads full of previous experiences, usually stressed the novel scenes and peculiar peoples they met. The visitors frequently superimposed their cultural baggage on the landscapes and Native men and women of Idaho. As a result, the first written "literature" of Idaho depicts places and peoples as varied as the travelers themselves.[3]

The first of these well-known nineteenth-century explorers, Meriwether Lewis and William Clark and their Corps of Discovery, as well other travelers who followed, provide revealing glimpses of themselves and new scenes and humans. Lewis and Clark were struck with the poverty, hunger, and generally wretched state of the "Snake" (Shoshoni) Indians but considered the more "civilized" Nez Perce among the friendliest and most advanced Natives they had encountered. In the rugged Rocky Mountains, the Nez Perce were "most admireable pilots" who saved the explorers much time—and perhaps their lives. The Lewis and Clark Expedition, overall, reacted both negatively and positively to the eating habits, dress, and sexual mores of Idaho's Natives.[4]

Other travelers also emphasized sociocultural novelties. Washington Irving, a notable American writer of the first half of the nineteenth century, never visited Idaho. Nonetheless, in his books *Astoria* (1836) and *The Adventures of Captain Bonneville* (1837), Irving provided romantic depictions of it as a "wild and sublime region" but also one featuring "a desolate and awful waste" in its southern parts. As missionary Narcissa Whitman crossed the Snake River Valley, she filled her diaries with biblical images of upper rooms, inns for the night, and comparisons of her experiences with the Jewish Exodus and Christian's journey in *A Pilgrim's Progress*. Catholic missionary Nicolas Point more often saw God's hand in the successes of Indian hunting and the abundance of animal life for hunters in this Far West.[5] For all these travelers and writers, as for others like David Thompson, Alexander Ross, and many overlanders on the Oregon Trail, the twin subjects of supreme interest were the novel terrains of Idaho and the Native residents they met, friends and foes. As "frontier" writers, they frequently stressed contact with new sights and new peoples in their accounts.

Between the end of the exploration and overland trail era and the later post–Civil War years, poet and essayist Joaquin Miller epitomized the eastern romantic influences at work on frontier literature. Something of a rough, a "splendid poseur" one writer called him, Miller filled such sketches as "Rough Times in Idaho" and "'Idahho'" with frenetic escapades, picturesque frontier character types, and Indians Miller calls "perfect savages." Written in a runaway style and often a jumble of extravagant diction and tortured syntax, these sketches, as well as Miller's poems, aspired (unsuccessfully) to move beyond mere literary description to literary achievement.[6]

In the decades surrounding 1900, Idaho and the rest of the Pacific Northwest lagged behind contemporary literary currents swirling across the United States. For example, northwestern writers such as Frederic Homer Balch and Abigail Scott Duniway remained tied to the romance novel form that Nathaniel Hawthorne pioneered before the Civil War. Residents of the region also retained the Local Color literary traditions of such westerners as Mark Twain and Bret Harte longer than did authors in other western subregions. Writers in the Pacific Northwest were slow, too, to adopt the new literary realism, naturalism, and regionalism that surfaced from the 1870s into the 1920s. Why? Were Idaho and the Pacific Northwest a cultural backwater reluctant to embrace these emerging literary movements? Or, as two writers claimed in the 1920s, were faculty members at the region's public schools and colleges and universities failing to teach their students to think analytically and reluctant to introduce the literary trends that captured western writers Hamlin Garland, Frank Norris, Willa Cather, and Jack London in other subregions of the West?[7]

The most notable of the late nineteenth-century authors in Idaho is Mary Hallock Foote, whose writings epitomize the Local Color movement that invaded the post–Civil War West. A talented illustrator and author, Foote accompanied her energetic but largely unsuccessful engineer husband to several sites in the West before moving to Idaho in 1884 and staying until 1895. Her novels *The Chosen Valley* (1892), *Coeur d'Alene* (1894), and *The Desert and the Sown* (1902), as well as other short and longer works of fiction, combine the familiar ingredients of Local Color writing—provincial settings, local dialects, and folk customs and dress—with romantic and sentimental plots.[8]

The daughter of a comfortable Quaker farm family in New York's Hudson River Valley, Foote brought west a trunkload and more of her suffocating sense of class (an unusual emphasis in most western fiction of the time) to her writing. In Foote's fiction, miners, farm laborers, and enlisted servicemen (as well as their wives and daughters) are never the equals of mine owners, engineers, farm and ranch owners, and military leaders. In her decade in Idaho, Foote never grew accustomed to the pioneer circumstances that surrounded her in Boise—and up the Boise canyon. Revealingly, she wrote later that "I love my West when I am in the East." Importing her eastern genteel biases, Foote spoke of "dark Idaho," a place with its "thousands of acres of desert empty of history."[9] Most of Foote's Local Color fiction, much of it appearing in the lordly *Century Magazine* (edited by Richard Watson Gilder, the husband of her best girlhood friend), gained a good deal of favorable attention and won the praise of Owen Wister and others treating the West literarily. As a writer and as an artist, Foote illustrated well the shaping influences of a rather snobbish eastern writer who attempted to depict Idaho scenes and residents so new and often alienating to her.

If writers such as Miller and Foote endeavored to produce an Idaho lit-erature based on brief residences in the state or shadowed by their biases and blindnesses, Vardis Fisher was the initial twentieth-century writer of Idaho to produce first-rate regional fiction and gain a national reputation. More than any other Idaho author, Fisher provided a bridge from the earlier descriptive Local Color writers to the later postregional authors writing from the 1960s onward. Born and reared in a fundamentalist Mormon fam-ily in backcountry eastern Idaho, Fisher, by intense personal effort, gained a Ph.D. with high honors in English literature at the University of Chicago. After teaching stints at the University of Utah and New York University, where he became a close friend of noted author Thomas Wolfe, Fisher did come home again. He came back to Idaho and launched a writing career, first of regional novels, then the huge Testament of Man series, and finally a string of western historical novels. Drawing on his literary connections outside Idaho and his voracious reading and driven by his inordinate desire to understand his own roots, Fisher turned out seven novels between 1928 and 1937 (including, for example, *Toilers of the Hills* [1928], *Dark Bridwell* [1931], *In Tragic Life* [1932], and *April: A Fable of Love* [1937]) that featured the central theme of regionalists: how physical and human landscapes of places shape the identities and histories of those specific places. In display-ing similarities to the writings of other western regionalists of the 1920s and 1930s, such as the works of Willa Cather and H. L. Davis, Fisher's Ida-ho novels illustrate his concern for comprehending the meanings of his fictional Antelope Hills country of eastern Idaho as well as his drive for personal understanding.[10]

These motivations eventually drove Fisher in two other directions as a novelist. First, he cast a wider intellectual net, commencing the monumen-tal task of tracing fictionally humankind's pilgrimage through history in his twelve-volume Testament of Man series (1943–60). In this mammoth undertaking, Fisher drove deeply into the major mysteries of western civi-lization: What were the essential natures of men and women, had these identities changed over time, and what roles had religion and culture played in shaping humankind's history? These fictional histories, taxing and time-consuming in their construction, were not successful financially and pushed

FIGURE 9.1. Vardis Fisher is probably Idaho's best-known author. His work symbolizes the western regional literature popular in the first half of the twentieth century. Photo courtesy of Idaho State Historical Society, 68-22.5.

Fisher toward writing more salable western historical fiction. In his final years, the sales record for *Tale of Valor*, a novel about Lewis and Clark (1958), and *Mountain Man* (1965) mirrored the earlier success of his most widely read novel, *The Children of God* (1939), a searching examination of the origins and early leadership of the Mormon Church. Altogether, Fisher wrote twenty-six novels. He also directed the New Deal's Federal Writers' Project, part of the federal Works Progress Administration (WPA), in Idaho and produced several works of nonfiction. He serves as the most illuminating example of Idaho's regional literary development from the 1920s through 1960s and became the first native Idaho writer to be nationally recognized.[11]

From 1940 onward, the literary scene in Idaho wobbled in several directions. One writer, Frank C. Robertson, turned out dozens of popular Westerns featuring frontier conditions in a Wild West. Novelist James Stevens, building on his earlier *Brawny-Man* (1926) and Paul Bunyan stories, produced a superior regional novel about workers in the Pacific Northwest in *Big Jim Turner* (1948). Other writers turned to the gender, ethnic, and personal memoir emphases characteristic of postregional writing. Grace Jordan spun an inviting tale about her family's experiences in backcountry Idaho in *Home Below Hells Canyon* (1954), much as Annie Pike Greenwood (*We Sagebrush Folks* [1934]) and Nelle Portrey Davis (*Stump Ranch Pioneer* [1942]) had done earlier. Mary Clearman Blew and Kim Barnes added notably to the personal memoir genre emphasizing women's experiences—Blew in her *All But the Waltz* (1991) and Barnes in *In the Wilderness: Coming of Age in an Unknown Country* (1997) and *Hungry for the World: A Memoir* (2001). Meanwhile, Janet Campbell Hale, part Native American, drew on her own life as a mixed-race woman in the novel *The Jailing of Cecilia Capture* (1985). Another novelist, Ruthanne Lum McCunn, attracted much attention with her fictional treatment of the Chinese pioneer woman Polly Bemis in *Thousand Pieces of Gold* (1981). Tom Spanbauer dealt with controversial sexual identities, a popular subject for much postregional literature, in his novel *The Man Who Fell in Love with the Moon* (1992).

Since 1980, the Idaho writer attracting the widest attention has been Marilynne Robinson. Raised in the panhandle and a graduate of Coeur d'Alene High School, Robinson went east to Ivy League Brown University for her bachelor's degree and returned to Seattle for a doctorate in English and a dissertation on Shakespeare at the University of Washington. Her first novel, *Housekeeping* (1981), won wide acclaim. She did not publish her second novel, *Gilead*, until 2004, but it won the only Pulitzer Prize awarded to an Idaho-born writer of fiction. Most recently she has published *Home* (2008), the sequel to *Gilead*, which is set in the same small Iowa town and employs most of the same characters.

Housekeeping illustrates Robinson's superb achievements as a postregional writer. Although placed in the forests of northern Idaho and smelling of the wet woods and limpid lakes of the interior Northwest, the novel is not primarily a work of regional fiction. Instead, character, language, and ideas count most in this compelling novel. As Robinson told an interviewer, "It's like a foundling story. The eastness or westness of it . . . I don't think of it as particularly more or less likely to occur anywhere."[12] For Robinson, a sense of "lonesome," of aloneness or individualism, became the key concept in dealing with the West. The author wanted to portray her two heroines, Ruthie and her Aunt Sylvie, as nomads, as wanderers, warmed and encour-

aged by "housekeeping," which she thought of as "a regime of small kind-
nesses, which, together, make the world salubrious, savory, and warm."[13]

Robinson's versatility as a writer and her superior stylistic achievements
are even more evident in *Gilead*. It is a book primarily about men, with a
seventy-something, small-town pastor at the center. Knowing his remaining days will be few, he sets out to write a letter of explanation and encouragement to his much-cherished only child, a seven-year-old son. Set in
the Midwest, this smoothly written and adeptly constructed postregional
novel focuses, first of all, on character and feeling more than on place or
sense of place. The shaping experiences of the pastor's life are the spiritual
and family inheritances from his father and grandfather, both also pastors.
Antislavery backgrounds and the Iowa small town influence the structure
and plot of the novel, but most of all his journey is a test of moral character.
In his warm and sustaining love for his wife and son and his congregants
and in his reluctant and then redemptive care for the prodigal son of a fellow pastor, he embodies a healing balm of Gilead. Elegantly phrased in an
appealing minimalistic style, Robinson's first-rate novel clearly deserves
accolades as an outstanding work of postregional fiction. It is plainly the
best book by an Idaho-born author.

ART IN IDAHO

The first artists to view and paint Idaho were, like the earliest writers, passing through, on their way to other destinations. They, too, brought strong
predilections about lands and peoples that they superimposed on the new
landscapes and humans they met in the West. Several visitors came to Idaho
in the decades following 1840, all brought different artistic backgrounds,
and nearly all were "frontier" artists in chiefly emphasizing the new sites
and peoples they encountered.[14]

The first of the artists was Charles Preuss, who accompanied John
Charles Frémont west on several of his explorations. A topographer by background, the German-born Preuss was clearly more addicted to facts than
to the romantic, seven-league fantasies of the expedition's leader. In the
early 1840s, after a trip through Idaho, Preuss sketched *The American Falls
of Lewis Fork [Idaho]* (1845). Available only as a lithograph, this no-nonsense
sketch of the Idaho scene strikes viewers as unvarnished realism: Preuss is

showing what he saw, uncolored by the novelty or possible sublimity of the scene.[15]

A half dozen years later, William Tappan, a trained artist, and George Gibbs, an untrained but enthusiastic painter, traveled with the Osborne Cross–William Loring train along the Oregon Trail. Tappan executed sketches of Fort Hall and Fort Boise that reveal his interest in but lack of perspective on these frontier sites. Along with others, Gibbs took a side trip to Shoshone Falls, which he declared "one of nature's greatest wonders."[16] Gibbs's drawing, *Shoshonee Falls of the Snake River, August 15, from below* (1849), provides a straightforward, unadorned sketch of this natural wonder that so caught his attention.

An even more talented and experienced artist, John Mix Stanley, accompanied several Pacific Railroad surveys in the West. By the time Stanley came west with the Isaac Stevens Expedition in 1853, he had had a decade of experience traveling and painting in the trans-Mississippi West. His watercolor *Coeur d'Alene Mission, St. Ignatius River* (1853), compact in its coverage of the mission, nonetheless idealistically contextualizes the scene in a romantic foreground and backdrop of an unspoiled lake, richly abundant bushes and trees, and looming mountains. At much the same time, German artist Gustavus Sohon, traveling with Stevens and later with Captain John Mullan, provided dozens of portraits of Indians, western landscapes, and fort and mission scenes. Contemporaries and later scholars often salute Sohon's authenticity as an artist, calling him the most reliable delineator of Indians living in the northern Rockies.[17]

The best known of the first artists to paint Idaho is George Catlin. He had produced hundreds of portraits of northern Plains Indians from the 1830s onward but did not come farther west for another generation. In 1855, while traveling on horseback, Catlin ascended the Snake River to the Salmon River Valley, which he praised as "one of the most verdant and beautiful valleys in the world."[18] Encountering a Crow Indian encampment in the valley, he lingered long enough to execute *A Crow Village and The Salmon River Mountains* (1855), and then turning back west, he stopped to paint *Mesa Falls of the Snake River* (1855). Both of these oil paintings vividly express Catlin's wonderment at the landscape and Indian scenes that spilled out before him.

The contrasting paintings of the Shoshone Falls by Thomas Moran and John Henry Hill are revealing examples of the differences among late nine-teenth-century artists viewing Idaho. A disciple of the artistic teachings of John Ruskin, the English art critic, Moran closely studied individual scenes but felt free to infuse these settings with dramatic color and light to create landscapes of grandeur and sublimity. He idealized and heightened nature rather than furnishing exact pictures of what he saw. Moran's *Shoshone Falls, Snake River, Idaho* (ca. 1875) illustrates this tendency to romanticize details. By contrast, Hill's *Shoshone Falls* (1871) plays down color and light, presenting instead "settings free of superfluous grandeur." Realism of detail in Hill's watercolor contrasts sharply with the idealism of Moran's painting. In Hill's "unwavering reverence for nature," writes one critic, "he chose to create a desolate and pristine vista free of inhabitants or embellishment."[19] In these two artistic renderings of Shoshone Falls, Idaho's most-painted scene, romantic and realistic painterly influences from the American East and Europe clashed in the far-off West.

In the late nineteenth century, Mary Hallock Foote was a key figure in the development of art in Idaho, as she was in the region's literature. Be-sides contributing markedly as a portrayer of Idaho terrains and peoples, Foote provided notable illustrations illuminating women's roles in early Idaho. More than any other artist of her time (roughly the 1870s to about 1910), Foote turned out dozens of artworks dealing with family experienc-es, particularly women's activities. Some centered on women's "civilizing" roles, as in *The Irrigating Ditch* (1889) and in other woodcuts included in the Pictures of the Far West series published in *Century Magazine* in 1888 and 1889. Other paintings, such as *The Coming of Winter* (1888) and *Afternoon at a Ranch* (1889), present women as domestic figures, as wives and daugh-ters. Even more intriguing are still other illustrations dealing with families, again chiefly women, caught between competing cultural forces. *The Engi-neer's Mate* (1895) depicts an eastern woman in tension between her genteel background and the new, chilling challenges of an arid and culturally barren landscape near isolated Kuna, Idaho. Or, in *The Orchard Windbreak* (1889), Foote revealingly portrays a young woman as a mediating figure, with a deer (symbolizing a natural West) nuzzling at her breast and her "civilized" West serving as a backdrop. Unlike her contemporaries Frederic Remington

FIGURE 9.2. Mary Hallock Foote was a notable author and artist. This woodcut illustration, *The Orchard Windbreak*, depicts women as nurturers between nature and settlement. From *Century Magazine* (February 1889), 501.

and Charlie Russell, Foote depicts a domestic West that features women as central civilizing figures; they are a region apart from the wild, unruly cowboys, soldiers, and Indians of Remington and Russell. In adapting her eastern and socially conforming ways to pioneer art, Foote provides still another example of transregional influences at work in Idaho.[20]

Artistic trends in twentieth-century Idaho moved in several directions. Like some contemporary writers, a few painters followed the frontier or Local Color traditions well past 1900. Others gradually accepted regional approaches to art, and still others became postregionalists. But the steps from frontier to region to postregion, discernible in literary Idaho, were neither as clear nor as steady in artistic works. There were too many ragged edges of diversity, provincialism, and uncertainty among artists to allow for clear, simple paths of transition and definition.

Some tentative patterns emerged, however. A rather superficial regionalism reached a popular high point in the 1930s, undoubtedly through the important financial support of the Federal Art Program of the WPA, which encouraged several painters to prepare murals and other scenes of local and regional subjects for Idaho public buildings, including post offices and county structures. Among these artists were Cecil Smith, Ethel Lucile Fowler, and Alfred Dunn, all of whom dealt in a celebratory manner with farm and ranch life and small-town Idaho. Contemporaries Archie Boyd Teater, Fletcher Martin, and Minerva Kohlhepp Teichert were equally positive in their artistic treatments of mining and lumber camps, historical celebrations, and pioneer scenes.[21] Unfortunately none of these artists moved notably beyond Local Color regionalism. They seemed too satisfied with surface realism, not much interested in painting probing treatments of landscape-and-setting-shaping experiences like those of the well-known midwestern triumvirate of painters Thomas Hart Benton, Grant Wood, and John Steuart Curry.

Since 1940, Idaho art has been slow to demonstrate modernity. Seemingly, neither Idaho artists nor the state's public has embraced the new artistic trends coursing through the nation and other parts of the American West. For example, Idaho seems to lack the explicit influences of Abstract Expressionist western artists such as Jackson Pollock, Clyfford Still, and Mark Rothko; Figurative painters David Park and Richard Diebenkorn; and Photo Realists, Pop Artists, or Conceptualists. Furthermore, no artist in Idaho has gained anything like the national reputation accorded the four painters of the Northwest School in neighboring Washington, Mark Tobey, Morris Graves, Kenneth Callahan, and Guy Anderson. Nor have Idaho artists gained regional or national notoriety for their experimental works dealing with the racial/ethnic, gender, or environmental themes so popular among western postregional artists.[22]

But there is evidence of continued artistic activity in Idaho even if not well known outside the state. Of particular importance are the art instructors and artists in residence at the state's college campuses. The most prominent of the campus instructors is Mary Kirkwood, who taught at the University of Idaho for forty years (1930–70). Gradually moving from figurative and realistic traditions to more experimental modes of composition, she encouraged her students to embrace the new techniques without becoming slaves to them. Thomas Raymond Nielson, Conan Mathews, and Max Peter played similar professorial roles at Idaho State College (now Idaho

State University), Boise Junior College (now Boise State University), and the College of Idaho, respectively.

The Boise Art Museum has also been a welcoming outlet for Idaho artists and a haven for art enthusiasts of the region. First organized as an association in 1931, it became the Boise Gallery of Art in 1937 and the Boise Art Museum in 1988. The museum has assembled a strong collection of local and regional artworks and sponsored exhibits of Asian, Native American, and recent northwestern art, among others. Recently the museum has displayed important paintings by the renowned expressionist Georgia O'Keeffe and Photo Realist Chuck Close, who grew up in western Washington. Early in the twenty-first century, the Boise Art Museum remains the premier site for artistic exhibits and other happenings in the state.[23]

Despite these encouraging developments on college campuses and at the Boise Art Museum, Idaho's artistic growth lags behind the expansion of literary activities in the state and artistic developments in Oregon and Washington. Idaho art seems less open to outside influences than it did in earlier years and in no way embraces, for instance, the Asian art so influential in major state art museums to the west. True, important exhibits of experimental and recent national and international artistic trends continue to come to the state, but they have not sparked widely recognized artworks from within the state. No recent anthology of the art of the Pacific Northwest features Idaho paintings, and no authority on Northwest regional art deals extensively with artworks from Idaho. Scholars need to examine post-1940 artistic trends in Idaho more closely to discern why this cultural lag has occurred.

ETHNIC CULTURE IN IDAHO: THE BASQUES

The Basques are a very small group in Idaho. In fact, some observers have grossly overestimated Euskaldunak (Basque) numbers in the state. According to the best, although shaky, numbers available from the U.S. Census since 1980, Idaho Basques have never numbered more than 7,000 persons, with 4,332 in 1980, 5,587 in 1990, and 6,637 in 2000.[24] Increasingly less rural and agricultural, most of the state's Basques are congregated within seventy-five miles of Boise. Even though much smaller in size than many minority ethnic and racial groups in Idaho, such as those examined in chap-

ter 7 in this volume, the Euskaldunak, in the words of a leading Idaho historian, "are perhaps the most well-known . . . of Idaho's European ethnics."[25]
Perhaps because many Americans, especially journalists and recent tourists
to the West, have romanticized the Amerikanuak (American Basques) as
lonely sheepherders in a wide-open West, the group has garnered notoriety
well beyond its modest numbers.

The frontier, regional, and postregional stages useful for understanding
literary and artistic Idaho are much less helpful for studying Basque culture. Basque history moved through different stages of development. The
pioneer or earliest period of the Idaho Basques began at the end of the nineteenth century and extended into the 1920s and 1930s when the Euskaldunak had begun to establish a recognizable identity in the state. A series of
events helped to sustain and then advertise their presence, even though
they tended to isolate themselves from non-Basques. First, there were the
Basque boardinghouses, restaurants, and jai alai courts. Next came a Mutual Aid Society and support for another Basque institution, the Catholic
Church of the Good Shepherd. By 1920, Boise had become the home of the
largest Basque colony in the Pacific Northwest, with its sphere of cultural
influence circling out to Jordan Valley and Ontario, Oregon, to the west and
to Shoshone and Pocatello to the east. The first annual Sheepherders' Ball
began in the late 1920s, and the community later participated in Boise's Music Week. Some of these events and the formation of the Euskaldunak Club
in 1949, the establishment of the Basque Center in 1950, and the launch-
ing of the Oinkari Basque Dancers in 1960, all enhancing the Basques' cultural reputation, also signaled that Basque culture was expanding beyond
the confines of its inward-looking period to enter a more cosmopolitan,
outward-looking stage. Since the 1960s, the mushrooming Basque Block in
downtown Boise, the Basque Studies program at Boise State University, and
sporadic conferences and other gatherings have increased the renown of
Basque culture in Idaho and established important links with non-Basques
in the state and surrounding regions.[26]

The Basques of Idaho illustrate a cultural group whose reputation has
spread from local, to regional and national, and to international prominence, even if within a limited sphere. By the early twentieth century,
Nampa and Boise had become the transregional economic and cultural cen-

ters for Basques in Idaho, Oregon, and northeastern Nevada. In the 1930s, journalists and Sunday supplement writers were featuring stories of the Basques in lively narratives of lonely sheepherders, vivacious dancers, and sturdy but exotic westerners. U.S. and Spanish newspapers were also covering Idaho Basque reactions to the Spanish Civil War of the late 1930s. After World War II, when Basques throughout the American West began to organize larger ethnic clubs, picnics, and cultural festivals, Idaho, Nevada, and California (and sometimes Wyoming) vied to be considered the leading area of Basque settlement. In 1973, with the establishment of an umbrella group, the North American Basque Organizations (NABO), Basques in Idaho competed with those in Nevada and California for national dominance. Finally, when the Basques of Boise sponsored the first Jaialdi International Basque Cultural Festival in 1987 and followed with others in 1990, 1995, 2000, 2005, and 2010 that sometimes drew up to twenty-five thousand Basques from the United States and Europe, the Idaho Basques had truly achieved international recognition.[27]

After a slow start, largely because of their tendency to remain isolated from other groups and their desire to keep their own culture alive, Basques began to study themselves even as they continued their self-preservationist ways. Home-grown scholar Joe Eiguren established language classes in the 1960s, Jay Hormaechea taught dance classes, and Idaho secretary of state Pete Cenarrusa helped secure an educational grant to teach the Basque language and culture and Basque dancing and to foster student exchanges between Idaho and Basque communities in Spain and France. In addition, authors such as John Bieter, Mark Bieter, and Gloria Totoricagüena have written thorough books on Idaho and Boise Basques.[28]

The North American Basque Organizations umbrella group has been particularly eye-opening for Idaho Basques. Hailing primarily from the Bizkaia (Vizcaya) province in the northwestern section of the Basque country in northern Spain, Idaho Basques were not well acquainted with their Basque cousins from the other three Spanish and three French Basque provinces before the 1970s. But the group forced representatives from Idaho to work with other Basque representatives, particularly from Wyoming, California, and Nevada. More recently the huge Jaialdi gatherings every five years in Boise illustrate the dual centripetal and centrifugal tendencies at work in Amerikanuak culture—looking inward to retain language, dance, and music, and looking outward to introduce Basque culture to non-Basques, particularly through musical, dance, and recreational celebrations and competitions.

Meanwhile, after World War II, economic and social changes were transforming Basque culture. Fewer Idaho Basques remained in the livestock business, as demand for wool fell off nationally and not many northwesterners became connoisseurs of lamb. No large numbers of Basque herders were migrating from the Old World to the American West. Concurrently, third- and fourth-generation American Basques were moving to towns and cities in the Northwest, with a variety of Boise jobs and computer and technological positions in Portland and Seattle the largest draws. Even while language and culture programs were encouraging young people to speak Euskera (the Basque language), take part in dance and language classes, and participate in Basque clubs, the results were not in every way encouraging. Younger Basques were assimilating into mainstream American culture, becoming less and less like their immigrant ancestors. Ironically, as these dramatic changes and increased complexities arose among the Basques, non-Basques, especially smitten tourists, retained their image of the Amerikanuak of the past. They held on to their outmoded views of Basque herders in tents and sheep wagons, leading romantic and free but lonely lives under the big sky.[29] These contradictory perspectives on the Basques, between reality and myth, continue into the twenty-first century.

This snapshot overview of Idaho Basques suggests one approach to the study of ethnic culture, or perhaps it indicates that one way of studying culture is through ethnicity and another way to study ethnicity is through cultural expressions. This story is chiefly a transitional narrative, from a pioneer era devoted essentially to self-preservation, through ethnicity maintenance, gradually shifting toward a more cosmopolitan or outward-looking stage of ethnic culture. With Idaho Basques, that transition began in the 1930s and continued through the 1950s. Since that time, Basques in Idaho have tried to hold on to the unique ingredients of their culture even as they have reached out to other groups, Basques and non-Basque, through organizations and celebrations. They have tried to become—and remain—Basques and Americans.[30]

THINKING ABOUT IDAHO CULTURAL HISTORY

At this point, three questions merit specific attention: (1) Are there key generalizations to be made about Idaho's cultural history? (2) What major comparisons and contrasts can be drawn between Idaho and other state cultures? (3) What other questions about the state's cultural history remain to be addressed? These queries—though little more than stated here—help us to think analytically about cultural trends in Idaho since 1800.

These questions have not surfaced in most histories of Idaho, but once raised, they encourage consideration of the transitions from frontier to regional to postregional and the outside-in transregional emphases in Idaho's culture. As "frontier" authors and artists, most nineteenth-century writers and painters who dealt with Idaho in their works came from elsewhere and superimposed their ideas and predispositions on the places and peoples they visited and on their new homes. Between the late nineteenth century and the 1920s and 1930s, Idaho's writers especially and a few artists also became regionalists, commencing to show how landscapes and historical experiences in Idaho shaped human character and identity. Undoubtedly the national regionalist movement of the interwar years and the New Deal cultural programs of the 1930s influenced—if not sparked—this transition. The third transition occurred after the 1960s. Like other writers and artists of the American West, several in Idaho became postregionalists—that is, while the shaping power of place remained in their works, ethnic and racial, class and gender, and environmental themes became even more important in their writings and artworks. The novels of Marilynne Robinson and several women memoirists, in particular, illustrate this transition to postregionalism.[31]

One should consider, too, how few Idaho writers and artists have enjoyed a national reputation. Except for Mary Hallock Foote, Vardis Fisher, and more recently Marilynne Robinson, Idaho authors and painters have been little known throughout the country. Charlie Russell, Wallace Stegner, H. L. Davis, Ken Kesey, Mark Tobey, and Morris Graves, to mention a half dozen writers and artists from the surrounding states of Montana, Utah, Oregon, and Washington, have achieved national status. Why not more attention and critical recognition for others from Idaho? Have the conservative worldviews, the traditional religious affiliations, and the agriculture-based and rural inhabitants of the state discouraged emphases on literature and the arts? Have the state and its legislative bodies been much less interested in sponsoring cultural production than in supporting programs for businesses, farmers, and other entrepreneurial endeavors? Despite their severely limited budgets, have universities and colleges in the state invested noticeably in centers, programs, faculty positions, or conferences that promote these fields? Studies of state, academic, and community funding for literature and the arts might answer these probing and necessary questions. Recent emphases on creative writing at the University of Idaho, on western literature and Basque studies at Boise State University, and on Mormon culture at Brigham Young University–Idaho suggest models to be emulated.[32]

Other questions about cultural currents in Idaho remain to be examined. Are most residents much interested in supporting literary and artistic emphases in the state? Why, for example, is there no large book review section in a leading newspaper in Idaho? Have schools and colleges strongly encouraged critical examination of the state's literary and artistic achievements in their offerings? How much might we learn about the state, its cultures, and ourselves if we devoted more attention to Idaho's literature and art, as well as to cultural groups like the Basques and their cultural productions?

The paucity of thorough research and writing on the cultural currents of Idaho has its downsides and upsides. Nearly every subtopic of Idaho's cultural history—literary, artistic, religious, educational, and popular cultural subjects, among others—has received insufficient attention from scholars and others interested in the state's history. We are just beginning—or have not yet begun—to scout out Idaho's cultural terrain. But ambitious students will not find many guideposts on their journeys toward understanding Idaho's cultural history. They will have to blaze their own trails in their pioneering studies.[33]

There is a positive side to this lacuna. Almost all cultural topics beckon. The lives of authors, artists, religious and educational figures, and popular cultural leaders—as well as individual works, ideas, and events—merit more examination. We have books on Vardis Fisher and Mary Hallock Foote, but other Idaho cultural figures deserve extended articles or book-length studies, including James Stevens, Annie Pike Greenwood, Marilynne Robinson, and Mary Clearman Blew. We have no extensive literary history of the state and but one very brief artistic overview. The Basques and other ethnic groups have received a good deal of attention, and yet no one has done the extensive, thorough study of these groups and their cultural contributions throughout Idaho.

In the end, one must conclude that, with apologies to another source, the fields are whitened unto harvest, but the workers have been too few. Anyone interested in the cultural history of Idaho faces a pleasant prospect: the research possibilities are large and endless.

NOTES

1   The frontier, regional, and postregional stages of western cultural history receive extensive treatment in Richard W. Etulain, *Re-imagining the Modern American West: A Century of Fiction, History, and Art* (Tucson: University of Arizona Press, 1996). For helpful discussions of Idaho and Pacific Northwest cultural patterns, see Peter Boag, "Mountain, Plain, Desert, River: The Snake River Region as a Western Crossroads," in David M. Wrobel and Michael C. Steiner, eds., *Many Wests: Place, Culture, and Regional Identity* (Lawrence: University Press of Kansas, 1997), 177–203, and John M. Findlay, "A Fishy Proposition: Regional Identity in the Pacific Northwest," in Wrobel and Steiner, *Many Wests*, 37–70. Arizona as another example of an "outside-in" culture in the American West is examined in Richard W. Etulain, "Contours of Culture in Arizona and the Modern West," in Beth Luey and Noel J. Stowe, eds., *Arizona at Seventy-Five: The Next Twenty-Five Years* (Tucson: Arizona State University and Arizona Historical Society, 1987), 11–53. Judith Austin makes useful distinctions between the interior and coastal sections of the Pacific Northwest in her essay "Desert, Sagebrush, and the Pacific Northwest," in William G. Robbins, Robert J. Frank, and Richard E. Ross, eds., *Regionalism and the Pacific Northwest* (Corvallis: Oregon State University Press, 1983), 129–47.

2   Three essays that discuss cultural trends in the American West and point out research opportunities in the field are Howard R. Lamar, "Much to Celebrate: The Western History Association's Twenty-Fifth Birthday," *Western Historical Quarterly* 17 (October 1986): 397–416; Richard W. Etulain, "Shifting Interpretations of Western American Cultural History," in Michael P. Malone, ed., *Historians and the American West* (Lincoln: University of Nebraska Press, 1983), 414–32; Etulain, "Research Opportunities in Twentieth-Century Western Cultural History," in Gerald D. Nash and Richard W. Etulain, eds., *Researching Western History: Topics in the Twentieth Century* (Albuquerque: University of New Mexico Press, 1997), 147–66.

3   The most useful collection of Idaho literature, by far, is James H. Maguire, ed., *The Literature of Idaho: An Anthology* (Boise: Hemingway Western Studies, Boise State University, 1986). Also see the collected essays in Idaho Humanities Council, *Tough Paradise: The Literature of Idaho and the Intermountain West* (Boise: Idaho Humanities Council, 1995).

4   Gary E. Moulton, ed., *The Lewis and Clark Journals: An American Epic of Discovery* (Lincoln: University of Nebraska Press, 2003), 183, 188–89, 331.

5   The quotes from Washington Irving, Narcissa Whitman, and Nicolas Point appear in Maguire, *The Literature of Idaho*, 66, 67, 70, 72.

6   "Rough Times in Idaho," in *Selected Writings of Joaquin Miller*, ed. Alan Rosenus (n.p.: Orion Press, 1977), 105–16, and "'Idahho,'" in ibid., 117–23; M. M. Marberry, *Splendid Poseur: Joaquin Miller—American Poet* (New York: Thomas Y. Crowell Company, 1953).

7   H. L. Davis and James Stevens, *Status Rerum: A Manifesto, Upon the Present Condition of Northwestern Literature, Containing Several Near-Libelous Utterances, Upon Persons in the Public Eye* (The Dalles, OR: n.p., 1927).

8   The most useful critical study of Mary Hallock Foote is Lee Ann Johnson, *Mary Hallock Foote* (Boston: Twayne Publishers, 1980); the best biographical study is Darlis A. Miller, *Mary Hallock Foote: Author-Illustrator of the American West* (Norman: University of Oklahoma Press, 2002). See also James H. Maguire, *Mary Hallock Foote*, Boise State College Western Writers Series 2 (Boise: Boise State College, 1972); Christine Hill Smith, *Social Class in the Writings of Mary Hallock Foote* (Reno: University of Nevada Press, 2009).

9   Mary Hallock Foote to Helena [de Kay Gilder], letter 358, May 23, 1888, Mary Hallock Foote Letters, Henry E. Huntington Library, San Marino, CA; *A Victorian Gentlewoman in the Far West: The Reminiscences of Mary Hallock Foote*, ed. Rodman W. Paul (San Marino, CA: The Huntington Library, 1972), 265.

10 The most thorough biography of Vardis Fisher is Tim Woodward, *Tiger on the Road: The Life of Vardis Fisher* (Caldwell, ID: Caxton Printers, 1989); the most helpful literary critical study is Joseph M. Flora, *Vardis Fisher* (New York: Twayne Publishers, 1965). We are badly in need of a full, updated study of Fisher as a western writer.

11 John R. Milton, *Three West: Conversations with Vardis Fisher, Max Evans, Michael Straight* (Vermillion: Dakota Press, University of South Dakota, 1970); Richard W. Etulain, "Western Fiction and History: A Reconsideration," in Jerome O. Steffen, ed., *The American West: New Perspectives, New Dimensions* (Norman: University of Oklahoma Press, 1979), 152–74.

12 Nicholas O'Connell, "Marilynne Robinson," in *At Trail's End: Interviews with Twenty Pacific Northwest Writers* (Seattle: Madrona Publishers, 1987), 220–30, quote on 229.

13 Marilynne Robinson, "My Western Roots," in Barbara Howard Meldrum, ed., *Old West—New West: Centennial Essays* (Moscow: University of Idaho Press, 1993), 165–72, quote on 171.

14 The most thorough account of Idaho's artistic heritage is Sandy Harthorn and Kathleen Bettis, *One Hundred Years of Idaho Art, 1850–1950* (Boise: Boise Art Museum, 1990). See also Leonard Arrington, *History of Idaho* (Moscow: University of Idaho Press, 1994), 2:223–31, 251–52; Steve Siporin, ed., *Folk Art of Idaho* (Boise: Idaho Commission on the Arts, 1984).

15 Patricia Trenton and Peter H. Hassrick, *The Rocky Mountains: A Vision for Artists in the Nineteenth Century* (Norman: University of Oklahoma Press, 1983), 39–40, 43; Harthorn and Bettis, *One Hundred Years*, 15.

16 Trenton and Hassrick, *The Rocky Mountains*, 97–98, 100; Harthorn and Bettis, *One Hundred Years*, 16–17.

17 Robert Taft, *Artists and Illustrators of the Old West, 1850–1900* (New York: Charles

Scribner's Sons, 1953), 1–21, plates 5 and 7; Trenton and Hassrick, *The Rocky Mountains*, 83–84, 85–89.

18 Trenton and Hassrick, *The Rocky Mountains*, 280–82, 287; Harthorn and Bettis, *One Hundred Years*, 18.

19 *The American West: Out of Myth, into Reality*, Peter Hassrick, guest curator (Washington, DC: Trust for Museum Exhibitions, 2000), 131–32, 134–35. Peter Boag provides an extensive discussion of the motivations behind Moran's artistic treatment of Shoshone Falls in his essay "Thomas Moran and Western Landscapes: An Inquiry into an Artist's Environmental Values," *Pacific Historical Review* 67 (February 1998): 41–66.

20 Barbara Taylor Cragg, Dennis M. Walsh, and Mary Ellen Williams Walsh, eds., *The Idaho Stories and Far West Illustrations of Mary Hallock Foote* (Pocatello: Idaho State University Press, 1988); Richard W. Etulain, *Telling Western Stories: From Buffalo Bill to Larry McMurtry* (Albuquerque: University of New Mexico Press, 1999), 32–41, 157–58; Rodman W. Paul, "When Culture Came to Boise: Mary Hallock Foote in Idaho," *Idaho Yesterdays* 20 (Summer 1976): 2–12.

21 For a brief overview of some of these artists and their works, see Arrington, *History of Idaho*, 2:227–29. See also the pertinent discussions in Harthorn and Bettis, *One Hundred Years*, 78–79, 88–90, 96, 101, 106–7, 111.

22 Etulain, *Re-imagining the Modern American West*, 182–207; Harthorn and Bettis, *One Hundred Years*, 104–5.

23 Boise Art Museum, www.boiseartmuseum.org (accessed June 28, 2011).

24 William A. Douglass, "Calculating Ethnicity through the U.S. Census: The Basque Case" (unpublished essay, undated, ca. 2004). The most thorough annotated list of sources on the Amerikanuak (American Basques) is William A. Douglass and Richard W. Etulain, eds., *Basque Americans: A Guide to Information Sources* (Detroit: Gale Research Company, 1981). The best overall study is still William A. Douglass and Jon Bilbao, *Amerikanuak: Basques in the New World* (Reno: University of Nevada Press, 1975).

25 Arrington, *History of Idaho*, 2:283.

26 John Bieter and Mark Bieter, *An Enduring Legacy: The Story of Basques in Idaho* (Reno: University of Nevada Press, 2003); Gloria Totoricagüena, *Boise Basques: Dreamers and Doers* (Reno: University of Nevada Press, 2004).

27 Nancy Zubiri, *A Travel Guide to Basque America: Families, Feasts, and Festivals* (Reno: University of Nevada Press, 1998); Richard W. Etulain, "Basque Beginnings in the Pacific Northwest," *Idaho Yesterdays* 18 (Spring 1979): 26–32.

28 Joe Eiguren, *How to Learn to Speak Basque* (n.p.: n.p., 1968); Angeline Kearns Blain, "Juanita 'Jay' Hormaechea and the Boise Heritage School of Basque Dancing," in Richard W. Etulain and Jeronima Echeverria, eds., *Portraits of Basques in the New World* (Reno: University of Nevada Press, 1999), 192–211, 278–81; Bieter and Bieter, *An Enduring Legacy*; Totoricagüena, *Boise Basques*.

29 Bieter and Bieter, *An Enduring Legacy*; William A. Douglass, "Lonely Lives under the Big Sky," *Natural History* 82 (March 1973): 28–29; Douglass, "The Vanishing Basque Sheepherder," *American West* 17 (July–August 1980): 30–31, 59–61; Etulain and Echeverria, *Portraits of Basques in the New World*, esp. the essays about Juan Achabal (also John Archabal), 83–96; Juanita "Jay" Hormaechea, 192–211; and Pete Cenarrusa, 172–91.

30 Some of these ideas about Basque culture receive expanded coverage in Richard W. Etulain, *Basques of the Pacific Northwest* (Pocatello: Idaho State University Press, 1991).

31 Cultural currents in the American West are traced in Richard W. Etulain, *Beyond the Missouri: The Story of the American West* (Albuquerque: University of New Mexico Press, 2006), esp. chs. 10–15.

32 For a model for one kind of cultural study in Idaho, see Carol Lynn MacGregor, "The Cultural Life of Boise, Idaho, 1950–2000," in Richard W. Etulain and Ferenc M. Szasz, eds., *The American West in 2000: Essays in Honor of Gerald D. Nash* (Albuquerque: University of New Mexico Press, 2003), 85–104.

33 For extensive lists of western topics available to scholars studying Idaho cultural currents, see the essays listed in note 2.

Writer Vardis Fisher tells the story of publishing the
Idaho Guide with the Works Progress Administration.

Then about that time, the Works Progress Administration started the Federal Writers Project and I—out of the blue I had an offer to be the Idaho director at that, which I was for four years, and that took care of 1935 to 1939. . . .

My four years there were very busy years for me. As a matter of fact, I was still quite an innocent person, you know. When I took that job, I thought they meant that, I thought this was a serious—to be a serious spending of the taxpayers['] money. So, I took my job seriously. I suppose you remember who H. G. Merriam was. He was, you know, chairman of the department, University of Montana, for a long time, and he was made Montana director. He sent me a long telegram, a very long telegram, between 150 and 200 words, said, "Don't take this seriously; you're not going to accomplish anything here, you know. But just draw your salary and play the game, because nothing will be accomplished in this." Well, that outraged me. I was determined, as a matter of fact, I was determined to get the Idaho guide out first. And, of course, I did. Became a national—something of a national sensation. They tried to—the Washington office tried to kill— stop the Idaho guide. They didn't want it published because it'd be such an embarrassment to all the big states that had so much more money in their projects and such huge staffs. . . . We had nobody in Idaho; unemployed writers didn't exist in Idaho. . . . So we had no staffs. So they sent a man out from Washington. They called me long distance several times and said, "You must not go ahead." I had this huge advantage that J. H. Gibson from Caxton Printers in Caldwell, Idaho[,] said, we'll publish this book, and I was determined it was going to be published. And they called me several times and said, "We'll send a man out to stop you." And they did send the assistant director, who was a—in those years rather a distinguished novelist, he came out to stop us from publishing that book. We got him drunk by—we took him to Gibson's home and got him drunk, and I put him on the train and sent him back to Washington, and we went ahead and published the guide.

* * *

A Basque man, Thomas Zabala, reflects on acculturation in Idaho.

INTERVIEWER: Your parents were really the transition generation between the old country, the old ways, and this newfound country. When you were raised, were you raised in a Basque tradition or did your parents raise you very much in American ways?

ZABALA: In a sense I had a foot in both cultures, because my grandparents were here and we had that influence as far as the food, the language, and that. My parents, for whatever reasons, chose not to teach us the language, and my folks both speak Basque and Spanish fluently, and they often use that to our disadvantage—to their advantage, to our disadvantage, at times. But for whatever reasons, they chose to, and in our case, to Americanize us, I guess. And at this point in my life I am regretting that I didn't take the time, or that they didn't take the time to tell us more about the culture, our heritage, and that. It's embarrassing at times for me now, because there are occasions when I would relish that, and my fear, necessarily, is that my son, who will carry on my name and that, will really not have the benefit of that knowledge of experience unless he were to take it upon himself to take some of the opportunities that are available now and are becoming more and more available through the local community here and the university. . . .

INTERVIEWER: Do you think Idaho is an easy place to retain one's cultural cast, or—

ZABALA: I think it is. At least particularly the past that the Basques have here. I think there is a very strong past, and one that we're seeing today of people that are stepping forth and are very proud of that heritage and are doing a lot to reinforce it and to get their children knowledgeable and sympathetic to the importance of knowing about where they came from and what accomplishments they have been able to make. Whether you're a professional or a blue-collar worker, whatever, it's all very important, and we've come a long way. We've conquered the language problems. We're getting very educated people in every walk of life in this community, and the Basques have been an essential part of the growth of not only our immediate area here within the state of Idaho but in the entire Pacific Northwest. Politicians, professional people, blue-collar workers, they've stepped right in, just as other cultures have, and made it all work.

NOTE

Vardis Fisher was interviewed by John Milton, South Dakota Public Television, March 20, 1967, transcript (OH1030) from Idaho Oral History Center/Idaho State Historical Society, 11–13. Used with permission of South Dakota Public Television.

Thomas Zabala was interviewed by Peter Morrill, November 15, 1989, Idaho Educational Public Broadcasting System/Idaho Public Television, transcript (OH1043) Idaho Oral History Center/Idaho State Historical Society, 3–4. Used with permission of Idaho Public Television.

10
Telling Stories
Idaho's Historians

JUDITH AUSTIN

I DAHO'S WRITTEN HISTORY IS BUILT ON THE WORK OF GENERA-
tions of people who undertook to record their and others' experiences.
Professional, academically trained historians; local and regional historians;
even early travelers and settlers, journalists past and present, pioneer politicians: these and others have been historians of Idaho and have helped
make possible the work of their successors in recording and analyzing the
state's history. Their own story—that is, how they have approached the
state's history and how much they have linked it to the wider history of
region and nation—has expanded and matured over time; so have the detail
and richness of their work.

What follows is by no means an exhaustive identification of Idaho historians local, public, or academic. It is a look at who has produced Idaho
history in many diverse forms and, where possible, from what perspectives.
The chapter is framed around multiple types of historians, including leading citizens who wrote themselves into their histories; local historians toil-
ing away in small communities, nearly anonymous to the larger profession
but valued throughout Idaho's historical circles, who preserved history and
memories for their particular regions; public historians dedicated to bringing Idaho's past alive for institutions and the public at large; and traditional
academic historians who have taken Idaho as their subject in order to illu-
minate broader concerns.[1] Surveying these myriad voices and approaches,
we can both appreciate Idaho's history further and better understand the
work required to produce our historical knowledge.

PRECURSORS TO HISTORY

Explorers, traders, and journalists who came to or through what is now Idaho wrote about contemporaneous events and circumstances that they unquestionably helped shape. Those who stayed cared and wrote about what brought groups and communities to the area.

In many ways, as Richard Etulain also notes in chapter 9 in this volume, the earliest English-language historians of what is now Idaho were members of the Lewis and Clark Expedition, whose journal entries include information about the Native bands they encountered.[2] They were followed by fur trappers, especially those brigade leaders who worked for the Hudson's Bay Company and were required to keep journals.[3]

Once Euro-American settlement began, a handful of journalists (some also promoters of Idaho) not only provided snapshots of Idaho through their writing but also attempted to explain something of why the area was as it was. The earliest was C. Aubrey Angelo, a correspondent for the *Liverpool Courier* who settled in California but wrote two books on Idaho in the mid-1860s.[4] A second was William Armistead Goulder, a correspondent for Boise's *Idaho Statesman*. He sent dispatches to the paper from northern Idaho, where he lived in the late 1860s, and toured the whole territory for the newspaper in 1876. Some of his dispatches have been reprinted with annotation, as have his reminiscences. A generation later, Charles S. Walgamott wrote columns for the *Idaho Citizen* in Twin Falls for many years. Robert Strahorn, originally a journalist who became a publicist for the Union Pacific, wrote about the territory's "resources and attractions," with due attention paid to how they came to be, to draw settlers to the eighteen-year-old territory.[5]

LEADING CITIZENS AND HISTORY

The most immediate successors to those men wrote about Idaho's history more intentionally, and they had even more impact on the form that history took. They were early active citizens of the territory, often engaged in its political life, as Laura Woodworth-Ney and Tara A. Rowe discuss in chapter 6 in this book.

For instance, Thomas Donaldson, author of *Idaho of Yesterday*, moved to Boise in 1869 to become the registrar at the General Land Office; he thereafter held a number of appointive positions in and for the territory. Donaldson knew the leading citizens of Boise and the participants in territorial government during his years in Idaho. His preface begins: "This book is not a history; it contains too much truth." Although Donaldson's point that participants in events cannot write a detached history of them may be well taken, in his case, "truth" may not be applicable to the whole contents of the book.[6]

John Hailey's *History of Idaho* is much drier than Donaldson's work and at times nearly encyclopedic in its data. Hailey served two terms as Idaho's delegate to Congress (1873–74, 1885–86), was warden of the state penitentiary from 1899 to 1906, and in 1907 became the first secretary (that is, director) of the Idaho State Historical Society, the position he still held when his history was published.[7]

Perhaps the most prominent of this group is William J. McConnell. The title page of his *Early History of Idaho* identifies him as "Ex.-U. S. Senator and -Governor Who was present and cognizant of the events narrated." Primarily a territorial history, the book predates McConnell's years in public office. He writes somewhat unkindly, if gently, of the positive tone of Hailey's book and quotes liberally from William Goulder in his introductory paragraph.[8]

Fred T. Dubois's "The Making of a State" is an autobiography of another significant Idaho politician. Dubois served two terms as a delegate to Congress from Idaho Territory and two discontinuous terms as a U.S. senator after statehood, the larger context of which Katherine G. Aiken examines in chapter 4. He is best known as the main force behind the anti-Mormon movement in Idaho, and he applied that force in part as the United States marshal in Idaho between 1882 and 1886.[9]

The primary author of one of the best-known early histories of Idaho is unknown, but his or her reliance on participants is acknowledged. In 1884, a San Francisco publisher drew on the expertise of some Idaho community leaders—notably Milton Kelly, a Boise pioneer and judge who by this time was publishing Boise's leading newspaper—to produce a large-folio history of Idaho Territory. The book, which includes statistical data and is promotional in tone, contains more than 150 maps, lithographs, and wood engravings depicting homes, farms and ranches, businesses, and public buildings.

It offers a fascinating view of the territory and of its residents' understanding of their history at a particular moment.[10]

The first straightforward narrative history of Idaho is part of Hubert Howe Bancroft's multivolume *Works*, all on the western United States, and of the subseries *History of the Pacific States of North America*. While *History of Washington, Idaho, and Montana, 1845–1889* carries Bancroft's name, it was in fact written by Frances Fuller Victor. Bancroft's books were, when possible, based on interviews with people who had participated in the events discussed; Victor's unsigned introductory note refers to "hundreds of dictations"—not exactly oral history as we know it, but a rich resource nonetheless. The chapters on Idaho carry the prospective state's history right down to discussion of issues that might block statehood—notably Mormon franchise—despite adoption of a state constitution by Idaho voters.[11]

"Mug books"—books with volumes that include profiles of prominent individuals—are a ubiquitous and special class of history, and the first few were among Idaho's earliest narrative histories. The very first, published in 1899, is *An Illustrated History of the State of Idaho, Containing a History of the State of Idaho from the Earliest Period of its Discovery to the Present Time, together with Glimpses of its Auspicious Future; Illustrations, including Full-Page Portraits of some of its Eminent Men, and Biographical Mention of Many Pioneers and Prominent Citizens of To-day*. The publishers described the book as "[p]repared by a number of writers, and deriving its information from various sources." The title and description capture well the nature of such works.[12]

The successors to the *Illustrated History* are multivolume works with a common structure of history and biographies in separate volumes. The first was Hiram T. French's *History of Idaho*, composed of one volume of history and two of biographical sketches of significant figures in the state that were, judging by tone and content, written by either the individuals themselves or close friends and family. They are nonetheless valuable, detailed accounts of those people deemed important in Idaho in 1914. French's work was followed by James H. Hawley's *History of Idaho: Gem of the Mountains*. Again, the first volume is history—with an emphasis on political history, not surprising given that Hawley had been both mayor of Boise and an Idaho governor as well as a leading attorney. The succeeding three volumes contain biographical sketches, beginning with Hawley's own. In 1933, Byron Defenbach, a former mayor of Sandpoint, state senator, and state treasurer, published *Idaho: The Place and Its People*. The first volume is essentially a history of Idaho Territory; only about a tenth of the book deals with the state's history, and the other volumes are laudatory biographical sketches. The final (and much later) example of this sort of history set is *History of Idaho*, by Merrill D. Beal and Merle W. Wells. Unlike their predecessor mug-book authors, both were trained historians who published widely. Theirs is a two-volume narrative history; the mug book is the third volume.[13] These mug books and histories by leading politicians lack some detachment; however, they capture a perspective important in the early years of Idaho's political and economic development. As such, they provide almost unparalleled insights into Idaho's elite.

IN THE FIELD: LOCAL HISTORIANS

A second category of participant-historians is that of local or regional historian. Not all authors of local histories have been directly involved in the events and developments they have written about, of course, but in many cases they have relied on information from those who were. They tend to understand well the impact of their history on those communities—and understand the role of social strata. Often, without their efforts, the history of those places and people who make up the state would have been lost. Many, perhaps most, of these community histories reach an audience no larger than the community itself and descendants of its founders, especially those written before the 1970s. Some communities are fortunate to have had local historians who worked for many years not only to gather and write (though rarely to interpret or place in broader context) their histories but also to create historical societies and museums, making that history even more accessible.[14] Virginia Ricketts was such a historian for the community of Jerome and, more broadly, Jerome County and the Twin Falls North Side irrigation tract. For years, she wrote newspaper columns about the area, many of which have been compiled into books. Julie Hyslop has played much the same role as Ricketts in Silver City and Owyhee County. While many others have written about that area, Hyslop's encouragement has made much of that writing possible.[15]

Many local and regional accounts were triggered by the national bicentennial observance in 1976 and Idaho's centennial celebration in 1990. For example, Helen Lowell and Lucile Peterson, residents of Parma, wrote a history of the lower Boise Valley as a bicentennial project. While some of its early material is based as much on legend as on fact, Lowell and Peterson relied on reminiscences of fellow longtime residents for much of the more recent history. Another bicentennial history of an area—the Stanley Basin—was written primarily by Esther Yarber. In this, as in Yarber's earlier history of the area to the north and east of Stanley Basin, part of the book is about community and part about individuals and families, a sort of mini–mug book, a common pattern in such local histories.[16]

Several other regional histories are worth special note for providing perspectives that are otherwise unavailable. Among them is *Between These Mountains: History of Birch Creek Valley, Idaho*, in which Pearl M. Oberg describes the life and near death of a part of east-central Idaho that was settled because of mining and ranching. Cecil Dryden describes life along the Clearwater River of north-central Idaho from the early days of the Nez Perce to the early part of the twentieth century in *The Clearwater of Idaho*. Dryden taught history for a number of years, and her professional approach shows through, but this is still primarily a memoir of an area rather than straight narrative history.[17]

Sister M. Alfreda Elsensohn is an atypical local historian. A member of the Benedictine community at St. Gertrude's Convent (now St. Gertrude's Monastery) in Cottonwood, she wrote a two-volume history of north-central Idaho, *Pioneer Days in Idaho County*. While mostly anecdotal, it is solidly researched. Sr. Alfreda also wrote *Idaho Chinese Lore*, which deals primarily with the Chinese experience in northern Idaho but includes chapters on the Boise–Boise Basin area, Pocatello and the Wood River Valley, and Silver City and Nampa; and *Polly Bemis*, about one of the best-known Chinese immigrants in Idaho's history.[18]

Local historians have at times been a specific type of "public" historian—unpaid but officially designated county historians who were assigned responsibilities by the state through the Idaho State Historical Society. In 1931, the Idaho legislature modified the statute that laid out the responsibilities of the Idaho Historical Society (as it was then known) to include appointing county historians "to cooperate with the Historical Society of the State of Idaho in the performance of its duties."[19] These county historians were asked to provide stories—"historical sketches"—some of which were published in the society's biennial reports. Other assignments for the county historians of the 1940s included tracking down information on ghost towns in their counties and compiling "First Facts" scrapbooks.[20]

When H. J. Swinney became the first professional director of the historical society in 1957, he assessed the role of county historians. In his 1958–59 biennial report, he commented that only twenty-two of the forty-four counties had designated historians when he arrived, and he had made only two further appointments—one of whom, Annie Laurie Bird, had already been "asked to do so a number of times in the past, but no definitive duties were ever assigned." Swinney told her that county historians' responsibilities would be to "keep track of matters of historical interest within their counties—celebrations, inquiries, important historic sites, and so on."[21] By the time Swinney left the society in 1965, the position of county historian had apparently disappeared. Two county historians remain well known beyond their own areas. Robert G. Bailey, a Lewiston newspaperman, produced something of a classic. His *River of No Return: A Century of Central Idaho and Eastern Washington History and Development, together with the Wars, Customs, Myths, and Legends of the Nez Perce Indians* is a set of vignettes of the area's history, including his own experiences. Bailey's *Hell's Canyon: Seeing Idaho through a Scrapbook* draws on other publications (e.g., an Idaho State Automobile Association pamphlet on Hells Canyon and how to get there) and as much on his own experiences as on anything else.[22] Bailey interviewed a great number of people for this second book. It is rather folksy in tone but fun to read.

The other widely known and prolific county historian, in this case, of Canyon County, is Annie Laurie Bird. Miss Bird (no one dared call her anything else) published four books: histories of the Boise Valley, Nampa, and Fort Boise and a brief biography of Thomas McKay, the founder of the fort. She also produced a series of articles on Idaho's territorial governor William Henson Wallace for *Idaho Yesterdays* and *Pacific Northwest Quarterly* that, put together, would have made a fifth book.[23]

Most of these county historians were amateurs. Yet the books and articles they wrote, the museums they operated, and the materials they collected have enriched our understanding of Idaho. Using their community connections, they preserved much of the past that otherwise would too easily have disappeared. In this way, local historians did much to build the state's history and make it easier for other historians to contribute their own perspectives.

IN THE FIELD: PUBLIC HISTORIANS

Idaho ultimately developed its own version of the county historian: the state historian, a state employee trained academically in history. The first person to hold that office had in fact been doing the work and providing the leadership it entailed for many years before the position was created in the late twentieth century. When Merle Wells began his work in Idaho, the idea of a "public historian" was decades in the future. Nonetheless, his professional career modeled what the term means, using academic training for local and public historical purposes.

Wells's academic teaching career was relatively brief. On leave from doctoral work at the University of California, Berkeley, he taught at his alma mater, the College of Idaho, during World War II; taught in Pennsylvania for a few years after he completed his doctorate; and for many years taught a course in Idaho history at Boise State University. Strictly speaking, his work can be defined as local history only because Idaho as a whole was his locale. He was, however, the quintessential public historian. Long before the job title was created, Wells was *the* state historian. His emphasis was on political history. Social history did not much interest him, and even his work on anti-Mormonism in Idaho emphasized the politics far more than the social or religious prejudice involved in the matter.

Wells's most important contribution was his role in preserving the state's historical record, both written and built. Beginning in the early 1950s (after he rescued historic state records from a closet in the state capitol) and continuing nearly until his death in 2000, he worked with extraordinary energy to provide resources for historians and, eventually, preservationists. He not only was Idaho's first state historic preservation officer, beginning in the mid-1970s, but also significantly shaped the nation's historic preservation program by insisting to colleagues in other states and in the

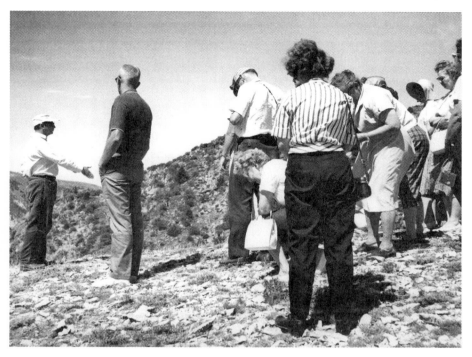

FIGURE 10.1. The Idaho State Historical Society has long been dedicated to preserving the state's history. State historian Merle Wells led this field trip to New York Summit near Silver City, Idaho, on July 8, 1961, showing the importance of being in the field and engaging the public. Photo courtesy of Idaho State Historical Society, 61-100.85a.

federal government on the use of rational, down-to-earth procedures and approaches. As the first editor of the Idaho State Historical Society's journal, *Idaho Yesterdays*, he provided a venue and encouraged many others to write Idaho's history.[24]

Despite his visibility, the best-known and most widely distributed of Wells's work is anonymous. Beginning in 1957, he worked with the state highway department to develop a series of highway markers around the state; anyone familiar with his prose style can tell which of the hundreds of signs he wrote. Even before that, in the 1940s, he wrote articles for the biennial reports of Idaho's secretary of state and the historical society. As soon as Wells began working formally with the historical society as a "consulting historian," he began the Reference Series; from a paragraph to several pages long, each reference contains information about a particular person, place, or event in Idaho. As with the highway markers, readers familiar with his writing can identify those that Wells wrote himself, even though they are unsigned. In addition, numerous unsigned articles, from a paragraph to several pages, appear in *Idaho Yesterdays*.

In addition to these very public roles, Wells was a scholar and a prolific author. His bibliography, in manuscript form and probably incomplete, is ten pages long. A bibliographic essay, by no means exhaustive, was published in a memorial issue of *Idaho Yesterdays*.[25] His only monograph, *Anti-Mormonism in Idaho, 1872–92*, is based on his doctoral dissertation and reflects both his interest in the territorial period and his focus on particular actors in historical events. One of his best-known works, *Gold Camps and Silver Cities*, also stems from his interest in the territorial era and some of the more entrepreneurial efforts of the time.[26]

Probably the most unusual publication to carry his name considers what a huge, early, federally financed irrigation project had done for and to the Boise Valley—and whether that project should be expanded. Wells and others laid out the history of and reasons for the valley's growth in the early twentieth century and surrounded that narrative with vast amounts of statistical data on population, native flora and fauna, and crops.[27] He took a great deal of pleasure in his involvement in such an atypical task, and it fits well with the work of such a public-minded historian.

Idaho's written history has benefitted from the work of other public historians as well. One, Arthur Hart, was a longtime colleague of Wells's, emeritus director of the Idaho State Historical Society, and probably the most visible nonacademic historian in the state. Trained in art history, Hart became director of the society's museum in 1969 and of the society as a whole in the mid-1970s. Early in his Idaho career, he surveyed the state's architectural history *for Idaho Yesterdays*; this was a particular interest of his and one that led to his election as a fellow of the American Institute of Architects. Other articles published there include one on preserving Idaho's heritage, written for the national bicentennial, and a history of the society. His newspaper columns, which he still writes for the *Idaho Statesman*, deal primarily with Boise's history and are based largely on newspaper research. Hart's books fall into two categories: those on a general topic and those written for a particular institution or organization. The former address such varied topics as barns, aviation, photography, baseball, steam trains, Boise's Chinatown, and the domestic life of the city's early residents. Topics for the latter include the cities of Eagle and Boise, Boise's architectural history, the Boise Police Department and Fire Department, the Boise Children's Home, Boise's Arid Club, the Western Idaho Fair, the Ada County Courthouse, and the nineteenth-century Boise Basin.[28] Obviously, Hart's interests are eclectic. The books, like his columns, rely heavily on newspaper research, but he has also conducted wide-ranging interviews with participants in events when possible, which have been preserved for future researchers.

A third historian with close ties to the Idaho State Historical Society is Keith Petersen, who has a particular interest in northern Idaho and in matters of public policy. Petersen has written one of the best community histories of Idaho, *Company Town: Potlatch, Idaho, and the Potlatch Lumber Company*. Meanwhile, his *River of Life, Channel of Death: Fish and Dams on the Lower Snake* deserves broader circulation at a time when the issue of Snake River dams and fish survival is so public. It built in part on research that Petersen and his wife, Mary Reed, did for the U.S. Army Corps of Engineers on the history of development on the Lower Snake River. An earlier interest in state parks resulted in *Harriman State Park and the Railroad Ranch: A History*, prepared as a working document for managers of the park, donation of which was the final impetus for creating a full-fledged state Department of Parks and Recreation.[29]

Petersen is also the author of *This Crested Hill: An Illustrated History of the University of Idaho*, published in anticipation of the university's centennial in 1989, and *Educating in the American West: One Hundred Years at Lewis-Clark State College, 1893–1993*. He is the former director of the Latah County Historical Society, an editor at the Washington State University Press, an independent historian, the former coordinator of Lewis and Clark activities, interim director of the Idaho State Historical Society, and, at this writing, the state historian and deputy director of the Idaho State Historical Society. In the early 1980s, Petersen was on the staff of the society's project "Working Together: A Regional Approach to Community Traditions and History in Idaho." Out of that came not only meetings, consultations, and activities around the state but *Historical Celebrations: A Handbook for Orga-*

nizers of Diamond Jubilees, Centennials, and Other Community Anniversaries,
in which Petersen shared in very practical ways his experiences in "working
together."[30]

A fourth public historian, much of whose work has been published, is
Susan Stacy, a former city land-use planner. While she has noted that "participants in public life have an excellent reason to write and study history"
in order to broaden their perspective on their work and responsibilities, she
instead brought her experiences in government and planning to her historical research and writing. Her study of the Boise River as it flows through
the state capital is an excellent example. So is the work she has done on
the nuclear facility in eastern Idaho. *Legacy of Light: A History of the Idaho
Power Company* is more straightforward institutional history; *Tom and Julia
Davis: "Some Good Place," Boise, Idaho* is a study of a couple and their role in
shaping a community.[31]

These are by no means the only public historians whose work is invaluable for understanding Idaho's history. Their work is, however, among the
most available to general readers, as well as scholars. Working for public
institutions, they and other public historians have ensured that Idaho has
built and preserved an enviable historical record.

BROADER CONTEXTS: ACADEMIC HISTORIANS

Historians who are based in academia both in and beyond Idaho have studied and written about many aspects of the state's history; a few are especially notable. Among the earliest is C. J. Brosnan, the first to write a history
of Idaho intended as a textbook. When his *History of the State of Idaho* was
first published, he was superintendent of schools in Nampa; when the second edition appeared seventeen years later, he was a professor of history at
the University of Idaho.[32]

Southeastern Idaho was the academic and intellectual base for
Merrill D. "Sam" Beal. His work was by no means confined to his coauthor-
ship of *History of Idaho*, the combination history and mug book popularly
known as "Beal and Wells." Probably the best known of his other works is
"I Will Fight No More Forever": Chief Joseph and the Nez Perce War, a thor-
oughly researched and thoughtfully written account of the war and its aftermath—and a cooperative effort between the National Park Service, which

was in the process of establishing the Nez Perce National Historical Park, and Idaho State College (now Idaho State University), where Beal taught. It was not Beal's only work for the park service; *The Story of Man in Yellowstone* drew on his doctoral dissertation, completed at Washington State University in 1944.[33]

Beal had other interests as well. *Intermountain Railroads: Standard and Narrow Gauge* (republished as *The Utah and Northern Railroad: Narrow Gauge*, with the chapter on northern Idaho railroads deleted) is in large part the story of the longest narrow-gauge railroad in the country, begun by Mormon pioneers in northern Utah and southeastern Idaho and serving the mining camps of Montana before it was taken over by the local component of the Union Pacific. The story is as much social history as railroad or business history. Beal had earlier considered the history of the whole region in *A History of Southeastern Idaho*. At the time, he was teaching at Ricks College, and while there he also published *The Snake River Fork Country: A Brief History of Peaceful Conquest of the Upper Snake River Basin* (under the pseudonym Samuel D. Beal). He moved to Idaho State College in 1947 when it became a four-year institution and taught there until his retirement in 1965. Four years after he joined the faculty and fifty years after the Academy of Idaho, the institution's forerunner, was founded, Beal began work on *History of Idaho State College*. His memoir is *Sixty Years of Educational Endeavors in Idaho, 1924–1984*.[34]

Carlos Schwantes, at this writing a professor of transportation studies and history at the University of Missouri, Saint Louis, taught for many years at the University of Idaho. His doctoral work was in labor history, and much of his early writing reflects that background. But several of Schwantes's books deal more generally with Idaho and the Pacific Northwest. *In Mountain Shadows: A History of Idaho* is minimally annotated and wonderfully illustrated, with sidebars and personal notes that make the volume—based on sound scholarship—more accessible to the general reader. Schwantes has a sharp eye for images that capture a story, and that gift is demonstrated in *So Incredibly Idaho: Seven Landscapes That Define the Gem State*. Most of the photographs in this book were taken by Schwantes, and they and his narrative go a long way toward explaining Idahoans' sense of themselves and others' sense of the state and its people. In *The Pacific*

Northwest: An Interpretive History, Schwantes approaches the region as a hinterland, though not as an isolated area, and he works to avoid the "heroic nature–heroic men" approach that he believes has characterized most of the earlier writing about the region.[35]

A number of historians have published articles in historical journals that together make up a significant part of Idaho's historical literature. The most prolific is Hugh Lovin, retired from the history department at Boise State University. His two streams of research, on irrigation projects and on the more liberal influences in Idaho's politics, have led to both invaluable studies and good reading. Subjects range from anti-German and Red Scare activities during World War I to the Non-Partisan League and Socialists to the travails of early settlers on irrigation tracts and the management of such tracts from afar. Lovin's work on Carey Act irrigation projects in particular is very valuable given that Idaho was by far the most successful state in using this public-private mode of developing irrigation projects.[36]

Brigham D. Madsen had a remarkably varied career as a scholar and academic administrator. He began teaching in Pingree, Idaho, before moving on (with a doctorate in history from the University of California, Berkeley) to teach at all three of Utah's universities (and serve as both vice president and acting director of libraries at the University of Utah). He was also an assistant director of training for the Peace Corps and director of training for Volunteers in Service to America and ran a construction company. Much of his published work on Idaho concerns Native American individuals and groups in eastern Idaho, a field that is still far too underdeveloped.[37]

James Gentry has taught for many years at the College of Southern Idaho in Twin Falls. He began work on *In the Middle and on the Edge: The Twin Falls Region of Idaho* in anticipation of the city's centennial after completing his doctorate in history at the University of Utah. His dissertation was on "English writers who interpreted individual shires in the late seventeenth century," arguably a good beginning point for writing in the late twentieth and early twenty-first century on a particular region and community in Idaho. As its title implies, Gentry's book sets the south-central Idaho city in context both geographically and historically.[38]

Many academic historians have come to Idaho history as part of larger topics and contexts, such as natural resources. For instance, Clark Spence is a distinguished historian of the American mining frontier. Raised in Glenns Ferry, Idaho, he has written two books that set Idaho's mining history in broader context: *British Investments and the American Mining Frontier, 1860–1901* and *Mining Engineers & the American West: The Lace-Boot Brigade, 1849–1933*, which goes beyond the "digging" to tell the often colorful story of a different sort of miner. More specifically on Idaho is *For Wood River or Bust: Idaho's Silver Boom of the 1880s*, a study of events in Idaho's mining history that had been sorely neglected. In retirement, Spence continues researching and writing on Idaho history.[39]

Environmental history is another topic on which historians have focused, as Kevin R. Marsh demonstrates in chapter 3 of this book. Several works have dealt with water. Among them is Karl Boyd Brooks's *Public Power, Private Dams: The Hells Canyon High Dam Controversy*. Brooks is a lawyer and former Idaho state legislator who brings both his legal and his governmental experience to the story of the debates surrounding the damming of the Snake River in the 1950s. His second book is a history of environmental law that includes a chapter on noted Idaho lawyer Bruce Bowler. It is another of the many recent studies that put Idaho's experience in a wider context. A second monograph about water, both environmental and social history, is Mark Fiege's *Irrigated Eden: The Making of an Agricultural Landscape in the American West*. Drawing substantially from the papers of the major irrigation projects across the Snake River Plain, Fiege considers the political, environmental, and especially social processes and impact of putting water on the land of that arid plain.[40]

Besides water, environmental historians have focused on forest and park lands. Stephen J. Pyne, the foremost historian of fire in the United States, wrote an account of one of Idaho's most memorable "natural disasters," setting the Great Fires of 1910 in the broader contexts of forest management and science. In *Year of the Fires: The Story of the Great Fires of 1910*, Pyne discusses the impact of the fires on later government policies and procedures nationally and even globally.[41] J. M. Neil has returned to his native state (where he managed Idaho's observance of the national bicentennial in 1976) to research and write on aspects of Idaho's conservation history.[42] Thomas R. Cox, a longtime faculty member at San Diego State University, now a resident of McCammon, has written on Idaho's state parks in both broad and narrow contexts. *The Park Builders: A History of State Parks in the Pacific Northwest* devotes a chapter to Governor Robert E. Smylie's efforts to establish an Idaho parks department. Cox's research on Idaho for *The Park Builders* led him to further research and writing on the Coeur d'Alene Indians, whose history is closely related to that of northern Idaho's Heyburn State Park.[43]

While Rodney Frey and Robert McCarl show in chapter 2 in this book that the history of Idaho's indigenous peoples is becoming better known, Cox's writing on the Coeur d'Alenes and Brigham Madsen's on the Shoshone is dwarfed, at least in volume, by research and writing on the Nez Perce. The Nez Perce have drawn more scrutiny for two primary reasons: the missionary experience on the reservation and the dramatic aspects of the so-called Nez Perce War of 1877. The core work on the Nez Perce remains Alvin Josephy's engagingly written and enormously informative *The Nez Perce Indians and the Opening of the Northwest*. It is in many ways the foundation for all later work by non–Nez Perce on the history of the Nimíipuu.[44] The Nez Perce have published their own history, *Noon Nee-Me-Poo (We, the Nez Perces): Culture and History of the Nez Perces*. It was preceded by *Nu Mee Poom Tit Wah Tit (Nez Perce Legends)*. Both were prepared under the direction of Allen P. Slickpoo, Jr.[45]

The Nez Perce War has been the subject of many books. The most recent study, *The Last Indian War: The Nez Perce Story* by Elliott West, interweaves the political and cultural history of both sides in compelling language. The first military episode was studied by John D. McDermott in *Forlorn Hope: The Battle of White Bird Canyon and the Beginning of the Nez Perce War*, which is based on research for the Nez Perce National Historic Park.[46]

The best-known accounts of missionary work among the Nez Perce are written or edited by Clifford M. Drury. A Presbyterian minister who taught for many years at San Francisco Theological Seminary, Drury brought to light much primary-source material, especially from the American Board of Commissioners for Foreign Missions, which sent Protestant missionaries to the inland Northwest in the first place. Drury also published a biography of the Nez Perce leader Lawyer and an article drawn from that book.[47] Major work on later missionaries among the Nez Perce was done by Allen and Eleanor Morrill. Their *Out of the Blanket: The Story of Sue and Kate McBeth*,

Missionaries to the Nez Perce takes the missionary story from the death of Henry Harmon Spalding, first missionary to the Nez Perce, to 1915, when Kate McBeth died. Its straightforward narrative draws heavily from the McBeth sisters' correspondence and journals, and it offers an excellent portrait of both the sisters and the Nez Perce as viewed through the McBeths' eyes. Kate McBeth herself wrote *The Nez Perces since Lewis and Clark*, history presented very much from the perspective of a missionary.[48]

While histories of particular ethnic groups other than Native Americans are comparatively scarce, Laurie Mercier, Errol D. Jones, and Richard W. Etulain show in chapters 7–9 in this volume that the situation is improving. In addition, J. Patrick Bieter did a remarkable job of encouraging the study of the Basque experience in Idaho. Bieter was a high-school history teacher and then a faculty member at Boise State University. He married into the Basque community in Boise and conducted many interviews with its members. Bieter was instrumental in establishing Boise State's Basque studies program in the Basque country. He published only journal articles, but, as is the case for so many Idaho historians, his influence has extended far beyond his readers. Bieter's son John P. Bieter, also a historian by training and profession, is continuing his father's work both in the Basque studies program at Boise State and in research on the Basques. John and his brother, Mark, have written a book-length history of the Basques in Idaho.[49]

Asian Americans have also received scholarly attention. Two Idaho historians have written from very different perspectives about the Japanese experience in the state. Robert C. Sims, now retired from Boise State University, continues his research on the Minidoka relocation camp at Hunt, Idaho. Eric Walz, a member of the history faculty at Brigham Young University–Idaho, drew from the experience of the Japanese family who owned the farm next to his family's farm in eastern Idaho and wrote about the lives of the Japanese who settled in the interior West before World War II.[50] Liping Zhu offers both new insight and a very different perspective on the Chinese experience in the West. Focusing on Idaho City between 1863 and 1910, Zhu has determined that the Chinese population there did indeed have a real chance at a good life: equity in the courts, the opportunity to gain wealth, and stability in the community that was far greater than Euro-American stability, especially in the early years of mining in Boise Basin.

Zhu, a native of Shanghai, now teaches at Eastern Washington University.[51]

Although their approach to their work is different from that of public or local historians, academic historians have used their training to place Idaho within broader historical trends. In doing so, they demonstrate links and contexts that are often missing or downplayed in other studies. The historians discussed above demonstrate clearly the diverse history of Idaho and its connections to other historical traditions.

AN EXEMPLAR: LEONARD ARRINGTON

No study of Idaho's historians would be complete without considering Leonard Arrington, who represents each of the categories of historian discussed here. Arrington was an academic historian: he had a Ph.D. in economics, taught at Utah State and Brigham Young Universities, was a mentor to other historians, and wrote for fellow historians. But he left academia to become the first professionally trained head of the Office of Church History of the Church of Jesus Christ of Latter-day Saints, supervising its collections and encouraging the use by Mormons and non-Mormons alike of materials related to the history of the Mormon community. Toward the end of his life, Arrington wrote local history, including several articles based in large part on his and his family's experiences but also using solid historical documentation about the Twin Falls area where he grew up, and about his own life.[52]

Arrington first combined his training in economics and his interest in the history of his home state in his doctoral dissertation, published in 1958 as *Great Basin Kingdom: An Economic History of the Latter-day Saints, 1830–1900*, which goes well beyond Mormon history. Thereafter, he wrote economic and business history (including a history of the Utah-Idaho Sugar Company that is one of the very few scholarly histories of businesses in the state), histories of Mormon activity and individuals, and stories of his own life and community. Throughout his career, he made a point of submitting articles to *Idaho Yesterdays*, sharing his work with general readers in his home state.[53]

In 1990, Arrington, then seventy-two, was offered an opportunity to bring together all his knowledge of and commitment to Idaho in one project. Idaho's Centennial Legislature adopted legislation that gave the Idaho

State Historical Society $100,000 for the writing, editing, and publishing of "a comprehensive and definitive work or treatise on the history of Idaho for Idaho's Centennial."[54] The law, sponsored by Senator Laird Noh (whose family's farm was adjacent to the Arringtons'), suggests the legislature's awareness of the importance of having a "lasting legacy" of the centennial celebration as well as a comprehensive, modern history of the state. Such a history might be a balance to the innumerable and ephemeral centennial events that were taking place across Idaho. None of that is particularly remarkable; the unusual aspect of the law was its naming of a particular "suitable" author: Leonard Arrington.[55]

The resulting two-volume work is in most respects a traditional history covering the topics assigned by the legislature. In also being very readable, it appeals to the general audience its author and sponsors hoped to reach, and it reflects Arrington's use of a wide variety of sources. Arrington brought to the project his expertise as a historian; his familiarity with primary sources and with work done by his predecessors in academic, public, and local history; and his commitment—by no means uncritical—to his native state. It is an exemplary effort.

CONCLUSION

In the two decades since the centennial history was published, all sorts of historians have researched and written much more about Idaho. Eventually, someone will build on that work, as well as what Arrington had access to, in order to study Idaho's history as a whole from a fresh perspective. The resources are ever richer.

Each of us has stories to tell: of ourselves, our families, the various communities geographic and otherwise of which we are a part. Together, these individual stories explain (and perhaps define) the storyteller's place in the world. Historians in general, and in particular the historians discussed in this essay and who have written the preceding chapters, build their work on such stories in order to tell more layered and nuanced stories of broader scope. They, and we, must work through many layers of story created over time and space to understand and tell the broader story of Idaho's religious, political, ethnic, cultural, and environmental history and, ultimately, the story of Idaho's place today.

NOTES

1   Perhaps to a greater degree than is true of other places, there are relatively few book-length studies on Idaho's history, which is instead addressed in shorter articles. Space limitations prevent full citation of all the relevant articles; however, representative samples are cited in this chapter.

2   Lewis's and Clark's own accounts of the time the expedition spent in Idaho are found in *Through the Rockies to the Cascades* and *From the Pacific to the Rockies*, vols. 5 and 7 of *The Definitive Journals of Lewis & Clark*, ed. Gary E. Moulton (Lincoln: University of Nebraska Press, 1988 and 1991). For further information on the expedition's time in Idaho, see articles by John Peebles in *Idaho Yesterdays* 8, 9, and 10 (1964–66) and in Steve Russell, *Lewis and Clark across the Mountains: Mapping the Corps of Discovery in Idaho* (Boise: Idaho State Historical Society, 2007).

3   Many of the journals have been published, first by the Hudson's Bay Record Society and, since its demise in 1983, by the Rupert's Land Record Society through McGill-Queens University Press. Like the accounts of the Lewis and Clark Expedition, they are both raw material for historians and an attempt by the writers to understand the history of the country through which they were passing.

4   C. Aubrey Angelo, *Idaho: A Descriptive Tour and Review of Its Resources and Route, Prefaced by a Sketch of British Misrule in Victoria, V.I.* (1865; Fairfield, WA: Ye Galleon Press, 1969); *Sketches of Travel in Oregon and Idaho: With map of South Boise* (New York: printed for the author by L. D. Robertson, 1866; repr., Fairfield, WA: Ye Galleon Press, 1988).

5   William Armistead Goulder, "The 'Statesman' in North Idaho," *Idaho Yesterdays* 27 (Winter 1984): 2–19; "Our North Idaho Correspondent: William A. Goulder to the *Statesman*," *Idaho Yesterdays* 32 (Spring 1988): 20–29; "Rocky Bar and Atlanta in 1876," *Idaho Yesterdays* 17 (Spring 1973): 12–25; *Reminiscences: Incidents in the Life of a Pioneer in Oregon and Idaho* (Boise: Timothy Regan, 1909; repr., Moscow: University of Idaho Press, 1990). Charles S. Walgamott, *Six Decades Back* (Caldwell, ID: The Caxton Printers Ltd., 1936; repr., Moscow: University of Idaho Press, 1990), is based on the two-volume *Reminiscences of Early Days: A Series of Historical Sketches and Happenings in the Early Days of Snake River Valley*, published in 1926 and 1928 by the *Idaho Citizen*. Robert Strahorn wrote *Resources and Attractions of Idaho Territory* (Boise, 1881; repr., Moscow: University of Idaho Press, 1990) in his role as a Union Pacific publicist—and with the imprimatur of the Idaho territorial legislature. Strahorn was instrumental in the establishment of towns along the Union Pacific subsidiary Oregon Short Line and its branches across southwestern Idaho, notably Caldwell.

6   Thomas Donaldson, *Idaho of Yesterday* (Caldwell, ID: The Caxton Printers Ltd., 1941), quotation on 9. The volume was edited by his son and published forty-three years after his death.

7   John Hailey, *History of Idaho* (Boise: Syms York Company, 1910).

8   William J. McConnell, *Early History of Idaho* (Caldwell, ID: The Caxton Printers Ltd., 1913), 19.

9   Fred T. Dubois, *Fred T. Dubois's "The Making of a State"* (Rexburg: Eastern Idaho Publishing Company, 1971). Dubois's manuscript, edited by Louis J. Clements, ends with Dubois's first term in the Senate.

10   *History of Idaho Territory Showing its Resources and Advantages; with Illustrations*
     Descriptive of its Scenery, Residences, Farms, Mines, Mills, Hotels, Business Houses,
     Schools, Churches, &c. from Original Drawings (San Francisco: Wallace W. Elliott &
     Co., Publishers, 1884; repr., Fairfield, WA: Ye Galleon Press, 1973).

11   Hubert Howe Bancroft, *History of Washington, Idaho, and Montana, 1845–1889* (San
     Francisco: A. B. Bancroft, 1890), quotation from viii. Victor's note also alerts read-
     ers that parts of the history of what is now Idaho can be found in earlier volumes:
     History of the Northwest Coast and *History of Oregon*, vols. 27 and 28, subseries vols.
     22 and 23 (San Francisco: A. B. Bancroft, 1884); vols. 29 and 30, subseries vols. 24
     and 25 (San Francisco: A. B. Bancroft, 1886, 1888). The interviews are at the Bancroft
     Library, University of California, Berkeley.

12   *An Illustrated History of the State of Idaho* . . . (Chicago: The Lewis Publishing Com-
     pany, 1899), quotation from iii.

13   Hiram T. French, *History of Idaho* (Chicago: Lewis Publishing Company, 1914); James
     H. Hawley, *History of Idaho: Gem of the Mountains* (Chicago: S. J. Clarke Company,
     1920); Byron Defenbach, *Idaho: The Place and Its People* (Chicago: American Historical
     Society, 1933); Merrill D. Beal and Merle W. Wells, *History of Idaho* (Chicago: Lewis
     Historical Publishing Company, 1959).

14   This dynamic surrounding professionalism is interpreted helpfully through the lens
     of gender by Laura Woodworth-Ney and Tara A. Rowe in chapter 6 in this volume.

15   Ricketts wrote columns in the *Twin Falls Times-News* and the Jerome *North Side
     News* for many years, and several volumes of them have been published. She was a
     major force in the creation and development of the Jerome County Historical Soci-
     ety. Hyslop was a very active participant in the Owyhee County Historical Society,
     and most of her writing was published in its various periodicals and multiauthor
     books.

16   Helen Lowell and Lucile Peterson, *Our First Hundred Years: A Biography of Lower Boise
     Valley, 1814–1914* (Parma: printed by the authors, 1976); Esther Yarber and Edna R.
     McGown, *Stanley-Sawtooth Country* (n.p.: printed by the author, 1976); Yarber, *Land
     of the Yankee Fork* (Denver: Sage Books, 1963).

17   Pearl M. Oberg, *Between These Mountains: History of Birch Creek Valley, Idaho* (Jeri-
     cho, NY: Exposition Press, 1970); Cecil Dryden, *The Clearwater of Idaho* (New York:
     Carlton Press, 1972).

18   M. Alfreda Elsensohn, *Pioneer Days in Idaho County*, 2 vols. (Caldwell, ID: The Caxton
     Printers Ltd., 1947–51); Elsensohn, *Idaho Chinese Lore* (Cottonwood: Idaho Corpora-
     tion of Benedictine Sisters, 1971); Elsensohn, *Polly Bemis* (Cottonwood: Idaho Cor-
     poration of Benedictine Sisters, 1979).

19   *General Laws of the State of Idaho* . . . *1931*, 61. The only material on the subject in the
     historical society's archives consists of correspondence dated 1942–47 and 1958–59
     with individuals around the state who had been asked to serve as their counties'
     historians.

20   It is clear from the correspondence between the society's directors and prospective
     county historians that some appointees were uncomfortable with their inability
     to gather as much material as they believed the historical society wanted, and a
     number of people simply turned down the offer of appointment, frequently suggest-
     ing other possible individuals. Administration Files, Idaho State Historical Society,
     AR12, Idaho State Archives, Boise. Unfortunately, whatever materials the county

historians submitted to the historical society have not been located in its files, although they may be unidentified among the society's files of ephemera.

21 Annie Laurie Bird, Nampa, to H. J. Swinney, April 5, 1958; Swinney to Bird, April 3, 1958, ibid.

22 Robert G. Bailey, *River of No Return: A Century of Central Idaho and Eastern Washington History and Development, together with the Wars, Customs, Myths, and Legends of the Nez Perce Indians*, rev. ed. (Lewiston, ID: R. G. Bailey Publishing Company, 1947), originally published in 1935; Bailey, *Hell's Canyon: Seeing Idaho through a Scrapbook* (Lewiston, ID: printed by the author, 1943). Bailey is reputed to have been the navigator on the presumed first run of the Salmon River, captained by Harry Guleke, in 1903.

23 Annie Laurie Bird, *Boise the Peace Valley* (Caldwell, ID: The Caxton Printers Ltd., 1934); Bird, *My Home Town* (Caldwell, ID: Caxton Printers, Ltd., 1968); Bird, *Old Fort Boise* (Parma, ID: Old Fort Boise Historical Society, 1971); Bird, *Thomas MacKay* (Caldwell, ID: The Caxton Printers Ltd., 1972); and articles on Wallace in *Idaho Yesterdays* (1957, 1958, 1959, 1966). She also published material in *Pacific Northwest Quarterly* (1945) and *Oregon Historical Quarterly* (1939). At least two other county historians, both apparently appointed in the 1940s, published books about their counties. Barzilla W. Clark was appointed Bonneville County historian after serving not only as mayor of Idaho Falls but as governor of Idaho. Olive Groefsema was designated Elmore County's historian sometime in the 1940s; her history of the county is, as the author notes, built from a scrapbook she gathered together in the late 1940s, one of her responsibilities as county historian. Barzilla W. Clark, *Bonneville County in the Making* (n.p.: n.p., 1941); Olive Groefsema, *Elmore County: Its Historical Gleanings; A Collection of Pioneer Narratives, Treasured Family Pictures, and Early Clippings about the Settling of Elmore County, Idaho* (n.p.: n.p., 1949).

24 Wells also wrote the state's archives law. Technically, the society's director was the state historic preservation officer and Wells was his deputy, but it did not work that way in practice.

25 Judith Austin, "Merle Wells's Writings," *Idaho Yesterdays* 44 (Winter 2000): 61–64.

26 Merle Wells, *Anti-Mormonism in Idaho, 1872–92* (Provo, UT: Brigham Young University Press, 1974). He published a number of articles in *Pacific Northwest Quarterly* beginning in 1949 and in *Idaho Yesterdays* beginning in 1959. *Gold Camps and Silver Cities* was first published as Bulletin 22 of the Idaho Bureau of Mines and Geology in 1964 and republished by the bureau in 1983; in 2002, it was reissued, much more heavily illustrated, by the University of Idaho Press.

27 H. H. Caldwell and Merle Wells, project investigators, for and in cooperation with the Idaho Water Resource Board, "Economic and Ecological History Support Study for a Case Study of Federal Expenditures on a Water and Related Land Resource Project, Boise Project, Idaho and Oregon" (Moscow: Idaho Water Resources Research Institute, University of Idaho, 1974). The author, a participant in the project, suspects that Wells was pleased with the report's lack of support for expanding the Bureau of Reclamation's Boise irrigation project.

28 Arthur Hart, "Architectural Styles in Idaho: A Rich Heritage," *Idaho Yesterdays* 16 (Winter 1972–73): 2–9; Hart, "The Future of Our Heritage," *Idaho Yesterdays* 21 (Spring 1977): 18–21; Hart, "Preserving Our Past: The Antecedents of the Idaho State Historical Society," *Idaho Yesterdays* 24 (Winter 1981): 2–10. His books have

been published by commercial publishers, the institutions and organizations that commissioned them, and a private nonprofit, Historic Idaho.

29 Keith Petersen, *Company Town: Potlatch, Idaho, and the Potlatch Lumber Company* (Pullman: Washington State University Press; Moscow, ID: Latah County Historical Society, 1987); Petersen, *River of Life, Channel of Death: Fish and Dams on the Lower Snake* (Lewiston, ID: Confluence Press, 1995); Mary Reed and Keith Petersen, *Harriman State Park and the Railroad Ranch: A History* (Boise: Idaho Department of Parks and Recreation, 1984). Reed and Petersen also wrote *Virgil T. McCroskey: Giver of Mountains* (Pullman: Department of History, Washington State University, 1983) to accompany a traveling exhibition on McCroskey, donor of the land that is now Mary Minerva McCroskey State Park in the Palouse country of north-central Idaho. They pursued that topic further in Petersen and Reed, "For All the People, Forever and Ever: Virgil McCroskey and the State Parks Movement," *Idaho Yesterdays* 28 (Spring 1984): 2–15.

30 Keith Petersen, *This Crested Hill: An Illustrated History of the University of Idaho* (Moscow: University of Idaho Press, 1987); Petersen, *Educating in the American West: One Hundred Years at Lewis-Clark State College, 1893–1993* (Lewiston, ID: Confluence Press, 1993); Petersen, *Historical Celebrations: A Handbook for Organizers of Diamond Jubilees, Centennials, and Other Community Anniversaries* (Boise: Idaho State Historical Society, 1986). Petersen's earliest published work in Idaho history, "Frank Bruce Robinson and Psychiana," *Idaho Yesterdays* 23 (Fall 1979): 9–15, 26–29, is on a most unusual mail-order business in Moscow; a later publication, *Psychiana* (Moscow: Latah County Historical Society, 1991), provides more detail on Robinson's movement.

31 Susan Stacy, *When the River Rises: Flood Control on the Boise River, 1943–1985* (Boulder: Institute of Behavioral Science, Natural Hazards Research and Applications Information Center, University of Colorado; Boise: College of Social Sciences and Public Affairs, Boise State University, 1993), xiii; *Proving the Principle: A History of the Idaho National Engineering and Environmental Laboratory, 1949–1999* (Idaho Falls: Idaho Operations Office of the Department of Energy, 2000); *Legacy of Light: A History of the Idaho Power Company* (Boise: Idaho Power Company, 1991); and *Tom and Julia Davis: "Some Good Place," Boise, Idaho* (Boise: T & J Publishing Company, 2007).

32 C. J. Brosnan, *History of the State of Idaho*, rev. ed. (New York: Charles Scribner's Sons, 1935), originally published in 1918.

33 Merrill D. Beal, *"I Will Fight No More Forever": Chief Joseph and the Nez Perce War* (Seattle: University of Washington Press, 1963); Beal, *The Story of Man in Yellowstone* (Caldwell, ID: The Caxton Printers Ltd., 1949; repr., Yellowstone National Park, WY: Yellowstone Library and Museum Association, 1956). In his preface, Beal notes that he intended his primary audience to be visitors to the park (8).

34 Merrill D. Beal, *Intermountain Railroads: Standard and Narrow Gauge* (Caldwell, ID: The Caxton Printers Ltd., 1962); Beal, *The Utah and Northern Railroad: Narrow Gauge* (Pocatello: Idaho State University Press, 1980); Beal, *A History of Southeastern Idaho* (Caldwell, ID: The Caxton Printers Ltd., 1942); Beal, *The Snake River Fork Country: A Brief History of Peaceful Conquest of the Upper Snake River Basin* (Rexburg, ID: n.p., 1935); Beal, *History of Idaho State College* (Pocatello: printed by the author, 1952); Beal, *Sixty Years of Educational Endeavors in Idaho, 1924–1984* (Pocatello: Idaho State University Press, 1984).

35 Carlos Schwantes, *The Pacific Northwest: An Interpretive History* (Lincoln: University of Nebraska Press, 1989), xix. See also Schwantes, *In Mountain Shadows: A History of Idaho* (Lincoln: University of Nebraska Press, 1991); Schwantes, *So Incredibly Idaho: Seven Landscapes That Define the Gem State* (Moscow: University of Idaho Press, 1996); Schwantes, ed., *Encounters with a Distant Land: Exploration and the Great Northwest* (Moscow: University of Idaho Press, 1994); and Schwantes and Thomas G. Edwards, eds., *Experiences in a Promised Land: Essays in Pacific Northwest History* (Seattle: University of Washington Press, 1986).
      In addition to labor and the landscape, Schwantes has both a scholarly and a personal interest in transportation, a field critical to understanding Idaho's history. A pair of books demonstrates that interest both intellectually and visually: *Railroad Signatures across the Pacific Northwest* (Seattle: University of Washington Press, 1993) and *Long Day's Journey: The Steamboat & Stagecoach Era in the Northern West* (Seattle: University of Washington Press, 1999). Two more recent books also focus on transportation's impact on the broader West: *Going Places: Transportation Redefines the Twentieth-Century West* (Bloomington: Indiana University Press, 2003) and Schwantes and James P. Ronda, *The West the Railroads Made* (Seattle: University of Washington Press, 2008).

36 Lovin's work on political history has been published since the early 1970s in both *Idaho Yesterdays* and *Pacific Northwest Quarterly*. His work on irrigation history appears almost exclusively in *Idaho Yesterdays*.

37 Madsen's works include *The Bannock of Idaho* (Caldwell, ID: The Caxton Printers Ltd., 1958); *The Lemhi: Sacajawea's People* (Caldwell, ID: The Caxton Printers Ltd., 1979); *The Northern Shoshoni* (Caldwell, ID: The Caxton Printers Ltd., 1980); *The Shoshoni Frontier and the Bear River Massacre* (Salt Lake City: University of Utah Press, 1985), the first volume in the press's Utah Centennial Series; *Chief Pocatello* (Salt Lake City: University of Utah Press, 1986; repr., Moscow: University of Idaho Press, 1999); *Glory Hunter: A Biography of Patrick Edward Connor* (Salt Lake City: University of Utah Press, 1990); "The 'Almo Massacre' Revisited," *Idaho Yesterdays* 37 (Fall 1993): 54–64, which challenges a long-held (and long memorialized) belief about Native American–Anglo relationships in southeastern Idaho. Another related book is Betty M. Madsen and Brigham D. Madsen, *North to Montana! Jehus, Bullwhackers, and Mule Skinners on the Montana Trail* (Salt Lake City: University of Utah Press, 1980). Madsen's autobiography, published in 1998, is a graceful account of a person who has lived in many worlds; see *Against the Grain: Memoirs of a Western Historian* (Salt Lake City, UT: Signature Books, 1998).

38 James Gentry, *In the Middle and on the Edge: The Twin Falls Region of Idaho* (Twin Falls: College of Southern Idaho and Twin Falls Centennial Commission, 2003), xv. Gentry also wrote *The College of Southern Idaho, 1945–1985: The Development of the Institution*, a chronology with a short narrative (Twin Falls: The College of Southern Idaho, 1987).

39 Clark Spence, *British Investments and the American Mining Frontier, 1860–1901* (Ithaca, NY: Cornell University Press for the American Historical Association, 1958); Spence, *Mining Engineers and the American West: The Lace-Boot Brigade, 1849–1933* (New Haven, CT: Yale University Press, 1970); and Spence, *For Wood River or Bust: Idaho's Silver Boom of the 1880s* (Boise: Idaho State Historical Society; Moscow: University of Idaho Press, 1999).

40 Karl Boyd Brooks, *Public Power, Private Dams: The Hells Canyon High Dam Contro-versy* (Seattle: University of Washington Press, 2006); Brooks, *Before Earth Day: The Origins of American Environmental Law, 1945–1970* (Lawrence: University Press of Kansas, 2009); Mark Fiege, *Irrigated Eden: The Making of an Agricultural Landscape in the American West* (Seattle: University of Washington Press, 1999). At this writing, Brooks is on leave from Kansas as administrator of Region 7 of the Environmental Protection Agency, adding another sort of experience to his résumé.

41 Stephen J. Pyne, *Year of the Fires: The Story of the Great Fires of 1910* (New York: Viking Press, 2001). Timothy Egan's *The Big Burn: Teddy Roosevelt & the Fire That Saved America* (Boston: Houghton Mifflin Harcourt, 2009) has added to the literature on the 1910 fire. Egan's larger story encompasses the president as well as his chief forester, Gifford Pinchot.

42 J. M. Neil, *To the White Clouds: Idaho's Conservation Saga, 1900–1970* (Pullman: Washington State University Press, 2005). Other articles by Neil have been published in *Idaho Yesterdays*.

43 Thomas R. Cox, *The Park Builders: A History of State Parks in the Pacific Northwest* (Seattle: University of Washington Press, 1988); Cox, "Tribal Leadership in Transition: Chief Peter Moctelme of the Coeur d'Alenes," *Idaho Yesterdays* 23 (Spring 1979): 2–9, 25–31; Cox, "Weldon Heyburn, Lake Chatcolet, and the Evolving Concept of Public Parks," *Idaho Yesterdays* 24 (Summer 1980): 2–15.

44 Alvin Josephy, *The Nez Perce Indians and the Opening of the Northwest* (New Haven, CT: Yale University Press, 1965). Forty-two years later, and two years after Josephy's death, his *Nez Perce Country* (Lincoln: University of Nebraska Press, 2007) was published. Josephy's account linking the Nez Perce experience to the land they called home—originally written for the National Park Service as an introduction to the Nez Perce National Historical Park—is introduced by Jeremy Five Crows, who speaks even more directly to the link between the land and his people.

45 Allen P. Slickpoo, Jr., *Noon Nee-Me-Poo (We, the Nez Perces): Culture and History of the Nez Perces* (n.p.: The Nez Perce Tribe of Idaho, 1973); Slickpoo, *Nu Mee Poom Tit Wah Tit (Nez Perce Legends)* (n.p.: The Nez Perce Tribe of Idaho, 1972).

46 Elliott West, *The Last Indian War: The Nez Perce Story* (New York: Oxford University Press, 2009); John D. McDermott, *Forlorn Hope: The Battle of White Bird Canyon and the Beginning of the Nez Perce War* (Boise: Idaho State Historical Society, 1978; repr., Caldwell, ID: Caxton Press, 2003).

47 Clifford M. Drury, *Henry Harmon Spalding, Pioneer of Old Oregon* (Caldwell, ID: The Caxton Printers Ltd., 1936). The following works by Drury were published by the Arthur H. Clark Company, Glendale, CA: *The Diaries and Letters of Henry H. Spalding and Asa Bowen Smith relating to the Nez Perce Mission, 1838–1842* (1958); *First White Women over the Rockies: Diaries, Letters, and Biographical Sketches of the Six Women of the Oregon Mission who made the Overland Journey in 1836 and 1838*, vol. 1: *Mrs. Marcus Whitman, Mrs. Henry H. Spalding, Mrs. William H. Gray, and Mrs. Asa B. Smith* (1963) and vol. 3: *Diary of Sarah White Smith (Mrs. Asa B. Smith), Letters of Asa B. Smith, and other documents relating to the 1838 Reinforcement to the Oregon Mission* (1966); *Chief Lawyer of the Nez Perce Indians, 1796–1876* (1979). The article based on his book *Chief Lawyer* is "Lawyer, Head Chief of the Nez Perce 1848–1875," *Idaho Yesterdays* 22 (Winter 1979): 2–12.

48 Allen Morrill and Eleanor Morrill, *Out of the Blanket: The Story of Sue and Kate Mc-*

Beth, Missionaries to the Nez Perce (Moscow: University Press of Idaho, 1978); Kate McBeth, *The Nez Perces since Lewis and Clark* (New York: Fleming H. Revell Company, 1908; repr., Moscow: University of Idaho Press, 1993).

49 See, by J. Patrick Bieter, "Reluctant Shepherds: The Basques in Idaho," *Idaho Yesterdays* 1 (Summer 1957): 10–15; "Letemendi's Boarding House: A Basque Cultural Institution in Idaho," *Idaho Yesterdays* 37 (Spring 1993): 2–10; and "Basques in Idaho," *Idaho Yesterdays* 41 (Summer 1997): 22–32. The book written by John P. Bieter and Mark Bieter is *Enduring Legacy: The Story of Basques in Idaho*, Basque Series (Reno: University of Nevada Press, 2000).

50 Robert C. Sims, "The Japanese American Experience in Idaho," *Idaho Yesterdays* 22 (Spring 1978): 2–10; Sims, "'You Don't Need to Wait Any Longer to Get Out': Japanese American Evacuees as Farm Laborers during World War II," *Idaho Yesterdays* 44 (Summer 2000): 7–13; Eric Walz, "Idaho Farmer, Japanese Diarist: Cultural Crossings in the Intermountain West," *Idaho Yesterdays* 39 (Fall 1995): 2–12. Walz's doctoral dissertation at Arizona State University deals with the same subject in a wider geographic context.

51 Liping Zhu, *A Chinaman's Chance: The Chinese on the Rocky Mountain Frontier* (Niwot: University Press of Colorado, 1997).

52 Leonard Arrington, "Recalling a Twin Falls Childhood," *Idaho Yesterdays* 25 (Winter 1982): 31–40; Arrington, "The Influenza Epidemic of 1918–1919 in Southern Idaho," *Idaho Yesterdays* 32 (Fall 1988): 19–29; Arrington, "'Doing to Learn': Idaho Future Farmers in the 1930's," *Idaho Yesterdays* 43 (Summer 1999): 25–31.

53 Leonard Arrington, *Great Basin Kingdom: An Economic History of the Latter-day Saints, 1830–1900* (Cambridge, MA: Harvard University Press, 1958; repr., Seattle: University of Washington Press, 1966). After Arrington's death, Merle Wells wrote an appraisal of him as a historian of Idaho and the Great Basin, "Leonard J. Arrington, July 2, 1917–February 11, 1999," *Idaho Yesterdays* 43 (Spring 1999): 3–4. Arrington's thoughtful memoir is *Adventures of a Church Historian* (Urbana: University of Illinois Press, 1998). He published numerous articles in *Idaho Yesterdays* between 1962 and 1991.

54 *General Laws of the State of Idaho Passed by the Second Regular Session of the Centennial Idaho Legislature* . . . (Boise: By authority of the Secretary of State, 1990), 665–66. The resulting book is *History of Idaho*, 2 vols. (Moscow: University of Idaho Press; Boise: Idaho State Historical Society, 1992).

55 Arrington himself had some qualms about being specified in the legislation. He was not reluctant to take on such a project in retirement, but he was concerned that Merle Wells—an old and close friend—might wish to take it on himself. Wells was delighted that Arrington was willing to research and write the state's centennial history. Leonard Arrington and Merle Wells, conversations with the author, winter or early spring 1990.

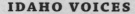
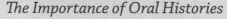

IDAHO VOICES
The Importance of Oral Histories

Robert C. Sims discusses the importance of oral histories.

INTERVIEWER: During the writing that stems from your interviewing, do you have any feelings about ways to integrate using those kinds of sources in traditional kinds of writing?

SIMS: Well, it depends on the way you seek to do the writing—at least what your purposes are in it. Now the study I mentioned earlier about Japanese-American contributions to Idaho's economic growth doesn't really call that much for analyzing the human experiences. It's much more a study of impact, just as the topic suggests. But if the writing is intended to be more of a history of a people or a history that partakes of people's feelings as well as discrete economic circumstances, then obviously it has a lot of impact. A lot of things that I have available to me, information that I got out of those interviews, I think really form the heart of the things I'll be trying to write about when I write about Camp Minidoka. Because that really is the thing I'm trying to deal with there. Not an administrative history of the camp as much as a history of the people who were in the camp. And that kind of information that you can get from an oral interview is far preferable to some statistical analysis or some flow chart of administrative responsibility for the camp. Even though I have those things and understand how the camp was operated, the benefit of the oral interviews give me some sense of what it was like to exist in there. You just can't replace that.

* * *

Merle W. Wells describes the poor state of historical records in Idaho in the 1940s.

INTERVIEWER: Were there any problems, Merle, initially getting access to those records [i.e., state papers]?

WELLS: Oh, no, other than the way they were arranged and all that. . . .
We had a frightful time getting at the governor's files. That we knew were
in governor's vault and that was years trying to find somebody who knew
where our governor's vault was. . . . [W]e finally found a custodian there who
actually knew where they were. And I remember, quite clearly, he opened
it up and I looked at it a little and really wanted to get in although I didn't
have much time right then. I was about to go back down. But I decided not
even to try to look at it at all. Because that vault was filled tighter than any
other I've ever seen. I was positive that if we began to look at it then, we'd
never be able to get them in and the door shut again.

INTERVIEWER: *(Laughter)* Is that right?

WELLS: Oh yes, they were just solid right at the door. And, we could see,
the only way you'd be able to get in there and look at them would be to take
everything out, or at least, well, maybe not quite everything. There'd be
some—but it was really tight there. [But if I took any out, it would have
been impossible to get them back in.] Even if we'd had a governor's mouse
that wanted to get in, he wouldn't have had space. So, about that next summer, I went in and got permission not only to look at them but to get the
whole thing organized because it was plain that we'd never be able to get
them back in once we got them out. Short of having the same kind of problem that nobody could find anything.

NOTE

Robert C. Sims was interviewed by Stacy Ericson, January 18, 1981, Boise, ID, transcript (OH1266) Idaho Oral History Center/Idaho State Historical Society, 3. Used
with permission of Idaho State Historical Society.

Merle W. Wells was interviewed by William E. Tydeman, December 5, 1991, Boise,
ID, transcript (OH1299) Idaho Oral History Center/Idaho State Historical Society,
234–35. Used with permission of Idaho State Historical Society.

Contributors

Katherine G. Aiken is a professor of history at the University of Idaho, where she served as dean of the College of Letters, Arts & Social Sciences from 2006 to 2013 and is currently interim provost and executive vice president. She has written articles dealing with Idaho's first woman member of the U.S. Congress, Gracie Pfost; environmental history; twentieth-century Idaho history; and the Coeur d'Alene mining district. Her books are *Harnessing the Power of Motherhood: The National Florence Crittenton Mission, 1883–1925; Idaho's Bunker Hill: The Rise and Fall of a Great Mining Company, 1885–1982;* and, with Kevin Marsh and Laura Woodworth-Ney, *Idaho: The Enduring Promise.* She is the Idaho Humanities Council chair and a member of the State Department of Education Professional Standards Commission.

Judith Austin retired in 2002 as historian and coordinator of publications at the Idaho State Historical Society. She received her B.A. in history at Duke University and her M.A. in the history of education at Teachers College, Columbia University. After four and a half years as an editor in New York City, she joined the staff of the society in 1967. For twenty-seven years, she was the editor of the society's journal, *Idaho Yesterdays.* She is active in the Western History Association and is the secretary-treasurer of the Conference of Historical Journals.

Richard W. Etulain is professor emeritus of history at the University of New Mexico. A specialist on the history and literature of the American West, he has authored or edited more than forty-five books on western and U.S. cultural topics. Among his best-known books are *Conversations with Wallace Stegner on Western History and Literature* (1983, rev. ed. 1996), *The American West: A Twentieth-Century History,* with Michael P. Malone (1989, 2nd ed. 2007), *Re-imagining the Modern American West: A Century of Fiction, History,* *and Art* (1996), *Telling Western Stories: From Buffalo Bill to Larry McMurtry* (1999), and *Beyond the Missouri: The Story of the American West* (2006). His writings have won several awards, and he has served as president of both the Western Literature and Western History Associations. *Lincoln and Oregon Country Politics in the Civil War Era* (2013) is his latest book.

Rodney Frey is a professor of ethnography at the University of Idaho. Over the past thirty-five years, he has been associated with and conducted various applied collaborative projects with the Apsáalooke (Crow of Montana), the Schitsu'umsh and Nimíipuu (Coeur d'Alene and Nez Perce of Idaho), the Confederated Warm Springs Tribes of Oregon, and other area tribes. Among his primary teachers, to whom he acknowledges his indebtedness, are Tom and Susie Yellowtail and Alvin Howe (Apsáalooke), Lawrence Aripa and Cliff SiJohn (Schitsu'umsh), Josiah and D'Lisa Pinkham (Nimíipuu), and Rob and Rose Moran (Little Shell Chippewa and Warm Springs). Among the books he has published in collaboration with his teachers are *Landscape Traveled by Coyote and Crane: The World of the Schitsu'umsh (Coeur d'Alene Indians)* (2001) and *Stories That Make the World: Oral Literature of the Indian Peoples of the Inland Northwest* (1995).

Jill K. Gill is a professor and graduate coordinator in the History Department at Boise State University. Her research and teaching interests bridge religious, racial, and political history in the twentieth-century United States, and she is the author of *Embattled Ecumenism: The National Council of Churches, the Vietnam War, and the Trials of the Protestant Left* (2011). She is currently exploring the history of black/white dynamics in Idaho as part of a book-length project.

Errol D. Jones is a professor emeritus of history at Boise State University, where he taught courses in U.S. and Latin American history from 1982 to 2007. He continues to be active in research and writing the history of Latinos in Idaho. His most recent publications include "The Shooting of Pedro Rodriguez," in *Idaho Yesterdays* (2005); with Kathleen R. Hodges, "A Long Struggle: Mexican Farmworkers in Idaho, 1918–1935," with Kathleen R. Hodges, in *Memory, Community, and Activism: Mexican Migration and Labor in the*

Pacific Northwest, edited by Jerry Garcia and Gilberto Garcia (2005); "Idaho," in *Latino America: A State-by-State Encyclopedia*, edited by Mark Overmyer-Velázquez (2008). He was guest editor and contributor for a special issue of *Idaho Landscapes,* "La Cultura Mexicana" (2011).

Kevin R. Marsh is a professor and the chair of the History Department at Idaho State University. He teaches courses in Idaho history, environmental history, and the twentieth-century United States. Marsh is also the editor of *Idaho Yesterdays* and has served as a board member of the Idaho Humanities Council. He is the author of *Drawing Lines in the Forest: Creating Wilderness Areas in the Pacific Northwest* and co-author with Katherine G. Aiken and Laura Woodworth-Ney of *Idaho: The Heroic Journey*, the centennial publication of the Idaho State Historical Society. He has published articles on environmental history in the *Western Historical Quarterly*, *Oregon Historical Quarterly*, and several anthologies and encyclopedias.

Robert McCarl is a professor in the Sociology Department at Boise State University. He has worked with the Idaho tribes in various public programming and research-related projects since 1986, including participation on the research team that assisted in the Coeur d'Alene lake claim for the United States Department of Justice. In addition to his work with Indian people, McCarl has published a number of articles and monographs on the study of work, occupational culture, and ethnography in the workplace.

Laurie Mercier is the Claudius O. and Mary W. Johnson Distinguished Professor of History at Washington State University. She is the author of *Anaconda: Labor, Community and Culture in Montana's Smelter City* (2001) and coeditor, with Jaclyn J. Gier, of *Mining Women: Gender in the Development of a Global Industry* (2009) and *Speaking History: Oral Histories of the American Past, 1865–Present* (2009). In 1989 and 1990, Mercier codirected the Idaho Ethnic Heritage Project with Carole Simon-Smolinski.

Tara A. Rowe is an independent scholar, editor, and political blogger. She has written extensively about Idaho history and politics. While attending Idaho State University, Rowe catalogued the congressional papers of Richard Stallings. She is the former assistant editor of *Idaho Landscapes*. Her current writing project is a history of the state psychiatric hospitals in Idaho during the first half of the twentieth century.

Adam M. Sowards is an associate professor of history at the University of Idaho, where he also directs the Program in Pacific Northwest Studies. A historian of the North American West and environmental history, Sowards has published two books, including, most recently, *The Environmental Justice: William O. Douglas and American Conservation* (2009), and numerous articles and essays in regional and environmental history, as well as the history of science.

Laura Woodworth-Ney is provost and vice president for academic affairs at Idaho State University. The former chair of the university's Department of History, she serves as executive editor of the Center for Idaho History and Politics and is the founding coeditor of the Idaho State Historical Society's *Idaho Landscapes*. From 2003 to 2008, she served as editor-in-chief of *Idaho Yesterdays* and currently serves as the editor of a scholarly book series published by the University of Arizona Press. She is a prolific scholar and historian, having published nearly thirty articles, book reviews, and scholarly encyclopedia entries, as well as three books.

Index

A

abortion, 99, 125
Ada County, 129–30, 227
Adams, Lloyd, 83–84
Adath Israel, 116
Affiliated Tribes of Northwest Indians, 34
affirmative action, 219
African Americans, 116, 117, 167, 169, 175–79, 185, 186, 187, 199–200; occupations of, 176–77; organizations of, 177; segregation of, 177–78, 191, 199
African Methodist Episcopal Church, 116, 179
Agricultural Adjustment Administration, 85
Agricultural Labor Law, 218
agriculture, 49, 50, 52, 54, 56, 57, 58, 79, 80, 83, 84, 85, 113, 141, 158, 168, 176, 180, 183, 184, 185, 203, 207–8, 209–10, 211, 225
Ahavath Beth Israel, 116, 117
Ah Fong, C. K., 174
Aid to Families with Dependent Children, 157–58
Alberta, 15
alcohol, 26
Alexander, Moses, 82–83, 116
Alien Land Law, 180–81, 182, 185
Allen Chapel African Methodist Episcopal Church, 178
allotment, 30, 31
Amalgamated Sugar Company, 204
American Civil Liberties Union, 127
American Falls, 213, 221
American Falls Dam, 59
American Indian Movement, 33
American Smelting and Refining Company (ASARCO), 66, 92
America's Promise Ministries, 128
Anderson, Clinton, 73
Anderson, Guy, 249
Andrus, Cecil, 66, 91–92, 96, 99, 125, 218
Angelo, C. Aubrey, 264
Anne Frank Human Rights Memorial, 130, 131
anti-Chinese movement, 169, 173
anti-communism, 89, 123
anti-Japanese movement, 180
anti-Mormonism, 78, 120–21, 265
anti-vice campaigns, 143
Appaloosa, 46
Archabal, Juan, 189
Arid Club, 101
Arizona, 199, 205, 212, 238
Armijo, Joe, 224
Armitage, Susan, 147, 160
Arriaga, Pia Unamuno, 190
Arrington, Leonard, 4–5, 50, 140, 280–81
Arrow Lakes, 15
Arrowrock Dam, 59
Aryan Nations, 4, 9, 127–29, 130, 131, 1767
Ashby, LeRoy, 81
Asians, 139, 167, 169, 186, 192, 279–80; racial-ization of, 181
Atlantic Ocean, 44
Axtell, Horace, 22

B

Bailey, Robert G., 269
Bairfield, Ophelia, 177
Balch, Frederic Homer, 240

Baldridge, Cora A. McCreighton, 165–66
Baldridge, H. Clarence, 64
Bancroft, Hubert Howe, 266
Bannaqwate. *See* Bannock
Bannock, 15, 17, 30–31, 36, 38, 46, 47, 48, 112–13
Bannock Hotel, 177
Bannock Stake Academy. *See* Brigham Young
    University—Idaho
Barkan, Elliott, 168
Barnes, Kim, 157, 244
Barnes, Verda, 87
Basque Block, 251
Basque country, 185, 188
Basque Museum and Cultural Center, 191
Basques, 4, 9, 113, 168, 169, 188–91, 192, 239,
    250–53, 261–62, 279; boardinghouses of,
    189–90; as herders, 188
Batt, Phil, 223
Beal, Merrill, 145, 267, 274–75
Bear Hunter, 27
Bear Lake County, 77, 85, 99
Bear Paw, 37
Bear River Massacre, 27, 35
beaver, 27, 45, 49
Beaverhead Range, 44
Bemis, Charlie, 173
Bemis, Polly Nathoy, 146, 152–53, 153*fig.*, 160,
    173, 244
Benewah County, 83
Bengoechea, Joe, 189
Benson, Ezra Taft, 99
Benton, Thomas Hart, 249
Berain, Jess, 224
Bethel Baptist Church, 178
Bieter, John, 252, 279
Bieter, Mark, 189, 252, 279
Bieter, Patrick, 189, 279
Big Creek, 75
Big Hole, 28, 37
Bilbao, Guisasola, 190
Billings, 180
Bird, Annie Laurie, 269
Bishop Kelly High School, 114
bison, 25, 46
Bitterroot Mountains, 44
Bitterroot Salish, 31
Bizkaia, 188, 252

Blackburn, George, 191
Blackfeet, 46
Blackfoot, 122, 204
Black History Museum, 116
Black Jack Mine, 53*fig.*
Blackman, George Washington, 175
Blackman Peak, 175
blacks. *See* African Americans
Blaine County, 221, 227
Blew, Mary Clearman, 244, 256
blister rust, 86
Board of Medical Examiners, 174
Boise, 4, 58, 77–78, 79, 113–14, 115, 116, 119,
    122, 123, 126, 129, 143, 157, 170, 174, 176,
    179, 189, 190, 191, 199–200, 206, 219, 227,
    228, 251, 252, 265, 268, 269
Boise, Tom, 88
Boise Art Museum, 250
Boise County, 175
Boise Junior College. *See* Boise State Univer-
    sity
Boise Mosque and Islamic Center, 116
Boise Payette Lumber Company, 64
Boise Project, 59, 60
Boise River, 18, 50, 58, 59, 61
Boise State University, 114, 221–22, 227, 250,
    251, 255, 270, 276, 279
Boise Trades and Labor Council, 208
Boise Valley, 59, 60
Bolshevik Revolution, 83
Bonner County, 129
Bonners Ferry, 15, 34, 173
Boone, William Judson, 114
Borah, William E., 80, 81, 82*fig.*, 82, 83, 84,
    85, 86
Bosnia, 116
Bottolfsen, Clarence A., 140
Boulder Mountains, 66
Boundary County, 128
Bowler, Bruce, 73, 277
"Boys of Boise," 97, 122–23
bracero program, 7, 118, 209–11. *See also* Lati-
    nos: and bracero programs
Brady, James, 56
Brady, Jerry, 87
Brigham City, 18, 35
Brigham Young University—Idaho, 115, 255

British Columbia, 15

Brooks, Karl, 61–62, 277

Brosnan, Cornelius J., 138, 274

Brown, Charles, 54

Brownlee Dam, 90

Bruneau River, 18

Bryan, William Jennings, 80

Buck, Carl, 140

Buck, Kellogg, 156

Buck Eye Mao Joss House, 172*fig.*

Budge, Homer, 99

buffalo. *See* bison

Buffalo Horn, 28

Bunker Hill and Sullivan Mining and Concentrating Company. *See* Bunker Hill Company

Bunker Hill Company, 52–53, 54, 74, 79, 186, 224

Bureau of Indian Affairs, 33, 35

Burke, 186

Burley, 204, 205, 215

Butler, Richar, 128

Butters, MaryJane, 159–60

C

Cache Valley, 27

Cahmeawait, 44

Caldwell, 114, 143, 145, 159, 180, 212, 213, 215, 216, 217, 220, 228

Caldwell Tribune, 189

California, 22, 124, 170, 182, 186, 188, 191, 198–99, 202, 205, 209, 212, 252

California Volunteers, 27

Callahan, Kenneth, 249

camas, 48, 149

Camas Prairie, 28

Camp Downey, 118

Canada, 28

Canyon County, 175, 210, 217, 224, 225, 226, 269

capitalism, 8, 51, 52, 86

Carey Act (1894), 58, 80

Carr, Greg, 130

Cartee, Lafayette, 143

Carter, Jimmy, 93, 95

Castle Peak, 66, 92

Cataldo, Joseph, 111

Cataldo Mission. *See* Sacred Heart Mission

Cathedral of the Rockies

Cather, Willa, 241, 242

Catholic Church of the Good Shepherd, 251

Catholic Diocese of Boise, 212

Catholicism and Catholics, 108, 109, 110–11, 113, 114, 119, 120, 123, 125, 128–29, 187, 206, 213, 216

Catlin, George, 239, 246

cattle. *See* ranching

Caxton Printers, 260

Cayuse, 46

celery, 59*fig.*

Celilo Falls, 25

Cenarrusa, Pete, 252

Central Intelligence Committee, 95

Century Magazine, 241, 247

chain migration, 168

Challis National Forest, 66

Charity Boarding School, 32

Chavez, Cesar, 91, 118

Chenoweth, Helen, 96–97

Cherokee Nation v. Georgia (1831), 29

China, 174

Chinese, 4, 6, 152–54, 168, 169–74, 177, 178, 179, 180, 185, 189, 190, 191, 202, 204268, 279–80; Chinatowns, 171, 174; labor resentment toward, 171–73; massacres of, 169, 173–74; and mining tax, 169; organizations of, 171; population characteristics of, 170–71

Chinese Empire Reform Association, 171

Chinese Exclusion Act (1882), 170, 173, 174

Chipp, Nettie, 155*fig.*

Christian Identity, 5, 9, 128, 130

Christianity, 49

Church, Bethine, 86, 106

Church, Frank, 62, 64–65, 66, 73, 86, 89, 92, 93, 94–95, 106, 218

Church Committee, 95

churches, 6, 109, 113, 122, 180, 187, 189, 212

Church of God in Christ, 116

Church of Jesus Christ, Christian, 128

Church of Jesus Christ of Latter-day Saints, 5, 35, 51, 76, 77, 78, 83, 93, 94, 97, 99, 101, 108, 124–25, 127–28, 131, 137, 280. *See also* Latter-day Saints

Church of the Good Shepherd, 113

Citizens for Civic Unity, 223

civil liberties, 81, 89, 183–84

civil rights, 88, 89, 125, 217, 219, 223, 224

Civil War, 27, 77

Civilian Conservation Corps, 86

Claggett, William, 79

Clark, Barzilla, 86

Clark, Chase, 86, 182

Clark, C. Worth, 86

Clark, William, 18, 44, 239. *See also* Lewis and Clark Expedition

Clark Fork River, 15

Clarks Fork, 173

Clearwater River, 16, 21, 28, 46, 50, 77, 149, 268

Clinton, Bill, 97, 100

Cobb, Calvin, 56

Cobb, Jerry, 74–75

Coeur d'Alene (city), 128–29, 180

Coeur d'Alene (Native Americans), 15, 16, 19, 21, 27, 36, 37, 38, 46–47, 48, 111, 278; and education, 32; employment, 34–35; and epidemics, 25; and executive orders, 30; and farming, 30, 111; and fur trade, 26; and missionaries, 31–32, 111; oral traditions of, 19, 24; tribal government of, 34; and war, 27

Coeur d'Alene Casino Resort Hotel, 34, 37

Coeur d'Alene Indian Reservation, 30, 31, 34

Coeur d'Alene mining district. *See* Silver Valley

Coeur d'Alene mining wars, 80

Coeur d'Alene River, 16, 52, 53

Colfax, 54

Colianni, Aldemo, 187

Colianni, Tony, 187

College Assistance Migrant Program, 221–22

College of Idaho, 114, 145, 250, 270

Collier, John, 33–34

Colored Baptist Church, 116, 178

Columbia Basin, 47, 61

Columbian Club, 143–44, 155, 156, 165

Columbia Plateau, 3

Columbia River, 15, 25, 45, 48, 62, 86

Columbia Valley Authority, 86

Colunga, Elias, 206–7

Colville, Indian Reservation, 16, 28, 31

Comanches, 25, 46, 48

Community Council of Idaho, 219

Conklin, Emily, 165

Conner, Colonel Patrick, 27

conservation, 8, 56, 57, 277

conservatism, 61, 76, 83

Constitution, 29

Corps of Discovery. *See* Lewis and Clark Expedition

Cottonwood, 114, 268

county historians, 269

Cox, Thomas R., 277–78

Craig, Larry, 96, 100, 225

Crapo, Mike, 66

Cristobal Columbus lodge, 187

Cuoio, Vito, 187

Curry, John Steuart, 249

Custer, 175

D

Daily Idahonian, 118

dams, 8

Darrow, Clarence, 80

Davis, "Bud," 91

Davis, H. L., 242, 254

Davis, Nelle Portrey, 244

Davis v. Beason (1890), 78

Dawes Severalty Act (1887), 30, 34

Day, Ernie, 73–74

Deary, 176

D'Easum, Dick, 140

Deep Ecology, 131

Defenbach, Byron, 138, 139

DeMary, Elizabeth, 156

Democratic Party, 78, 79, 80, 81, 84, 87, 88, 91, 92–93, 94, 95–97, 99, 100–101, 120–21, 166

Democrats. *See* Democratic Party

Derr, Allen, 97

DeSmet, 32

DeSmet, Pierre-Jean, 111

diphtheria, 25

disease, 25, 46, 47, 49

Diversion Dam, 59

Donaldson, Thomas, 264–65

Douglas, William O., 62

Downey, 118

Drexel, Katherine, 111

Driggs, 206, 208

drought, 57
Drury, Clifford M., 278
Dryden, Cecil, 268
DuBois, Fred, 56, 78, 79, 265
Duck Valley Reservation, 16, 18, 28, 30, 35, 36
Dunbar, Henrietta C., 165
Duniway, Abigail Scott, 138, 141, 146, 152, 160, 240
Dunn, Alfred, 249
Dust Bowl, 84
Dworshak, Henry, 90, 96
Dye, Eva Emory, 152

E

Easton, Stanley, 64
Edmunds Act (1882), 78
Egyptian Theater, 116
Eiguren, Joe, 252
Eisenhower, Dwight, 89, 99, 212
El-Ada, Inc., 217
11th Hour Remnant Messenger, 128, 129
Elsensohn, M. Alfreda, 268
Emmett, 180, 181
Employment Security Agency, 216
Endangered Wilderness Act, 95
Eng, Owen, 172*fig.*
environmental history, 45
environmentalism, 131
environmentalists, 90, 92, 96
Environmental Protection Agency, 74
Episcopal Church and Episcopalians, 114
Equal Rights Amendment, 124–25
Espionage Act, 83
Ethics Act (1978), 94
Euskal, Herria. *See* Basque country
Euskaldunak Club, 251
Euskera, 253
evangelicals, 123, 124, 125, 126
Evans, John, 96
Executive Order 9066, 182
Explosive Devices Act, 129

F

Fair Labor Standards Act, 211
Falk, Leo, 116
Farmer-Labor Party, 81
Farm Placement Service's Annual Worker

Plan, 212
farms and farming. *See* agriculture
Farm Security Administration, 85, 209, 212
Farmway Village, 212
Farm Worker Appreciation Day, 215
farmworkers, 118, 225. *See also* Latinos: and labor conditions
Federal Art Program, 248
Federal Bureau of Investigation, 95
Federal Council of the Churches of Christ, 182
federal government, 8, 27, 28–29, 31, 33, 34, 55, 58, 60, 61, 65, 76, 77, 84, 85, 86, 90, 91, 94, 118
Federal Writers' Project, 243, 260
Fiege, Mark, 60, 277
fire, 48, 84, 277
First Presbyterian Church, 114
First United Church of Christ, 130
First United Methodist Church, 114
Fisher, Vardis, 238, 242–43, 243*fig.*, 254, 255, 260–61
Flake, Kathleen, 123
Flathead (Native Americans), 16, 47
Flathead Indian Reservation, 15, 16, 31
Fontes, Manuel, 202
Foote, Arthur, 58, 59, 142
Foote, Mary Hallock, 58, 140, 142, 238, 239, 241–42, 247–48, 248*fig.*, 254, 255
forest reserves. *See* national forests
forests, 54, 56, 86; debates about, 55
Fort Boise, 246, 269
Fort Bridger Treaty, 30
Fort Hall, 246
Fort Hall Indian Reservation, 16, 17, 28, 30–31, 34, 35, 36, 113
Fort Sherman, 79
Fort Vancouver, 49
Foster, Flora Mason, 144
Fouch, Althea E., 144
14 Word Press, 128
Fowler, Ethel Lucile, 249
Franklin, 27, 51, 52, 77, 114
Franklin County, 99
Freemont County, 85, 122
free silver, 80
French, Hiram T., 138, 139, 266
French, Permeal, 140

Friends Church, 115
Fritzen, Mary Jane, 139
Fuentes, Humberto, 217, 218
Fujii, Fumiko Mayeda, 181
Fujii, Hajimu "Henry," 180, 181, 198–99
Fujimoto, Masayoshi, 180
Fujimoto, Toji, 181
fur trade and traders, 26–27, 46, 49, 52, 167, 264

G

gambling, 97. *See also* Native Americans: and
    gaming
Garden City, 174
Garland, Hamlin, 241
Garreau, Joel, 149
Gates, Charles, 148
gender history, 142, 146–47, 156, 160
General Land Office, 265
Gentleman's Agreement (1908), 181
Gentry, James, 276
Ghost Dance religion, 32–33, 113
Gibbs, George, 246
Gibson, J. H., 260
Gilded Age, 77, 121
Glendora Ranch Gang, 88
Glenns Ferry, 217
Glover, John, 55
gold, 50
Goldwater, Barry, 87, 91
Gooding, Frank, 80, 140
Gospel Hump Wilderness Area, 65, 95
Gossett, Charles, 105–6
Goulder, William Armistead, 264, 265
Governor's Migratory Labor Committee, 213,
    215
Grangeville, 65, 95
Graves, Morris, 249, 254
grazing. *See* ranching
Great Basin, 3, 48, 112–13
great depression, 8, 84, 86, 118, 156, 207,
    208–9, 209
Great Northern railroad, 179, 186
Great Plains, 46, 48, 113
Greek Orthodox Church, 117
Greeks, 187, 202
Green Creek, 106
Greene, Elizabeth, 130

Greene, Mamie, 176
Greenleaf, 115
Greenleaf Friends Academy, 115
Greenwood, Annie Pike, 141, 142, 158, 244, 256
Gritz, Bo, 128
Grover, William, Jr., 60
Guido, Sam, 187
guns, 47, 115

H

H-2A temporary visas, 214
Hailey, 173, 175, 190, 227
Hailey, John, 138, 139, 143, 265
Haines, John, 82, 140
Hale, Janet Campbell, 244
Hale, Shelley, 178
Hamilton, Joe, 177
Hansen, Connie, 94
Hansen, George, 93–94
Hansen, Orval, 94
Harding, Ralph, 99
Hardy, William Riley, 178
Hart, Arthur A., 140, 145, 146, 174, 272–73
Hashitani, Henry, 181
Hausladen, Gary J., 150
Hawkins, Ora B., 144
Hawley, James H., 138, 140, 266–67
Hawthorne, Nathaniel, 240
Haywood, William "Big Bill," 80, 83
Head Start, 217, 218
health care, 159
Heaton, John, 46
Hebard, Grace, 152
Heffernan, Michael, 152
Helena, 142
Hellgate Treaty (1855), 31
Hells Canyon, 17, 45, 61–62, 90, 269, 277
Hells Canyon Dam, 90
Hells Canyon National Recreation Area and
    Wilderness Area, 62, 90
Heyburn, Weldon, 56
Heyburn State Park, 63, 86, 278
High Hells Canyon Dam, 61–62, 89, 277
High School Equivalency Program, 221–22
Hill, John Henry, 247
Hindus, 116, 119
Hines, Gloria, 178

Hisom, William C. "Doc," 175–76
Hispanic Business Association, 219
Hispanics. *See* Latinos
historians and historical profession, 3, 4, 7, 144–45, 146
historical geography, 150
homosexuality, 123, 125, 137
Hoover, Herbert, 85
Hormaechea, Jay, 252
horses, 24–25, 46
hospitals, 114
House Bill 142, 82
House Bill 217, 223
Howard, Minnie, 156
Howard, Oliver, 28
Hudson's Bay Company, 26, 49
Humboldt River, 26
Hune, Shirley, 154
Hunt (Minidoka) High School, 183
Hunt, Lucy Peña, 217
Hunt, Nelson Bunker, 94
hydroelectricity, 60, 61
Hyslop, Julie, 267

I

Idaho: art and artists in, 245–50; communities in, 6, 109, 118, 126, 156, 185, 214; congressional districts, 87–88, 94; conservatism in, 9, 76, 91, 94, 100; constitution, 60, 78–79, 98; as crossroads, 45, 67, 146; culture, 6, 238–56; discrimination in, 6, 7, 118, 167–68, 170, 175, 177, 178, 180–81, 187, 198–200, 204, 206, 208, 210, 222–27, 228; diversity of, 7, 67, 146; economy of, 50, 61, 79, 84, 86, 121–22, 149, 156–57, 168, 191, 203, 214, 227, 253; ethnic composition of, 4, 167–92, 201–2; environment, 4, 6, 44–67, 77, 92, 93, 95; geography of, 3, 44–45, 47, 76–77, 149; governors, 77, 87; history and historians of, 4, 5, 9, 108, 138–43, 149, 154, 160, 255–56, 263–81; legislature, 79, 87, 90, 97, 100, 125, 143, 169, 175, 180, 198, 213, 218, 222–23, 224, 226, 268, 280–81; liberalism in, 89; literature, 239–45; Native Americans in, 13–38, 14*map*; paradoxes of, 4, 5; politics of, 3–4, 5, 9, 65, 76–101, 109, 119–21, 138–39, 149, 165–66, 276; race relations, 6, 118; refugees in, 116; religion and, 108–31; statehood, 7, 52, 78, 79, 148; territorial status, 77–78, 148, 169, 175, 202, 265; uniqueness of, 4–5; violence, 6; women, 6, 115, 122, 138–60
Idaho Association of Counties, 226
Idaho Citizen, 264
Idaho Citizens Alliance, 125
Idaho Citizens-Committee for Civil Rights, 222
Idaho City, 50, 113, 115, 154
Idaho Commission on Hispanic Affairs, 224–25
Idaho Community Action Network, 222
Idaho Conservation League, 96
Idaho Council of Churches, 118
Idaho Department of Labor, 227–28
Idaho Earth Institute, 131
Idaho Falls, 86, 115, 122, 129, 204, 208–9, 220
Idaho Farm Workers Services, Inc., 217
Idaho First National Bank, 101
Idaho High School Athletic Association, 183
Idaho Human Rights Commission, 223–24, 225
Idaho Migrant Council, 217, 218, 219–20, 224
Idaho National Guard, 208
Idaho Power Company, 61, 86, 89, 90, 101
Idaho Primitive Area, 64, 82
Idaho Property Owners Association, 99
Idaho State Automobile Association, 269
Idaho State Board of Education, 219–20
Idaho State Board of Education Task Force on Hispanic Education, 220
Idaho State Department of Employment, 214, 215
Idaho State Department of Health, 214
Idaho State Federation of Labor, 208
Idaho State Historical Society, 10, 139, 143–44, 145, 182, 265, 268–69, 271, 272, 273, 280–81
Idaho Statesman, 56, 97, 165, 179, 180, 227, 228, 264
Idaho State University, 145, 149, 249, 275
Idaho Sugar Beet Growers Association, 208
Idaho Sugar Companies, 121–22
Idaho Supreme Court, 99, 174
Idaho Test Oath, 78, 99, 120
Idaho Values Alliance, 125–26
Idaho Wildlife Federation, 63, 73
Idaho Yesterdays, 142, 145, 269, 271, 272, 280
Image de Idaho, 219, 224

Image del Sudeste, 219
immigrants, 146, 156, 168, 181, 190, 192. *See also specific ethnic groups*
Immigration Act (1965), 174
immigration legislation, 8, 168, 173, 181, 185, 204. *See also* Chinese Exclusion Act (1882); Immigration Act (1965); Immigration Reform and Control Act (1986); Johnson-Reed Immigration Act (1924); Walter-McCarran Act (1952)
Immigration Reform and Control Act (1986), 225
Inchausti, Maria Epifania, 190
Indian Gaming Regulatory Act (1988), 34
Indian Presbyterian Church, 111–12, 112*fig.*
Indian Reorganization Act (1934), 8, 34
Indian reservations, 15
Indians. *See* Native Americans
Industrial Workers of the World, 83
Ink Spots, 177
Interfaith Alliance, 126
Interfaith Sanctuary, 131
Irish, 113
irrigation, 45, 51, 56, 57, 58–60, 63, 80, 272, 276
Irving, Washington, 240
Issei. *See* Japanese
Italians, 113, 167, 169, 185–88, 202; occupations of, 186–87
Italy, 185

J

Jackson, Sheldon, 114
Jackson, Teton, 140
Jaialdi International Basque Cultural Festival, 252
Japan, 181
Japanese, 6, 156–57, 168, 169, 179–85, 190, 191, 198–99, 204, 279; and baseball, 182, 183; composition of community, 181; labor resentment toward, 180; and land laws, 180–81, 198–99; organizations of, 181–82
Japanese American Citizens League, 182, 185
Japanese Association of America, 181
Japanese Association of Western Idaho, 180
Japanese Committee on International Friendship among Children, 182
Japanese internment, 156, 182–83

Japanese Northwest Fourth of July Baseball Tournament, 182
Jehovah's Witness, 110
Jerome, 114, 126
Jerome County, 267
Jesuits, 31–32, 111
Jews, 82, 115–16, 129, 167, 206
Johansen, Dorothy O., 148
John Birch Society, 94
Johnson, James, 55
Johnson, Lena L., 179
Johnson, Lyndon, 87, 218
Johnson, Sonia, 124
Johnson-Reed Immigration Act (1924), 169, 173, 190
Jones, Frank, 73
Jones, Joseph Taylor ("J.T.") 177
Jordan, Grace Edgington, 90, 140, 141, 242
Jordan, Len, 61, 62, 66, 90, 91, 93, 94, 97, 140, 141
Jordan Valley, 113
Joseph, 28
Josephy, Alvin, 278
Juarez, Javier Tellez, 228
Julia Davis Park, 126
Junior Chamber of Commerce, 126–27

K

Kalispel (Native Americans), 15–16, 27, 31, 36, 38, 48; and fur trade, 26
Kalispel Indian Reservation, 16, 31
Kamiah, 111–12,
Kellogg, 53, 54, 186, 224
Kellogg, Noah, 52
Kellogg-Briand Pact, 81
Kelly, Milton, 265
Kempthorne, Dirk, 127
Kesey, Ken, 254
Ketchum, 173, 227
King, Martin Luther, Jr., 223
Kiowa, 32
Kirkwood, Mary, 249
Kootenai, 15, 31, 35, 36, 38, 42–43, 48; and fur trade, 26; and war, 35
Kootenai County Task Force on Human Relations, 128–29
Kootenai Indian Reservation, 15, 34

Kootenai River, 15
Kootenay River, 15
Krishna Temple, 116
Ktunaxa. *See* Kootenai
Ku Klux Klan, 178–79, 206
Kullyspell House, 26, 49
Kuna, 247

L

Labor Relation Board, 211
labor unions, 170, 188
Labrador, Raul, 101
Ladies Aid Societies, 115
Lake Coeur d'Alene, 16, 24, 74
Lake Pend Oreille, 16, 26, 49
Landon, Alf, 85
Lapwai, 45, 49
LaRocco, Larry, 97
Latah County, 55, 118, 176
Latinos, 6, 9, 118, 123, 139, 156, 159, 167, 169,
    187, 192, 201–28; and bracero programs,
    203–4, 209–11; and citizenship, 226;
    and cultural celebrations, 215, 216*fig.*;
    discrimination toward, 204, 205–6, 208,
    210, 213, 222–27, 228; and education, 205,
    211, 214, 215, 216, 218–19, 219–22, 226, 227;
    and labor conditions, 204, 206–7, 209–10,
    211–12, 213–14, 217, 224, 227–28; and labor
    strikes, 207–8, 210, 217–18; and language,
    214–15, 218, 219–20, 221, 224, 226; Mexi-
    can officials and, 205, 206–7, 208, 210, 226,
    227; population characteristics of, 201–2;
    occupations of, 202–3, 205*fig.*
Latter-day Saints, 6, 51, 52, 58, 78, 99, 108–9,
    112, 114–15, 119–22, 123, 124–25, 126,
    127–28, 136, 138, 139, 167, 275
Lau v. Nichols (1974), 219
Lawyer, Mrs. 23*fig.*
LDS Hospital, 115
Lead Creek, 74
League of Women Voters, 144
Lee, Quon, 172*fig.*
Lemhi Indian Reservation, 17, 31
Lemhi Pass, 44, 47
Lemhi Shoshone, 17, 44, 67, 152
Lewinsky, Monica, 97, 100
Lewis, Meriwether, 18, 44, 239. *See also* Lewis

and Clark Expedition
Lewis and Clark Expedition, 26, 44, 45, 47, 48,
    67, 151–52, 239–40, 264
Lewis-Clark State College, 157, 273
Lewiston, 10, 114, 115, 157, 186; as territorial
    capital, 77–78, 148
Lewiston Women's Christian Temperance
    Union and Tsceminicum Club, 156
Life magazine, 92
limited English proficient, 219–20, 221
Lincoln, 122, 203
Local Color, 142, 239, 240, 241, 248, 294
Lochsa River, 67
logging. *See* timber
Lombardi, Maria, 187
London, Jack, 241
Looking Glass, 28
López, Isidro "Blackie," 222
López, Pedro, 217
Lost River, 141
Lost Trail Pass, 67
Lovin, Hugh, 276
Lowell, Helen, 268
Lucerta, Pagoaga, 190
Lukens, Fred, 165–66
Lukens, Magdalena Fritchle, 165–66
lumbering. *See* timber
Lyon, Caleb, 55

M

Madison County, 99
Madsen, Brigham D., 276, 278
Magic Valley, 58, 227
Malad, 106, 114
Malheur County, 184
Malicious Harassment Law, 129
Marshall, John, 29
Martin, Fletcher, 249
Martin Luther King Jr. Day, 129
Mathews, Conan, 249
McBeth, Kate, 278
McBeth, Sue, 111, 278
McCarthy, Joseph, 89
McClure, James, 87, 91, 93, 100
McConnel, M. G., 207–8
McConnell, William, 79, 138, 139, 140, 265
McCunn, Ruthanne, 152, 244

McDermott, John D., 278
McDevitt, Gertrude, 144, 145
McDowell, Linda, 150
McKague, Shirley, 226
McKay, Thomas, 269
McVety, William J. A., 204
Medlicot, Carol, 152
Mennonites, 118, 216
Meridian, 129, 226
Merriam, H. G., 260
Mexican Revolution, 203
Mexicans and Mexican Americans. *See* Latinos
Mexico, 47, 202, 209, 222
Middle Fork of the Salmon River, 64
Migrant Education Program, 217
migrant laborers. *See* Latinos: and labor conditions
Miles, Colonel Nelson, 28
Miller, Clara, 136
Miller, Joaquin, 240, 242
Milner Dam, 58, 63
Mine Owners' Association, 53
Minico High School, 221
Minidoka internment camp, 182–83, 184, 279
Minidoka Project, 59
Minidoka School District, 221
mining and miners, 50, 52, 63, 66, 74–75, 77, 79, 105, 113, 154, 167, 168, 169–70, 175, 185, 188, 191, 202, 277, 279–80
Minnick, Walt, 100–101
missionaries and missions, 31, 37, 43, 49, 109, 110–11, 113, 167, 278–79
Miss Nara, 182
Missoula, 57
Missouri River, 44
Monpelier, 106, 114
Montana, 15, 25, 175, 176, 254
Moore, Charles C., 84, 140
Moore Inn, 177
Moran, Thomas, 239, 247
Mormons. *See* Latter-day Saints
Morrill, Allen, 278–79
Morrill, Eleanor, 278–79
Morris-Knudsen Company, 101
Morrison, John T., 140
Moscow, 79, 117–18, 173, 176, 186
Mountain Home, 18, 61, 180, 190

Moyer, Charles, 80
mug books, 266
Mullan, John, 246
Muslims, 116

N

Nampa, 89, 114, 122, 180, 183, 210, 219, 220, 222, 251, 268, 269, 274
Nampa Trades and Labor Council, 208
Nash, Alice Beath, 144
Nathoy, Lalu. *See* Bemis, Polly
National Association for the Advancement of Colored People, 179
National Committee for an Effective Congress, 89
National Congress of American Indians, 34
National Council of Churches Migrant Ministry, 212, 213, 215
National Federation of Women's Clubs, 155
national forests, 55–56, 57, 65
National Origins Act (1924). *See* Johnson-Reed Immigration Act (1924)
National Park Service, 63, 93, 274–75
National Wildlife Federation, 92
Native Americans, 6, 8, 9, 13–38, 47–48, 111, 139, 146, 150, 159, 167, 203, 210, 246; and Animal Peoples, 18–19, 20, 21, 24, 32, 35; and disease, 25, 47; and executive orders, 28–29, 30; and federal relations, 28–29; and gaming, 34; and horses, 24–25, 26fig., 46; intertribal trade15–16, 25; lands of, 18–19, 20, 22, 31; oral traditions of, 18, 20–21, 22–24; and pan-Indian identity, 112; population estimates of, 25; self-determination, 9; subsistence practices of, 47–48; tribal sovereignty of, 27, 28–30, 33, 34, 35, 36; treaties with, 28–29; values of, 22, 32; women, 139. *See also specific tribes*
nativism, 168
Nazarenes, 114
Neil, J. M., 277
Nevada, 17, 19, 22, 30, 96, 170, 188, 190, 201, 252
New Deal, 61, 81, 85, 86, 87, 254
Newe. *See* Shoshone
Newlands Act. *See* Reclamation Act (1902)
New York Canal, 59

Nez Perce, 15, 16, 36, 37, 38, 46, 47, 48, 49, 67,
    111–12, 186, 203, 239, 278; and diseases,
    25; and fur trade, 26; and horses, 25; oral
    traditions of, 20; and Treaty of 1863, 28;
    Wallowa bands of, 28; and war, 27
Nez Perce Indian Reservation, 16, 34
Nez Perce War of 1877, 16, 27–28, 151, 274, 278
Nielson, Thomas Raymond, 249
Nimíipuu. See Nez Perce
Nisei. See Japanese
Noble, Edward, 177
Noble, Mary, 177
No Child Left Behind, 221
none-zone, 109, 131
Nonpartisan League, 81
Norris, Frank, 241
North American Basque Organizations, 252
North Dakota, 81
Northern Pacific railroad, 179
Northern Paiute, 15, 18, 22, 25, 28, 30, 36, 38,
    47, 48, 113
Northern Shoshone, 16, 18
North Idaho College, 130
Northwest coast, 48
Northwest Company, 49
Northwestern Band of Shoshone Nation, 16,
    18
Northwest Nazarene University, 114
Northwest Passage, 44
Northwest School, 249
Notus Farm Labor Committee, 210
Numa. See Northern Paiute

O

Oakland, 188
Obama, Barack, 100, 101, 227
Oberg, Pearl M., 268
Obregón, Alvaro, 206
Occupational Safety and Health Administra-
    tion, 94
Office of Economic Opportunity, 217, 218
off-road vehicles, 66
Ogden, 57
Ogden, Peter, 26
Oinkari Basque Dancers, 1960
Oliver, Lincoln, 119
Oliver, Mamie, 119, 178

Oneida, Marion, 190
Oneida County, 99
One Percent Initiative, 99
Ontario (Oregon), 183, 184, 185, 217, 251
oral history, 10
Order, the, 129
Oregon, 16, 17, 18, 28, 108–9, 148, 175, 176, 182,
    183, 184, 198–99, 201, 216, 252, 254
Oregon Short Line railroad, 58, 179
Otazua, Victor, 189
Otter, C. L. "Butch," 100, 224–25, 226
overgrazing, 50, 56, 57
overland trails, 45, 240, 246
Owyhee Canyonlands, 66
Owyhee County, 191, 267
Owyhee Initiative, 66
Owyhee Mountains, 50
Owyhee Plaza Hotel, 116, 166, 176
Owyhee River, 18
Oxbow Dam, 90

P

Pacific Northwest, 4, 50, 54, 61, 62, 212, 241
Pacific Northwest Quarterly, 269
Pacific Ocean, 44, 149
Paddy Cap, 28, 30
Paffile, John, 186
Paffile, Phoebe, 186
Pagoaga, Joe, 190
Paiute, 16, 25, 66
Palouse (Native Americans), 27
Palouse (region), 50, 54
Palouse (town), 54
Palouse River, 54
Panama Canal Treaty, 94, 95
Paris, 114
parochial schools, 114
Paul, 204
Payette, 122
Payette River, 18, 61
Pecora, Mike, 186
Peltier, Leonard, 33
Peña, Rudy, 224
Pend Oreille River, 16
Peoples Party. See Populist Party
Perez, Rita, 208–9
pesticides, 211, 228

Peter, Max, 249
Petersen, Keith, 273–74
Peterson, Lucile, 268
Pettibone, George, 80
Pfost, Gracie, 89–90
Phelps, Fred, 126
Pierce, 170, 175
Pinchot, Gifford, 56
Pinkerton detectives, 80
Pittman, Key, 85
Pocatello, 16, 18, 35, 56, 85, 94, 115, 116, 149,
    157, 176, 177, 178, 179, 182, 187, 188, 199,
    204, 219, 251, 268
Pocatello Forest Reserve, 56
Pocatello Women's Club, 155, 156
Point, Nicolas, 240
pollution, 53–54, 74–75
polygamy, 52, 78, 120–21, 127–28, 136
Poorman Mine, 186
Pope, James P., 85, 86
Populist Party, 80
Portland, 50, 141, 253
potato, 45, 84
Potlatch, 187
Potlatch Lumber Company, 55
Powell, Cynthia S., 140
Powell, John Wesley, 51
Presbyterians, 111, 114–15
President's Committee on Migrant Labor, 212
Preston, 114, 210
Preuss, Charles, 245–46
Priest River, 113, 129, 186, 187
primary elections, 81
prior appropriation, 60
Progressive era and movement, 58, 61, 83, 156;
    values of, 60
Progressive Party, 81, 88
prohibition, 82–83, 122, 166
Proposition 1, 125, 130, 137
prostitution, 142, 154
Protestantism and Protestants, 108–9, 110,
    113, 115, 119, 120, 122, 123–24, 125, 156, 213
Psychiana, 117–18
public historians, 270–74
public lands and policy, 55–56, 57, 93, 96
Puget Sound, 47, 62
Pullman, 186
Pyne, Stephen J., 277

Q
Qlispé. See Kalispel
Quakers, 115

R
"Rabbit and Jack Rabbit," 19–20, 21, 22, 37
racism, 175, 177, 184, 192, 224, 228
Racketeer Influenced and Corrupt Organiza-
    tions Act, 226
railroads, 52, 54, 58, 60, 79, 80, 179–80, 185,
    186, 202, 203, 204, 275
Rainbow Family of Living Light, 131
ranching, 50, 52, 57, 85, 113, 185, 188–89, 202
Reagan, Ronald, 95
Reberger, Phil, 95
reclamation, 58, 59
Reclamation Act (1902), 58–59, 80
recreation, 62, 63, 64, 67
Reed, Ella Cartee, 143
Reed, George H., 143
Reed, George W., Jr., 144
Reed, Mary, 273
Reed, Simeon, 53
Reed v. Reed (1971), 97
regional history, 142, 143, 146–47
regions and regionalism, 147–48, 158, 254
Remington, Frederic, 247–48
Republican Party, 64, 78, 79, 81, 83–84, 87,
    88–89, 90, 91, 93, 94, 95–97, 100–101, 110,
    119–20, 123, 124, 126, 166, 226, 227
Republicans. See Republican Party
Rexburg, 94
Rexburg Tabernacle, 115
Rhodes, William, 175
Ricards, Sherman, 191
Ricketts, Virginia, 267
Ricks College. See Brigham Young University–
    Idaho
Ridenbaugh, Mary, 156
Rigby, 114
Risch, Jim, 100
Rivera, Mike, 204
River of No Return Wilderness Area, 64, 73, 95
Roberts, Margaret S., 144
Robertson, Frank C., 243
Robinson, Frank Bruce, 117–18
Robinson, Marilynne, 238, 244–45, 254, 256
Rockefeller, Nelson, 91

Rocky Mountains, 3
Rodriguez, Antonio, Sr., 222
Ronda, James P., 48
Roosevelt, Franklin D., 81, 85, 86, 182
Rosebud Women's Club, 178
Rose Hill cemetery, 178
Ross, Alexander, 240
Ross, C. Benjamin, 85–86, 105–6, 140, 207, 208
Ross, Claudia, 144
Ruddock, H. N., 60
Rupert, 59, 143, 159
Rupert Culture Club, 155, 156
Ruskin, John, 247
Russell, Charlie, 248, 254
Russia. *See* Soviet Union
Russian thistle, 57
Rutledge, Richard H., 64

S

Sacajawea, 44, 151–52, 160
Sacred Heart Mission, 27, 30, 32, 111
Sagebrush Rebellion, 96
Sahaptian language, 16
Saint Michael's, 114
Sala, Louis, 185–86
Saleesh House, 26
Sali, William "Bill," 100, 227
Salishan language, 16
salmon, 48, 96
Salmon River, 17, 18, 50, 62, 67, 77, 89, 152, 173, 246
Salt Lake City, 4, 205
Samaria, 114
same-sex marriage, 99–100
Samuelson, Don, 66, 91–92, 99, 213
Sanctuary, 119
San Diego Fruit and Produce, 207
Sandpoint, 128
San Francisco, 174
San Francisco Elevator, 175
Sawtooth National Recreation Area, 66, 93, 175
Sawtooth Range, 17, 63, 66, 74
Sawtooth Wilderness Area, 66
Scharff, Virginia, 152
Schismatic Catholics, 127
Schitsu'umsh. *See* Coeur d'Alene
Schwantes, Carlos, 76, 148, 275–76

Seattle, 174, 180, 253
Self-Determination Act (1975), 34
Self-Governance Act (1995), 34
Selway Bitterrot Wilderness Area, 67, 74
Senate Bill 1221, 223
Settle, Eugene, 176
Seventh Cavalry, 113
sheep. *See* ranching
Sheepherders' Ball, 251
Shelley, 204
Shellworth, Harry, 64
Shoshone (Native Americans), 15, 16, 17, 25, 30, 36, 46, 47, 48, 112–13, 239, 278; and fur trade, 26; and war, 27, 28
Shoshone (town), 190, 251
Shoshone County, 168
Shoshone Falls, 63, 246, 247
Shoup, George L., 79
Sierra Club, 90, 92, 96
Silver City, 53*fig.*, 171, 175, 268, 271*fig.*
Silver Purchase Act (1934), 85–86
Silver Valley, 53, 79, 170, 186
Simplot, Gay, 100
Simplot, J. R., 100, 101
Simplot Company, 100, 101
Simpson, Mike, 66
Sims, Robert, 184, 279
Sioux, 32–33
Sitting Bull, 33
Six Compaies, 171
slavery, 78
Slickpoo, Allen, 42, 278
smallpox, 25, 47
Smelterville Flats, 74
Smith, Cecil, 249
Smith, Elmo, 184
Smith, Jean Conly, 63
Smith, Joseph, 137
Smith, Joseph F., 121
Smith, Listoria, 177
Smith, Vernon, 97
Smylie, Robert E., 91, 97, 98*fig.*, 98, 278
Snake River, 10, 16, 18, 59, 60, 61, 62, 63, 86, 149, 175, 246, 277
Snake River Plain, 48, 49, 58, 60, 62, 84, 149, 179–80, 203, 207, 240, 277
Sohon, Gustavus, 246

Soldiers of the Sacred Heart, 32
Solis, Tony, 217
Southern Baptist Convention, 124
Southern Central Idaho League, 183
southern Europeans, 173, 185–91
Southern Idaho Migrant Ministry, 118
South Fork Coeur d'Alene River, 74–75
Southwest Idaho Migrant Ministry, 213, 217
Soviet Union, 81, 83, 88
Spalding, Eliza, 49, 50, 111
Spalding, Henry, 49, 50, 58, 111
Spanbauer, Tom, 244
Spanish Civil War, 252
Spanish traders, 25
Spence, Clark, 276–77
Speno, Frank, 186
Spokane, 4, 27, 98, 183
Spokane (Native Americans), 16, 27
Spokane County, 184
Spokane House, 26
Spokane River, 16, 26
Stacy, Susan, 274
Stallings, Richard, 94, 96
St. Alphonsus, 114
St. Anthony's, 113, 187
Stanley, John Mix, 239, 246
Stanley Basin, 268
Stapilus, Randy, 76
state history, 139, 142, 143, 145, 146–47, 148,
    150, 160
St. Bernard's, 113
St. Catherine's, 187
Stegner, Wallace, 254
Steptoe, Colonel Edward, 27
Steunenberg, Frank, 63, 79, 80, 81, 140
Stevens, Issac, 246
Stevens, James, 243, 254
St. Gertrude's Monastery, 268
St. Joe River, 16
St. John's Cathedral, 113
St. Joseph's, 113
St. Luke's, 114
St. Margaret's, 114
St. Maries, 128
Stoll, Steven, 50
St. Paul's Baptist Church, 116, 119, 178
Strahorn, Robert, 264

suffrage, 122, 138–39, 166
sugar beets, 121–22, 179–80, 183, 208–9
Sun Belt, 124
Sunshine Mine fire, 224
Superfund site, 54
Swinney, H. J. "Jerry," 145, 269
Symms, Steve, 65, 73, 95–96

T

Table Rock cross controversy, 126–27, 130, 131
Tappan, William, 246
taxes, 80, 85, 91, 97–99, 105–6, 128
Taylor, Glen, 88, 89
Taylor, Nancy, 130
Taylor Grazing Act (1934), 57, 85
Tea Party Movement, 101
Teater, Archie Boyd, 249
Teichert, Minerva Kohlhepp, 249
television, 89
Temple Beth Israel, 116, 117fig.
Temple Emanuel, 116
temples, 109, 115
Ten Commandments, 126–25
Tennessee Valley Authority, 86
termination policy, 30, 33
Teton County, 99, 208
Teton Dam disaster, 94
Tetonia, 94
Teton Valley, 207
Texas, 177, 205, 210, 214, 215, 222
Thiessen, Betty Meloy, 139
Thompson, David, 49, 240
Thompson Falls, 26
Tigner, Rosa, 177, 199–200
timber, 52, 54–55, 63, 79, 83, 176, 202
timber famine, 55
Tobey, Mark, 249
Tobias, Nelle, 131
Totoricagüena, Gloria, 252
tourism, 45
trade networks, 7, 48, 49, 50
transportation, 50, 149
Treasure Valley, 50, 225, 227
Treasure Valley Community College, 217
Treasure Valley Council for Church and Social
    Action Community Ministries Center, 119
treaties, 28–30

Treaty of Ruby Valley (1863), 30
Treaty of Versailles, 81
Trice, Amy, 42–43
Trienen, Sylvester, 114
Trueblood, Ted, 73
Turner, Frederick Jackson, 146
Tuttle, Daniel, 114
Twain, Mark, 240
Twin Falls, 58, 59fig., 115, 126, 183, 190, 204, 208, 212, 213, 220, 264, 276, 280
Twin Falls Daily News, 206
Twin Falls Syringa Club, 155

U

Umatilla, 16, 28
Uniform Hate Crimes Reporting Act, 129
Union Pacific Railroad, 177, 204, 264, 275
Unitarian Universalists, 119, 130
United Farm Workers, 91, 217
United Japanese Association Council, 180
United Nations, 96
United Order, 120
University of Idaho, 79, 149, 222, 249, 255, 273, 274
Urquides, Jesús, 202
U.S. Army, 27–28, 202, 203
U.S. Congress, 28, 30, 55, 66, 78, 81, 86, 87, 89, 94, 96, 169, 225
U.S. Department of Education Office for Civil Rights, 220
U.S. Employment Service, 209
U.S. Forest Service, 55, 56, 57, 63, 64, 65, 90, 93
Usk, 31
U.S. Public Health Service, 210–11
U.S. Senate, 81, 84, 86, 88, 90, 91, 94, 95–96, 100, 180
U.S. Supreme Court, 29, 78, 97, 126, 168
U.S. Treasury Department, 80, 85
Utah, 17, 27, 35, 77, 109, 149, 199, 201, 254
Utah-Idaho Sugar Company, 179, 203, 204
Utah Migrant Council, 217
Utah Sugar Companies, 120–21
Utes, 46
Uto-Aztecan language, 17, 18

V

Valentine, Gaetano, 187
Vasquez, Robert, 226
Victor, Frances Fuller, 266
Vietnam War, 95
Vineyard Church, 131
Vitale, Kathy, 186–87, 188
Vizcaya. *See* Bizkaia

W

Walgamott, Charles S., 264
Walkup, Al, 224
Wallace, 56, 186
Wallace, Henry, 88
Wallace, William Henson, 269
Walla Walla, 50
Wallowa Lake, 16
Walter-McCarran Act (1952), 174, 185
Walz, Eric, 279
Warm Springs (Native Americans), 16
War on Poverty, 218
War Relocation Authority, 184
Warren, 173
Washington, 16, 55, 108–9, 148, 175, 176, 182, 183, 201, 254
Washington, Hattie, 177
Wassmuth, Bill, 128–30
water rights, 60
Watkins, Mary Sanders, 178
Weaver, Randy, 128
Weippe Prairie, 44
Welker, Herman, 89
Wells, Joe, 176
Wells, Lou, 176
Wells, Merle, 139, 145, 146, 267, 270–72, 271fig.
Weppner, Genie Sue, 137
West, Elliott, 46, 50, 278
Western Federation of Miners, 80
Western Historical Quarterly, 147
Western History Association, 147
Weyerhaeuser, Frederick, 55
Weyerhaeuser syndicate, 55
Wheeler, Burton K., 85
White, Richard, 57
White Bird (location), 28, 37
White Clouds, 66, 92
whiteness, 168, 173, 188, 190

white supremacists, 128

Whitman, Marcus, 50

Whitman, Narcissa, 50, 240

Wild and Scenic Rivers Act, 62

Wilder Labor Center, 216

wilderness, 63–64, 66, 73, 93

Wilderness Act (1964), 64, 65, 73–74

Wilderness Gateway, 67

Wilderness Society, 73

Wilkins, Kitty, 146

Willey, Norman B., 140

Wilson, Jack, 32–33

Wilson, Woodrow, 166

Wister, Owen, 241

Wodziwob, 113

Women's Christian Temperance Union, 122, 155

women's clubs, 143, 145, 154–55

women's history. *See* gender history

Wood, Grant, 249

Wood River Valley, 268

Woodruff, Wilford, 78

Woodword, Tim, 228

Woodworth-Ney, Laura, 59–60

Worcester v. Georgia (1832), 29

Works Progress Administration, 243, 248, 260

World War I, 81, 83, 166, 168, 186, 203, 204

World War II, 8, 61, 86, 118, 156, 182–83, 184, 190, 209–10

Worster, Donald, 51

Wounded Knee, 33, 113

Wovoka, 114

Wright, George

Wyoming, 17, 25, 149, 252

X

Xu, Yixian, 140

Y

Yakama (Native Americans), 16, 27

Yakama Indian Reservation, 28

Yarber, Esther, 268

"Yellowstone Jack," 179

Yellowstone National Park, 28

Young, Brigham, 112

Yrazabal, Florentina, 190

Yribar, Juan, 189

Yribar, Teresa, 189

Z

Zabala, Thomas, 261–62

Zhu, Liping, 170, 279–80